THE AMES FOUNDATION

FOUNDED 1910

BY CONTRIBUTIONS OF THE FRIENDS OF

JAMES BARR AMES

FOR THE PURPOSE OF CONTINUING
THE ADVANCEMENT OF LEGAL KNOWLEDGE
AND AIDING THE IMPROVEMENT
OF THE LAW

The second publication issued under the auspices of the Ames Foundation is

A BIBLIOGRAPHY OF EARLY
ENGLISH LAW BOOKS

The Ames Foundation

A BIBLIOGRAPHY
OF
EARLY ENGLISH LAW BOOKS

COMPILED FOR THE AMES FOUNDATION
By JOSEPH HENRY BEALE
ROYALL PROFESSOR OF LAW IN HARVARD UNIVERSITY

CAMBRIDGE
Harvard University Press
1926

THE UNIVERSITY PRESS, CAMBRIDGE, U.S.A.

TABLE OF CONTENTS

PREFACE

SINS of omission and of commission in this book are better known to the author than they can be to any user. The author is neither a trained bibliographer nor an experienced copyist. He has had no sufficient chance to examine the books in any large library except that of the Harvard Law School. A few weeks in London and in Cambridge, a day in Oxford and in Washington, an hour in Manchester and in San Francisco, have been supplemented by the kind assistance of the librarians at the Columbia Law School, the New York State Library, the Henry E. Huntington Library and Art Gallery at San Gabriel, and the Library of Congress in Washington.

With no qualifications and few opportunities, it may be asked why did the author attempt the task? The answer is simple if not sufficient; because no one else had done it or seemed likely to do it. The work claims no scientific merit; it is only a check-list by which those who handle law-books of the period may estimate their wares.

In the first chapters, an effort has been made to give enough of the title-page and colophon of each book to identify it. The collation also is only for the purpose of making sure of the whole text. Size, type, and contents, so important in a scientific bibliography, have been omitted. An attempt at further identification has been made, however, by reference to the devices reproduced in McKerrow's "Printers' and Publishers' Devices in England and Scotland" and by reproducing in an appendix the most important woodcuts not found in McKerrow.

In the fourth chapter an attempt has been made to date the books, especially in the case of the printers Pinson and Tottel. This is the only contribution which the author has attempted to make to knowledge of the subject; and the dating is of the most tentative sort.

The table is at once an index to the books and an attempt to indicate the places in which each may be found. This is sadly incomplete, especially for books, other than Year Books, printed later than 1550. An effort has been made, however, to make the list complete for the libraries in which the searcher is most likely to find what he seeks.

Three men are chiefly responsible for the upbuilding at the Harvard Law School of its collection of these old books: James Barr Ames, in whose honor the Foundation which is publishing this bibliography was organized, my dear old master, wise and foreseeing, who loved the past as it was the builder of the present, who fostered the collection of these historical monuments of our law; John Hines Arnold, librarian under whose skilful and sagacious administration most of the books in that library were gathered; George Dunn, who devoted his life to collecting a remarkable library of these books which on his death came to swell the Harvard library. At the feet of these three men I lay this unworthy offering.

J. H. BEALE.

HARVARD LAW SCHOOL, September 1, 1926

BIBLIOGRAPHY OF EARLY ENGLISH LAW BOOKS

BIBLIOGRAPHY OF EARLY ENGLISH LAW BOOKS

CHAPTER I

Statutes

SECTION 1. COLLECTIONS

a. Nova Statuta

S 1. No title-page. [Machlinia c. 1485.]
Colla. 310 leaves unnumbered.
Colo. None.

S 2. No title-page. [Pynson c. 1507.]
Colla. Table, 29 leaves+a–z 8's+A, Q 8's, +A 8, B 9, C 8, D–F 6's, G 4, D 8, E 6, F 6, G 3.
Colo. ℭ Emprynted by my/Rycharde Pynson./ [On reverse of last leaf, McK. 9b.]

b. Magna Carta

S 3. T.p. & calendar lacking.
Colla. [1]–154+[2].
Colo. . . . Londoñ/cum solerti cura ac diligētia prudē-/tissimi viri, honestissimiqz Richardi/Pynson. (Regis ĩpressor exptissim')/nuperrime exaratus. Millesimo quingē-/tesimo. viii. tercio id' Septēbris./ [On reverse, McK. 32.]

S 4. No title-page.
Colla. Calendar, 6 leaves, +table, 9 leaves with colophon dated 1514 [with device McK. 32 b]+A–N 12's.
Colo. Impresse in civita-/te Londoñ per Ri-/chardum Pynson/ Regis impressorē./

S 5. No title-page.
Colla. Calendar, A 6; table, A 10 [with colophon and device McK. 32 b]; A–L 12's+N 10+[2].
Colo. ℭ Liber magne carte cum alijs statutis explicit. Im-/press. Londini. Anno Ver-/bi ĩcarnati. M.D.xix. Die/xxv. mensis Maij, per Ri-/chardū Pynson regiū Im-/pressorem cum privilegio/a rege indulto./

S 6. No title-page.
Colla. [6]+i–cxlvi+[9].
Colo. In parochia/sancti Clementis sub intersignio/sancti Georgii. cum solerti cura ac/diligentia viri Roberti Redman/ nuprime exoratus. Anno Incar-/nationis dñice. Millesimo quin-/gentesimo. xxv. nono idus Maii./

S 7. Title-page missing.
Calendar and 4 leaves of table missing.
Colla. [A 6], A 10, [A 12],+xiii–cliiii. [+1 missing].
Colo. Missing. [At end of table, McK. 3 b.]

S 8. ¶ Magna/Carta in F./whereunto is added/more statutz than e-/uer was imprynted/in any one boke be-/fore this tyme, with/an Alminacke & a/Calender to/know the/mootes./Necessarye for all/yong studiers of/the lawe./Anno Domini. M./CCCC.-XXIX.
Colla. T.p.+[6]+1–148+[4].
Colo. None. [followed by Secunda Pars, 1539.]

S 9. Magna/Carta, cũ alijs an-/tiquis statutis, q°/rum catalogum/in fine ope-/ris repe/ries./ [Title in border 27.]
Colla. T.p.+2–150+[3].
Colo. ¶ Impressus Londini in edibus/Thome Bertheleti regii/impressoris, Anno/dom. 1531./mense/Nouembr̄. Cum/priuile-/gio.

S 10. The boke/of Magna Carta,/with diuers other sta-/tutes, whose names ap-/pere in the nexte lefe fo-/lowynge; translated /into Englyshe./. . . . /☞ Anno Dñi./1534./[Title in border 29.]
Colla. T.p.+[3]+1–193+[6].
Colo. Imprynted/at London in Fletestrete,/by me Robert Redman,/dwellyng at the/sygne of/the/George, nexte to Saynt/Dunstones/church./ ¶ Cum pri-/uilegio Re-/gali. [Device, McK. 41 on reverse.]

S 11. ❧: The/great Charter cal-/led ĩ latyn Magna Car-/ta with diuers olde/statutes whose/titles appere/in the next/leafe/Newly correctyd./&c. [In border 29.]
Colla. T.p.+[3]+1–211+[4]. [On +iv rev. is cut 25.]
Colo. ❧: Thus en-/deth the boke called Magna/Carta, trãslated out of latyn/and Frenshe into Englysh/by George Ferrerz. And/Imprynted at London in/Fletestrete by Elisabeth/wydow of Robert Redmã/dwellyng at the sygne/of the George next/to saynte Dun-/stones chur/che./ ¶ Cum priuilegio/ad imprimen-/dum solum./[McK. 3 d.]

S 12. Magna/Carta cum/aliis antiquis/statutis,/quorum/cata-/lo-/gum in fine/operis/repe-/ries./Anno. M.D.XL./
Colla. T.p.+2–148+[tab. 4].
Colo. ¶ Impressus Londini in aedibus/Thomae Bertheleti regii /impressoris. Anno/dom. 1541./Cum priuilegio ad imprimen-/dum solum./

S 13. ❧ The great/Charter called in la-/tyn Magna Carta;/with diuers olde/statutes whose/titles appere/in the next/leafe/Newly corrected./&c. [In border, McK. 86.]
Colla. T.p.+[3]+1–209+[4].
Colo. ¶ Thus endeth the boke/called Magna Carta,/translated out of/Latyn/and Frenshe into En-/glysshe By George/ Ferrerz.

Impryn-/ted at London/in Paules/church yerde at the signe/of the Maydens heed by/Thomas Petyt./M.D.XLii./ ☞ Cum priuilegio ad Impri-/mendum solum./

S 14. [Magna Carta. Petit 1552. Herbert].

S 15. Magna/Carta et cete-/ra antiqua statuta nunc no-/uiter per diuersa exempla/ria examinata et sum-/ma diligentia/castiga-/ta et correcta &c. . . . /Londini./☞ In aedibus Thome Marshe./ 1556./
Colla. T.p.+[11]+2–160.
Colo. None.

S 16. ☙ Magna/Charta, cum statu-/tis quae Antiqua vocantur, iam re-/cens excusa, & summa fide/emendata, inxta vetusta/exemplaria ad Parlia-/menti rotulos exa-/minata:/quibus accesserunt nonnulla/nunc primum typis edita: . . . /apud Richardum/ Totelum./12. Iun./1556./&c.
Colla. T.p.+[7]+1–170+[2].
Colo. None.

S 17. Magna/Charta cum statu-/tis &c./nunc primum typis edita/ apud Richardum Tottelum./12. Inn./1556./
Colla. T.p.+[7]+1–170+[2].
Colo. None.

S 18. ¶ Magna/Charta, cum statutis,/&c. . . . /per Richardum/ Tottell./Anno domini. 1576./ ¶ Cum priuilegio ad impri-/mendum solum./
Colla. T.p.+[6]+1 bl.+[1]–247.
Colo. ¶ Imprinted at London in Flee-/testreete within Temple barre/at the Signe of the Hand and/Starre, by Richard Tot-/tel, the 8. day of March./1579./

S 19. ☙ Magna/Charta, cum statutis,/&c./ per Richardum/ Tottell./ Anno domini 1576./ ¶ Cum priuilegio ad impri-/mendum solum./
Colla. T.p.+[6]+1 bl.+[1]–247.
Colo. ¶ Imprinted at London in/Fleetestrete within Temple barre/at the Signe of the hande and/Starre, by Richard Tottell./ the 8. day of Marche./1576./

S 20. ¶ Magna Charta cum/statutis, &c./per Richardum/Tottill./ Anno Domini 1587./Cum Priuilegio ad impri-/mendum solum./
Colla. T.p.+[6]+1 bl.+[1]250+[1].
Colo. ¶ Imprinted at London/in Fleetestrete, within Tem-/ple Barre, at the Signe of the Hand/and Starre by Richarde/Tottell, Anno/Do. 1587./

c. Secunda Pars

S 21. Secunda/pars/ve-/terum sta-/tu-/torum./ [In border 27.]
Colla. T.p.+[3]+1–76.
Colo. ¶ Impressus Londini in edibus/Thome Bertheleti regii/ impressoris, Anno/dom. 1532./Mense/Ianuar̄. Cum/priuile-/gio./

S 22. Secun-/da pars/vete-/rum/statu-/to-/rum/Anno. M.D.XL./
Colla. T.p.+[3]+1–80.
Colo. ❧ Londini in aedibus Tho-/mae Bertheleti typis/ impress./Cum priuilegio ad impri-/mendum solum./Anno. M.D.XL./
[Two copies in H. differ in fol. 32 rev. line 18.]

S 23. Secun/da pars/vete-/rum/statu-/to-/rum/Anno. M.D.L.VI./
Colla. T.p.+[3]+1–80.
Colo. ¶ Imprinted at London in/Fletestrete nere to S. Dun-/ stones Churche, by Tho/mes Marshe./ Anno. M.D.L.VI./

S 24. ❧ Secun-/da pars ve-/terumStatutorum./❧/Anno. M.D.L.VI./
Colla. T.p.+2–72.
Colo. ¶ Londini in aedibus Ri-/chardi Tottelli,/Anno do. 1556./ Cum priuilegio ad impri-/mendum solum./

S 24a. Secunda/Pars Veterum/Statutorum/Anno. M.D.LVI./
Colla. T.p.+2–72.
Colo. ¶ Londini in aedibus Ri-/chardi Tottelli,/Anno. do. 1556./Cum priuilegio ad impri-/mendum solum./

d. Great Book of Statutes

S 25. ¶ The great boke of statutes cō-/teynyng all the statutes made in the parliamentes from the/begynnyng of the fyrst yere of the reigne of kyng Edwarde the thyrd tyll/ the begynnyng of the. XXV. yere of the moste gracyous reigne/of our soueraigne lorde kyng Henry the. VIII./
[Over cut 7; 8 on reverse.]
Colla. T.p.+[7]+A 6, B 4, C 4, +[4]+A–Y 6's+A–I 6's, K 4 +A–L 6's,+A–N 6's, D 4.
Colo. ¶ Imprynted at London by Ro-/bert Redman, Cum priui-/legio Regali.

S 26. ¶ The great boke of statutes cō-/teynyng all the statutes . . . tyll/the begynnynge of the. xxxiiii. yere of the most gracyous raigne/of our soueraigne lorde Kyng Henry the. viii./
[Over cut 7; 8 on reverse.]
Colla. T.p.+[23]+A–M 6's, N 4, O–V 6's, X–Y 4's+A–I 6's, K 4+A–L 6's+A–K 6's, L 8.
Colo. ¶ Imprynted at London in Fletestrete at the sygne of/the George by Wyllyam Myddylton./Cum priuilegio &c.

e. Statutes from 1225

S 27. ❧ In this volume/are conteined the statutes made/and established from the time/of Kyng Henry the thirde,/ . . . &c./Anno. M.D.XLIII./
Colla. T.p.+[7]+A–h 8's+i 6: [On reverse of last leaf, McK. 80.]
Colo. Londini in officina Thomae Berthe-/leti typis impress./ Cum priuilegio ad imprimen-/dum solum./Anno. M.D.XLIII.
[No. 17 above.]

S 28. In this vo-/lume are/conteined the statutes/made and established/from the time of king/Henry the thirde,/ unto the first yere/&c./Imprinted at London in Fléet-/stréete by Henry Wykes,/ Anno Domini/1551./
[In border 18 state 4.]
Colla. As in S 27. Except title and table, this is identical with S 27. Last leaf wanting.
Colo. None.

S 29. In this vo-/lume are/conteined the statutes/made and established/from the time of king/Henry the third,/&c./Imprinted at London in Fleete-/streete by Henry Wykes. Anno Domini/1564./
Colla. as in 1. This is a complete reprint, made page by page with the original.
Colo. [on reverse of i 6, following McK. 80] Londini in officina Thomae Ber-/theleti typis impress./Cum priuilegio ad imprimen-/dum solum./Anno M.D.XLIII./

S 30. In this vo-/lume are con-/teyned the Statutes, made/and established from the time of/Kinge Henrye the/thirde, &c. . . . / Anno Domini./1577./ [In border 45.]
Colla. T.p.+[7]+A–Qq 8's, Rr–Tt 6's, A–F 8's, G–I 6's.
Colo. ¶ Here endeth the statutes of kynge/Henry the seventh./God save the Kinge./

f. Statutes at Large

S 31. The/whole volume of sta-/tutes at large,/which at anie/ &c. . . ./At London/Printed for Christopher Barker, Printer/to the Queenes most excel-/lent Maiestie./1587.
[Title in border 50.]
Colla. T.p.+[7]+1–1043,+1–786.
Colo. None.

g. Collected Statutes

HENRY THE EIGHTH

S 32. ❧ The Second Volume/conteyninge those Statutes,/which haue ben made in/the tyme of the most vic/torious reigne of our/ most gracious soue-/raigne lorde kyng/Henry the/Eyght./❧/ ❧ Londini in aedibus Thome Bertheleti/Typographi regii excus./Anno uerbi incarnati. M.D.XLIII./Cum priuilegio.
Colla. T.p. & table [7].

S 33. ❧ The Second Volume/conteyning those Statutes,/which haue ben made in/the tyme . . . &c./❧ Londini in aedibus Thomae Bertheleti/Typographi regius excus./Anno uerbi incarnati. M.D.XLIII./Cum priuilegio.
Colla. T.p. & table [6].

S 34. ❧ The Second volume/conteinyng those Statutes/whiche haue ben made/in the tyme of the most/victoriouse reigne/of kyng Henrie/the Eight./With a table to the whole./❧ Londini in

aedibus Thomae Bertheleti./Anno uerbi incarnati. M.D.LI./ Cum priuilegio . . ./❦/
Colla. T.p. & table, [8].

S 35. The Seconde/volume./Conteining those Statutes/whiche haue been made in/the time of the moste vic-/torious reygne of kyng/ Henry the eight, with/a Table to the/whole./Anno. 1563./ ¶ Imprinted at London in Flete-/streete by Thomas Powell./ Cum priuilegio &c.

S 36. The second/volume,/conteininge/those Statutes which haue beene/made in the time of the moste victori-/ous reigne of Kinge Henry/the eight, with a table/to the whole./❧ ❧ Anno. 1575./Imprinted at London in Fleete-/streate neare to S. Dunstones Church by Thomas/Marshe./
Colla. T.p. & table [7].

EDWARD THE SIXTH

S 37. ❧ A table to all the Sta-/tutes made in the/tyme of the/ most vi-/ctori-/ous Reigne of Kynge/Edward the/sixte./❦/ ❧ Londini in aedibus/Thomae Bertheleti./Aeno verbi incar-/nati. M.D.LIII./Cum priuilegio./ [Title in border 18, state 4.]
Colla. T.p.+[3].

S 38. ❧ A table/to al the Statutes made from/the beginning of the raigne of/Kyng Edwarde the. vi. unto this/present. xii. yeare of the reigne/of oure moste gratious/and soueraigne Ladye/ Queene Elizabeth./(.˙.)/In aedibus Richardi/Tottelli./Cum priuilegio./ [Title in border 22.]
Colla. T.p.+[6].

SECTION 2. ABRIDGMENTS

a. The Great Abridgment

S 39. No title-page.
Colla. [4]+A–N 8's.
Colo. None.

S 40. No title-page.
Colla. [7]+i–clxxxviii.
Colo. ¶ Explicit abbreuiamentum Statutoꝝ/im̄pssū/per Ricardū Pynson Et totaliter finitū nono/die Mensis Octobris. Anno dn̄i Mill' mo qua/tcentesimo Nonagesimo nono./ [Device, McK. 3 b.]

S 41. No title-page.
Colla. [7]+i–clxxxviii.
Colo. ¶ Explicit abbreuiamentū statutoꝝ im̄pssum/ꝑ Richardū Pynson & totaliter finitum nono/die Mensis octobris. Anno dn̄i Mill' mo qua-/tcentesimo Nonagesimo nono./ [Device, McK. 3 b.]

S 42. ¶ Le breggement de toutes/les estatutes: ausi bien des vielles/ come des nouelles, nouellemēt/abbreges, correctes, et amen-/des par Guillame Owein/du medile temple. Et/imprimes ꝑ Richard/ Pynson tanqz al/xiii. an du tresui-/ctorieux et soue-/raigne roy/ Henry le/viii./

Colla. T.p.+[4]+1 bl.+i–ccv+1 bl.

Colo. ¶ Explicitum abbreuiamentum statutoꝝ impressū/ Londini per Richardum Pynsonū regium/impressorem. Anno domini Millesimo/quingentesimo vigesimo primo./Die octavo mensis Maij/Cum priuilegio/a rege in-/dul-/to./ [Device, McK. 3 b.]

S 43. ¶ Le Breggement/de toutz les estatutz, auxi/bien des veillez cōe dez no/uellez, nouellemēt abrig-/gez, correctez et amēdez &c. . . . /Anno dn̄i. M.D.xxviij./

Colla. T.p.+[7]+i–ccv+[1].

Colo. ¶ Explicitum abbreuimentum statutoꝝ impressū/Londini per Richardum Pynsonū regium/Impressorem. Anno domini Millesimo/quingentesimo vigesimo primo./Die octavo mensis Maij/Cum priuilegio/a rege in-/dul-/to./

S 44. [An abridgment/of the Statutes/In English/Enprinted/by/John Rastell/1527./]

Colla. [T.p.?] [table],+i–cclxiiii.

Colo. ¶ Enprynted in the chepesyde at the syg-/ne of the mere mayde next to poulys ga-/te the. xxii. day of Decēber in the. xix/yere of the reygne of oure so/uerayne lorde kinge Henry/ the. viii./ ¶ Per me Johannem Rastell./Cum Priuilegio Regali./ [Device, McK. 37 on reverse.]

S 45. ¶ Magnum ab-/breuiamentū/statutorum/Anglie/usqz ad an-/ num. xv. H. viii./inclusiue./

Colla. T.p.+[7]+i–cccxxiii+[5].

Colo. (on third unnumbered leaf). ¶ Johānes Rastel imprimi/ me fecit. i. die Decembris/, anno dn̄i. M.ccccc./xxviii./ ¶ Cum priuilegio regali/. [Two pages of errata, and device McK. 37 at end.]

S 46. Le bregemēt de tou/tes les estatutes: ausi bi-/en des vielles come des/nouelles: nouellemēt im/primes per Robert Red-/mā tanqz al. xviii. an du/tresuictorieux et so/ueraigne roy/Henry le/viii./ Cū gratia et priuilegio./ [Title in border, McK. 81.]

Colla. T.p.+[3]+i–cc.

Colo. Lacking.

S 47. Here begynnith the hole/abrygemēt of al the sta/tutz aswel the olde as/the new with diuers/other tytles & sta/tutes whiche/ were/never impryntyd before/in englysshe . . . &c. . . . / [Title in border McK. 81.]

Colla. T.p.+[3]+i–ccxxlii+[1].

Colo. Here endyth the/hole abrydgemēt/of al the statutz . . . &c./Imprynted at Lon-/don in Saynt/Donstons/Pa-/ryshe at the/signe of the Ge/orge by me Robert/Redman the yeere of our/lorde. M.CCCCC.XXVIII./Cum gratia & priuile-/gio a rege indulto./

S 48. ¶ The grete ab-/bregement of the/statutys of En-/glond untyll/ the. xxii. yere/of kyng/Henry the. viii./Cum priuilegio/Regali./
Colla. T.p.+[7]+i–ccxciii+[11].
Colo. None.

S 49. ¶: The greate/abbrydgement of/all ye statutes of Eng-/lande, untyll the. xxx yere/of the reygne of our moste/drad soueraygne lorde kynge/Henry the eyght &c./ [In border 29.]
Colla. T.p.+[7]+I–CCCCXV+[11].
Colo. ❧ Imprynted at/London in Fletestrete,/at the sygne of the George/nexte to Saynt Dunstones/churche, by me Roberte/ Redman./Cum priuilegio,/Regali./ [Device, McK. 3 c on reverse.]

S 50. [Title-page lacking.]
Colla. T.p.+[5]+i–cccxi+[10].
Colo. ¶ Imprynted by Robert Redman./Cum priuilegio a rege/ indulto./ [No. 22.]

S 51. ¶: The greate/abbrydgement of/all ye statutes of Eng-/lāde, untyl the. xxxiii. yere/of the reygne of our moste/drad soueraygne lord king/Henry the eyght. . . . &c./ [Title in border 29.]
Colla. T.p.+[7]+I–CCCXXI+[8]. [Cut 22.]
Colo. ❧ Imprynted at/London in Fletestrete by me wyl-/lyam Myddylton dwellynge/at the sygne of the George/nexte to saynte Dun-/stones churche./In the/yere of our Lorde. M/ CCCCC./XLII./ ¶ Cum priuilegio/ad imprimen-/dum solum./ [Device, McK. 93 on reverse.]

S 52. ¶: The great/Abredgement of all the/Statutes of Englande/with the abredgemētes of the/statutes made in the. XXXIII. yere/ &c. . . . [Device, McK. 86.]
Colla. T.p.+[8]+I–CCCXXI+[9].
Colo. ❧ Imprynted at/London in Paules church yarde/at the Sygne of the May-/dens heed by Thomas/Petyt. In the yere /of our Lorde/God./M.D.XLII./Cum priuilegio ad im-/primendum solum./ [Device, McK. 86. Sill-piece only.]

S 53. ¶ The newe greate/abredgement brefly con-/teynynge, all thactes and statu-/tes of this Realme of England,/untyll the. xxxv. yere of the reigne/of oure late noble Kynge of moste/worthye and famous memorye/Henry the. viii./(whose soule/God pardone) . . . &c. . . . /Excusum Londini in officina/Thomae Gaultier./Anno Domini 1551./ [In border, McK. 101.]
Colla. T.p.+[7]+i–ccclxxxi+[10]+1 bl.
Colo. ¶ Imprynted at London by Richard/Kele, dwellyng in Lombard/strete nere unto the stockes/market at the signe of/ the Egle. In the/yere of our/Lorde/M.D.LI./

S 54. ¶ The newe greate/abredgement brefly con-/teynynge, all thactes and statu-/tes &c. Excusum Londini in officina/Thomae Gaultier/Anno Domini 1551./ [In border, McK. 101.]

Colla. T.p.+[7]+i–ccclxxxi.+[10].
Colo. ¶ Imprinted at London by/Wyllyam Seres dwellyng/at Peter Colledge beside/Powles. In the/yere of our/Lorde/M.D.LI./ Cum priuilegio.

S 55. ¶ The newe greate/abredgement brefly con-/teynynge, all thactes and statu-/tes of this Realme of England,/untyll the. xxxv. yere of the reigne/of oure late noble Kynge of moste/worthye and famous memorye/ . . . &c. . . . /([Excusum Londini in officina/ Thomae Gaultier] printed over by an ornamental bar)/Anno Domini 1551./ [In border, McK. 101.]
Colla. T.p.+[7]+i–ccclxxi+[10].
Colo. ¶ Imprinted at London in Flete-/strete by Wyllyam Powel dwel-/lyng at the signe of the George/nexte to saincte Dun-/stones churche. In/the yere of our/Lorde/M.D.LI./

S 56. [Great abridgement of the Statutes. Petit 1552.]

b. Rastell's Statutes

S 57. A colleccion of/all the statutes (from the/ begynning of Magna Carta/unto the yere of our Lorde,/1557) . . . &c./In aedibus Richardi Tottelli./Cum priuilegio ad impri-/mendum solum./
Colla. [6]+1–550.
Colo. ¶ Imprinted at London/in Fletestrete within Temple Barre, at the/signe of the hande & starre, by Richard Tottyll./ And finished the. 16. day of October./Anno domini. 1557./Cum priuilegio.

S 58. ❧ A colleccion of all/the statutes (from the begynning of/ Magna Carta unto the yere of/our Lorde. (1557.) whiche/were before that yere/imprinted./Whereunto be addyd the collection of/the statutes, made in the fourth and/fifth yeres of the reignes of king Phi-/lip and Quene Mary, and also the/statutes made in the first yere/of the raigne of our soue-/raygne lady Queene/ Elizabeth./&c. . . . / ¶ In aedibus Richardi Tottelli./1559/Cum priuilegio ad imprimen-/dum solum./
Colla. T.p.+[5]+1–580.
Colo. ❧ Imprinted at Lon-/don in Fletestrete, within Temple/barre at the signe of the hande and/starre by Richard Tottell. And finished/the. ix. daye of Nouēber in the yere/of our Lord/1559./Cum priuilegio./

S 59. ❧ A colleccion of all/the statutes (from the begynning of/ Magna Carta unto the yere of/our Lorde. 1557) whiche/ were before that yere/imprinted./Whereunto be addyd the colleccion of/the statutes, made in the fourth and/fift yeres of the reignes of kyng Phi-/lip and Quene Mary, and also the/statutes made in the fyrst yere/of the raigne of our soue-/rayne Lady Quene/ Elizabeth./ . . . &c. . . . /In aedibus Richardi Tottelli./1559./ Cum priuilegio ad imprimen-dum solum./
Colla. T.p.+[5]+1–580.
Colo. ¶ Imprinted at London/in Fletestrete within Temple

Barre, at the/signe of the hande & starre by Richard Totty/ll. And finished the. 9. day of Nouember./Anno domini. 1559./Cum priuilegio./

s 60. A collection/of all the statutes, from the/begynning of Magna Carta,/unto the yeare of our Lorde (1557.)/&c. . . . /In aedibus Richardi Tottelli./Anno. 1565. die/Maij 26./ ¶ Cum Priuilegio Regiae Maiestatis./

Colla. T.p.+[7]+1–619.

Colo. ¶ Imprinted at Lon-/don in fletestrete within Temple/ Barre at the signe of the hande and/starre by Rycharde Tottel, the/xxvi. daye of May./An. 1565./Cum priuilegio ad impri-/ mendum solum./

s 61. (T.p. lacking.)

Colla. T.p.+[5]+1–618.

Colo. ☙ Imprinted at Lon-/don in fleetestrete within temple/ Barre at the signe of the hand and/starre by Rychard Tottel, the/last daye of October/An. 1566./Cum priuilegio./

s 62. ¶ A collection/of all the statutes, from/the beginning of Magna Charta,/unto this present yeare of our/Lorde God. 1568./In aedibus Richardi Totelli/Anno. 1568. decimo ter-/tio Nouembris./ Cum priuilegio &c.

Colla. T.p.+[5]+1–634.

Colo. ☙ Imprinted at Lon-/don in fletestrete within Temple/ Barre at the signe of the hand & starre,/ by Richard Tottill, in the/year of our lorde/1568./Cum priuilegio./

s 63. ¶ A collection/of all the statutes, from/the beginning of Magna charta,/unto this present yere of our/Lorde God 2572./In aedibus Richardi Tottelli./Añ. 1572. vicesimo quarto./Ianuarij./ Cum priuilegio Regiae Maiestatis./

Colla. T.p.+[7]+1–664.

Colo. ¶ Imprynted at Lon-/don in Fletestrete within Temple barre/at the signe of the Hand and starre, by/Rychard Tottyl. Anno/1572./Cum priuilegio./

s 64. ¶ A collection/of all the statutes, from/the beginning of Magna charta,/unto this present yere of our/Lorde God. 1574./In aedibus Richardi Tottelli./Añ. 1574. vicesimo sexto/Iulij./Cum priuilegio Regie Maiestatis./

Colla. T.p.+[7]+1–689.

Colo. ¶ Imprinted at London in/Fletestrete within Temple barre/at the signe of the Hand and starre,/By Rychard Tottel. Anno./1574./Cum priuilegio.

s 66. ❧ A collection of all the/Statutes, from the beginning of Magna/Charta, unto this present yeare of/our Lord God 1579 . . . &c. . . . /Anno Domini./1579./

Colla. T.p.+[43]+1–639+[12].

Colo. ¶ Imprinted at London by Christopher Barker/Printer to the Queenes Maiestie./

s 67. ❧ A collection in English, of the/Statutes nowe in force, continued from the beginning of Magna/Charta, made in the 9. yeere of the reigne of King H. 3. untill/the ende of the Session of Parliament holden in the 23. yeere of the Reigne of our gra-/tious Queene Elizabeth . . . &c . . . /❧ Imprinted at London by/Christopher Barker, Printer to the/Queens most excellent maiestie./

Colla. T.p.+[31]+1–559+[17].

Colo. ❧ Imprinted at London by/Christopher Barker, printer to the/Queenes Maiestie./1583./

s 68. ❧ A Collection in English, of the/Statutes nowe in force, continued from the beginning of Magna/Charta, made in the 9. yeere of the reigne of King H. 3. untill/the ende of the Session of Parliament holden in the 23. yeere of the reigne of our gra-/tious Queene Elizabeth &c . . . /❧ Imprinted at London by/Christopher Barker, Printer to the/Queenes most excellent Maiestie./

Colla. T.p.+[30]+1 bl.+1–559+1 bl.+[20].

Colo. ❧ Imprinted at London by/Christopher Barker, printer to the/Queenes Maiestie./

s 69. ❧ A collection in English, of the/Statutes now in force, continued from the beginning of Mag-/na Charta, . . . &c. . . . / ❧ Imprinted at London by the/Deputies of Christopher Barker, Printer to the/Queenes most excellent Maiestie./Anno 1588./

Colla. T.p.+[31]+1–596+[16].

Colo. None.

s 69a. ❧ A Collection in English, of the/Statutes now in force . . . / ❧Imprinted at London by the/Deputies of Christopher Barker, Printer to/the Queenes most excellent Maiestie/Anno 1591./

Colla. T.p.+[29]+1–528+[16].

Colo. None.

s 70. ❧ A collection in English, of the/Statutes now in force, continued from the beginning of Mag-/na Charta, . . . &c . . . / ❧ Imprinted at London by the/Deputies of Christopher Barker, Printer to/the Queenes most excellent Maiestie./Anno 1594./

Colla. T.p.+[31]+1–552+[14].

Colo. None.

s 70a. ❧ A Collection in English, of the/Statuts now in force . . . / ☙ Imprinted at London by Charles/Yetsweirt Esq./Cum priuilegio Regiae Maiestatis./Anno 1595./

Colla. T.p.+[30]+1–562 pp.+[14].

Colo. None.

s 71. ¶ A collection in English, of the/Statutes now in force, continued from the/beginning of Magna Charta . . . &c./❧ Imprinted at London by Thomas/Wight and Bonham Norton./Anno Dom. 1598./

Colla. T.p.+[31]+1–552+[36].

Colo. None.

c. Pulton's Penal Statutes

S 72. [Pulton's Penal Statutes. Tottel 1560. Dibdin.]

S 73. An abstract of all the/penall Statutes which be generally in force and use, . . . &c./collected by Fardinando/Pulton/of Lincoln Inne/Gentleman./ . . . &c. . . . /
¶ In aedibus Richardi Tottelli./Anñ Dominj. 1577./ ¶ Cum Priuilegio Regie Maiestatis./
Colla. T.p.+[7]+1–418.
Colo. Imprinted at Lon-/don in Fleetestrete, within Temple/ Barre at the signe of the hand and/Starre by Richard Tottyl, the/ first day of Nouember/1577./ ¶ Cum Priuilegio./

S 73a. An abstract of al the/penall Statutes which be generall, in force and use . . . /In aedibus Richardi Tottelli./Anno Dominj. 1577/ ¶ Cum Priuilegio Regiae Maiestatis./
Colla. T.p.+[5]+323+[11].
Colo. Imprinted at Lon-/don in Fleetestrete, within Temple/ Barre at the signe of the hand and/Starre by Richard Tottyl, the /27. day of Ianuary./1577./ ¶Cum priuilegio./

S 74. An Abstract of all the/penal Statutes which be general, in force/ and use . . . &c./[McK. 193 a]/Imprinted at London by Christopher/Barker, printer to the Queenes Maiestie./Anno. 1579. Octob. 20./Cum priuilegio ad imprimendum solum./
Colla. T.p.+[7]+1–376.
Colo. Imprinted at London/by Christopher Barker, Printer to/the Queenes Maiestie./Cum privilegio ad imprimen/dum solum./An. Do. 1579./

S 74a. The same, without date on the title-page.

S 75. An Abstract of all the/penal Statutes which be general, in force and/use, . . . &c. . . . / ¶ Collected by Fardinando Pulton of Lincolnes Inne, Sythence the Parliament holden Anno. 23. Elizabeth, and by him corrected/and amended./&c./McK. 193b/ Imprinted at London by Christopher/Barker, printer to the Queenes Maiestie./Anno. 1581. Septembris. 30./Cum priuilegio ad imprimendum solum./
Colla. T.p.+[7]+1–368.
Colo. Imprinted at London/by Christopher Barker, Printer/ to the Queenes Maiestie/ ¶ Cum priuilegio ad imprimendum solum./An. Do. 1581./

S 76. An abstract of all the/penal Statutes which be general, in force and/use . . . &c. . . . /[McK. 193 b]./
☙ Imprinted at London by Christopher/Barker, printer to the Queenes Maiestie./Anno. 1586. Octobris. 12./Cum priuilegio ad imprimendum solum./
Colla. T.p.+[7]+1–404.
Colo. Imprinted at London/by Christopher Barker, Printer/ to the Queenes Maiestie./ ¶ Cum priuilegio ad imprimendum solum./

S 77. ☞ An abstract of all/the penal Statutes . . . &c. . . . /[McK. 193 a]/Imprinted at London by Christo-/pher Barker, Printer to the/Queenes Maiestie./Cum priuilegio ad imprimendum solum./
Colla. T.p.+[7]+1–418.
Colo. ☜ Imprinted at Lon-/don by Christopher Barker, Prin-/ter to the Queenes Maiestie./Cum priuilegio ad imprimendum solum./

S 77a. An abstract of all the pe-/nall statutes . . . . /☞ Imprinted at London by the Deputies/of Christopher Barker, printer to the Queenes/most excellent Maiestie./Anno 1592./Cum priuilegio ad imprimendum solum./
Colla. T.p.+[7]+1–368.
Colo. ¶ Imprinted at London by the Depu-/ties of Christopher Barker, Printer/to the Queenes most excellent/Maiestie./Anno 1592./Cum priuilegio ad imprimendum solum.

S 78. An abstract of all the pe-/nall Statutes . . . &c. . . . /At London,/Printed by Iane Yetsweirt, widow of Charles/Yetsweirt Esq. late deceased. 1596./Cum priuilegio Regiae Maistatis./
Colla. T.p.+[7]+1–390.
Colo. None.

S 79. An/Abstract of all the penall/Statutes . . . &c./At London,/ Printed by Thomas Wight/1600./Cum Priuilegio Regiae Maiestatis./
Colla. T.p.+[8]+1–349, incomplete.
Colo. None.

d. Abridgments of Session-Laws

S 80. Statuta de An. xxi. Henrici. VIII./ ¶ Here after foloweth an abbryd-/gement of the statutes, made in the parlya-/ment helde in the. xxi. yere of Kynge/Henry tge eyght./
Colla. A, B 8's.
Colo. ¶ Cum gratia et priuilegio.

S 81. Statuta de Anno. xxii. H. VIII./The abredgemēt of the statutes/ made in the parlyament holden in the./xxii yere of the rayne of kynge/Henry the eyght./
Colla. A 8, B 10.
Colo. ¶ Imprynted at London in/Fletestrete, by Robert Red/ man dwellynge in saynt Dunstones/parysshe, next the churche./ at the sygne of the./George./

S 82. The abregemēt/of the statutys made in the/parlyamēt holden in/ the. xxii. yere of/ the/rayne of/kynge Henry/the/eyght./
Colla. A, B 8's.
Colo. None.

S 83. ¶ Statuta Anno. xxiii. H. VIII./ ¶ Here after foloweth an abrege-/ment of the statutes made in the parlya-/ment holden in the. xxiii. yere of/kynge Henry the eyght./
Colla. A 8, B 4.

Colo. ¶: Imprynted/at Londō in Fletestrete/by me Elizabeth late wyfe to/Robert Redman dwel-/lynge at the sygne of/the George nexte saynt/Dunstones/churche./Cum priuilegio./

s 84. The abregemēt/of the statutes/made in the par-/liamēt holden in/the. xxiii. &. xxiiii/yere of the reyn/of kynge/Henry the/eyghte./

Colla. A–C 8's.

Colo. Prynted by W. Rastell in/Fletestrete in saynt/Brydys chyrch/yarde./Anno a Christo nato/1534./Cum priuilegio./

s 85. The abregemēt/of statutes made/in the parlyment/holdē ī the. xxiiii/and. xxv. yere of/the reygne of/kynge Hen-/ry the/VIII./

Colla. A–E 8's, F 4.

Colo. ¶ Imprynted at/Lōdon in Fletestrete by me Wyl-/lyam Myddilton dwellynge at the/sygne of the Gorge, next to/Saynte Dunstones/Churche./Cum priuilegio./

s 86. The abredgemēt of/the statutes made/in the parlyamēt/holdē in the. xxiiii/and, xxv. yere of/the reygne of/kyng Hen-/ry the/viii./ [Cut 22.]

Colla. A–E 8's+F 2.

Colo. ¶ Imprynted at London in Flete-/strete, by me Robert Redman,/dwellyng at the sygne/of the George,/nexte to Saynt/Dunstones/church./Cum priuilegio./

s 87. Statuta de An. xxvi. Henrici viii./

Colla. A, B 8's.

Colo. ¶ Imprynted at London in/Fletestrete by me Roberte/Redman./

s 88. Statuta de An. xxvi. Henrici. viii./
¶ Here after foloweth an abbryd-/gement of the statutes, made in the parlya-/ment holden in the. xxvi. yere of kynge/Henry the eyght./ [Cut 22.]

Colla. A, B 8's.

Colo. ¶ Imprynted by me Robert Redman.

s 89. The abregemente of the statutz/made in the. xxvii & xxviij yere/of the reygne of kyng Hen/ry the eyghte./

Colla. A–F 8's.

Colo. ❧ Imprynted/at London in Fletestrete, by me/Roberte Redman, dwellynge, at the sygne of the George,/nexte to Saynte Dunsto-/nes Churche./Cum priuilegio ad imprimen-/dum solum./

s 90. The abregemēt/of the statutes/made ī the par-/lyament holden/in the. xxvii. &/xxviii. yere of/Henry the/viii./

Colla. A–F's.

Colo. ¶ Imprinted by me Ro-/bert Redman dwellyng/at the sygne of the/George./ ¶: Cum pri-/uilegio Re-/gali./ [Device, McK. 41.]

s 91. ❧ The Abrege/ment of the statutes ma/de in the. xxxj. yere of the reyg-/ne of our most drad souerayne/Lorde kynge Henry the eyght,/&c. . . . /

Colla. [10].

Colo. ☙ Imprynted/at London in Fletstrete,/by me Roberte Redman,/dwellynge at the syg-/ne of the George,/nexte to saynt/Dunsto-/nes/Churche./

S 92. ¶ The abregement of the sta/tutes of Anno. xxxi. Henrici. VIII./

Colla. A 8.

Colo. None.

S 93. ¶ Here begynneth the Abre-/gement of the statutes made/in the xxxii. yere of the reygne/of kyng Henry the/eyght./

Colla. A 8, B 6.

Colo. ☙: Imprynted/at London in Fletstrete/by me Elysabeth late wyfe/to Robert Redman/dwellyng at the sygne/of the George nexte/to Saynt Dunsto/nes chur-/che./ ¶ Cum priuilegio/ ad imprimen-/dum solum./ (Last leaf blank with device on reverse.)

S 94. ☙ The Abregemẽ/tes of the statutes made in the. xxxiii./yere of the reygne of our souereygne/lorde kyng Henry the. viii./

Colla. A–C 8's, D 6.

Colo. ¶ Imprynted at London/in Fletestrete at the sygne of/ the George by me Wyl-/lyam Mydylton./ [Cut 29. Device, McK. 93 on reverse.]

S 95. ¶ The abregemẽ-/tes of the statutes made in the/xxxiii. yere of the raygne of our soue-/raygne lorde kyng Henry the. viii./

Colla. 1–xxx+[2].

Colo. ☙ Imprynted at/London in Paules church yarde/at the sygne of the May-/dens heed by Thomas/Petyt. In the yere/ of our Lorde/God./M.D.xlii./Cum priuilegio ad im-/primendum solum./

SECTION 3. SESSION LAWS

RICHARD III

The First Year

S 96. Statuta apđ. Westmonasteriũ edita Annȯ primo re-/gis Ricardi tercii./

Colla. A–B 8's. T.p. (probably blank) and last leaf (blank) lacking.

Colo. None.

HENRY VII

The First to the Fourth Year

S 97. ¶ The kynge our souereyn lorde henry the seuenth after the/ conquest by the grace of god kyng of Englonde & of Fra-/unce and lorde of Irlonde at his parlyamẽt holden at West-/mynster the seuenth daye of Nouembre in the first yere of/his reigne, to thonour of god & holy chirche, and for the co/men profyte of the royame, bi thassent of the lordes spiritu/ell & temporell, and the comens in the sayd parliamẽt assẽ-/bled, and by auctorite of

the sayd parlyamente, hath do to be/made certein statutes & ordenaunces in maner & fourme fo-/lowyng.
Colla. aii–viii, b–d 8's, E ix [+1 bl?]; ai probably blank.
Colo. None.

S 98. ℂ The Kynge our souereyn lorde henry the seventh . . . &c.
Colla. a–d 6's, e 8.
Colo. ℂ Enpryñted at westmynster by/me wynken de worde./

S 99. Anno. i Henrici VII. [Cuts 5, 6.]
Colla. aii–vi (which is blank), b–e 6's, f 8.
Colo. ℂ Emprynted at London withoute Tempell/Barre, in Saynt Clementys parysshe,/by me Iulyan Notary dwellynge/at the syne of the thre kynges./In yᵉ yere of our lorde a./M.CCCCC.VII.

The Seventh Year

S 100. Anno vij° Henrici Septimi/&c.
Colla. a 6.
Colo. Enprynted at westmestre by/wynkyn de worde./

S 101. Anno. vii. Henrici. VII./ [Cuts 5, 6.]
Colla. AA 8.
Colo. ℂ Enprynted at London withoute Tempell/Barre, in Saynt Clementys parysshe,/By me Iulyan Notary dwellynge/ at the syne of the thre kynges./In yᵉ yere of our lorde a./ M.CCCCC.VII./

The Eleventh Year

S 102. Anno xi° Henrici vii./Statuta bonum publicum/concernencia edita in parliamento ten/to apud westmonasterium. xiiij. die/ Octobris Anno regni illustrissimi/Dñi nostri Regis Henrici septimi xi°. [No. 5 redrawn on reverse.]
Colla. A 8, B–E 6's.
Colo. None. [McK. 10, on reverse of last leaf.]

S 103. Anno. xi. Henrici. vii./Statuta bonū publicum concernēcia . . . &c.
Colla. A 8, B–D 6's.
Colo. None.

S 104. Anno XI° Henrici VII./ [Cuts 5, 6.]
Colla. T.p.+[1]+Aa–Gg 6's.
Colo. ℂ Enprynted at London withoute Tempell/Barre, in Saynt Clementys parysshe,/By me Iulyan Notary dwellynge/ at the syne of the thre kynges./In yᵉ yere of our lorde a./ M.CCCC.VII./ [At the end Notary's device, McK. 26 and 28.]

S 105. ℂ The statutes concerning the common wele. . . .
Colla. A 8, B–E 6.
Colo. Lacking.

The Nineteenth Year

S 106. Anno xix henrici VII./Statuta/Bonum publicū concernantia, &c.
[Large capital S. A chain border surrounds each page of print.]

Colla. A–C 8's (last leaf blank).

Colo. ¶ Here endeth the statues/holden at Westmēstyr the/ XXV. daye of Ianiuere in yᵉ/XIX. yere of yᵉ moste nobyil/ reigne of kynge henry the/VII. Enprynted in london/within seynt Helens be/Guillam Faques yᵉ kyng/prynter. [W. Faques' device, McK. 14 & 15.]

S 107. No title-page: [Cuts 5, 6.]

Colla. A–B 6's, C–E 4's.

Colo. ¶ Enprynted at London without Tempelle,/Barre in Saynt Clementys parysshe/By me Iulyan Notary dwellynge/ at the syne of the thre kynges/In yᵉ yere of our lorde a./ M.CCCCC.VII./ [At end, Notary's device, McK. 26 & 28.]

All the Years

S 108. ¶ Statuta. VII. perlamentoꝝ Henrici VII.

Colla. T.p.+[1]+A 6, B 4, C 8, D 4, E 8, F–G 6's, F 4, G 8, H–I 6's, K 4, L 8, M 4, N–O 8's, P 2, Q 6, P 4, Q 8, R 4, S 8.

Colo. ¶ Here endeth the statutes./ ¶ Enprynted at London in Fletestrete/at the sygne of the sonne, by Wynkyn/de Worde. In the yere of our lorde a./M.CCCCC.VIII./[de Worde's device, McK. 10.]

S 109. [First years not found; title-page of nineteenth year.] Anno. XIX./Henrici. VII./ ¶ Statuta/in parliamēto apud Westmonesteriū vicesimo/quīto die Ianuarii Anno regni metuedissimi regis Anglie/&c . . . [Cut 7.]

Colla. [A–K]+l 6, m 8, n 4.

Colo. (at end of 19th year) ¶ Emprented at London in Fletestrete at the/signe of the George by Saint Dūstones/chyrche By me Rycharde Pyn-/son Squyer and prenter/unto the kynges/ noble grace./ [Pynson's device, McK. 9 b.]

HENRY VIII

The First Year

S 110. Anno primo. Henrici. viij./ ¶ A Reuocation &c. [Title-page lacking; probably cut 7.]

Colla. A 6, B 4, C 6, D 4.

Colo. ¶ Here endeth the Statutis holden at Westmyn-/ster the. xxi. daye of Ianuary in the firste yere of yᵉ/moste noble reygne of Kynge Henry the. viii. En/prynted in London by his cōmaundement in Flet/strete: at the Sygne of the George, by Richarde/Pynson, prynter unto his noble grace. With the/ pryuylege of our moste gracious Soueraygne lor/de kynge Henry the. viii. graunted to his trusty &/welbelouyd seruaunte Richarde Pynson, prynter unto his moste noble grace, that noo man within /this his Realme of Englonde, prynte nor sell, but/suche as the sayde Rycharde shal therunto thynke/beste by the space of. two yeres./

S 110a. ❡ The Acte of the Kynges Reuenues./ [Over No. 7; No. 8 on reverse.]
Colla. A 6, B 4, C 2.
Colo. ❡ Here endeth the statutes holden at Westmynster the. xxi. day of Ia-/nuary in the firste yere of the most noble reygne of Kynge Henry the./viii. Enpryntedin London by his commaũde-ment in Flestrete: at the/Sygne of the George. By Rycharde Pynson: prynter unto his noble/grace./ [over McK. 9 c.]

S 111. Title lacking.
Colla. [A 6, B 4?]
Colo. ❡ Here endeth the Statutis holden at westmynster the/ xxi. daye of January in y[e] firste yere of the most noble rey-/gne of Kynge Henry y[e] viii. Enprynted in London by me/Rychard Faques dwellyng in Poulys churche yerde at/the sygne of the Maydyn hed./ [McK. 31a.]

S 112. ☙ Anno Primo/Henrici Octavi./The kyng our souerayn/lorde Henry the. VIII. after the conquest, by the grace of god/Kynge of Englande and of Fraunce, and lorde of Irelande,/at his parlya-ment holden at westmynster the. XXI. day of/Ianuary, in the fyrste yere of his mooste noble reigne: to/the honour of god and hollye churche, and for the common weale/and profyte of this his realme, by the assente of the lordes/spyrytuall and temporall and the commons in this/present parlyament assembled, and by au-/ctoritie of the same: hath do to be or-/dayned, made, and enacted cer-/tayne statutes and ordi-/naunces in maner/and fourme/folow-/yng./ ❧ [Title in 18 lines. In border 18, state 2.]
Colla. T.p.+ii–x.
Colo. Thomas Berthelet regius impressor/excudebat. Cum privilegio. [Cut 16.]

S 113. ☙ Anno primo/Henrici Octavi./The kyng our soverain/lorde Henry the. VIII./&c./❧ [Title in 16 lines.]
Colla. T.p.+ii–x.
Colo. Thomas Berthelet excudebat./Cum priuilegio.
[Separate act, broadside.]
❡ An acte declarynge the establysshment of the successyon of the kynges moste royall/maiestie in the imperyall crowne of this realme./
Colla. One sheet.
Colo. Tho. Berth. regius impress. excudebat, Cũ. priuilegio.

S 114. ☙ Anno primo/Henrici/Octavi./ ❡ The kynge our soueraigne lorde/Henrie the eight &c. [In border 16, state 5.]
Colla. A 6, B 4.
Colo. ❡ Imprinted at London in Fletestreete by Thomas Powell.

S 115. Anno primo/Henrici/VIII./The king oure soueraigne lorde &c. [In border of straight lines.]
Colla. A 6, B 4.
Colo. None.

THE THIRD TO THE SEVENTH YEAR

S 116. Anno Regni Regis Henrici. viii. Tertio/Statuta/ ¶ The Kynge our soueraygne lorde Henry the. VIII. after the/Conquest by the grace of God kyng of Englande & of Frau̅/ce, and lorde of Irlande, at his Parlyament holden at west-/mester, the fourth day of Februarij. In the thyrde yere of his/moost noble Reygne to the honoure of god and holy Chur-/che, and for the Comon well & profyte of this his Royalme,/by the assent of the Lordes spirituall and temporall, and the/Comons in this his present Parlyament assembled, and by/ auctoryte of the same hath do to be ordeyned made and ena-/cted certayne Statutes, and ordynaunces in maner & four-/me folowynge./ [The title-page is dominated by the great S, which is prolonged into the head of a large bird. It occurs on the title-page of all Pynson's statutes of this reign. A separate title-page to the fourth year, but a continuous register. On reverse of each title-page, cut 8.]

Anno regni Regis Henrici. viii. Quarto./Statuta./ ¶ The Kynge our souerayne lorde Henry the. VIII. &c.

Colla. A 6, B 4, C 6, D 4, E 4.

Colo. None. Pynson's device on reverse of last leaf, the obverse being blank.

S 117. ¶ Anno sexto Henrici. viii./Statuta./ ¶ The Kyng our souerayne lorde Henry the. viii. &c.

Colla. A–B 6, C–D 4.

Colo. . . . Enprynted by the cōmaundment of oure Souereygne lorde the Kynge & his Counsell by (Rycharde Pynson) prynter unto his moste noble grace, dwellyng in Lōdon in Fletestrete, at the sygne of the George, besyde Supet Dunstane's Churche.

S 117a. Anno Sexto. Henrici. viii./Statuta/¶ The Kynge our Soueraygne lorde Henry the. viii. . . . [No. 8 on reverse.]

Colla. A–B 6's, C–D 4's.

Colo. ¶ Here endeth the Statutes holden at Westmester the. v. day/of Februarii. In the. vi. yere of the moost noble reygne of Kyn-/ge Henry the. viii. Enprynted by the co̅maundement of oure/Souereygne lorde the Kynge & his Counsell by (Rycharde/ Pynson) prynter unto his moste noble grace, dwellyng in Lō/ don in Fletestrete, at the sygne of the George, besyde Seynt/ Dunstanes Churche./ [over McK. 9 c.]

S 117b. Anno Septimo. Henrici. viii../Statuta/¶ The kynge our Souereygne lord Henry the. viii. . . . [Cut No. 8 on reverse.]

Colla. A 6, B 4, C 6.

Colo. (on C 5 *rev.*) ¶ Here endeth the Statutes holden at Westmester the. xii. daye of Nouembre. In the. vii. yere of/the moost noble Reygne of Kynge Henry/the. viii. Emprynted by the cōmaun-/dement of our Soueraygne lorde/the Kynge & his Counseyll by/(Richarde Pynson) Pryn/ter unto his moost noble/ grace, dwellynge in/London in Flete-/strete, at the Sy/gne of the Ge/orge./

[Cut No. 7 on C 6 *obv.*; McK. 9 c on C 6 *rev.*]

S 118. ☙ Anno tertio/Henrici Octavi./The Kyng our soverayn/lorde Henry the. VIII. after the conquest, by the grace of god/kynge of Englande and of Fraunce, and lorde of Irelande,/at his parlyament holden at westmynster the. iiii. daye of/February, in the thyrde yere of his mooste noble reygne &c./❧/ [Cut 16. A separate title-page to each of the years, 3, 4, 6, 7.]
Colla. T.p.+ii–l (for 53).
Colo. Thomae Berthelet regius impressor excudebat. Cum/privilegio ad imprimendum solum. [Cut 17, state 3. A separate colophon for each year.]

S 119. ☙ Anno tertio/Henrici Octavi./The kyng our souerayne/ lorde Henry the. VIII. &c./❧/ [Separate title-page for each year, that for the fourth year dated M.D.LII.]
Colla. T.p.+II–XLVII (for 53).
Colo. Tho. Bertheleti. Cum priuilegio ad imprimendum solum./ [Cut 17. Separate colophon for each year.]

S 120. ❧ Anno tertio/Henrici/Octavi./ ¶ The kynge our soueraygne lorde/Henry the eyght &c. [In border 18, state 5. Separate title-page for each year.]
Colla. A–H 6's, I 4.
Colo. ¶ Imprinted at London in Fletstreete by Thomas Powell./Cum priuilegio ad imprimendum solum./

S 121. Anno tertio/Henrici/VIII./The kynge our soueraygne lorde &c./ ❧ ☙/ [In border of straight lines. Separate title-page for each year.]
Colla. A 4, B–H 6, I 4.
Colo. None.

THE FOURTEENTH AND FIFTEENTH YEAR

S 122. [Pynson.]
Conjectural.

S 123. ☙ Anno XIIII et/XV. Henrici Octavi./The kynge our Soverayne/lorde Henry the. VIII. after the conquest, by the grace of god/kynge of Englande and of Fraunce, defender of the faythe,/ and lorde of Irelande, at his parlyament holden at London/the. xv. day of Apryll, in the. xiiii. yere. &c./❧/ [Cut 16, state 2.]
Colla. T.p.+II–XV+1 blank.
Colo. Thomas Berthelet regius impressor/excudebat. Cum priuilegio.

S 124. ☙ Anno XIIII et/XV. Henrici Octavi./The kynge our soueraine/lorde, Henry the. VIII . . . &c. . . ./❧/
Colla. T.p.+[i]+iii–xiiii.
Colo. Thomas Berthelet excudebat./Cum priualegio./

S 125. ❧ Anno XIIII. et/XV. Henrici/Octavi./ ¶ The kynge our soueraigne lorde/Henrie the eight &c. [In border 18, state 5.]
Colla. A 6, B 8.
Colo. None.

S 126. Anno XIIII. et XV./Henrici/VIII./The kynge our soueraygne lorde &c. . . . [In border of straight lines.]
Colla. A 6, B 8.
Colo. None.

The Twenty-first Year

S 127. Statuta/in parliamento apud westmonasteri-/um tertio die Nouembris. Anno regni metuendissimi Anglie et Fran-/cie regis fidei defensoris, ac domini Hibernie Henrici octavi vicesimo/ primo Tento, Bonum publicum concernantia./
Colla. A–D 4's, E 6.
Colo. None. [McK. 44 on reverse of last leaf.]

S 128. Statuta/in parliamento apud westmonasteri-/um &c.
Colla. A–D 4's, E 6.
Colo. None. No device.

S 129. Statuta/in parliamento/apud Westmonasterium tertio/&c.
Colla. A–D 4, E 6.
Colo. None. [McK. 37 on reverse of last leaf.]

S 130. Anno. XXI./Henrici/VIII./Statuta ad Remp./spectantia . . . &c./ [In border 18, state 3.]
Colla. T.p.+II–XXVII.
Colo. Londini in aedibus Thomae Ber-/theleti Regii Impres-/ soris./Cum priuilegio.

S 131. ❧ Anno. XXI./Henrici/VIII./Statuta ad Remp./spectantia &c. [In border 18, state 4.]
Colla. T.p.+II–XXVII.
Colo. Londini in aedibus Thomae Ber-/tholeti Regii impres-/ soris./Cum priuilegio.

S 132. ❧ Anno XXI./Henrici/Octavi./Statuta ad Remp./spectantia &c. . . . /Excudebat Londini,/Anno. 1562./ [In border 18, state 5.]
Colla. A–D 6's, E 4 (last leaf blank).
Colo. Londini in aedibus Thomae/Bertheleti Regii Im-/pres- soris./
(One copy in the British Museum has "Bertholeti" in the colophon).

S 133. Anno XXI./Henrici/VIII./Statuta ad Remp./spectantia &c. [In border of straight lines.]
Colla. A–D 6's, E 4 (last leaf blank).
Colo. None.

The Twenty-second Year

S 134. Anno XXII. H. VIII./Statuta bonū pu-/blicum concernen-/tia, edita in pliamento &c.
Colla. T.p.+II–XXIIII.
Colo. ¶ God saue the kynge./Tho. Berthelet regius impressor excudebat./Cum priuilegio./

S 135. Anno XXII. H. VIII./Statuta bonū pu-/blicum concernen-/tia, edita &c./☞ ☜/❧/
Colla. T.p.+ii–xxiiii.
Colo. ¶ Thomas Berthelet regius impressor/excudebat. Cum priuilegio./

S 136. Anno vicesimo se-/cundo Henrici/Octavi./Statuta bonum publi-/cum concernantia &c./❦/
[Line 20 of title is the word primū.]
Colla. T.p.+II–XXIIII.
Colo. Tho. Berthelet regius impressor excudebat./Cum priuilegio./

S 137. Anno vicesimo se-/cundo Henrici/Octavi./Statuta bonum/publicum concer-/nentia &c./
Colla. T.p.+II–XXIIII.
Colo. Tho. Berthelet regius impressor excudebat./Cum priuilegio./

S 138. Anno vicesimo se-/cundo Henrici/Octavi./Statuta bonum publi-/cum concernantia &c.
[Line 20 of title is the word primum: 31 lines in t.p.]
Colla. T.p.+II–XXIIII.
Colo. Tho. Berthelet regius impressor excudebat./Cum priuilegio./

S 139. Anno vicesimo se-/cundo Henrici/Octavi./Statuta bonum publi/cum concernantia edita in/parliamento &c. (29 lines)./❦/
Colla. A–D 6's.
Colo. ¶ Imprinted at London in Fleetestreete, by Thomas Powell./

S 140. Anno XXII./Henrici/VIII./Statuta bonum publicum/concernantia &c. [In border of straight lines.]
Colla. A–D 6's.
Colo. None.

THE TWENTY-THIRD YEAR

S 141. Anno. XXIII. H. VIII./The kynge our soueraigne lorde/Henry the eight by the grace of god/kynge of Englande and of Fraunce,/ &c. [Title in border 18, State 1.]
Colla. T.p.+II–XXIIII.
Colo. God saue the kynge./ ¶ Imprinted at London in Fletestret by Thomas/Berthelet, printer to the kynges moste/noble grace. Cum priuilegio./ [Cut 17, state 1. McK. 80 on reverse of last leaf.]

S 142. Anno XXIII. H. VIII./The kynge our soueraigne lorde/Henry the eight by the grace of god/kynge of Englande and of Fraunce,/ &c. [In border 18, state 2.]
Colla. T.p.+II–XXVIII.
Colo. God saue the kynge./ ¶ Imprinted at London in Fletestrete by/Thomas Berthelet, printer to/the kynges most noble/

grace. Cum pri-/uilegio./ [Colophon first on xxiv reverse, followed by cut 17 in state 1. Colophon repeated on xxviii, followed by cut 16.]

S 143. Anno XXIII. H. VIII./The kynge our soueraygne lorde/&c. [In border 18, State 2.]
Colla. T.p.+ii–xxviii.
Colo. God saue the/kynge./ ¶Imprynted at London in Fletestrete by/Thomas Berthelet prynter to/the kynges most noble/ grace. Cum pri-/uilegio./ [Cut 17, state 2.]

S 144. Anno XXIII. H. VIII./The kynge oure soueraigne lorde/Henry the eight &c. [Title in border 18, state 43.]
Colla. T.p.+ii–xxviii.
Colo. God saue the kynge./Tho. Berthelet regius impressor excudebat./Cum priuilegio./❧/ [Cut 17, state 3. Another colophon on leaf XXIV.]

S 145. ❧ Anno. XXIII. Henrici Octavi./The king our soueraigne lord/Henry the eyght . . . &c./❧/
Colla. A–D 6's, E 4.
Colo. (at end) ¶Imprynted at London in Fletestrete by/Thomas Berthelet prynter to/the kynges moste noble/grace. Cum pri/uilegio./ [Another colophon on D 6.]

S 146. Anno XXIII. H. VIII./The kynge oure soveraigne lorde/Henry the eight . . . &c./ [In border 18, state 4.]
Colla. T.p.+II–XXVIII.
Colo. ❧ God save the kynge. ❧/Tho. Berthelet regius impressor excudebat./Cum priuilegio./ [Cut 17 in state 5.]

S 147. ❧ Anno XXIII./Henrici/Octavi./The kynge our soueraigne lorde Henry/&c. [In border 18, state 5.]
Colla. A–D 6's, E 4.
Colo. ❧ God save the Kynge. ❧/Tho. Berthelet regius impressor excudebat./Cum priuilegio./ [On D 6 rev., cut 17, state 6.]

S 148. Anno XXIII./Henrici/VIII./The Kynge our Soueraygne Lorde/&c. [In border of straight lines.]
Colla. A–D 6's, E 4.
Colo. None.

The Twenty-fourth Year

S 149. ❧ Anno XXIIII/Henrici/VIII./Actis made/in the Session of this present parlya-/mente &c. ❧/Londini in aedibus Tho-/mae Bertheleti Re-/gii impressoris./Cum priuilegio.
Colla. T.p.+ii–xviii.
Colo. None. [Cut 17 in state 1.]

S 150. ❧ Anno XXIIII/Henrici/VIII./Actis made/in the Session of this presente parlya-/mente &c./❧/Londini in aedibus Thomae Berthe-/leti regii im-/pres-/soris. Excus./Anno. M.D. XXXVIII./Cum priuilegio./

Colla. T.p.+II–XVIII.
Colo. None. [Cut 17 in state 2.]

S 151. Anno XXIIII/Henrici/VIII./Actis made in/the session of this present parliament,/&c. . . . /❦/Londini in aedibus Thomae Ber-/theleti typis impress./Cum priuilegio ad imprimen-/dum solum./Anno. M.D.XLVI./
Colla. T.p.+II–XVII+V.
Colo. None. [Cut 17 in state 4.]

S 152. ❧ AnnoXXIIII./Henrici/VIII./Actis made/in the Session of this presente parlya-/mente . . . &c./❦/Londini in aedibus Thomae /Bertheleti Regii/Impressoris/excus./Anno M.D.XXXVIII./ Cum priuilegio./
Colla. T.p.+II–XVIII.
Colo. None. [Cut 17 in state 6.]

S 153. Anno XXIIII/Henrici/VIII./❧Actes made in/the session of this present parly-/amente &c. . . . /❦/Londini in aedibus Thomae Berthe-/leti Regii impressoris/Excus./Anno. M.D.XXXVIII./ Cum priuilegio./ [In border 18, state 5.]
Colla. A–C 6's.
Colo. None. [Cut 17, state 6.]

S 154. Anno XXIIII./Henrici/VIII./Actes made in the session of/&c. . . . [In border of straight lines.]/
Colla. A–C 6's.
Colo. None.

THE TWENTY-FIFTH YEAR

S 155. ❧ Anno. XXV./Henrici/VIII./Actis made/in the session of /this present Parliment/&c. . . . ☙ Londini in aedibus Tho-/mae Bertheleti re-/gii impressoris./Cum priuilegio a re-/ge indulto./
Colla. T.p.+II–XXXVII [for 41].
Colo. None. [Cut 17, state 1.]

S 156. ❧ Anno. XXV./Henrici/VIII./Actis made/in the session of/ this present parliment/&c. . . . Londini in aedibus Tho-/mae Bertheleti re-/gii impressoris./Cum priuilegio &c.
Colla. T.p.+II–XLI (irregular).
Colo. None. [Cut 17, state 1.]

S 157. ❧ Anno. XXV./Henrici/VIII./Actis made/in the session of /this present parliment/&c. . . . ❧/❧ Londini ☙/in officina Thomae Bar-/theleti typis/impress./Cum priuilegio ad impri-/mendum solum.
Colla. A–G 6's (last leaf blank).
Colo. None. [Cut 17, state 4.]

S 158. ❧ Anno. XXV./Henrici/VIII./Actis made/in the session of /this present Parliment/&c. . . . /❧❧ Londini ☙/in officina Thomae Bar-/theleti tipis/impress./Cum priuilegio ad impri-/mendum solum.

Colla. T.p.+II–XLII [for 41] + 1 blank.
Colo. None. [Cut 17, state 6.]

S 159. ❧ Anno XXV./Henrici/Octavi./Actes made in the session/ of this present parliament &c. . . . /Excudebat Londini,/Anno M.D.LXII./ [In border 18, state 5.]
Colla. A–G 6's (last leaf blank).
Colo. None.

S 160. ❧ Anno XXV./Henrici/Octavi./Actes made/in the session of this/present Parliament &c. . . . /Excudebat Londini,/Anno. M.D.LXII./ [In border 45.]
Colla. A–G 6's (last leaf blank).
Colo. None.

The Twenty-sixth Year

S 161. Anno. XXVI./Henrici/VIII./Actes made in the/session of this presente parly-/ament &c. . . . /Tho. Berthelet/excudebat./Cum priuilegio./ [In border 18, state 2.]
(The Table on the reverse ends *Finis Tabule.*)
Colla. T.p.+II–XXVII.
Colo. Thomas Bertheletus re-/gius impressor ex-/cudebat./ [Cut 17, state 2, on reverse, McK. 80.]

S 162. Anno. XXVI./Henrici/VIII./Actes made in the/session of this presente parly-/ament &c. . . . /Tho. Berthelet/excudebat./ Cum priuilegio. [In border 18, state 2.]
(The table on the reverse ends *Finis Tabulae.*)
Colla. T.p.+II–XXVII.
Colo. Thomas Bertheletus re-/gius impressor ex-/cudebat./ [Cut 17, state 2. No McK. 80, on reverse.]

S 163. Anno XXVI./Henrici/VIII./Actes made in the/session of this presente parly-/ament &c. . . . /Tho. Berthelet/excudebat./ Cum priuilegio./ [In border 18, state 3.]
(The table on the reverse ends *Finis Tabule.*)
Colla. T.p.+II–XXVI (for 27).
Colo. Thomas Bertheletus re-/gius impressor ex-/cudebat./ (No cut or device.)

S 164. Anno. XXVI. Henrici/Octavi./Actes made in the session of/ this present parlyament . . . &c. . . . /❦/Thomas Berthelet regis/impressor excudebat./Cum priuilegio ad im-/primendum solum./
Colla. A–C 6's, D 8.
Colo. ❧ Thomas Bertheletus re-/gius impressor ex-/cudebat./ ❧ Cum privilegio &c./

S 165. Anno. XXVI./Henrici/VIII./Actes made in the/session of this present parlia-/ment . . . &c. . . . /Tho. Berthelet/Excude-bat./Cum priuilegio./ [In border 18, state 4.]
Colla. T.p.+II–XXVI.
Colo. Thomas Bertheletus excudebat./Cum priuilegio ad im-primendum solum.

S 166. ❧ Anno XXVI./Henrici/Octavi./Actes made in the session/ of this present parliament . . . &c. . . . / ¶ Imprinted at London in Flete-/streete by Thomas Powell./ [In border 18, state 5.]
Colla. A–C 6's, D 8.
Colo. None.

S 167. Anno XXVI./Henrici/VIII./Actes made in the session of/this presente parliamente . . . &c. . . . /❧❧/ [In border of straight lines.]
Colla. A–C 6's, D 8.
Colo. None.

THE TWENTY-SEVENTH YEAR

S 168. Anno XXVII./Henrici/VIII./Actes made in the/session of this present parly-/ament holden upon prorogation at/Westm̄, the. IIII. day of February,/in the. XXVII. yere of the reygne/ . . . &c. . . . /Tho. Berthelet/Excudebat./Cum priuilegio./ [In border 18, state 2.]
[a ii, first line, Gloucester.]
Colla. T.p.+II–XLVII.
Colo. None. [Cut 17, state 2.]

S 169. Anno XXVII./Henrici/VIII./Actes made in the/session of this present parly-/ament . . . &c./Tho. Berthelet/Excudebat./ Cum priuilegio./ [In border 18, state 3.]
[a ii, first line, Glocester]
Colla. T.p.+II–XLVII.
Colo. None. [Cut 17, state 3.]

S 170. Anno XXVII./Henrici/VIII./Actes made in the/session of this present parly-/ament . . . &c. . . . /Thomas Berthelet/typographus regius excudebat./Anno. M.D.XLVI./Cum priuilegio ad impri-/mendum solum./ [In border 18, state 4.]
Colla. T.p.+II–XLVI.
Colo. None. [Cut 17, state 3.]

S 171. Anno XXVII./Henrici/VIII./Actes made in the/session of this present parli-/ament . . . &c. . . . /Imprinted at London/in Fletestrete by/Thomas Powell./An. M.D.LVII./Cum priuilegio ad impri-/mendum solum./ [In border 18, state 5.]
Colla. T.p.+II–XLVI (irregular).
Colo. None. [Cut 17, state 6.]

S 172. ❧ Anno XXVII./Henrici/Octavi./❧ Actes made in the sessi-/on of this present parliament . . . &c. . . . /Imprinted at London in Fletestrete/by Thomas Powell./Anno Christi,/ 1562./ [In border 18, state 5.]
Colla. A–G 6's, H 4.
Colo. None. [Cut 17, state 6.]

S 173. Anno XXVII./Henrici./Octavi./Actes made in/ . . . &c. . . . /

☞/Imprinted at London in Fletstrete/by Thomas Powell/ Anno Christi./1562./ [In border of straight lines.]
Colla. A–G 6's, H 4.
Colo. None.

THE TWENTY-EIGHTH YEAR

S 174. Anno. XXVIII./Henrici/VIII./Actes made in the/parliament begōne and hol-/den at Westm̄,/the. VIII. daye of/ . . . &c./ Tho. Berthelet re-/gis impressor/excudebat,/Cum priuilegio./ [In border 18, state 2.]
Colla. T.p.+II–XXVI.
Colo. None.

S 175. The same, leaves not numbered.

S 176. Anno XXVIII./Henrici/VIII./Actes made in the/parlyament begōne and hol-/den . . . &c./Tho. Berthelet/ excudebat./Cum priuilegio./ [In border 18, state 2.]
Colla. T.p.+II–XXVI.
Colo. None. [Cut 17, state 2.]

S 177. Anno XXVIII./Henrici/VIII./Actes made in the/parliament begōne and hol-/den at Westm̄, the. VIII. daye of/ . . . &c./ Tho. Berthelet re-/gis impressor ex-/cudebat,/Cum priuilegio./ [In border 18, state 4.]
Colla. A–C 6's, D 8.
Colo. None. [Cut 17, state 4.]

S 178. Anno XXVIII/Henrici/VIII./❧ Actes made in/the parliamente begunne and hol-/den at Westminster the. viii. day of/ . . . &c. /❦/Tho. Berthelet excudebat./Cum priuilegio./ [In border 18, state 5.]
Colla. A–C 6's, D 8.
Colo. None. [Cut 17, state 6.]

S 179. Anno XXVIII./Henrici/VIII./Actes made in the Parlia-/ment . . . &c./❧☙/ [In border of straight lines.]
Colla. A–C 6's, D 8.
Colo. None. [Cut 17, state 6.]

THE THIRTY-FIRST YEAR

S 180. ❧ Anno Tricesimo Primo/Henrici Octavi./Henry the/VIII. by the Grace/of God Kynge . . . &c. . . . /❧/ Londini./ ❧ Anno verbi in-/carnati/M.D.XXXIX./
Colla. T.p.+II–XXIX.
Colo. Londini in aedibus Thomae Berthe-/leti typis impress./ Cum priuilegio ad imprimen-/dum solum./Anno. M.D.XXXIX. [Cut 17, state 3.]

S 181. ❧ Anno Tricesimo Primo/Henrici Octavi./Henry the/VIII. by the Grace/of God kynge . . . &c. . . . /❧☙/❦/❧Londini./ ❧ Anno verbi in-/carnati./M.D.XXXIX./
Colla. T.p.+II–XXIX.

Colo. Londini in aedibus Thomae Berthe-/leti typis impress./ Cum priuilegio ad imprimen-/dum solum./Anno M.D.XXXIX./ [Cut 17, state 3.]

S 182. ❧ Anno Tricesimo Primo/Henrici Octavi./Henry the/VIII. by the Grace/of God Kyng &c. . . . /❦/Londini./❧ Anno verbi in-/carnati./M.D.XXXIX.

(In line 7 of the title "fayth.")

Colla. T.p.+II–XXVI (for 29).

Colo. Londini in aedibus Thomae Berthe-/leti typis impress./ Cum priuilegio Ad imprimen-/dum solum./Anno. M.D.XLVI/ [Cut 17, state 5.]

S 183. ☙ Anno Tricesimo Primo/Henrici Octavi./Henry the/VIII. by the Grace/of God Kyng of England/ . . . &c. . . . /❦/ Londini/❧ Anno verbi in-/carnati./M.D.XXXIX/

(In line 7 of the title, "faith.")

Colla. T.p.+II–XXV (for 29).

Colo. Londini in aedibus Thomae Berthe-/leti typis impress./ Cum priuilegio ad imprimen-/dum solum./Anno, M.D.XLVI./ [Cut 17, state 6.]

S 184. The same, with "Londidi" in place of "Londini" in the imprint.

S 185. ☙ Anno XXXI./Henrici/Octavi./ ❡ Henry the eyght by/ the grace of god king/&c. . . . /❧/Excudebat Londini./1562. [In border 18, state 5.]

Colla. A–E 6's (last leaf blank).

Colo. Tho. Berthelet regius impressor excudebat./Cum priuilegio. [Cut 17, state 6.]

S 186. Anno XXXI./Henrici/VIII./Henry the viij. by the/grace of God king &c. . . . / [In border of straight lines.]

Colla. A–E 6's (last leaf blank).

Colo. None.

THE THIRTY-SECOND YEAR

S 187. ❧ Anno XXXII./Henrici Octavi/In the parlyament begon/at Westm̄, the XXVIII. of Apryl, the xxxi yere/ . . . &c./❧ Anno M.D.XL. ❧/

Colla. T.p.+II–LXVIII (colophon)+A, B 6's (colophon) +A 4 (last l. bl.).

Colo. (at end) Londini ex aedibus Thomae Bertheleti/regii impressoris./Cum priuilegio &c.

S 188. ❧ Anno XXXII./Henrici Octavi./In the Parlyament begon/at Westm̄, the.xxviii. of Apryll, the. xxxi. yere/of the reygne. . . . &c./❦/Anno. M.D.XL./

Colla. T.p.+II–LXXII.

Colo. Londini ex aedibus Thomae Bertheleti/Cum priuilegio ad impri-/mendum solum./

S 189. ❧ Anno XXXII./Henrici Octavi/In the parlyament begon/ at Westm̄, the. XXVIII. of Apryll, the. XXXII. yere/&c. . . . ❦/Anno. M.D.XL.

Colla. T.p.+II–LXVII (for 72)+A, B 6's [Cut 17, state 4.]
Colo. God save the Kinge./LONDINI ex aedibus Thomae Bertheleti/regii impressoris./Cum priuilegio &c.

S 190. ❧ Anno XXXII./Henrici Octavi./In the parlyament begon/at Westm̃ the. XXVIII. of Apryll, the. XXXII. yere/ . . . &c. . . . /❦/Anno. M.D.XL./
Colla. T.p.+II–LXVII.
Colo. God save the Kynge./LONDINI ex aedibus Thomae Bertheleti./Cum priuilegio &c.

S 191. ❧ Anno XXXII./Henrici Octavi/In the parlyamente begon/at Westm̃. the. xxviii. of Apryll, the. xxxii. yeare of/ . . . &c. . . . /❦/Anno. M.D.XL./
Colla. T.p.+II–LXVII (for 72).
Colo. Londini ex aedidus Thomae Bartheleti./Cum priuilegio ad impri-/menbum solum./

S 192. ❧ Anno XXXII./Henrici Octavi/In the parliament be-/gon &c. . . . /Anno MDXL./
Colla. T.p.+[I]+III–LXXII.
Colo. None.

The Thirty-third Year

S 193. Anno Tricesimo/Tertio Henrici/Octavi./Henry the. VIII/by the grace of/God Kyng of Englande, Fraunce,/and Ireland, defender of the fayth,/and of the Churche of Englande/ . . . &c./victory-/ouse/reygne, wherein were esta-/blyshed these actes/folowynge./ [In border 18, state 3.]
Colla. T.p.+II–LXIX.
Colo. Londini ex officina Thomae Ber-/theleti typis impress./Cum priuilegio ad imprimendum/solum./❧ Anno. M.D.XLII./[Cut 17, state 4.]

S 194. Anno Tricesimo/Tertio Henrici/Octavi./Henry the. VIII./by the grace of/God Kyng. . . . &c./vyctory-/ouse/reygne, wherein were esta-/blysshed these actes/folowinge./ [In border 18, state 3.]
Colla. A–L 6's, M 4 (last leaf blank).
Colo. Londini ex officina Thomae Ber-/theleti typis impres./Cum priuilegio ad imprimendum/solum./❧ Anno M.D.XLII./[Cut 17, state 4.]

S 195. Anno Tricesimo/Tertio Henrici/Octavi./Henry the. VIII./by the grace of/God kyng . . . &c./vyctory-/ouse/reygne, wherein were esta-/blysshed these actes/folowynge./ [In border 18, state 3.]
Colla. T.p.+[5]+VII–XXXVI+G–L 6's, M 4.
Colo. Londini ex officina Thomae Ber-/theleti typis impress./Cum priuilegio ad imprimendum/solum./❧ Anno. M.D.XLII./[Cut 17, state 4.]

S 196. Anno Tricesimo/Tertio Henrici/Octavi./Henry the. VIII./by the grace of/God kyng. . . . &c./vyctori-/ouse/reygne, wherein were esta-/blyshed these actes/folowyng./ [In border 18, state 4.]

Colla. T.p.+[5]+VII–LXIX+i-blank.

Colo. Londini ex officina Thomae Ber-/theleti typis impress./ Cum priuilegio ad imprimendum/solum./Anno M.D.XLII./ [Cut 17, state 6.]

S 197. ❧ Anno XXXIII./Henrici/Octavi./Henry the. viii. by the grace/of God kynge of Englande, Fraunce, and/Ireland . . . &c./ [In border 18, state 5].

Colla. A–L 6's + M 4 (last leaf blank).

Colo. Tho. Berthelet regius impressor excudebat./Cum priuilegio./ [Cut 17, state 6.]

S 198. ❧ Anno XXXIII./Henrici Octavi./Henrye the VIII. by/the Grace of God . . . &c. . . . /acts folowinge./☞ ☜/❧ ❧/ [In border of straight lines.]

Colla. A–L 6's, M 4 (last leaf blank).

Colo. Tho. Berthelet regius impressor excudebat./cum priuilegio./

The Thirty-fourth and Thirty-fifth Year

The General Laws occupy signatures A–F. Three signatures are occupied by the act for a Subsidy, and two for the Ordinance in Wales.

S 199. ❧ Anno tricesimo quar-/to et quinto Henri-/ci octavi./Actes made in the session of/this present parliament holden upon proroga-/tion, &c. . . . /Imprinted at London in Fletestrete by Thomas/Barthelet printer to the kynges hyghnes, the/fyrste day of Iune, the yere of our/Lorde. M.D.XLIII./Cum priuilegio &c.

Colla. A–E 6's, F 4, +A–C 6's.

Colo. ❧ Imprinted at London in Fletestrete by Thomas/ Barthelet printer to the kynges highnes, the fyrste/day of Iune, the yere of our Lorde./M.D.XLIII./Cum priuilegio &c.

S 200. ❧ Anno tricesimo quar-/to et quinto Henri-/ci octavi./Actes made in the session of/this present parlyament . . . &c. . . . ❧ Imprinted at London in Fletestrete by Thomas/Barthelet printer to the kynges hyghnes, the/firste day of Iune, the yere of our/Lorde. M.D.XLIII./Cum priuilegio ad imprimendum solum.

Colla. A–E 6's, +F 4+G–I 6's+A 6+B 8.

Colo. Thomas Barthelet regis impressor excudebat./Cum priuilegio ad impri-/mendum solum. . . . /☞ ❧ ❧ ☜/

(Also a Colophon on I 6).

S 201. ❧ Anno tricesimo quar-/to et quinto Henri-/ci Octavi./Actes made in the session of/this present parlyament . . . &c./❧/ Imprinted at London in Fletestrete by Thomas/Barthelet printer to the kynges hyghnes, the/firste day of Iune, the yere of our/ Lorde. M.D.XLIII./Cum priuilegio ad imprimendum solum.

Colla. A–K 6's, L 8.

Colo. (at end) Imprinted at London in Fletestrete by Thomas/ Berthelet printer to the kynges highnes, the. iii./daie of Ianuarie, the year of our lorde./M.D.XLVII./Cum priuilegio ad imprimendum solum./ [Cut 17, state 6.] (Also a colophon on I. 6).

S 202. ❧ Anno tricesimo quar-/to et quinto Heri-/ci octavi./Actes made in the session of/this present parlyament holden upon proroga-/tion at westm̃ . . . &c. . . . /Imprinted at London in Fletestrete, in the house/of Thomas Barthelet./Cum priuilegio ad imprimendum solum./

Colla. A–E 6's, F 4, G 6, H 4, I 3.

Colo. None.

S 203. Anno XXXIIII. et. V./Henrici/Octavi./ ¶ Actes made in the session of this present/parliamente holden upon prorogacion at/ Westminster &c. . . . /Excudebat Londini./1562./[In border 18, state 5.]

Colla. A–E 6's, F 4, G 6, H 4, I 4.

Colo. None.

S 204. Anno XXXIIII./et XXXV. Hen-/rici Octavi./Actes made in the/&c. . . . /❧/❧ ❧/ [In border of straight lines.]

Colla. A–E 6's, F 4, G 6, H 4, I 4.

Colo. None.

THE THIRTY-FIFTH YEAR

S 205. ❧ Henry the/eyght by the grace of/God kyng of Englande Fraunce and/ . . . &c. . . . /❧/❧Londini.❧/In aedibus Thomae Bertheleti regii im-/pressoris typis excusum./Anno uerbi incarnati. M.D.XLIIII./Cum priuilegio ad impri-/mendum solum./

Colla. A–D 6's, E 4, F 4.

Colo. (at end) Imprinted at London in Fletestrete by Thomas Bar-/thelet prynter to the kynges hyghnes, the. IX./daye of Apryll, the yere of our Lorde/M.D.XLIIII./Cum priuilegio ad impri-/mendum solum.

S 206. ❧ Henry the/eyght by the grace of/God kynge of Englande France and/Irelande . . . &c./❧/In aedibus Thomae Bertheleti regii im-/pressoris typis excusum./Anno uerbi incarnati M.D.XLIIII./Cum priuilegio ad impri-/mendum solum.

Colla. A–D 6's, E 4.

Colo. Thomas Berthelet regius impressor excudebat./Cum priuilegio ad impri-/mendum solum.

S 207. ❧ Henry the/Eyght by the Grace of/God kynge of Englande France and/&c. . . . /❧/❧ Londini ❧/In aedibus Thomae Bertheleti regii im-/pressoris typis excusum./Anno uerbi incarnati. M.D.XLIIII./Cum priuilegio ad imprimendum solum.

Colla. A–D 6's, E 4, F 4 (last leaf blank).

Colo. (at end) Imprinted at London in Fletestrete by Thomas Ber/thelet, rpynter to the kynges hyghnes, the. IX./daye of

Apryll, the yere of our Lorde/M.D.XLIIII./Cum priuilegio ad impri-/mendum solum./
(The colophon, except the first word, is in Italic. Another colophon on E 4).

S 208. ❧ Henry the/Eyght [&c., t.p. as in the preceding.]
Colla. A–D 6's, E 4, F 4 (last leaf blank).
Colo. (at end) Imprinted at London in Fletestrete by Thomas Ber/thelet, prynter to the kynges hyghnes, the. IX. daye of Apryll, in the yere of our Lorde/M.D.XLIIII./Cum priuilegio ad impri-/mendum solum./

S 209. ❧ Henry the/eyght by the grace of/God kynge of Englande Fraunce and/ . . . &c. . . . /❦/❧ Londini ☙/In aedibus Thomae Bertheleti regii im-/pressoris typis excusum./Anno uerbi incarnati. M.D.XLIIII./Cum priuilegio ad impri-/mendum solum./
Colla. A–D 8's, E 4, F 4 (last leaf blank).
Colo. ¶ Imprinted at London in Fletestrete by Thomas Barthelet/prynter to the kynges hyghnes, the. IX. daye of Apryll,/ the yere of our Lord. M.D.XLIIII./Cum priuilegio ad impri-/mendum solum./

S 210. ❧ Henry the/eyght . . . &c. . . . /❦/❧ Londini ❧/In aedibus Thomae Bertheleti regii im-/pressoris typis excusum. /Anno uerbi incarnati M.D.XLIIII./Cum priuilegio &c./
Colla. A–D 6's, E 4, F 4 (last leaf blank).
Colo. Imprinted at London in Fletestreate by Thomas/Berthelet printer to the kynges hyghnes, the IX./daye of Aprill, the yeare of our Lorde/M.D.XLIIII./Cum priuilegio &c./

THE THIRTY-SEVENTH YEAR

S 211. Statutes made in the/parliament, holden at westminster/in the. xxxvii. yere of the reygne . . . &c. . . . /❦/Thomas Berthelet/ typographus regius excudebat./Anno. M.D.XLVI./Cum priuilegio ad imprimen-/dum solum. [In border 19.]
Colla. A–F 6's, A–B 6's, C 4.
Colo. (at end) Londini in aedibus Thomae Ber-/theleti typis impress./Cum priuilegio ad imprimen-/dum solum./Anno. M.D.XLVI./(also on F 6). [Cut 17, state 5.]

S 212. Statutes made in the/parliament, holden at Westminster/in the. xxxvii. yere of the reigne of/the moste renoumed Henry/the eyght . . . &c. . . . /❦/Imprinted at London in Flete-/strete, by Thomas Powell./Cum priuilegio ad imprimen-/dum solum. [In border 19.]
Colla. A–F 6's.
Colo. Londini./1557./Cum priuiilegio ad impri-/mendum solum./ [Cut 17, state 6.]

S 213. ☙ Anno XXXVII./Henrici/Octavi./ ¶ Statutes made in the parliament, hol-/den at westminster . . . &c./❦/Imprinted at

London in Flete-/strete, by Thomas Powell./ Cum priuilegio ad imprimen-/dum solum./ [In border 18, state 5.]
Colla. A–F 6's.
Colo. None. [Cut 17, state 6.]

S 214. ☙ Anno XXXVII./Henrici/Octavi./Statutes made in/the parliament, holdē at Westminster . . . &c. . . . / [In border of straight lines.]
Colla. A–F 6's.
Colo. None.

EDWARD VI

The First Year

S 215. Statutes ma-/de in the parliamēt, begon/at Westmynster the iiii. day of No-/uembre, in the first &c. . . . /☙ Cum gratia &c. [In border 36.]
Colla. T.p.+[ii]–XXXVII+[1]+[4].
Colo. (at end) Excusum Londini, in aedibus Richardi Graftoni/Regii impressoris./Cum priuilegio ad imprimendum solum./ Anno domini. M.D.XLVIII./ [McK. 114.] (Another on XXXVII.)

S 216. ¶ Statutes/made in the parliamente,/begon at Westminster the fourthe/daie of Nouembre, in the firste yere/ . . . &c. . . . / ¶ Cum gratia, &c. [In border 36.]
Colla. T.p.+[ii]–xxxvi+[1]+[4].
Colo. (at end) Excusum Londini, in aedibus Richardi Graftoni/regii impressoris./Cum priuilegio ad imprimendum solum./ Anno domini. M.D.XLVIII./ [McK. 114.] (Another on xxxvi.)

S 217. ¶ Anno primo Edwar-/di sexti./ ¶ Statutes/made in the parliament be-/gon at westminster the fowerthe daye/of Nouember . . . &c. . . . / [In border, McK. 110.]
Colla. T.p.+ii–xxxvi+[4].
Colo. (at end) Excusum Londini, in aedibus Richardi Graftoni/regii impressoris./Cum priuilegio ad imprimendum solum./ Anno domini M.D.XLVIII.

S 218. Anno primo Edwar-/di Sexti./Statutes/made in the parlamente be-/gon at Westminstre the fowerth daie/of Nouembre . . . &c. . . . / [In border, McK. 110.]
Colla. T.p.+II–XXXVIII.
Colo. Excusum Londini in aedibus Richardi Graftoni/regii impressoris./Anno. M.D.XLVIII./Cum priuilegio ad imprimendum solum./

S 218a. ¶ Statutes/made in the Parliament be-/gon at Westminster . . . &c. [In McK. 110.]
Colla. T.p.+ij–xxxviij.
Colo. Excusum Londini, in aedibus Richardi Graftoni/ Regij Impressoris./Anno 1548./Cum priuilegio ad imprimendum solum./

S 219. Anno primo Edwar-/di sexti./Statutes/made in the parlamente be-/gon at Westminster the fowerthe daye/of Nouember . . . &c. . . . / [In border, McK.110.]

Colla. T.p.+II–XXXVIII.

Colo. ¶ Excusum Londini in aedibus Richardi Graftoni/regii impressoris./Anno. M.D.xlviii./ ¶ Cum privilegio ad imprimendum solum./

S 220. ¶ Anno primo Edwar-/di sexti./ ¶ Statutes/made in the parliament be-/gon at westminster the fowerthe daye/of Nouember . . . &c. . . ./ [In border, McK. 110.]

Colla. T.p.+II–38.

Colo. ¶ Excusum Londini, in aedibus Richardi Graftoni,/ regii impressoris./ ¶ Anno. M.D.xlviii./ ¶ Cum priuilegio.

THE SECOND AND THIRD YEAR

S 221. Anno secundo/et tertio Edovardi/sexti./❧ Actes/made in the session of this/present parliament, holden upon pro-/rogacion . . . &c. . . . / [In border, McK. 110.]

Colla. T.p.+ii–lxx (for 68).

Colo. Excusum Londini, in aedibus Richardi Graftoni/regii impressoris./Mense Aprilis. M.D.xlix./Cum priuilegio ad imprimendum solum./

S 222. Anno secundo/et tertio Edovardi/Sexti/❧ Actes/made in the session of this/present parliament, holden upon pro-/rogacion . . . &c. . . . / [In border, McK. 110.]

Colla. T.p.+[II]–LXX.

Colo. (in fine italic) Excusum Londini, in aedibus Richardi Graftoni/regii impressoris./Mense Iunii. M.D.xlix./Cum priuilegio ad imprimendum solum./

S 223. Anno secundo/et tertio Edvardi/sexti./❧ Actes/made in the session of this/present Parlament, holden upon prorogation . . . &c. . . . /.˙. / [In border, McK. 110.]

Colla. T.p.+ii–lxvi (for 68).

Colo. Richardus Graf-/tonus, Typographus Regius excudebat./ Anno Domini. 1552./Cum Priuilegio ad Imprimen-/dum solum./

S 224. Anno secundo, et tertio,/Edovardi sexti./ ¶ Actes/made in the session of this pre-/sent parliament, holden upon proro-/gation . . . &c. . . . / [In border, McK. 110.]

Colla. T.p.+2–lviii (alternately by signatures in arabic and Roman figures).

Colo. ¶ Richardus Graftonus/Typographus Regius excudebat./Anno Domini. 1552./Cum priuilegio.

S 225. Anno secundo/et tertio Edovardi/sexti./❧ Actes/made in the session of this/present parlament, holden uppon pro-/rogation . . . &c. . . . /˙§˙/ [In border, McK. 110.]

Colla. T.p.+II–LXVIII.

Colo. ¶ Richardus Graftonus/Typographus Regius excudebat./ Anno Domini. 1552./Cum priuilegio ad imprimen-/dum solum./

The Third and Fourth Year

S 226. Anno tertio/et quarto Edovardi/sexti./ Actes/made in the session of this present parliament, holden upon pro-/rogacion . . . &c. . . . /.˙./ [In border, McK. 110.]
Colla. T.p.+II–XXXII.
Colo. Richardus Grafton,/typographus Regius excudebat./ Mense Februarii./A.M.D.XLIX./Cum priuilegio ad imprimendum solum./

S 227. Anno III. & IIII./Edwardi sexti./ Actes /made in the Session of this/present parlament, holden upon pro-/rogation . . . &c. . . . /.˙./ [In border, McK. 110.]
Colla. T.p.+II–XXXII.
Colo. Imprinted at London by Ry-/chard Grafton, printer to the/kinges Maiestie./1553./Cum priuilegio ad Impri/mendum solum./

S 228. ¶ Anno. III & IIII./Edwardi sexti./ Actes /made in the session of this/present Parlament, holden upon pro-/rogation . . . &c. . . . /(˙.˙) [In border, McK. 110.]
Colla. T.p.+II–XXXII.
Colo. ¶ Imprinted at London by Richard/Grafton, printer to the/Kynges Maiestie./1553/Cum priuilegio ad impri-/mendum solum./

S 229. ¶ Anno. III. et. IIII./Edwardi sfxti./ Actes made/in the session of this present par-/lament, holden uppon prorogation . . . &c. . . . /(.˙.)/ [In border, McK. 110.]
Colla. T.p.+ii–xxxii.
Colo. Imprinted at London by Richard Grafton/Printer to the Kinges maiestie./1553./Cum priuilegio./

The Fifth and Sixth Year

S 230. Anno quinto/et sexto Edvardi/sexti./ Actes/made in the Session of this/present parlament, holden upō proro-/gacion . . . &c. . . . / [In border, McK. 110.]
Colla. T.p.+ii–xxxiii+1 blank (15 and 16 not numbered).
Colo. Richardus Graftonus,/typographus Regius excudebat./ Mense Aprili./Anno. M.D.LII./Cum priuilegio ad Imprimendum solum./

S 231. Anno quinto/et sexto Edvardi/sexti/ Actes/made in the session of this/present parlament, holden upō proro-/gation. . . . &c. . . . / [In border, McK. 110.]
Colla. T.p.+II–XXII+1 blank. (15 and 16 numbered.)
Colo. Richardus Grafton/typographus regius excude-/bat. Mense Aprili./1552./Cum priuilegio ad imprimendum solum./

S 232. Anno quinto/et sexto Edvardi/sexti./ Actes/made in the session of this/present parlament, holden upō proro-/gacion &c./ [In border, McK. 110.]
Colla. T.p.+ii–xxxii.

Colo. Richardus Graftonus,/typographus regius excudebat./ Mense Iunii./Anno. M.D.LII./Cum priuilegio &c.

s 233. ¶ Anno quinto/et sexto Edvardi/sexti./❧ Actes/made in the Session of this/present parlamente, holden upō proro-/gacion . . . &c./ [In border, McK. 110.]

Colla. T.p.+II–XXXII.

Colo. Richardus Graftonus,/typographus Regius excudebat./ Mense Iunii./Anno. M.D.LII. Cum priuilegio ad imprimendum solum./

s 234. ¶ Anno quinto et/sexto Edwardi/sexti./❧ Actes made/in the Sessiō of this present par-/liament, holden upon prorogacion . . . &c. . . . / [In border, McK. 110.]

Colla. T.p.+II–XXXIII+1 blank.

Colo. ¶ Richardus Graftonus/typographus Regius excudebat./ Mense Iunii./1552./Cum priuilegio ad imprimendum solum./

s 235. ¶ Anno quinto et/sexto Edvardi/sexti./❧ Actes/made in the session of this/presēt parlamente . . . &c. . . . / [In border, McK. 110.]

Colla. T.p.+ii–xxxiii+1 blank.

Colo. Richardus Graftonus/typographus regius excudebat./ Mense Iunii./Anno. M.D.LII./Cum priuilegio ad imprimendum solum.

The Seventh Year

s 236. Anno Septimo/Edwardi sexti./☙ Actes ❧/made in the Parlament hol-/den at Westminster, the first daie of/Marche &c. . . . /❦/ [In border McK. 110.]

Colla. T.p.+II–XXXVIII (for 44).

Colo. Londini in aedibus Richardi Graftoni/typographi Regii excusum./Mense Aprilis./Anno Domini. M.D.LIII./Cum priuilegio ad imprimendum solum./

s 237. Anno septimo/Edwardi sexti./☙ Actes ❧/made in the Parlamente hol-/den at Westminster, the first daie of/Marche &c. . . . /·.·/ [In border McK. 110.]

Colla. T.p.+ii–lxiiij [for 44].

Colo. (fine italic) Londini in aedibus Richardi Graftoni/typographi Regii excusum./Mense Aprilis./(Roman) Anno domini. M.D.LIII./(italic) Cum priuilegio ad imprimendum solum.

s 238. ¶ Anno septimo/Edwardi sexti./☙ Actes ❧/made in the parliament, holden at/Westminster, the first daie of March . . . &c. . . . /·.·/ [In border McK. 110.]

Colla. T.p.+ii–xliiii.

Colo. ¶ Londini in aedibus Richardi Graftoni/typographi Regii excusum./Mense Aprilis./1553./Cum priuilegio ad imprimendum solum./

s 239. [Title page lacking: a fragment of two leaves only.]

Colla. [T.p.+ii]–xliiii.

Colo. ¶ At Worcestre by Ihon Oswen, printer appointed/by the Kinges Maiestie, for the Principalitie of Wales,/and marches of the same./Anno Domini. M.D.LIII./Cum priuilegio, &c.

MARY: PHILIP AND MARY

First Year: First Parliament

S 240. Anno Mariae/primo./Actes/made in the Parliament be-/gonne and holden at Westmin-/ster the. v. daye of October, in the/ first year of the reigne of our most/gratious Soueraigne Ladye,/ Mary by ye grace of God, Quene/of England, Fraunce, & Ireland,/defender of the fayth, and of the/churche of Englande and of Ire-/lande, in earth the supreme head,/and there continued to the. xxi./day of the same moneth, that/is to saye, in the fyrst session/of the same parliament,/as foloweth./Cum priuilegio Regiae/Maiestatis. [In border 18, state 4.]

Colla. T.p.+II+1 blank +IV (table)+V–XXVII+i.

[Catchword a ii, *or:* a ii reverse ends "Finis."]

Colo. Excusum/Londini in aedibus Iohannis Cawodi/typographi Regiae Maiestatis./Anno. M.D.LIIII./Cum priuilegio ad imprimendum solum./

S 241. Anno Mariae/primo./Actes/made in the Parliament be-/gonne and holden at Westmin-/ster the. v. daye of October, in the/ first year of the reigne . . . &c. . . . [In border 18, state 4.]

Colla. T.p.+II–XXVII+[i].

[Catchword a ii, "by": a ii reverse ends "of none effect."]

Colo. Excusum/Londini in aedibus Iohannis Cawodi/typographi Regiae Maiestatis./Anno. M.D.LIIII./Cum Priuilegio ad imprimendum solum./

S 242. Anno Mariae/primo./Actes made in/the Parliament begon and/ holden at Westminster, the. v./day of October, in the fyrst yere of/ the reigne . . . &c. . . . [In border 38.]

Colla. T.p.+II–XXVII.

Colo. ¶ Excusum Londini in aedibus/Iohannis Cawodi, Typographi Regiae/Maiestatis./Anno Domini. M.D.LIIII./Cum priuilegio ad imprimendum solum./

S 243. Anno Mariae/primo./Actes made in/the parliament begun and/ holden at Westminster, the. v./day of October, in the fyrst yeere of/ . . . &c. . . . /❧/Cum priuilegio &c. [In border 38.]

Colla. T.p.+II–XXVII+1 blank.

Colo. ¶ Excusum Londini in aedibus/Iohannis Cawoodi, Typographi Regiae/Maiestatis./Anno Domini. M.D.LIIII./Cum priuilegio &c.

S 244. Anno Mariae primo./ ¶ Actes made in the/parliament begun and holden at/&c. [In border 38.]

Colla. T.p.+II–XXVII.

Colo. Excusum Londini in aedibus/Iohannis Cawodi, typographi regiae/maiestis./Anno Domini. M.D.LIIII./Cum priuilegio &c.

First Year: Second Parliament

S 245. Anno Mariae/primo./Actes/made in the Parliament be-/gonne and holden at Westminster/the seconde daye of Apryll, in the/ firste yeare of the reygne . . . &c./ [McK. 126.] [In border 38.]
Colla. T.p.+ii–xx; pp. 13 & 17 misnumbered.
Colo. ☞ Excusum/Londini in aedibus Iohannis Cawodi./ Typographi Regiae Maiestatis./Anno. M.D.Liiii./Mense maio./ Cum priuilegio Reginae mariae./

S 246. Anno Mariae/primo./Actes/made in the parlyamente be-/gonne and holden at Westminster/the seconde daye of Apryll, in the/firste yeare of the raygne . . . &c. . . . [In border 38.]
Colla. T.p.+II–XX; pages 13, 16 & 17 misnumbered.
Colo. EXCUSUM Londini in aedibus Iohannis/Cawodi Typographi REgiae/Maiestatis./Anno. M.D.Liiij./Mense Maio./Cum priuilegio Reginae Mariae.

S 247. Anno Mariae/primo./Actes/made in the Parliamente be-/gonne and holden at Westminster/the seconde daye of Apryll, in the/ firste yeare of the reygne . . . &c. . . . [In border 18, state 4.]
Colla. T.p.+II–XX.
Colo. Excusum/Londini in aedibus Iohannis Cawodi/Typographi Reginae Mariae./Anno. M.D.LIIII./Mense Maio./Cum priuilegio Reginae Mariae./

S 248. Anno Mariae/primo./Actes/made in the Parliamente be-/gonne and holden . . . &c. [In border 38.]
Colla. T.p.+ii–xx.
Colo. ☞ Excusum/Londini in aedibus Iohannis Cawodi/Typographi Reginae Mariae./Anno. M.D.LIIII./Mense Maio./ Cum priuilegio Reginae Mariae.

S 249. Anno Mariae primo./ ¶ Actes made in the/parliament begun and holden at/Westminster the second day of Aprill/ . . . &c. . . ./ Cum priuilegio Reginae/Mariae./ [In border 45.]
Colla. A–D 6's, E 2.
Colo. ¶ Excusum Londini in aedibus/Iohannis Cawoodi, typographi regiae/maiestatis./Anno Domini. M.D.LIIII./Cum priuilegio &c.

S 250. Anno Mariae primo./ ¶ Actes made in the/parliament begun and holden at/Westminster the second day of Aprill/ . . . &c. . . ./ Cum priuilegio Reginae/Mariae./ [In border 45.]
Colla. A, B 6's, C. D 4's.
Colo. Excusum Londini in edibus Iohannis Cawo-/di, typographi regiae ma-/iestatis./Anno. M.D.Liiii./Mense Maio./Cum priuilegio Reginae Mariae./

The First and Second Year of Philip and Mary

S 251. Anno primo & secundo Philippi/& Mariae/Actes/made at a Parliament, begon/and holdē at Westminster, the. xii./daye of

Nouember, in the fyrste/and seconde yeare . . . &c. . . . [In border 38.]

[Table, fo. 2, the first line is: "An Act touchyng letters patentes, and other writynges."]

Colla. T.p.+ii–xxxiv: pp. 11, 15, 31 & 33 misnumbered.

Colo. Excusum Londini in aedibus Iohannis Cawodi, Tipographi Regiae/Maiestatis Anno MDLV./

S 252. Anno primo & secundo Philippi/& Mariae./Actes/made at a Parliament, begon/and holdē at Westminster, the. xii./daye of Nouember in the fyrste/and seconde yeare . . . &c. . . . [In border 38.]

[Table, fo. ii, first line: "An Acte touching letters patentes, & other writinges."]

Colla. T.p.+ii–xxxiv.

Colo. Excusum Londini in aedibus Iohannis Cawodi, Typographi Regiae/Maiestatis. Anno M.D.LV./

S 253. Anno primo et secūdo Philippi/& Mariae./Actes/made at a Parliament begon/and holden at Westminster, the. xii/day of Nouēber, in the fyrst and se-/cond year of the reigne . . . &c./ [In border 38.]

Colla. T.p.+ii–xxxiii.

Colo. Excusum Londini in aedibus Iohannis Cawodi, Tipographi Regiae/Maiestatis Anno MDLV./

S 254. Anno primo & secundo Phi-/lippi & Marie./Actes made at a Par-/liament begon & holden at West-/minster the eleuenth day of Nouember, in the/first and seconde yere . . . &c. . . . [In border 37.]

Colla. T.p.+II–XXXIIII; pp. 13, 14, 32 & 33 misnumbered.

Colo. Excusum Londini in aedibus Iohannis Cawodi/Tipographi Regiae Maiestatis./Anno Domini. 1555./

S 255. Anno primo et secūdo Philippi/& Mariae./Actes/made at a parliament begon/and holden . . . &c. . . . [In border 45.]

Colla. T.p.+ii–xxxiiii (paging irregular).

Colo. Excusum Londini in aedibus Iohannis Cawodi tipographi/Regiae Maiestatis. Anno. M.D.LV./

S 256. Anno primo & secundo Philippi & Marie./Actes made at a par-/liament begun and holden at West-/minster the eleuenth day oƒ November/ . . . &c. . . . /(.˙.)/Cum priuilegio regiae maiestatis./ [In border 45.]

Colla. A 6, B 4, C–F 6's.

Colo. ¶ Excusum Londini in aedibus Iohannis/Cawooddi, typographi regiae/maiestatis./Anno Dom. 1555./

The Second and Third Year

S 257. Anno secundo et tertio Philippi/& Mariae./Actes/made at a Parliamente begon/and holdē . . . &c. [In border 38.]

Colla. T.p.+ii–lviii.

Colo. Excusum Londini in aedibus Iohannis Cawodi/Tipographi Regiae Maiestatis./Anno. M.D.LV./Cum priuilegio &c.

S 258. Anno secundo & tertio Phi-/lippi & Mariae./Actes made at a Par-/liament begon & holden at West-/minster the. xxi. day of October, in the se-/conde and thirde yere/&c. [In border 37.]
Colla. T.p.+ii–lviii; pp. 17, 23, 28, 34, 41, 43, 44, 47, 48 misnumbered.
Colo. Excusum Londini in aedibus Iohannis Cawodi/Tipographi Regiae Maiestatis./Anno Domini. 1555./Cum priuilegio regiae Maiestatis./

S 259. Anno secundo & tertio Phi/lippi & Mariae./Actes made at a Par-/liament begunne and holden at West-/minster the. xxi. day of October, in the seconde/and thirde yere . . . &c. . . . [In border 37.]
Colla. A–I 6's, K 4.
Colo. Excusum Londini in aedibus Iohannis Cawodi/tipographi regiae maiestatis./Anno Domini. 1555./Cum priuilegio &c.

S 260. Anno secundo & tertio Philippi/& Mariae./Actes/made at a Parliament, begon/and holdē at Westminster the. xxi./daye of October, in the seconde/and thyrde yeare . . . &c./ [In border 38.]
Colla. T.p.+ii–lviii; pp. 6, 15, 18, 24, 26, 34, 43, 44, 47 & 48 misnumbered.
Colo. Excusum Londini in aedibus/Iohannis Cawodi Typographi Regiae Maiestatis./Anno. M.D.LV./Cum priuilegio ad imprimendum solum./

S 261. Anno secundo & tertio Philippi/& Mariae./Actes/made at a Parliament, begon/and holdē at Westminster, the. xxi./daye of October, in the seconde/and thyrde yeare . . . &c./ [In border 38.]
Colla. T.p.+ii–lviii.
Colo. Excusum Londini in aedibus/Iohannis Cawodi Typographi/Regiae Maiestatis./Anno. M.D.LV./Cum priuilegio ad imprimendum solum./

S 261a. Anno Secundo et Tertio Philippi/& Mariae./Actes/made at a Parlyamente begon/and holdē at Westminster the. xxi./daye of October . . . . /[In made-up border with sill-piece McK. 129.]
Colla. T.p.+ii–lviii.
Colo. Excusum Londini in aedibus Iohannis Cavvodi/Tipographi Regiae Maiestatis./Anno. M.D.LV./Cum priuilegio regiae Maiestatis.

The Fourth and Fifth Year

S 262. Anno quarto et quinto, Philippi/& Mariae./❧ Actes/made at a Parliament begon/and holden at Westminster, the. xx/daye of Ianuary, in the fourth and/fift yeare . . . &c./ [McK. 126. In border 38.]
Colla. T.p.+II–XLI.

Colo. ❧ Excusum Londini/in aedibus Iohannis/Cawodi./ Tipographi Regiae Ma-/iestatis./Anno. M.D.LVIII./Cum priuilegio ad imprimen-/dum solum.

S 263. Anno quarto et quinto Philippi/& Mariae./Actes/made at a parliament begon/and holden at Westminster the. XX/day of Ianuary in the fourthe and/fifte yeare . . . &c. . . . / [In border 38.]
Colla. T.p.+II–XLI (irreg.) + 1 blank.
Colo. ¶ Excusum Londini/in aedibus Iohannis./Cawodi:/ Tipographi regiae ma-/iestatis./Anno. M.D.LVIII./Cum priuilegio &c.

S 264. Anno quarto et quinto, Philippi/& Mariae./Actes/made at a Parliament begon/and holden . . . &c. . . . / [McK. 126. In border 38.]
Colla. T.p.+ii–xli.
Colo. ❧ Excusum Londini/in aedibus Iohannis/Cawodi./ Tipographi Regiae Ma-/iestatis./Anno. M.D.LVIII./Cum priuilegio Regiae Maie-/statis.

S 265. ¶ Anno quarto & quinto Philippi/& Mariae./Actes made at a/ Parliament begun and holden at/Westminster, the. xx. day of Ianuary, in the/iiii & v. yere . . . &c. . . . [In border McK. 109.]
Colla. A–F 6's, G 4.
Colo. ¶ Excusum Londini in/aedibus Iohannis Cawodi,/ Tipographi Regiae Maiestatis./Anno. M.D.LVIII./Cum priuilegio Regiae Maiestatis./

S 266. Anno quarto & quinto Philippi & Mariae./Acts made at a par-/ liament begun and holden at West-/minster the twentieth day of Ianuarie . . . &c. . . . / [In border 45.]
Colla. A–F 6's, G 4.
Colo. ¶ Excusum Londini in aedibus Iohannis/Cawooddi, typographi regiae/maiestatis./Anno Dom. 1555./Cum priuilegio regiae ma-/iestatis./

ELIZABETH

The First Year

The general laws fill signatures A to F, and "A Subsidy of Tonnage and Pondage" occupies signatures A–C of a separate register.

S 267. Anno primo Regi-/nae Elizabethe./❧ At the/parliament be-/ gonne at Westmynster, the/xxiii of Ianuary in the fyrste/yeare of the reigne of oure So-/ueraigne Ladye, Elizabeth . . . &c./ Anno. 1. 5. 5. 9./ [McK. 126] [In border 36.]
Colla. T.p.+ij–xxxviij+i–v+1+B 6, C 4.
Colo. Imprynted at London, in Powles Churchyard,/ by Rychard Iugge, and Ihon Cawood, Printers/to the Quenes Maiesties./Anno. M.D.LIX./Cum priuilegio Regiae Maiestatis./

S 268. Anno Primo Regi-/nae Elizabethe./❧ At the/parliament be-/gonne at Westmynster, the/xxiii. of Ianuary in the fyrste/yeare of the reigne of oure So-/ueraigne Ladye, Elizabeth . . . . &c./Anno. 1. 5. 5. 9./ [McK. 126] [In border 36.]
Colla. T.p.+ii–xxxviii+i–xvi.
Colo. ¶ Imprinted at London in Poules Churchyarde/by Richarde Iugge, and Iohn Cawood, Printers to/the Quenes Maiestie./Anno. M.D.LIX./Cum priuilegio Regiae Maiestatis.

S 269. Anno primo regi-/nae Elizabethe./❧ At the/parliament be-/gonne at Westmynster, the/xxiii of Ianuary in the fyrste/yeare &c. . . . /Anno. 1. 5. 5. 9./ [In border 36.]
Colla. T.p.+ii–xxxviii+i–xvi.
Colo. ❧ Imprinted/at London in Poules Churche/yarde, bi Richarde Iugge, and Iohn Cawood,/printers to the quenes maiestie./Anno. M.D.LIX./Cum priuilegio &c.

S 270. Anno primo regi-/nae Elizabethe./❧ At the/parliament be-/gonne at Westmynster, the/xxiij of Ianuarye in the fyrste/yeare . . . &c. . . . /Anno. 1. 5. 5. 9./ [In border 36.]
Colla. T.p.+I+i–xxxviii+[i]–xvi.
Colo. ¶ Imprinted at London/in Powles Churchyarde, by/Richarde Iugge and Iohn Cawood, printers to/the quenes maiestie./Anno. M.D.LIX./ ¶ Cum priuilegio Regiae Maiestatis.

S 271. Anno primo reginae/Elizabethe./At the parliament/begunne at Westminster, the. xxiii. of/Ianuary, in the fyrste yeere of the reigne of/ . . . &c. . . . /1559./ [In border 37].
Colla. A–F 6's, +A–B 6's, C 4.
Colo. ❧ Imprinted at London by/Newegate Market, next unto Christes Churche,/by Richarde Iugge, printer to the Queenes/Maiestie./Anno. 1559./Cum priuilegio Regiae Maiestatis./

S 272. Anno primo regi-/nae Elizabethe./❧ At the/parliament be-gonne at Westminster, the/xxiii of Ianuary in the fyrst/yeare . . . &c. . . . /Anno. 1559./ [In border 37.]
Colla. T.p.+I+III–XXXVIII+A–B 6's, C 4.
Colo. ¶ Imprinted at London/in Powles Churchyarde, by/Richarde Iugge and Iohn Cawood printers to/the queenes maiestie./Anno. M.D.L.IX./Cum priuilegio Regia Maiestatis.

S 273. Anno primo reginae/Elizabethe./At the parliament/begunne at Westminster, the. xxiij. of/Ianuarie, in the fyrst yeere of the raigne of/ . . . &c. . . . /1559./ [In border 37.]
Colla. A–F 6's,+A–B 6's, C 4.
Colo. ❧ Imprinted at London by/Newegate Market, next unto Christes Church/by Richarde Iugge, printer to the queenes/maiestie./Anno. 1559./Cum priuilegio Regiae Maiestatis.

S 274. Anno primo reginae/Elizabethe./At the Parliament/begunne at Westminster, the. xxiii. of/Ianuarie, in the fyrst yere of the raigne of/ . . . &c. . . . /1559/ [In border 37.]
Colla. A–F 6's, +A–B 6's, C 4.

Colo. ❧ Imprinted at London in/Powles Churchyarde by Richarde Iugge and/Iohn Cawood, Printers to the Queenes/ Maiestie./Cum priuilegio Regiae Maiestatis./

THE FIFTH YEAR

The general acts fill signatures A to E. "An Act of one Fifteen" occupies, in a new register, three signatures; "An Act of the Queenes Maiesties free and generall Pardon" is in a single signature.

S 275. Anno quinto reginae/Elizabethe./At the parliament/holden at Westmynster the. XII. of/Ianuary, in the fyfth yere of the raigne/ . . . &c. . . . /Anno. 1563./ [In border 38.]

Colla. T.p.+ii–lxviii+A 6, B–C 8,+lxix–lxxii.

Colo. (at end of *pardon*). ¶ Imprinted at London in/Powles Churchyarde, by Rychard Iugge/and Ihon Cawood, printers to the/Queenes Maiestie./Cum priuilegio &c.

Colo. (at end of *subsidy:* apparently this was interpolated from another edition, see S 282). ❧ Imprinted at London by/ Richarde Iugge, printer to the/Queenes Maiestie./Cum priuilegio &c.

S 276. Anno quinto reginae/Elizabethe./At the parliament/holden at Westmynster the. XII. of/Ianuary, in the fyfth yere of the raigne/ . . . &c. . . . /Anno. 1563./ [In border 38.]

Colla. T.p.+II–LXXII (including *pardon*) +A–B 6's, C 8.

Colo. (after pardon) ¶ Imprinted at London in Powles Churchyarde by Richard Iugge/and Iohn Cawood, printers to/ the Queenes Maiestie./Cum priuilegio &c.

Colo. (after subsidy). ¶ Imprynted at London in Powles Church yarde/by Richard Iugge and Iohn Cawood, printers/to the Quenes Maiestie./Cum priuilegio &c.

S 277. Anno quinto reginae/Elizabethe./At the Parliament hol/den at Westmynster the. xii. of/Ianuary, in the fifth yere of the raigne/ . . . &c. . . . /Anno 1563./ [In border 38.]

Colla. T.p.+ii–lxxii+[1]+A, B 6's, C 8.

Colo. (at end) ¶ Imprinted at London/in Powles Churchyard, by Rychard Iugge,/and Ihon Cawood, printers to the Que-/nes Maiestie./Cum priuilegio &c.

S 278. Anno quinto Regi-/nae Elizabethe./At the/Parliament hol/den at Westmynster, the .xii. of/Ianuary, in the fifth yere of the reigne/&c. . . . /❧ Anno. 1563./ [In made-up border, the sill-piece being McK. 129.]

Colla. T.p.+2–73+[1]+A–B 6's, C 8.

Colo. ¶ Imprinted at London/in Powles Churchyard by Richard Iugge/and Iohn Cawood Printers to the Queenes Maiestie./Cum priuilegio Regiae Maistatis./

S 279. Anno quinto Reginae/El izabethe./At the/Parliament hol-/den at Westmynster the. xii. of/Ianuary, in the fifth yere of the raigne/ . . . /Anno 1563./ [In made up border, the sill-piece McK. 129.]

Colla. T.p.+2–72+[1]+A–B 6's, C 8.
Colo. ℂ Imprinted at London/in Powles Churchyard, by Richard Iugge,/and Ihon Cawood, Printers to the Que-/nes Maiestie./Cum priuilegio Regiae Maiestatis./

S 280. Anno quinto reginae/Elizabethe./ ¶ At the parliament holden at/Westminster the. XII. of Ianu-/ary, in the fyfth yere of the/ raigne . . . . . . /1563./ [In border Mc.K. 109.]
Colla. T.p.+II–LXXI+blank+A–B 6's+C 8 (last leaf blank).

Colo. ℂ Imprinted at London in/Powles Churchyarde by Rycharde/Iugge and Iohn Cawood/printers to the Queenes/ Maiestie./Cum priuilegio &c.

S 281. Anno quinto Regi-/nae Elizabethe./At the Parliament hol-/den at Westmynster . . . . . . /❧/Anno. 1563./ [In border 38.]
Colla. T.p.+II–LXXI+A–B 6's, C 8 (last leaf blank).
Colo. (at end) ℂ Imprinted at London/in Poules Churcheyarde, by Rycharde Iugge,/and Iohn̄ Cawood, prynters to the/ Quenes Maiestie./Cum priuilegio &c./

S 282. Anno quinto reginae Elizabethe./ ¶ At the Parliament holden at/ Westminster the. xii. of Ianua-/rie, in the fifth yeere of the/ reigne . . . &c. . . . /1563/ [In border 37.]
Colla. T.p.+II–LXXI (irregular)+blank+N–P 6's.
Colo. ❧ Imprinted at London in/Powles Churchyarde, by Richarde Iugge./Printer to the Queenes Maiestie./Cum priuiegio Regiae Maiestatis./

S 283. Anno quinto reginae/Elizabethe./ ¶ At the parliament holden at/Westminster the. xii. of Ianua-/rie, in the fyfth yeere of the/ raigne . . . &c./1563./ [In border, McK. 109.]
Colla. T.p.+II–LXXIIII (irregular)+blank+A–B 6's, C 8 (last leaf blank).
Colo. (at end). ❧ Imprinted at London in/Powles Churchyarde by Richarde Iugge, Priuter to the Queenes Maiestie./Cum priuilegio Regiae Maiestatis.

S 284. Anno quinto reginae Elizabethe./ ¶ At the parliament holden at/ Westminster the. XII. of Ianua-/rie, in the fifth yeere of the/ raigne . . . &c. . . . /.1563./ [In border, McK. 109.]
Colla. T.p.+II–LXXI+blank+A–B 6's, C 8 (last leaf blank).
Colo. (at end). ❧ Imprinted at London by/Richarde Iugge, printer to the/Queenes Maiestie./Cum priuilegio &c.

The Eighth Year

The general laws occupy signatures A to E. "An Acte of one Fyfteene" fills three signatures, and An act of Pardon one.

S 285. Anno octavo regi-/nae Elizabethe/At the Par-/liament by pro-/ rogation holden at Westmin-/ster the last day of Septem-/ber, in the eight yere of the reigne/ . . . &c. . . ./❧/Anno Christi. 1566./ [In border 38.]

Colla. T.p.+II–XXVIII+A–B 6's, C 4+F 6 (last leaf blank).

Colo. ❧ Imprinted at/London in Powles Churche/yarde by Iohn Cawood and Richarde/Iugge, printers to the Queenes/ Maiestie./Cum priuilegio Regiae Maiestatis./

S 286. Anno octavo Reginae/Elizabethe./At the Parliament/by prorogation holden at Westmin-/ster the last day of September, in the eyght/yere . . . &c. . . . /Anno Christi. 1566/ [In border 37.]

Colla. A–D 6's, E 4, +A–B 6's, C 5+1 blank+F 4.

Colo. ¶ Imprinted at London/in Powles Churchyarde by/ Rycharde Iugge, Prin-/ter to the Queenes/Maiestie./Cum priuilegio Regiae Maiestatis./

S 287. ¶ Anno octavo reginae Elizabethe./At the parliament/by prorogation holden at West-/minster the last day of September, in/ the eight yeere of the raigne . . . &c. . . . /Anno Christi. 1566./ [In border 37.]

Colla. A–D 6's, E 4, +A–C 6's (last leaf blank)+F 4.

Colo. (on second C 5) Imprinted at London by/Newgate Market next unto Christes/Churche, by Richarde Iugge, printer to the/Queenes Maiestie./Cum priuilegio &c.

S 288. Anno octavo, reginae/Elizabethe./At the parliament/by prorogation holden at Westminster the/last day of September, in the eyght yere of/the raigne . . . &c. . . . /Anno Christi. 1566./ [In border 37.]

Colla. A–D 6's, E 4, F–H 6's (last leaf blank), I 4.

Colo. ¶ Imprinted at London/in Powles Churchyarde by/ Richard Iugge, prin-/ter to the Queenes/Maiestie./Cum priuilegio &c.

THE THIRTEENTH YEAR

The general laws fill signatures A–G; an act for a subsidy occupies two signatures, an act of two fifteens fills three, and an act of pardon one.

S 289. Anno. xiii. Reginae Elizabethe./ ¶ At the parliament/begunne and holden/at Westminster the seconde of April,/in the. xiij. yere of the reigne . . . &c. . . . /1571./ [In border 37.]

Colla. A–G 6's+A–B 4's: +A–C 6's (with colophon): +¶ 6.

Colo. (at end) ¶ Imprinted at London in/Powles Churchyarde, by Richarde Iugge and/Iohn Cawood, printers to the Queenes/Maiestie./Cum priuilegio regiae maiestatis./

S 290. Anno. xiii. Reginae Elizabethe./ ¶ At the parliament/begunne and holden/at Westminster the second of Apryll,/in the. xiii. yere of the raigne . . . &c. . . . /1571./ [In border 37.]

Colla. A–G 6's+H 4+A–B 4's+A–B 4's, C 6+t 4.

Colo. Imprinted at London in/Powles Churchyard by Richarde/Iugge and Iohn Cawood, Printers to/the Queenes Maiestie. /Cum priuilegio Regiae Maiestatis./

S 291. Anno. xiii. Reginae Elizabethe./ ¶ At the parliament/begunne and holden/at Westminster the second of Apryll,/in the. xiii. yere of the raigne . . . &c. . . . /1571./ [In border 37.]
Colla. A–L 6's, M 4.
Colo. Imprinted at London in/Poules Churchyarde by Richarde/Iugge and Iohn Cawood, Printers to/the Queenes Maiestie. /Cum priuilegio Regiae Maiestatis./

S 292. Anno. xiij. Reginae Elizabethe./ ¶ At the Parliament/begunne and holden/at Westminster the seconde of April,/in the. xiij. yere of the raigne . . . &c. . . . /1571./ [In border 37.]
Colla. A–L 6's, M 4.
Colo. ☙ Imprinted at London by/Newgate Market next unto Christes Churche,/by Richarde Iugge, printer to the/ Queenes Maiestie./Cum priuilegio &c.

S 293. The same, without colophon.

S 294. Anno xiii. Reginae Elizabethe./ ¶ At the parliament/begunne & holden at Westminster/the second of April, in/the xiii yere of the reigne . . . &c. . . . /Imprinted at London by Christo-/pher Barker, printer to the/Queenes Maiestie./Cum priuilegio . . . &c./1578./ [In border 37.]
Colla. A–L 6's, M 4.
Colo. None.

THE FOURTEENTH YEAR

S 295. Anno. xiiii. Reginae Elizabethe./ ¶ At the parliament/begunne and holden/at Westminster the eight of May,/in the. xiiii. yeere of the raigne of our most/gracious soueraigne Lady Elizabeth,/ . . . &c. . . . /1572./ [In border 37.]
Colla. A–D 6's.
Colo. ☙ Imprinted at London in/Powles Church yarde by Richard Iugge,/printer to the Queenes Maiestie./Cum priuilegio &c.

S 296. Anno. xiiii. Reginae Elizabethe./ ¶ At the parliament/begunne and holden/at Westminster the eyght of May,/in the. xiiii. yere of the raigne of our most/gratious soueraigne Lady Elizabeth,/ . . . &c. . . . /1572./ [In border 37.]
Colla. A–D 6's.
Colo. ☙ Imprinted at London in/Powles Churche yarde by Richard Iugge,/printer to the Queenes Maiestie./Cum priuilegio Regiae Maiestatis./ [McK. 125a.]

THE EIGHTEENTH YEAR

The general laws occupy signatures A–F; "An Acte of two Fifteens" fills three signatures, and "An Acte of the Queenes Maiesties most free and general Pardon" fills one.

S 297. Anno. xviii. Reginae Elizabethe./At this present Sessi-/on of Parliament by prorogation holden/at Westminster the. viii. day of Fe-/bruary, in the. xviii. yeere . . . &c. . . . /1575./ [In border 45.]

Colla. A–E 6's, F 8+A–C 6's, +A 6.

Colo. ☞ Imprinted at London/by Richarde Iugge, Printer to the/Queenes Maiestie./Cum priuilegio Regiae Maiestatis./

S 298. [The same, except the collation.]

Colla. A–K 6's.

THE TWENTY-THIRD YEAR

S 299. Anno xxiii. Reginae Elizabethae./At this present Sessi-/on of Parliament by prorogation holden/at Westminster the xvi. day of Ia-/nuarie, in the xxiii. yeere . . . &c. . . . /Imprinted at Lon-/don by Christopher Barker, Printer to/the Queenes most excellent Maiestie./1581./ [In border 50.]

Colla. A–I 4's, +Aa 4, Bb–Cc 6's, Dd 2 (last leaf blank)+ ¶ 4, ¶ ¶ 4 (last leaf blank).

Colo. ☞ Imprinted at London/by Christopher Barker, Printer to the/Queenes most excellent Maiestie,/in Bacon house, neere/Foster lane./

THE TWENTY-SEVENTH YEAR

S 300. Anno xxvii. Reginae Elizabethae./ ¶ At the Parliament/begunne and holden at Westminster,/the xxiii. day of Nouember, in the/ xxvii. yeere . . . &c. . . . /Imprinted at London by Christo-pher/Barker, Printer to the Queenes most ex-/cellent Maiestie/ 1585./ [In border 50.]

Colla. A–H 6's, I 4, +Aa–Cc 6's, Dd 1, +1 blank, +Ee–Ff 4's.

Colo. ☞ Imprinted at London/by Christopher Barker, Printer to the/Queenes most excellent Maiestie,/in Bacon house, neere/ Foster Lane./

THE TWENTY-NINTH YEAR

S 301. Anno xxix. Reginae Elizabethae./ ¶ At this present Ses-/sion of Parliament by prorogation hol-/den at Westminster, the xv. day of/Februarie, in the xxix yeere . . . &c. . . . /Imprinted at London by Christo-/pher Barker, printer to the Queenes most/ excellent Maiestie./1587./ [In border 50.]

Colla. A 6, B 4, +Aa–Bb 4's, Cc–Ff 6's.

Colo. ☞ Imprinted at London by/Christopher Barker, Printer to the/Queenes most excellent/Maiestie./

THE THIRTY-FIRST YEAR

S 302. Anno xxxj. Reginae/Elizabethae./At a session of par-/liament holden at Westminster the/fourth day of Februarie, in the one and/thirtieth yeere of the reigne of our mostgra-/tious Soueraigne Ladie Elizabeth . . . &c. . . . / ¶ Imprinted at London by the De-/puties of Christopher Barker, printer/to the Queenes most excellent Maiestie./1589./ [In border 50.]

Colla. A–C 6's, D–E 4's, Aa–Cc 6's, Dd 8.

Colo. ☙ Imprinted at London by/the Deputies of Christopher Barker,/*printer to the Queenes most excellent*/Maiestie./

S 303. Anno xxxi. Reginae/Elizabethae./At a session of par-/liament holden at Westminster the/fourth day of Februarie, in the one and/thirtieth yeere of the reigne of our most gra-/tious soueraigne Ladie Elizabeth . . . &c. . . . / ¶ Imprinted at London .by the De-/puties of Christopher Barker, printer/to the Queenes most excellent Maiestie./1589./ [In border 50.]

Colla. A–C 6's, D–E 4's, Aa–Cc 6's, Dd 2, Ee 6.

Colo. ☙ Imprinted at London by/*the Deputies of Christopher Barker*,/printer to the Queenes most ex-/cellent Maiestie./

S 304. Anno xxxj. Reginae/Elizabethae./At a Session of Par-/liament holden at Westminster the/fourth day of Februarie, in the one and/thirtieth yeere of the Reigne of our most gra-/tious Soueraigne Lady Elizabeth . . . &c. . . . / ¶ Imprinted at London by the De-/puties of Christopher Barker, Printer/to the Queenes most excellent Maiestie./1589./ [In border 50. A fragment only, signatures A–C 6's.]

THE THIRTY-FIFTH YEAR

S 305. Anno XXV. Reginae/Elizabethae./ ¶ At the parliament/begun and holden at Westminster/the XIX. day of Februarie, in the/five and thirtieth yeere . . . &c. . . . / ¶ Imprinted at London by the Deputies of/Christopher Barker, prin-/ter to the Queenes most excel-/lent Maiestie./1593./ [In border 50.]

Colla. A–C 6's, D–E 4's, ℭ–ℭ ℭ 4's, Aa–Cc 6's, Dd 4, Ee 6.

Colo. Imprinted at London by the/Deputies of Christopher Barker, printer/to the Queenes most excellent Maiestie./

S 306. Anno xxv. Reginae/Elizabethae./ ¶ At the parliament,/begun and holden at Westminster/the xix. day of Februarie, in the/five and thirtieth yeere . . . &c. . . . / ¶ Imprinted at London by the Deputies of/Christopher Barker, Prin-/ter to the Queenes most excel-/lent Maiestie./1593./ [In border 50.]

Colla. A–E 6's, F 2, +K 6.

Colo. ☙ Imprinted at London by the Deputies of/Christopher Barker, Printer to the/Queenes most excellent Maiestie./

THE THIRTY-NINTH YEAR

S 307. Anno xxxix. Reginae/Elizabethae./At the parliament/begun and holden at Westminster/the xxiiii. day of October, in the xxxix./yeere . . . &c. . . . /1597/ ¶ Imprinted at London by the/deputies of Christopher Barker, Printer to/the Queenes most excellent Maiestie./ [In border 50.]

Colla. A–H 6's+I 4+Aa–Ee 6 (with colophon)+Ff- Gg 4's.

Colo. ¶ Imprinted at London by/the Deputies of Christopher Barker/Printer to the Queenes most excellent/Maiestie./

CHAPTER II

Decisions

SECTION 1. YEAR-BOOKS

EDWARD III

Year 7

R 1. ¶ De termino Hillarii. Anno regni Regis Edwardi tertii./Post conquestum Angliae. Quadragesimo septimo./ [Over cut 7.]
Colla. T.p.+ii–lxx.
Colo. ¶ Explicit annus quadragesimus septimus Edwardi tertii/Imprimendus in edibus Richardi Pynson Regi/Impressoris. Anno domini Millesimo quingentesimo decimo octa-/uo. Die uere mensis/Ianuarii deci-/mo nono./ [McK. 9 c.]

Years 1–10

R 2. Regis Edwardi Ter-/tii a primo ad decimum (inclusiue) anni/ &c. . . . Richardi/Tottelli./Anno post uerbum/natum. 1562./ Cum priuilegio./ [In McK. 110.]
Colla. T.p.+ii–dxlii.
Colo. ☞ Imprinted at London/in Fletestrete within Temple Barre, at the/signe of the hande & starre by Richard Tottyll./ Anno domini. 1562./Cum priuilegio./

R 3. 1596/Anni/decem priores, regis/Edwardi tertii,/ . . . &c. . . ./ Londini/In aedibus Ianae Yetsweirt relictae/Caroli Yetsweirt Armigeri./Cum priuilegio/Regiae Maiestatis./ [In McK. 168 b]
Colla. T.p.+2–404.
Colo. None.

Year 17

R 4. Hillar̄ desimo septimo. Edwardi tercii./
Colla. i–lxxx.
Colo. None. [J. Rastell, 1515.]

R 5. ¶ De termino Hillarii./Anno xvii. Edwardi tertii./
Colla. i–lxxx.
Colo. None. [Tottell, 1561.]

R 6. ¶ De termino Hillarii./Anno xvij. Edwardi tertii./
Colla. i–lxxx.
Colo. None. [Tottell, 1585.]

Year 18

R 7. Hill. Decimo octauo Edwardi tercii./
Colla. i–lx.
Colo. None. [J. Rastell, 1515.]

R 8. ℂ De termino Hillarii./Anno. xviii. Edwardi tertii./
Colla. i–lix.
Colo. None. [Tottell, 1561.]

R 9. ¶ De termino Hillarii./Anno. xviij. Edwardi tertii./
Colla. i–lix+[1].
Colo. None. [Tottell, 1585.]

Year 21

R 10. De termino Hillarii Anno. xxi. Edwardi. iii./
Colla. i–xliiii.
Colo. ℂ Explicit Annus uigesimus primus Edwardi/tercii. Impressus per Richardum Pin-/sonum regium impressorem./Cum priuilegio./

R 11. ℂ De termino Hillarii, anno regni regis/Edwardi tertii uicesimo primo./
Colla. i–liiii.
Colo. Londini in edibus Thome Bertheleti in vico fletestrete prope aquagiū/sitis sub intersignio Lucrecie excus. Anno dñi. 1527. mense Nouemb./Cum priuilegio a rege indulto./

R 12. ℂ De termino Hillarii anno/regni regis Edwardi tertii. xxi./
Colla. i–lxii.
Colo. ☙ Imprinted at London/in Fletestrete within Temple Barre, at the/signe of the hande & starre by Richard Tottyll./the. xii. daye of Maye./Anno domini. 1561./ ℂ Cum priuilegio./

R 13. ℂ De termino Hillarii anno/regni regis Edwardi tertij xxj./
Colla. i–lxii.
Colo. ¶ Imprinted at London in/Fleetestreat within Temple Barre at the signe/of the hand and starre by Richard Tottyll. the xij./day of May./Anno domini 1584./ ¶ Cum priuilegio./

Years 22–28

R 14. ℂ De termino Hillarii, Anno regni regis/Edwardi tertii post conquestum/vicesimo secundo./
Colla. [i]–c.
Colo. ℂ Impress. Londini in edibus Thome Bertheleti impressoris/regii. Anno domini. 1532. mense Nouembr̄./Cum priu-/ilegio./❧ ☙/.

R 15. ℂ De termino Hillarii anno regni/Regis Edwardi tertii post conquestum xxii./
Colla. i–c+[1] bl.
Colo. ☙ Imprinted at Lon-/don in fletestrete within temple/ Barre at the signe of the hand & starre./by Rychard Tottel, the xxiii./daye of Ianuarye./An. 1567/Cum priuilegio./

R 16. ¶ De termino Hillarii anno regni/Regis Edwardi tertii, post conquestum xxij./
Colla. i–c+[1] bl.

Colo. ¶ Imprinted at London in/Fleetestrete within Temple Barre at the signe/of the Hande and Starre, by Richard Tottyl./ Anno Dom. 1585/Cum priuilegio./

YEAR 24

R 17. ¶ De termino Hillarii Anno Regni Regis/Edwardi tertii post con/questum vicesi/mo quarto./

Colla. i–li.

Colo. ¶ Imprentyd by my Robert Redman./ ¶ Cum gratia & priuilegio a Rege indulto./

YEAR 29

R 18. Anno. xxix. E. tercii./ ¶ De termino Hilarii Anno regni Regis Edwardi tercii/post conquestum vicesimo nono./

Colla. i–lxiiii.

Colo. ¶ Imprinted at London/in Fletestrete by me/Robert Redman./ [McK. 44 on reverse.]

R 19. ¶ De termino Hillarii anno/regni regis Edwardi tertii xxix./

Colla. i–xlix+[1 bl.].

Colo. ☞ Imprinted at London/in Fletestrete within Temple Barre, at the/signe of the hande & starre by Richard Tottyll./ ¶ Cum priuilegio./An. domini. 1561./

R 20. ¶ De termino Hillarii anno/regni regis Edwardi tertij xxix./

Colla. i–xlix+[1 bl.].

Colo. ¶ Imprinted at London in/Fleetestrete within Temple Barre at the signe/of the Hande and stae, by Richad Tottyl./ Anno Dom̄. 1585./Cum priuilegio./

YEAR 30

R 21. Anno. xxx. E. tercii./ ¶ De termino Hillarii Anno regni Regis Ed-/wardi tercii, post conquestum tricesimo./

Colla. i–xlii.

Colo. ¶ Imprentyd at London/by me Robert/Redman.

R 22. De termino Hillarii anno regni/regis Edwardi tertii post conquestum. xxx.

Colla. i–xxxii.

Colo. ☞ Imprinted at London/in Fletestrete within Temple Barre, at the/signe of the hande & starre, by Richard Tottyll./ Anno domini. 1561./Cum priuilegio./

R 23. ¶ De termino Hillarii anno/regis Edwardi tertij post conquestum xxx./

Colla. i–xxxii.

Colo. Imprinted at London in/Fleetestrete within Temple Barre, at the Signe/of the hande and starre, by Richard Tottell./ Anno. Do. 1585./ ¶ Cum priuilegio./

YEAR 38

R 24. De termino Hillarii. Anno regni regis/Edwardi tercii post conquestum/tricesimo octauo/.

Colla. [i]–xliii.
Colo. ℭ Explicitus Annus. xxxviii. Edwardi tertii. Ex officina Pyn-/soniana. Cum priuilegio a rege indulto. Anno uerbi/incarnati. M.D.XX./Idibus Marciis./[McK. 44 on reverse.]

R 25. ℭ De termino Hillarii anno/regni regis Edwardi tertii. xxxviii./
Colla. i–xxxvi+[1 bl.]
Colo. ☞ Imprinted at London/in Fletestrete within Temple Barre, at the/signe of the hande & starre by Richard Tottyll./ Anno domini.. 1561./Cum priuilegio./

R 26. ¶ De termino Hillarii anno/regni regis Edwardi tertii. xxxviii./
Colla. i–xxxvii+[1 bl.]
Colo. ¶ Imprinted at London in/Fleetestrete within Temple Barre at the signe/of the Hande and Starre, by Richard Tottel./ Anno Dom. 1585/Cum priuilegio.

Year 39

R 27. Anno. xxxix. E. tercii./ ℭ De termino Hillarii Anno regni Regis Ed-/wardi tercii, post conquestum. xxxix./
Colla. i–l.
Colo. ℭ Imprentyd at London/in Fletestrete by me/Robert Redman./

R 28. De termino Hillarii anno regni/regis Edwardi tertii post conquestum. xxxix./
Colla. i–xxxviii.
Colo. ☞ Imprinted at London/in Fletestrete within Temple Barre, at the/signe of the hande & starre by Richard Tottyll./ Anno domini. 1561./Cum priuilegio./

R 29. ℭ De termino Hillarii anno/regis Edwardi tertij post conquestum xxxix./
Colla. i–xxxviii.
Colo. ¶ Imprinted at London in/Fletestrete within Temple barre at the signe of/the hand and stare by Richard Tottill./ Anno Domini 1585./

Year 40

R 30. Termino Hillarij Anno. xl. E. tertij./
Colla. i–xxx.
Colo. Impressum p Richardum Pynson./

R 31. ℭ Annus quadragesimus Ed-/wardi tercii nouiter impressus et castigatus, una cum/multis aliis casibus adjectis nuncq antea impressis./ [Cut 7] Ne moy reproues sans cause, quar mon entent est de bone amour./
Colla. T.p.+ii–lii.
Colo. ℭ Imprime a Lōdres par/moy Robert Redman le. x. iour de Marche, Lan/de grace. M.CCCCC.XXXIIII./Cum priuilegio regali./

YEAR 41

R 32. De termino Hillarij Anno regni Regis/Edwardi tercii. xli./
Colla. i–xxiv.
Colo. Impressum p̱ Richardum Pynson./

R 33. De termino Hillarii. An.xli. E. iii./
Colla. i–xxxviii.
Colo. ¶ Explicit annus qua-/dragesimus primus/Edwardi tercij./Imprynted at London in Fletstrete by me Robert/Redman dwellynge at the sygne of/the George./

YEAR 42

R 34. Anno regni Regis. E. iii. xlii./ ¶ De termino Hillarii Anno regni Regis Edwardi tertii/Post conquestum Quadragesimo secundo./
Colla. i–xxiiii.
Colo. ¶ Impressum per Richardum Pynson/Regis impressorem./ [McK. 9].

YEAR 43

R 35. De termino sancti Hillarii. Anno regni Regis/Edwardi tertii. xliii./
Colla. i–xvi.
Colo. ¶ Explicit Annus. xliii. Edwardi tertii./ ¶ Impressum per Richardum Pynson./ [McK. 9 c.]

YEAR 44

R 36. ¶ De termino Hillarii. Anno regni Regis Edwardi tertii./post conquestum Quadragesimo. iiii./
Colla. i–xli.
Colo. ¶ Impressum per Richardum Pynson/Regis impressorem./ [McK. 9 c.]

YEAR 45

R 37. Anno regni Regis. E. iii. xlv./ ¶ De termino Hillarii Anno regni Regis Edwardi tertii/Post conquestum Anglie Quadragesimo secundo./
Colla. i–xxiv.
Colo. ¶ Explicit Annus quadragesimus quintus./ ¶ Impressum per Richardum Pynson/Regis Impressorem./ [McK. 9 c.]

YEAR 46

R 38. ¶ De termino Hyllarii. Anno regni Regis Edwardi. iii./Post conquestum Anglie. xl.vi./
Colla. i–xxix+[1].
Colo. [Device, McK. 9 c] ¶ Impressum per Richardum Pynson/regis impressorem. Anno salutis./M.CCCCC.xvii./

YEAR 47

R 39. De termino Trinitatis. Anno regni regis/Edwardi tertii post conquestum/quadragesimo sep/timo./

Colla. [i]–xxx.

Colo. ¶ Annus. xlvii. E. iii. explicatus. Impressus Londini/ in edibus Richardi Pynsonis regii impressoris/Anno uerbi incarnati millesimo quingē-/tesimo uigesimo. Idibus quinqz/ mensis Iunii. Cum priui-/legio a rege in-/dulto./ [McK. 9 c on reverse.]

Year 48

R 40. De termino Hillarii./Anno regni Regis Edwardi tertii./Post conquestum quadrage-/simo octauo./

Colla. i–xxxii.

Colo. ¶ Explicit Annus. xlviii. Edwardi tertii. Imprimend'/ p Richardū Pynson Regis Impressorem Anno/dñi. M.D.xviii. die vero mensis Maii. x./

Year 49

R 41. ¶ De termino Hyllarii. Anno regni Regis Edwardi. iii./Post conquestum Anglie. xlix./

Colla. i–xxxii.

Colo. [Device, McK. 9 c] ¶ Impressum p Richardum Pynson/ Regis Impressorem./

Year 50

R 42. De termino Hillarii./Anno regni regis Edwardi tercii. post/Conquestum quinquagesimo./

Colla. i–xxvii+[1].

Colo. None. [McK. 9 c.]

Years 40–50

R 43. Regis pie memorie Ed-/wardi tertii a quadragesimo ad quin-/quagesimum . . . &c. . . . Anno domini./1555./☙ Londini in aedibus Ri-/chardi Tottelli./Cum priuilegio ad impri-/mendum solum./ [In McK. 110.]

Colla. T.p.+ii–xlix+ii–xxxii+ii–xxvi+i–xxxvi+ii–xlvi+ii–xxviii+ii–xxxiiii+ii–xxvi+i–xxxiiii+i–xxvii+i–xxvii.

Colo. ¶ Imprinted at London/in Fletestrete within Temple Barre, at/the signe of the hande & starre, by Richard/Tottel, the. xiii. daye of Ianuarye,/in the yere of oure/Lorde. 1556./ ☙ Cum priuilegio ad impri-/mendum solum./

R 44. ¶ Regis pie memorie Ed-/wardi tertii a quadragesimo/ . . . &c. . . . Anno domini./1565./ ¶ Londini in aedibus Ri-/chardi Tottelli./ ¶ Cum priuilegio ad impri-/mendum solum./ [In McK. 110.]

Colla. T.p.+ii–xlix+ii–xxxi+i–xxvi+i–xxxvi+ii–xlvi+ii–xxviii+ii–xxxiiii+ii–xxvi+i–xxxiiii+i–xxvii+i–xxvii.

Colo. ¶ Imprinted at Lon-/don in Fletestrete within Temple/ Barre at the signe of the hande and/starre by Rycharde Tottel, the/xv. daye of August./An. 1565./Cum priuilegio ad impri-/mendum solum./

R 45. ¶ Regis pie memorie Ed-/wardi tertii a quadragesimo ad quin-/quagesimum . . . /Anno Domini./1576./ ¶ Londini in aedibus Ri-/chardi Tottelli./Cum priuilegio ad impri-/mendum solum. [In McK. 110.]

Colla. (as in R 44)+[table, 26.]

Colo. ❧ Imprinted at London/in Fletestrete within Temple barre/at the signe of the Hand and starre,/by Rycharde Tottel/the seconde day of Marche./Anno. 1576./ ¶ Cum priuilegio ad impri-/mendum solum.

R 46. Regis/pie memo-/rie Edwardi/tertii, a qua-/dragesimo &c. . . ./ Londini in aedibus/Thomae Wight./Cum priuilegio./Anno Dom. 1600./

Colla. T.p.+2–49+2–31+1–26+1–36+2–46+2–28+2–34+2–26+1–34+1–27+1–27+[table, 26].

Colo. None.

LIBER ASSISARUM

R 47. Tabnla li. assāz [Pynson, 1517].

Colla. [2]+i–cliiii.

Colo. None. [Device, McK. 9 without border].

R 48. Tabula libri assisarū & plītorum corone/ [Device, McK. 37, 40].

Colla. T.p.+[3, table]+A–B 8's, c–z 6's, A–R 6's, S 8.

Colo. Assisarum liber & plitorū corone foelicit' explicit.

R 49. The same, without colophon.

R 50. ¶ Le liver des assi-/ses & plees del Corone moues & de-/pandantz denaunt les Iusticez sybien/. . . . &c. . . . /Anno domini/1561./ ❡ Londini in aedibus/Richardi Totteli./❦/ ❡ Cum priuilegio. [In McK. 110.]

Colla. T.p.+[3]+i–cccxxvi.

Colo. ❧ Imprinted at London/in Fletestrete within Temple Barre, at the/signe of the hande & starre by Richard Tottyll./the. xvi. daye of Ianuary./ ❡ Anno domini a uerbo nato. 1561./ ❡ Cum priuilegio./

R 51. ❧ Le liuer des/assises & plees del corone/moues & dependauntz deuant les/Iustices &c. . . . / ¶ Londini in aedibus Richar-/di Tottelli./Anno Domini. 1580./ ¶ Cum priuilegio. [In McK. 110.]

Colla. T.p.+[3]+A–H 4's+i–cccxxvi+[table, 10].

Colo. ❧ Imprinted at London/in Fletestrete within Temple Barre,/at the signe of the Hand and Starre, by/Rychard Tottel, the xvi. day/of Marche./ ¶ Anno Domine a uerbo nato. 1580./ Cum priuilegio ad impri-/mendum solum./

LIBER ASSISARUM *Abridged*

R 52. The/Abridge-/ment of the booke of/Assises/nowe newely imprinted/by Richard Tottill the/last day of Septem-/ber. Anno do./1555./Cum priuilegio./ [In McK. 98, with sill showing three cherubs.]

Colla. T.p.+1–165+[table, 2].

Colo. ℂ Imprin-/ted at London in Flite-/strete within Temple barre,/at the signe of the hande/and starre by Richard/Tottell./ ¶ Cum priuilegio/ad impri-/mndum solum./

R 53. ¶ The Abridge/ment of the Boke of/Assises . . . &c. . . . newlye im-/prynted by Ry-/charde Tottle, ye/laste daye of/ Septēber./An. Do./1555./ ¶ Cū priuilegio./ [In McK. 105.]
Colla. T.p.+1–165+[2].
Colo. ℂ Imprinted/at London in Fletestrete/within Temple barre, at the/signe of the hand & starre,/by Richard Tottel./ ☙ Cum priuilegio ad impri-/mendum solum./

HENRY IV

Year 7

R 54. ℂ De termino sctī Michaelis anno regni/Regis Henrici quarti. Septimo./
Colla. i–xli.
Colo. ℂ Imprssum ꝑ Richardum pynson./[McK. 9 b.]

Year 8

R 55. De termīo Michaelis Anno. viii. H. iiii.
Colla. i–xxii.
Colo. ℂ Explicit annus Octauus Henrici quarti. Impress./per Richardum Pynsonum regiū impresso-/rem. Cum priuilegio &c.

Year 9

R 56. ℂ De termino Pasche Anno. ix. Henrici. iiii./
Colla. i–xii.
Colo. ℂ Imprynted by me Robert Wyre, dwellynge at the/ Sygne of seynt Iohñ Euangelyst, in seynt/Martyns parysshe in the Felde, besyde/Charynge cross, in the Bysshop/of Norwytche rentz./ [McK. 67 a.]

Year 11

R 57. De termino Michaelis Anno. xi. Regis Henrici quarti./
Colla. A–P 8's [last leaf missing, blank or device.]
Colo. None. [Pynson].

Year 12

R 58. ℂ De termino sancti Michaelis Anno regni/Regis Henrici quarti. duodecimo./
Colla. i–xxvi.
Colo. None. [Pynson.]

Year 14

R 59. Annus. xiii. Henrici quarti./
Colla. A–F 6's, G 4.
Colo. None. [Pynson.]

Years 1–14

R 60. In hoc volumine/continētur omnes anni Regis Hē-/rici quarti ab anno primo usque/ad annum decimum quintum, non/modo impressorum, sed etiam ma-/nuscriptorum exemplarium colla-/tione emendati, et iam noui-/ter impressi opera &/impensis Richar-/di Totteli./ [In McK. 116.]
Colla. 330 leaves, each year separately numbered.
Colo. ¶ Imprynted at London/by Rycharde Tathyll dwellynge in Fletestrete by/twene the two Temple gates at the/sygne of the Hande and the/Starre. 1553. the. 26./day of Ianua-/ry./

R 61. In hoc volumine/continentur omnes anni regis Hen-/rici quarti &c . . . Richardi/Totteli./1562./Cum priuilegio ad impri-/mendum solum. [In McK. 110.]
Colla. 330 leaves, each year separately numbered.
Colo. ❧ Imprinted at Lon-/don in Fletestrete, within Temple/barre at the signe of the hande and/starre by Richard Tottell. And finished/the. ii. daye of January in the yere/of our Lord/1563./Cum priuilegio./

R 61a. A copy of this issue with uninked colophon.

R 62. ¶ In hoc volumine/continētur omnes anni Regis Henrici/quarti ab anno primo usque ad annum/decimum quintum &c. . . . & im-/pensis Richardi/Tottelli./1575./ ¶ Cum priuilegio ad impri-/mendum solum./ [In McK. 110.]
Colla. T.p.+i–cccxxviii.
Colo. ❧ Imprinted at London/in Fletestrete within Temple barre/at the signe of the Hand and starre,/By Rycharde Tottel./Anno. 1576./ ¶ Cum priuilegio./

HENRY V

Year 9

R 63. De Termino Pasche Anno nono Henrici quinti./
Colla. A 6, b 8.
Colo. ¶ Explicit Annus nonus Henrici quinti post conquest' nono termino/Pasche Anno Regis Henrici Sexti primo a quel t'me Babyngtō fuit/fait chief Iustic' de coēn banck. Hals, fuit fait Iustic' a mesme temps/& Iune chief Baron del Escheker &c./

R 64. De termino Pasche an. ix. Hen. quinti./
Colla. i–xiiii.
Colo. ¶ Imprinted at London in Fletestrete at/the signe of the George, nexte to saint Dunstones/churche by Wyllyam Powell./

Years 1–9

R 65. In hoc volumine conti-/nentur aliquot anni Regis Henrici quinti/ . . . &c. . . . /Anno Domini./1563. mensis Ianuarii/secundo./ In aedibus Richardi/Tottelli./Cum priuilegio./ [In McK. 110.]
Colla. T.p.+i–xiiii+i–xii+[1]+i–xiii+[1]+i–ix+i–xi+i–xv.

Colo. ☙ Imprinted at Lon-/don in Fletestrete, within Temple/ barre at the signe of the hande and/starre by Richard Tottell. And finished/the. xv. daye of Ianuary in the yere/of our Lord/ 1563./Cum priuilegio./

R 66. ¶ In hoc volumine conti-/nentur aliquot anni Regis Henrici/ quinti . . . &c. . . . Anno Do-/mini. 1563. Mensis Ianuarii/ secundo./In aedibus Richardi/Tottelli./Cum priuilegio./ [In McK. 110.]

Colla. (as in R 65.)

Colo. ☙ Imprynted at Lon-/don in Fletestrete within Temple barre/at the signe of the Hand and starre, by/Rychard Tottyl. Anno./1570./Cum priuilegio./

R 67. ¶ In hoc/volumine continen-/tur aliquot anni Regis Hen-/rici quinti . . . &c. . . . Anno/Domini/1587./In aedibus Richardi/ Tottelli./ ¶ Cum Priuilegio./ [In McK. 196.]

Colla. 1–14+1–2+[1]+1–13+[1]+1–9+1–11+1–15+[1].

Colo. ☙ Imprinted at London/in Fleetestrete within Temple Barre,/at the signe of the hand and Starre/by Richarde Tottyll./ 1587./(With separate title-pages and colophons for years 1 & 2, 5, and 7–9).

HENRY VI

Year 1

R 68. De termino Michaelis Anno primo Henrici sexti.

Colla. A–B 4's.

Colo. ¶ Et hec de Anno primo Henrici sexti dicta sufficiant./ Impress. per Richardum Pynsonum regium/impressorem Cum priuilegio a rege/indulto.

R 69. De termino Michīs Anno p'mo H. vi./

Colla. i–viii [for 10].

Colo. Imprynted by me Robert Redman dwellyng at the sy-/ ne of yᵉ George without tempule Barre in/sent Clemētis Paryshe deligently/ouersene et correctyd by a/well lernyd Gen-/tilman./

R 70. ¶ De termino Michaelis Anno regni/Regis Henrici sexti primo./

Colla. [i]–ix+[1 bl.].

Colo. ¶ Impressum Londini in aedibus Henrici Smyth, cōmo-rantis/extra Temple barre, in parochia sancti Cle-/mentis, sub intersignio Trinitatis./

R 71. [I Henry 6. Middleton]

R 72. ¶ De termino Michaelis anno/regni Regis Henrici sexti primo./

Colla. i–viii.

Colo. ☙ Imprinted at London/in Fletestrete within Temple Barre, at the/signe of the hande & starre by Richard Tottyll./ the. xxix. daye of Ianuary./Anno domini. 1556./ ¶ Cum priui-legio./

R 73. ¶ De termino Michaelis anno/regni Regis Henrici sexti primo./

Colla. i–viii.

Colo. ☙ Imprynted at Lon-/don in Fletestrete within Temple barre/at the signe of the Hand and starre, by/Rychard Tottyl. Anno./1570./Cum priuilegio./

R 74. ¶ De termino Michaelis anno/regni Regis Henrici sexti primo./
Colla. i–viii.
Colo. ☙ Imprinted at London/in Fleetestrete within Temple Barre,/at the signe of the Hand and starre by/Rychard Tottyl./ Anno/1584./ ¶ Cum priuilegio./

YEAR 2

R 75. ¶ De termino sancti Michaelis. Anno regni Regis/Henrici Sexti. ii./
Colla. Primo–xvi.
Colo. ¶ Impressum est hoc opus p̧ Richardū Pynson Regis Impressorē./ [McK. 9, without border.]

R 76. ¶ De termino sancti Michaelis. Anno regni Regis/Henrici Sexti. ii./
Colla. Primo–xvi.
Colo. [In McK. 81] Impressum London.' in/suburbiis vulgariter no/minatis Temple barre/de parochia scti Clemen/tis per Robertus redmā/impressorē ae biblio-/polas sub intersig-/nio scti Geor-/gii./

R 77. ¶ De termino Michaelis. Anno. ii./Henrici sexti./
Colla. i–xvi.
Colo. ☙ Imprynted at London in/Fletestrete at the sygne of the George next to/saynt Dunstones church by wyllyam Myddilton./In the yere of our Lorde. M.CCCCC.xlvii./The xviii. daye of July./

R 78. ¶ De termino Michaelis, Anno regni Regis/Henrici sexti secundo./
Colla. [i]–xvi.
Colo. ¶ Impressum Londini in aedibus Henrici Smyth, cōmorantis/extra Temple barre, in parochia sancti Cle-/mentis, sub intersignio Trinitatis./

R 79. ¶ De termino Michaelis anno/secundo Henrici sexti./
Colla. i–xvi.
Colo. ☙ Imprinted at London/in Fletestrete within Temple Barre, at the/signe of the hande & starre by Richard Tottyll./ the. xxix. daye of Ianuary./Anno domini. 1556./ ¶ Cum priuilegio./

R 80. ¶ De termino Michaelis anno/secundo Henrici sexti./
Colla. i–xvi.
Colo. ☙ Imprynted at Lon-/don in Fletestrete within Temple barre/at the signe of the hand and starre, by/Rychard Tottyl. Anno./1570./Cum priuilegio./

R 81. ¶ De termino Michaelis anno/secundo Henrici sexti./
Colla. i–xvi.

Colo. ☙ Imprinted at London/in Fleetestrete within Temple Barre,/at the signe of the Hand and starre by/Rychard Tottyl. Anno/1584./ ¶ Cum priuilegio./

Year 3

R 82. De termino Michaelis Anno/regni Regis Hērici sexti tertio./
Colla. [i]–lii.
Colo. ℂ Explicit Annus tertius Henrici sexti nouiter/ac diligenter impressus & non minimo labo-/re revis' Londoñ in academia ere ac im-/pensis honesti uiri Ricardi Pynson/Regii impressoris morā suā tra/hentis in Fletestrete sub si-/gno sctī Georgii Anno/ dñi. M.v.c.x. die ve-/ro. xii. Octobris./ [McK. 9 b on reverse.]

R 83. Determino Michaelis. Anno. iii. Henrici. vi./
Colla. i–lviii.
Colo. ℂ Explicit annus tertius Henrici sexti. Imprinted by/ Richarde Pynson, printer to the kyn-/ges most noble grace./

R 84. De termino Michaelis Anno. iii. H. vi./
Colla. i–lii.
Colo. ℂ Explicit Annus tercius Henrici sexti nouiter/ac diligenter impressus & non minimo labo-/re revis' Londoñ in academia ere ac/impensis honesti uiri Roberti/Redman moram suam tra-/hentz in Fletestrete sub/signo sctī Georgii A./M.vc.xxvii. die/ vero. xiiii/Octo-/bris.

R 85. ℂ De termino Michaelis, Anno. iii. Henrici sexti./
Colla. i–lviii.
Colo. ¶ Impressum Londini in aedibus Henrici Smyth, cōmorantis/extra Temple barre, in parochia sancti Cle-/mentis, sub intersignio Trinitatis./

R 86. ℂ De termino Michaelis anno. III,/regni regis Henrici sexti./
Colla. I–LVI.
Colo. ℂ Imprinted at London in fletestrete with-/in temple barre, at the signe of the hande and/starre, by Richard Tottill./ (☞ *)/Cum priuilegio./

R 87. ¶ De termino Michaelis anno./iii. regni regis Henrici. vi./
Colla. I–LVI.
Colo. ☙ Imprynted at Lon-/don in fletestrete within temple barre/at the signe of the Hand and starre, by/Rychard Tottel. Anno/1568./

R 88. ¶ De termino Michaelis anno/ iii. regni Regis Henrici vi./
Colla. I–LVI.
Colo. ¶ Imprinted at London/in Fleetestrete, within Temple Barre/at the signe of the Hand and Starre,/by Rycharde Tottell./ 1582./Cum priuilegio./

Year 4

R 89. ℂ De termino Michaelis. Anno. iiii. Henrici sexti./
Colla. A 6, B 4, C 6, D 4, E–F 6's.

Colo. ℭ Et hec de Anno quarto Henrici sexti dicta sufficiant./ Impress. per Richardum Pynsonum regium/impressorem Cum priuilegio a rege/indulto./

R 90. De Termino Michīs Anno Regni regis Henrici vi. iiii./
Colla. [I]–XXXII.
Colo. ℭ Explicit Annus Quart' Henrici Sexti./ ℭ Imprynted by me Robert. Redman/dwellynge at the Syne of the/George without tempull/Barre in sent Cle-/mentis Pa-/ryshe./ [McK. 81, with cut 23 inside.]

R 91. De Termino Michaelis Anno regis Henrici sexti. iiii./
Colla. [i]–xxxi+[1 bl.].
Colo. ¶ Explicit Annus Quartus Henrici Sexti./ ¶ Impressum Londini in aedibus Henrici Smyth, cōmorantis/extra Temple barre, in parochia sancti Cle-/mentis, sub intersignio Trinitatis./

R 92. ¶ De termino Michaelis anno/iiii. regni regis Henrici. vi./
Colla. I–XXXII.
Colo. ℭ Imprinted at London/in Fletestrete within Temple Barre, at the/signe of the hand & starre, by Richard Tottel,/ Anno. 1556./ [Device, McK. 121.]

R 93. Anno. iiii. H. vi./ ¶ De termino Michaelis anno/iiii regni regis Henrici. vi./
Colla. i–xxxii.
Colo. ❧ Imprynted at Lon-/don in fletestrete within temple barre/at the signe of the Hand and starre, by/Rychard Tottel. Anno./1568./

R 94. Anno. iiii. H. vi./ ¶ De termino Michaelis anno/iiii. regni Regis Henrici vi./
Colla. I–XXXII.
Colo. ¶ Imprinted at London/in Fleetestrete, within Temple Barre/at the signe of the Hand and Starre,/by Rycharde Tottell./ 1582./Cum priuilegio./

Year 7

R 95. De termino Michaelis, anno regni/regis Henrici sexti. septimo./
Colla. i–xlviii.
Colo. Tipographus Lectori./Tandem generosiss. lector hunc annum (ut vocant). vii. H. vi. absolui, qui/diutius in manibus herebat quam volebam. hoc feci ut castigatior exeat in publicū./ tamen si nō tibi satisfaciat omnibus in locis, ignoscas oro, et me tuo studio adiuua./Vale. Londini in edibus Thome Bertheleti. Anno domini. 1528. id'. vi. Aprilis./Cum priuilegio a rege indulto./

R 96. De termino Michaelis, anno regni/regis Henrici sexti, septimo./
Colla. i–xlviii.
Colo. ¶ Explicatus est annus. Vii. Henrici sexti./ ¶ Impressum Londini in aedibus Henrici Smyth, cōmorantis/extra Temple barre, in parochia sancti Cle-/mentis sub intersignio Trinitatis./

Year 8

R 97. De termino Michaelis, Anno regni/regis Henrici sexti, octavo./
Colla. Primo–xxxviii.
Colo. ℭ Explicatus est annus. viii. H. vi. Impressus Lōdini in edibus Tho. Bertheleti./sitis prope aquagium in vico Fletestrete, sub intersignio Lucrecie. anno/dñi. 1528. mense maio. Cum priuilegio a rege indulto./

R 98. ℭ De termino Michaelis, Anno regni/regis Henrici sexti, octauo./
Colla. Primo–xxxviii.
Colo. ¶ Impressum Londini in aedibus Henrici Smyth, cōmorantis/extra Temple barre, in parochia sancti Cle-/mentis, sub intersignio Trinitatis./

Years 7 and 8

R 99. ℭ De termino Michaelis Anno. vii. Hen. vi./
Colla. i–lxxxvi.
Colo. ☙ Expliciunt Anni. vii. et/viij. Henrici. vj. Imprynted at London in Flete-/strete at the sygne of the George nexte to saynt Dunstons churche by Wyl-/lyam Myddylton./ ℭ Cum priuilegio ad imprimendum solum./

R 100. De termino Michaelis, anno/regni regis Henrici sexti. septimo./
Colla. I–XLV+I–XXXVII.
Colo. ☙ Imprinted at London/in Fletestrete within Temple Barre, at the/signe of the hande & starre by Richard Tottyll./ And finished the. 12. day of Nouember./Anno domini. 1559./

R 101. ¶ De termino Michaelis anno/Regni Regis Henrici sexti septimo./
Colla. I–XLV+I–XXXVII.
Colo. ☙ Imprynted at Lon-/don in Fletestrete within Temple barre/at the signe of the Hand and starre, by/Rychard Tottyl. Anno./1570./Cum priuilegio./

R 102. ¶ De termino Michaelis anno/Regni Regis Henrici Sexti septimo./
Colla. I–XLV+I–XXXII.
Colo. ☙ Imprinted at London/in Fleetestrete within Temple Barre,/at the signe of the Hand and starre by/Rychard Tottyl. Anno/1584./Cum priuilegio./

Year 9

R 103. Anno nono Henrici sexti Termino Michaelis./ [Pynson 1500.]
Colla. A 8, B–C 6's, D 8, E 6, F 8, G 6, H 8, I–O 6's.
Colo. ℭ Explicit Annus Nonus Henrici vi[ti].

R 104. ℭ De termino Pasche. Anno regni Regis/Henrici sexti. ix./
Colla. Primo–LXVII+[1].
Colo. ℭ Impressum per (Richardum Pynson)/Regis Impressorem./ [Device, McK. 9 c.]

R 105. ℭ De termino Pasche, Anno regni Regis/Henrici sexti, nono./
Colla. Primo–lvii+[1 bl.].
Colo. ℭ Explicit Annus. ix.' Henrici. vi./ ¶ Impressum Londini in aedibus Henrici Smyth, cōmorantis/extra Temple barre, in parochia sancti Cle-/mentis, sub intersignio Trinitatis./

R 106. ℭ De termino Pasche, Anno nono Henrici sexti./
Colla. i–lxvii+[1 bl.].
Colo. ℭ Explicit Annus. ix.' Henrici. vi./ ¶ Impressum Londini in aedibus Henrici Smyth, cōmotantis/extra Temple barre, in parochia sancti Cle-/mentis, sub intersignio Trinitatis./

R 107. ℭ De termino Pasche, Anno nono Henrici sexti./
Colla. i–lxvii.
Colo. ℭ Impressum Londini in edibus Wilhelmi Powell, commorantis/intra Temple barre, in parochia Sancti Dun-/stani, sub intersignio diui Georgii./

R 108. ℭ De termino Pasche anno/regni regis Henrici. vi. nono./
Colla. i–lxvii+[1 lb.].
Colo. ☙ Imprinted at Lon-/don in Fletestrete, within Temple /barre at the signe of the hande and/starre by Richard Tottell the. xxii./day of Apryll in the yere/of our Lord/1562./Cum priuilegio./

R 109. ¶ De termino Pasche anno/regni regis Henrici sexti nono./
Colla. I–LXVII+[1 bl.].
Colo. ☙ Imprynted at Lon-/don in Fletestrete within Temple barre/at the signe of the Hand and starre, by/Rychard Tottyl. Anno./1570./Cum priuilegio./

R 110. ¶ De Termino Pasche Anno/Regni Regis Henrici vj. nono./ [Tottell.]
Colla. i–lxxvij.
Colo. None.

YEAR 10

R 111. ℭ De termino Michaelis. Anno. x. Henrici sexti./
Colla. A–E 6's (last two leaves blank).
Colo. ℭ Explicit annus decimus Henrici sexti: Im-/press. per Richardū Pynsonum regium/impressorem. Cum priuilegio./

R 112. De Termino Michaelis Anno. x. Henrici sexti./
Colla. A–E 6's (last two leaves blank).
Colo. ℭ Imprynted at London in Fletestrete at the sygne of/the George nexte to saynt Dunstans church/by Wyllyam Myddylton./

R 113. ℭ De termino Michaelis. Anno. x. Henrici sexti./
Colla. [i]–xxvii+[1 bl.].
Colo. ¶ Impressum Londini in aedibus Henrici Smyth, cōmorantis/extra Temple barre, in parochia sancti Cle-/mentis, sub intersignio Trinitatis./Finis./

R 114. ℭ De termino Michaelis anno/decimo Henrici sexti./
Colla. A–E 4's+F 6.

Colo. ☙ Imprinted at London/in Fletestrete within Temple Barre, at the/signe of the hande & starre by Richard Tottyll./ the. xxi. daye of Februarye./Anno domini. 1561./ ¶ Cum priuilegio./

R 115. ¶ De termino Michaelis anno/decimo Henrici sexti./
Colla. I–XXVI.
Colo. ☙ Imprynted at Lon-/don in Fletestrete within Temple barre/at the signe of the Hand and starre, by/Rychard Tottyl. Anno./1570./Cum priuilegio./

R 116. De termino Michaelis Anno decimo/Henrici sexti./
Colla. 1–26.
Colo. ☙ Imprinted at London/in Fleetestrete within Temple Barre,/at the Signe of the Hand and Starre/by Richarde Tottyll./1587./Cum priuilegio./

YEAR 11

R 117. De Termino Michaelis An. xi. H. vi.
Colla. I–LXXII.
Colo. ¶ Imprynted at London by/me Robert Redman./Cum priuilegio/Regali./

R 118. De termino Michaelis An. xi. H. vi.
Colla. i–lxix.
Colo. ¶ Explicit Annus. xi. Henrici Sexti./ ¶ Impressum Londini in aedibus Henrici Smyth, cōmorantis/extra Temple barre, in parochia sancti Cle-/mentis, sub intersignio Trinitatis./

R 119. ¶ De termino Michaelis anno. XI./regni regis Henrici sexti./
Colla. i–lvi.
Colo. ¶ Imprinted at London in fletestrete with-/in temple barre, at the signe of the hande and/starre, by Richard Tottill./(☞ *)/Cum priuilegio.

R 120. De termino Michaelis anno/xi. regni Regis Henrici sexti./
Colla. i–lvi.
Colo. ☙ Imprinted at Lon-/don in fletestrete within Temple/ Barre at the signe of the hand & starre,/by Richard Tottill, in the/yeare of our lorde/1567./

R 121. ¶ De termino Michaelis anno/xi. regni Regis Henrici sexti./
Colla. I–LVI.
Colo. ☙ Imprinted at London/in Fletestrete within Temple Barre,/at the signe of the Hand and Starre, by/Rychard Tottel, the xii. day/of Iune. 1582./Cum priuilegio./

YEAR 12

R 122. ¶ De termīo Michaelis. Anno. xii. Henrici sexti./
Colla. A–B 4's.
Colo. ¶ Et hec de Anno. xii. Henrici sexti dicta sufficiant./ Impress. per Richardum Pynsonum regium/impressorem. Cum priuilegio/a rege indulto./

R 123. ¶ De termino Michaelis. Anno. xii. Henrici sexti./
Colla. i–viii.
Colo. ¶ Explicit Annus. xii. Henrici sexti. Impryn-/ted at London in Fletestrete at the sygne of/the George nexte to saynt Dunstons/churche by Wyllyam/Myddylton./

R 124. ¶ De termino Michaelis. Anno. xii. Henrici sexti./
Colla. i–viii.
Colo. ❧ Imprynted at London/by me Richarde Tottle dwell-ynge in Fletestrete/at the signe of the hande and the starre/ within temple barre./☞ ❧/❧ ☜/

R 125. ¶ De termino Michaelis anno/duodecimo Henrici sexti./
Colla. i–viii.
Colo. ❧ Imprinted at Lon-/don in Fletestrete, within Temple/ barre at the signe of the hande and/starre by Richard Tottell the. viii./day of Apryll in the yere/of our Lord./1562./Cum priuilegio./

R 126. ¶ De termino Michaelis anno/duodecimo Henrici sexti./
Colla. i–viii.
Colo. ❧ Imprinted at London/in Fletestrete within Temple barre/at the signe of the Hand and starre,/by Rychard Tottel the/vi. day of December in the/yere of our Lord./1574./Cum priuilegio./

Year 14

R 127. Anno quarto decimo Henrici Sexti./
Colla. Primo–xxvii+[1 bl.].
Colo. ¶ Explicit ann.' xiiii. Henrici Sexti./Impressum per me Robertum/Redman. Cum gra' & pri-/uilegio a Rege cōcesso./

R 128. Anno quartodecimo Henrici sexti./
Colla. Primo–xxvii.
Colo. ¶ Explicit Annus. XIIII. Henrici/Sexti impressus/per me Wil-/helmum Meddelton./

R 129. Anno. xiiii. Henrici Sexti./
Colla. i–xxvi.
Colo. ¶ Explicit Annus decimus quartus Henrici sexti/Impressus per me Richardum/Tottelum./

R 130. ¶ Anno Decimo Quarto/Henrici sexti./
Colla. i–xxvi.
Colo. ❧ Imprinted at Lon-/don in Fletestrete, within Temple /barre at the signe of the hande and/starre by Richard Tottell the. xxii./day of Apryll in the yere/of our Lord/1562./Cum priuilegio./

R 131. ¶ Anno Decimo Quarto/Henrici sexti./
Colla. i–xxvi.
Colo. ❧ Imprinted at London/in Fletestrete within Temple barre/at the signe of the Hand and starre,/by Rychard Tottel the/vi. day of December in the/yere of our Lord./1574./Cum priuilegio./

R 132. ¶ Anno Decimo Quarto/Henrici sexti./ [Tottell.]
Colla. i–xxvi.
Colo. None.

YEAR 18

R 133. ¶ De termino Pasche. Anno. xviii. Henrici sexti./
Colla. A–B 6's+C 4+D–F 6's.
Colo. ¶ Explicit Annus decimus octauus Henrici sexti./ Impressum per me Richardũ Pynsonum/regium impressorem. Cum pri-/uilegio a rege indulto./

R 134. De termino pasche Anno. xviii. H. vi./
Colla. i–xxxiiii.
Colo. Imprentyd be my Robert Redman./ ¶ Cum gratia & priuilegio a/Rege indulto./

R 135. De Termino pasche. Anno. xviii. H. vi./
Colla. i–xxxiiii.
Colo. ¶ Imprinted by Rycharde Tottel./ ¶ Cum priuilegio ad imprimendum solum./

R 136. ¶ De Termino pasche anno/xviii Henrici sexti./
Colla. i–xxxiv.
Colo. ¶ Imprinted by Rycharde Tottel./ ¶ Cum priuilegio ad imprimendum solum./

R 137. ¶ De termino Paschae anno/xviij. regni Regis Henrici sexti./
Colla. i–xxxiiii.
Colo. ¶ Imprinted by Rycharde Tottel./ ¶ Cum priuilegio ad imprimendum solum./

YEAR 19

R 138. De Termino Michaelis Anno. xix. H. vi./
Colla. i–lxxx.
Colo. ¶ Imprentyd by my Robert Redman./ ¶ Cum gratia & priuilegio a/Rege indulto./

R 139. De termino Michaelis Anno. xix. H. vi./
Colla. i–lxxx.
Colo. Imprinted at London/in Fletestrete at the sygne of the George/by Wyllyam Myddylton./

R 140. De termino Michaelis. Anno. xix. H. vi./
Colla. i–lxxx.
Colo. Imprinted at London in Fletestrete within/Temple barre at the signe of the hande and starre,/by Richard Tottel./ Cum priuilegio ad imprimendum solum./

R 141. ¶ De termino Michaelis Anno. xix./regni regis Henrici sexti./
Colla. i–lxxx.
Colo. Imprinted at Lon-/don in fletestrete within Temple/ Barre at the signe of the hand & starre,/by Richard Tottill, in the/yeare of our lorde/1567./

R 142. ¶ De Termino Michaelis Anno XIX./regni regis Henrici Sexti./
Colla. i–lxxv.

Colo. ☙ Imprinted at London/in Fletestrete within Temple barre/at the signe of the Hand and starre,/by Rycharde Tottel in the/yeare of our Lorde./1567./

YEAR 20

R 143. De termino Michaelis. Anno xx° Henrici sexti./ [Pynson 1500.]
Colla. A–B 8's.+C–F 6's, +G 8.
Colo. ¶ Explicit Annus xx° Henrici sexti./

R 144. De termino Michaelis. Anno. xx. Henrici sexti./ [Pynson].
Colla. A 8+B–E 6's+F–G 4's. [Device, McK. 9 b.]
Colo. None.

R 145. De termĩo Michaelis. Anno. xx. Henrici sexti./
Colla. A–H 6's+I 2. [Device, McK. 44.]
Colo. ¶ Explicit Annus vigesimus Henrici sexti. . . . Impressum per Richardum/Pynsonum Cum priuilegio/a rege indulto./

R 146. De termino Michaelis./Anno. xx. Henrici, sexti./
Colla. 1–50.
Colo. ¶ Imprynted at London/by Rycharde Tottyll dwellyng in Fletestrete by/twene the two Temple gates at the/sygne of the Hande and the/Starre. 1553. the. 11/day of Septem-/bre./

R 147. ¶ De termino Michaelis. anno./XX. Henrici sexti./
Colla. i–xlvi.
Colo. ☙ Imprinted at London/in Fletestrete within Temple Barre, at the/signe of the hande & starre by Richard Tottyll./ the. xxix. daye of Ianuary./Anno domini. 1556./ ¶ Cum priuilegio./

R 148. ¶ De termino Michaelis Anno/xx. Henrici sexti./
Colla. I–XLVI.
Colo. ☙ Imprynted at Lon-/don in Fletestrete within Temple barre/at the signe of the Hand and starre, by/Rychard Tottyl. Anno./1570./Cum priuilegio./

R 149. De termino Michaelis Anno regni/Regis Henrici sexti vicesimo./ [Tottell].
Colla. [i]–xlvi.
Colo. None.

YEAR 21

R 150. De termino Michaelis Anno. xxi. Henrici sexti./
Colla. A 6+B 4+C 6+D 4+E 6+F 4+G 6+H 4+I 6+K 4+L 6+M 4+N 6.
Colo. ¶ Et hec de Anno. xxi. Henrici sexti dicta sufficiant./ Impress. per Richardum Pynsonum regium/impressorem Cum priuilegio a rege/indulto./

R 151. De Termino Michĩs. Anno. xxi. H. vi./
Colla. i–lxiii+[1 bl.].
Colo. ¶ Imprynted by my Robert Redman./ ¶ Cum priuilegio a Rege indulto./

R 152. ℂ De termino Michaelis anno. XXI./regni regis Henrici sexti./
Colla. i–lviii.
Colo. ℂ Imprinted at London in fletestrete with-/in temple barre, at the signe of the hande and/starre, by Richard Tottill./ (☞ *)/ ℂ Cum priuilegio./

R 153. De termino Michaelis anno XXI./regni regis Henrici sexti./
Colla. i–lviii.
Colo. ☙ Imprinted at Lon-/don in fletestrete within Temple/ Barre at the signe of the hand & starre,/by Richard Tottill, in the/yeare of our lorde/1567./

R 154. ¶ De termino Michaelis anno/xxi. regni Regis Henrici sexti./
Colla. i–lviii.
Colo. ☙ Imprinted at London/in Fletestrete within Temple barre/at the signe of the Hand and starre,/By Rychard Tottel the/10. day of Nouember in the/yere of our Lord./1575./

Year 22

R 155. ℂ De termino Michaelis. Anno. xxii. Henrici. VI./
Colla. A–E 6's+G 4+H–I 6's+K 4+L–M 6's.
Colo. ℂ Et hec de Anno. xxii. Henrici sexti dicta sufficiant./ Impress. per Richardum Pynsonum regium/impressorem.Cum priuilegio a rege/indulto./

R 156. ℂ De Termino sancti Michaelis Anno regni/Regis Henrici sexti uicesimo Secundo./
Colla. i–lxvi.
Colo. ℂ Enprented by my Robert Redman./Cum priuilegio a Rege indulto./

R 157. ℂ De termino sancti Michaelis anno/regni regis Henrici sexti· XXII./
Colla. i–lx.
Colo. ℂ Imprinted at London in fletestrete with-/in Temple barre, at the signe of the hande and/starre, by Richard Tottill./ (☞ *)/Cum priuilegio./

R 158. ℂ De termino Michaelis anno/xxii. Henrici sexti./
Colla. i–lx.
Colo. ☙ Imprinted at Lon-/don in fletestrete within Temple/ Barre at the signe of the hand & starre,/by Richard Tottill, in the/yeare of our lorde/1567./

R 159. ¶ De termino Michaelis anno/xxij. Henrici sexti./
Colla. [i]–lx.
Colo. ☙ Imprinted at London/in Fletestrete within Temple barre/at the signe of the Hand and starre,/by Rychard Tottel the/18. day of October in the/yere of our Lord./1575./

R 160. ℂ De Termino Michaelis Anno/xxii. Henrici sexti./
Colla. [i]–lx.
Colo. ☙ Imprinted at London/in Fletestrete within Temple barre/at the signe of the Hand and starre,/by Rycharde Tottel in the/yeare of our Lorde./1575./

Year 27

R 161. ¶ De Termino sancti Michaelis Anno regni Regis/Henrici Sexti-post conqm̄ vicesimo septimo./
Colla. i–x.
Colo. ¶ Imprynted by Richarde Pynson, prynter/unto the Kynges noble grace./ [Device, McK. 9 b.]

R 162. De termino Michaelis An. xxvii. H. vi./
Colla. i–xii.
Colo. ¶ Imprynted by me Robert/Redman./

R 163. ¶ De Termino sancti Michaelis Anno regni Regis/Henrici Sexti post conqm̄ uicesimo septimo./
Colla. [i]–x.
Colo. ¶ Imprinted at London in Fletestrete at the signe/of the hand, and starre by Richard Tottel,/dwelling within Temple barre./

R 164. ¶ De termino Michaelis anno/regni Regis Henrici vi. post conquestum. xxvii./
Colla. i–x.
Colo. ☞ Imprinted at Lon-/don in Fletestrete, within Temple/barre at the signe of the hande and/starre by Richard Tottell the. v./daye of Iune in the yere/of our Lord/1562./Cum priuilegio./

R 165. ¶ De termino Michaelis anno/regni Regis Henrici. vi. post conquestum. xxvii./
Colla. i–x.
Colo. ☞ Imprinted at Lon-/don in fletestrete within Temple/Barre at the signe of the hand & starre,/by Richard Tottill, in the/yeare of our lorde/1567./

R 166. ¶ De termino Michaelis anno/regni Regis Henrici. vi. post conquestum. xxvii./
Colla. i–x.
Colo. ☞ Imprinted at London/in Fletestrete within Temple barre/at the signe of the Hand and starre,/By Rychard Tottel the/xxix. day of Marche in the/yere of our Lord./1575./ ¶ Cum priuilegio./

Year 28

R 167. ¶ De Termino sancti Michaelis Anno regni Regis/Henrici Sexti post conqm̄ vicesimo Octauo./
Colla. i–xii.
Colo. ¶ Imprynted by Richarde Pynson, prenter/unto the kyngs noble grace./

R 168. ¶ De Termino sancti Michaelis Anno regni Regis/Henrici Sexti post conquestum/uicesimo octauo./
Colla. [i]–xii (16).
Colo. ¶ Imprinted at London by/me Robert Redman,/Cum priuilegio/Regali./

R 169. ¶ De termino sancti Michaelis anno./regni Regis Henrici Sexti post conquestum/uicesimo octauo./

Colla. i–xiii+[1 bl.].

Colo. ¶ Imprinted at London in Fletestrete,/within Temple barre, at the signe of the hande/and Starre, by Richard Tottle, the. xxx. day/of Ianuarie, the yere of our Lorde./1556./ ¶ Cum priuilegio ad Impri-/mendum solum./

R 170. De termino sancti Michaelis anno/regni Regis Henrici Sexti post conquestum/uicesimo octauo./

Colla. i–xiii+[1 bl.].

Colo. ☞ Imprinted at Lon-/don in fletestrete within temple/ Barre at the signe of the hand & starre./by Rychard Tottel, the xxx./daye of February/An. 1567./Cum priuilegio./

R 171. De termino sancti Michaelis anno./regni Regis Henrici Sexti post conquestum/uicesimo octauo.

Colla. i–xiii+[1 bl.]

Colo. ☞ Imprinted at London/in Fletestrete within Temple barre/at the signe of the Hand and starre,/By Rychard Tottel the/vii. day of Aprell in the/yere of our Lord./1575./

Years 30–31

R 172. ¶ De termino Michaelis Anno xxx. H. vi./

Colla. i–xviii.

Colo. ¶ Imprynted at London by/Robert Redman,/Cum priuilegio/Regalj./

R 173. ¶ De termino Michaelis Anno. xxx. H. vi./

Colla. i–xvi.

Colo. ☜ Imprynted at Lon-/don in Fletestrete at the/sygne of the George/by Wyllyam Myd-/dylton./

R 174. ☞ De termino Michaelis anno/xxx. Henrici sexti./

Colla. i–xvi.

Colo. ¶ Imprinted at London/in Fletestrete within Temple Barre, at the/signe of the hand & starre, by Richard Tottel,/ Anno. 1556./Cum priuilegio ad imprimendum solum./

R 175. De termino Michaelis anno regni/regis Henrici sexti post conqm̄ tricesimo./

Colla. i–xvi.

Colo. ☞ Imprinted at Lon-/don in fletestrete within temple/ Barre at the signe of the hand & starre./by Rychard Tottel, the xxvii/daye of February/An. 1567./Cum priuilegio./

R 176. ¶ De termino Michaelis anno regni/Regis Henrici sexti post conquestū xxx./

Colla. i–xvii.

Colo. ☞ Imprinted at London/in Fletestrete within Temple barre/at the signe of the Hand and starre,/By Rychard Tottel the/10. day of Nouember in the/yere of our Lord./1575./ ¶ Cum priuilegio./

YEAR 32

R 177. ℂ De Termino Trinitatis An. xxxii. H. vi./
Colla. i–xl.
Colo. ℂ Imprynted at London by/Robert Redman,/Cum priuilegio/Regali./

R 178. De Termino Trinitatis. An. xxxii. H. vi./
Colla. i–xl.
Colo. ☙ Imprynted at Lōdon in/Fletstrete at the sygne of the George/nexte to saynt Dunstons chur-/che by Wyllyam Myd/dylton./

R 179. ☙ De termino Trinitatis anno trisesi-/mo Secundo Henrici Sexti./
Colla. i–xxxiiii.
Colo. ℂ Imprinted at London/in Fletestrete within Temple Barre, at the/signe of the hand & starre, by Richard Tottel,/ Anno. 1556./Cum priuilegio ad imprimendum solum./

R 180. ℂ De termino Trinitatis anno Trisesi-/mo Secundo Henrici Sexti./
Colla. i–xxxiiii.
Colo. ❧ Imprinted at Lon-/don in fleetestrete within temple/ Barre at the signe of the hand and/starre by Rychard Tottel,/ An. 1566./Cum priuilegio./

R 181. ¶ De termino trinitatis anno/tricesimo secundo Hernici sexti./
Colla. i–xxxiiii.
Colo. ❧ Imprinted at London/in Fletestrete within Temple barre/at the signe of the Hand and starre,/by Rycharde Tottel./ Anno. 1576./ ¶ Cum priuilegio./

YEAR 33

R 182. ℂ De termino hillarii anno Henrici sexti. xxxiii°./(Lettou & Machlinia.).
Colla. 66 leaves without folio or signature.
Colo. ℂ Explicit annus xxxiii'/Henrici Sexti./

R 183. ℂ De termino hillarii anno henrici sexti. xxxiii. (Pynson, 1510).
Colla. T.p.+i–li.
Colo. ℂ Explicit annus xxxiii'/Henrici sexti./

R 184. ℂ De termino Hillarii. Anno. xxxiii. H. vi./
Colla. Primo–lxiii.
Colo. ℂ Explicit annus. xxxiii.' Henrici sexti/Impress. per me Robertū Redman/cōmorantem in perochia sancti/Dunstani ad signum/diui Georgii./Cum priuilegio./

R 185. ☙ De termino Hillarii anno/xxxiii. regni regis Henrici. vi./
Colla. i–lvi.
Colo. ℂ Imprinted at London/in Fletestrete within Temple Barre, at the/signe of the hand & starre, by Richard Tottel,/ the. vi. day of Marche./Anno. 1556./☙ Cum priuilegio ad imprimendum solum./

R 186. ¶ De termino Hillarii anno/xxxiii. regni regis Henrici. vi.
Colla. i–lvi.
Colo. ☙ Imprinted at Lon-/don in Fletestrete within Temple/ barre at the signe of the hande and/starre by Richard Tottell./ ye vi. day of March./1556./Cum priuilegio./

R 187. ¶ De termino Hillarii anno/xxxiii. regni regis Henrici sexti/
Colla. i–lvi.
Colo. ☙ Imprinted at London/in Fletestrete within Temple barre/at the signe of the Hand and starre,/By Rychard Tottel the/14. daye of Maye in the/yere of our Lord./1575./Cum priuilegio./

R 188. ¶ De termino Hillarii Anno/xxxiij regni Regis Henrici Sexti./ [Tottell.]
Colla. i–lvi.
Colo. None.

YEAR 34

R 189. Termino scī Michīs Anno. H. vi. xxxiiii.
Colla. [1 bl.]+92 leaves without pagination or signature.
Colo. Enp'te ꝑ moy Williā Maclyn en Holborn̄./

R 190. ¶ De termino Michaelis Anno. xxxiiii. H. vi./
Colla. A 6, B 4, C 6, D 4, E 6, F 4, G 6, H 4, I–L 6's.
Colo. ¶ Explicitur annus. xxxiiii. Henrici sexti. Impressus/ per Richardum Pynsonum regiū impresso-/rem. Cum priuilegio./

R 191. ☙ De termino Michaelis anno./XXXIIII. regni regis Henrici sexti./
Colla. i–liii+[1 bl.].
Colo. ¶ Imprinted at London/in Fletestrete within Temple Barre, at the/signe of the hand & starre, by Richard Tottel,/ the vi. day of Marche./Anno. 1556./☙ Cum priuilegio ad imprimendum solum./

R 192. ¶ De termino Michaelis anno/xxxiiii. regni Regis Henrici sexti./
Colla. i–liii.
Colo. ¶ Imprinted at Lon-/don in fletestrete within Temple/ Barre at the signe of the hande and starre/by Richard Tottel ye vi. of March,/Anno. 1556./Cum priuilegio ad imprimendum solum./

R 193. ¶ De termino Michaelis anno/xxxiiii. regni Regis Henrici sexti./
Colla. i–liii+[1 bl.].
Colo. ☙ Imprinted at London/in Fletestrete within Temple barre/at the signe of the Hand and starre,/By Rychard Tottel the/xiij. day of Aprell in the/yere of our Lord./1575./ ¶ Cum priuilegio./

R 194. ¶ De Termino Michaelis Anno/xxxiiii. regni Regis Henrici sexti./ [Tottell.]
Colla. i–liii+[1 bl.].
Colo. Explicit Annus xxxiiij. Henrici Sexti./

YEAR 35

R 195. ℂ De termino Michaelis anno regni regis. H. vi. xxxv°./ [Lettou & Machlinia.]
Colla. 70 leaves, without foliation or signature.
Colo. Explicit ann' xxxv°/Henrici Sexti./

R 196. ℂ De termino Michaelis anno regni/regis. H. vi. xxxv./ [Pynson.]
Colla. i–lvi.
Colo. ℂ Explicit ann'. xxxv° Henrici Sexti./

R 197. De Termino Michaelis An. xxxv. Henrici vi./
Colla. i–lxxvi.
Colo. ℂ Imprynted at London by/me Robert Redman,/Cum priuilegio./Regalj./

R 198. ¶ De termino Michaelis anno/XXXV. regni regis Henrici. vi./
Colla. i–lxiii+[1 bl.].
Colo. ℂ Imprinted at London/in Fletestrete within Temple Barre, at the/signe of the hand & starre, by Richard Tottel,/ Anno. 1556./

R 199. ℂ De termino Michaelis anno/XXXV. regni regis Henrici. vi./
Colla. i–lxiii+[1 bl.].
Colo. ❧ Imprinted at Lon-/don in Fletestrete within Temple/ barre at the signe of the hande and/starre by Richard Tottell./ 1556./

R 200. De termino Michaelis anno/xxxv. regni regis Henrici Sexti./
Colla. i–lxiii+[1 bl.].
Colo. ❧ Imprinted at London/in Fletestrete within Temple barre/at the signe of the Hand and starre,/By Rychard Tottel the/21. daye of Iune in the/yere of our Lord./1575./

R 201. ¶ De termino Michaelis Anno/xxxv. Regni Regis Henrici sexti./ [Tottell.]
Colla. i–lxiii+[1 bl.].
Colo. ℂ Explicit annus xxxv. Regis Henrici sexti./

YEAR 36

R 202. Michaelis. xxxvi. Henrici sexti [Lettou & Machlinia].
Colla. 39 leaves, without foliation or signature.
Colo. ℂ Explicit annus. xxxvi° Hen-/rici sexti Termino micahelis./

R 203. ℂ Anno tricesimo sexto Henrici sexti./
Colla. A–F 6's.
Colo. ℂ Et hec de Anno. xxxvi. Henrici sexti dicta sufficiant./ Impress. per Richardum Pynsonum regium/impressorem. Cum priuilegio/a rege indulto./

R 204, Anno trisecimo sexto Henrici sexti./
Colla. A 6, B 4, C 6, D 4, E 6, F 4, G 6.
Colo. ℂ Imprynted at London in Fletestrete at the sygne of/ the George by Wyllyam Myddylton./

R 205. Anno tricesimo sexto Henrici sexti./
Colla. i–xxxiiii.
Colo. ¶ Imprinted at London/in Fletestrete within Temple Barre, at the/signe of the hand & starre by Richard Tottle,/ Anno. 1557./Cum priuilegio ad imprimen-/dum solum./

R 206. Anno tricesimo sexto Henrici sexti./
Colla. i–xxxiiii.
Colo. ☞ Imprinted at Lon-/don in fletestrete within temple/ Barre at the signe of the hand & starre./by Rychard Tottel, the tenthe/daye of Marche/An. 1567./Cum priuilegio./

R 207. Anno xxxvi. H. vi./
Colla. i–xxxiiii.
Colo. ☞ Imprinted at London/in Fletestrete within Temple barre/at the signe of the Hand and starre,/By Rychard Tottel the/14. day of Nouember in the/yere of our Lord./1575./ ¶ Cum priuilegio./

Year 37

R 208. De termino Michīs anno. xxxvii. Henrici sexti./ [Machlinia.]
Colla. a–f 8's, g–h 6's.
Colo. None.

R 209. De termino Michaelis. Anno. xxxvii./H. vi./
Colla. A–G 6's, last leaf blank.
Colo. ¶ Et hec de Anno. xxxvii. Henrici sexti dicta sufficiant./ Impress. per Richardum Pynsonum regium/impressorem. Cum priuilegio/a rege indulto.

R 210. De termino Michaelis. Anno. xxxvii. H. vi./
Colla. i–xlii.
Colo. ¶ Imprynted at London in Fletestrete at the sygne/of the George nexte to saynt Dunstons/Churche by Wyllyam/ Myddylton./

R 211. ¶ De termino Michaelis. Anno./xxxvii. Henrici sexti./
Colla. i–xxxviii.
Colo. ¶ Imprinted at London in Fletestrete within/Temple barre, at the signe of the hande/and starre, by Richard Tottill./

R 212. De termino Michaelis. anno./xxxvii. Henrici sexti./
Colla. i–xxxviii.
Colo. ☞ Imprinted at Lon-/don in fletestrete within Temple/ Barre at the signe of the hand & starre,/by Richard Tottill, in the/yeare of our lorde/1567./

R 213. ¶ De termino Michaelis anno/xxxvii. Henrici sexti./
Colla. i–xxxviii.
Colo. ☞ Imprinted at London/at Fletestrete within Temple barre/at the signe of the Hand and starre,/By Rychard Tottel the/2. daye of Iune in the/yere of our Lord./1575./ ¶ Cum priuilegio./

YEAR 38

R 214. ℂ De termino Michaelis. Anno. xxxviii. H. vi./
Colla. i–xlvi.
Colo. ℂ Explicit./ℂ Here endeth the. xxxviii. yere of kynge Henry the syxte,/newely correctyd and amended, and imprynted by/me Robert Redman, dwellyng in Fletestrete/besyde saynt Dunstones churche, at the/sygne of the George./ ℂ Cum priuilegio./ [McK. 44.]

R 215. ¶ De termino Michaelis. anno/XXXVIII. regni regis Henrici. vi/
Colla. i–xl.
Colo. ℂ Imprinted at London/in Fletestrete within Temple Barre, at the/signe of the hand & starre, by Richard Tottel,/ Anno. 1556./☙ Cum priuilegio ad imprimendum solum./

R 216. ℂ De termino Michaelis anno/XXXVIII. regni regis Henrici. vi/
Colla. i–xl.
Colo. ❧ Imprinted at Lon-/don in fletestrete within temple/ Barre at the signe of the hand and/starre by Rychard Tottel,/ An. 1566./Cum priuilegio./

R 217. ¶ De termino Michaelis anno/xxxviii. regni Regis Henrici sexti./
Colla. [i]–xl.
Colo. ☙ Imprinted at London/in Fletestrete within Temple barre/at the signe of the Hand and starre,/By Rychard Tottel the/v. daye of Maye in the/yere of our Lord./1575./ ¶ Cum priuilegio.

YEAR 39

R 218. De termĩo Michaelis Anno. xxxix. Henrici sexti./
Colla. A 6, B 4, C 6, D 4, E 6, F 4, G 6, H 4, I 6, K–L 4's.
Colo. ℂ Et hec de Anno. xxxix. Henrici sexti dicta sufficiant./ Impress. per Richardum Pynsonum regium/impressorem Cum priuilegio a rege/indulto./

R 219. De Termino Michaelis Anno. xxxix. Henrici sexti./
Colla. A 6, B 4, C 6, D 4, E–G 6's, H 4, I 6, K 4, L 4.
Colo. ❧ Imprynted at London in/Fletestrete at the sygne of the George/nexte to saynt Dunstones church by/Wyllyam Myddylton./

R 220. ☙ De termino Michaelis anno/xxxix. Henrici sexti./
Colla. i–li+[1 bl.].
Colo. ℂ Imprinted at London/in Fletestrete within Temple Barre, at the/signe of the hand & starre by Richard Tottle,/ Anno. 1557./Cum priuilegio ad imprimendum solum./

R 221. ℂ De termino Michaelis anno/XXXIX Henrici sexti./
Colla. i–li.
Colo. ℂ Imprinted at Lon-/don in fletestrete within Temple/ Barre at the signe of the hand & starre, by/Richard Tottill, ye xvii day of/ May in the yeare of/our lorde. 1567./

R 222. ¶ De termino Michaelis anno/xxxix. Henrici sexti./
Colla. i–li.

Colo. ☙ Imprinted at London/in Fletestrete within Temple barre/at the signe of the Hand and starre,/By Rychard Tottel the/14. day of December in the/yere of our Lord./1575./ ¶ Cum priuilegio.

EDWARD IV

Year 1

R 223. De t'mino Michīs A. primo. E. iiii./
Colla. A 4 [first blank].
Colo. Per me Ricardum Pynson.

R 224. Edwardi iiii/
Colla. 3 leaves without foliation or signature.
Colo. Per me Ricardum Pynson.

R 225. De termino sctī Mich. An° Reg. E. iiii. primo./ [Pynson, 1508.]
Colla. i–viii.
Colo. Explicit scm. Townsend.

R 226. ¶ De termino Michaelis. Anno Reg. E. iiij. primo./ [Pynson, 1508.]
Colla. i–ix+[1 bl.].
Colo. Explicit scm. Townsend'.

R 227. ¶ De termino Michaelis. Anno. primo. E. iiii./
Colla. i–x.
Colo. ¶ Explicit scm. Townsend'. ¶ Imprynted at London in Fletestrete at the sygne/of the George by Wyllyam Myddylton./

R 228. De termino Michaelis Anno/primo Eduardi quarti./
Colla. i–x.
Colo. ¶ Imprinted at London in/Fleetestrete within Temple Barre at the signe/of the Hande and Starre, by Richard Tottill./ Anno. 1556./Cum priuilegio ad imprimendum solum./

R 229. ¶ De termino Michaelis anno/primo Edwardi quarti./
Colla. i–x.
Colo. ¶ Imprinted at Lon/don in fletestrete within Temple/ Barre at the signe of the hande and starre/by Richard Tottel,/ Anno. 1565./Cum priuilegio ad imprimendum solum./

R 230. ☙ De termino Michaelis anno/primo Edwardi quarti./
Colla. i–x.
Colo. ¶ Imprinted at London/in Fletestrete within Temple Barre, at the/signe of the hand & starre, by Richard Tottel,/ Anno. 1556./Cum priuilegio ad imprimendum solum./

R 231. ¶ De termino Michaelis Anno/primo Edwardi quarti./
Colla. i–x.
Colo. ¶ Imprinted at Lon-/don in fletestrete within Temple/ Barre at the signe of the hande and starre/by Richard Tottle,/ Anno. 1556./Cum priuilegio ad imprimendum solum./

R 232. [first page lacking.]
Colla. i–x.
Colo. ❧ Imprinted at London in/Fletestrete within Temple Barre, at the/signe of the Hand and Starre, by/Rychard Tottel./ 1582./Cum priuilegio ad imprimendum solum./

Year 2

R 233. De termĩo Pasche An° scdo E. iiii./
Colla. i–xxviii.
Colo. ¶ Explicit annus scdus. E. iiii. scdm Townsend/de novo impressus in academia, ere ac impensis/honesti viri Richardi Pynson Regii ĩpressoris./

R 234. ¶ De termino Pasche Anno secundo. E. iiii./
Colla. i–xxxi.
Colo. ¶ Explicit annus secundus E. iiii. scũm Tounsende./

R 235. ¶ De termino Pasche Anno secundo. E. iiii./
Colla. i–xxviii.
Colo. ¶ Explicit annus scds. E. iiii. scdm Townsend'./

R 236. ¶ De termino Pasche. Anno/secundo. Edwardi quarti./
Colla. i–xxvii.
Colo. Imprinted at London in fletestrete/within Temple barre at the signe of the/hand and starre by Richarde/Tottyll./Anno domini. 1558./ ¶ Cum priuilegio ad imprimendum solum./

R 237. ¶ De termino Pasche anno/secundo Edwardi quarti./
Colla. i–xxvii.
Colo. ¶ Imprinted at Lon-/don in fletestrete within Temple/ Barre at the signe of the hande and starre/by Richard Tottell./ Anno. 1566./Cum priuilegio ad imprimendum solum./

R 238. ¶ De termino Pasche anno/secundo Edwardi quarti./
Colla. i–xxvii+[1 bl.].
Colo. ¶ Imprinted at London/in Fletestrete within Temple Barre at/the signe of the Hand and Starre, by Rychard/Tottel in the yeare of our Lorde. 1572./Cum priuilegio.

R 239. ¶ De termino Pasche anno/secundo Edwardi quarti./
Colla. i–xxviii.
Colo. ¶ Imprinted at London/in Fleetstrete, within Temple Barre/at the signe of the hand and starre, by/Rycharde Tottel./ 1584./Cum priuilegio.

Year 3

R 240. De termino scẽ Triñ a° iii regni E. iiii/ [Pynson, 1496.]
Colla. A–C 8's, D–E 6's (last leaf blank).
Colo. None.

R 241. ¶ De termino scẽ Trinitatis anno iii. Edwardi quarti./ [Pynson, 1502.]
Colla. 32 leaves.
Colo. None.

R 242. De termino Trinitatis Anno. iii. Edwardi quarti./
Colla. A–B 6's, C 4, D 6, E 4, F 6 (last leaf blank).
Colo. ℂ Imprinted at London in Fletestrete, by/Richarde Pynson, prynter to the/kyng noble grace/.

R 243. De termino Trinitatis Anno. iii. Edwardi quarti./
Colla. i–xxxi+[1 bl.].
Colo. ℂ Explicit Annus tertius Edwardi tertii. Impryn-/ted at London in Fletstrete at the sygne of/the George nexte to saynt Dunstons/churche by Wyllyam/Myddylton./

R 244. ¶ De termino Trinitatis Anno. III./Edwardi quarti./
Colla. i–xxviii.
Colo. ¶ Imprinted at London in fletestrete within/Temple barre, at the sygne of the hand/and starre, by Richard Tottell./ An. do. 1558./Cum priuilegio ad impri-/mendum solum./

R 245. De termino Trinitatis Anno/tercio. Edwardi quarti./
Colla. i–xxviii.
Colo. ℂ Imprinted at Lon-/don in fletestrete within Temple/ Barre at the signe of the hande and starre,/by Richard Tottell./ Anno. do. 1566./Cum priuilegio ad imprimendum solum./

R 246. De termino Trinitatis Anno. III./regni regis Eduardi quarti./
Colla. i–xxviii.
Colo. ¶ Imprinted at London in/Fleetestrete within Temple Barre at the signe/of the Hande and Starre, by Richard Tottill./ Anno. 1566./Cum priuilegio ad imprimendum solum./

R 247. ¶ De termino Trinitatis anno/III. Edwardi quarti./
Colla. i–xxviii.
Colo. ¶ Imprinted at London/in Fleetstrete, within Temple Barre/at the signe of the hand and starre, by/Rycharde Tottel./ 1583./Cum priuilegio.

Year 4

R 248. De termino pasche A° iiii. E. iiii./ [Pynson, 1496.]
Colla. A–C 8's, D–E 6's, F–G 8's.
Colo. None.

R 249. ℂ De termino Pasche anno iiii. Edwardi iiii./ [Pynson, 1510.]
Colla. A–G 6's, H 8 (last leaf blank).
Colo. None.

R 250. ℂ De termino Pasche Anno. iiii. Edwardi quarti./
Colla. A 6, B 4, C–D 6's, E 4, F–G 6's, H 8 (last leaf blank).
Colo. ℂ Imprinted at London in Fletestrete, by/Richarde Pynson, prynter to the/kyng noble grace./

R 251. ℂ De termino Pasche Anno. iiii. Edwardi. iiii./
Colla. i–xlvii+[2 bl.].
Colo. ℂ Imprinted at London in Fletestrete at the sygne/of the George nexte to saynt Dunstons/Churche by Wyllyam/ Myddylton./ ℂ Cum priuilegio ad imprimendum solum./

R 252. ¶ De termino Pasche anno. IIII./Edwardi quarti./
Colla. i–xliiii.
Colo. Imprinted at London in fletestrete within/Temple barre, at the sygne of the hand/and starre, by Richard Tottyll./An. do. 1558./Cum priuilegio ad impri-/mendum solum./

R 253. ¶ De termino Pasche. anno. IIII./Edwardi quarti./
Colla. i–xliiii.
Colo. ¶ Imprinted at Lon-/don in fletestrete within Temple/ Barre at the signe of the hande and starre/by Richard Tottell./ Anno. 1558./Cum priuilegio ad imprimendum solum./

R 254. ¶ De termino Pasche Anno. IIII./Edwardi quarti./
Colla. i–xliiii.
Colo. ¶ Imprinted at London in/Fleetestrete within Temple Barre at the signe/of the Hande and Starre, by Richard Tottill./ Anno. 1558./Cum priuilegio ad imprimendum solum./

R 255. ¶ De termino Paschae anno/IIII. regni regis Edwardi quarti./
Colla. i–xliiii.
Colo. Imprinted at London/in Fleetstrete; within Temple Barre/at the signe of the hand and starre, by/Rycharde Tottel./ 1583./Cum priuilegio.

Year 5

R 256. De termino pasche A° V. E. iiii./ [Pynson, 1496.]
Colla. A 8, B 6 (last two leaves blank).
Colo. None.

R 257. ¶ De termino Pasche. anno v. Edwardi quarti./ [Pynson.]
Colla. A–B 6's.
Colo. None.

R 258. De termino Pasche. Anno. V. Edwardi quarti./ [Pynson, 1508.]
Colla. A 6, B 4.
Colo. ¶ Explicit annus quintus/Edwardi quarti./

R 259. ¶ De termino Pasche Anno. V./Edwardi quarti./
Colla. i–viii.
Colo. ¶ Imprinted at London/in Fletestrete within Temple Barre, at the/signe of the hand & starre by Richard Tottle./ Anno. 1557./Cum priuilegio ad imprimendum solum./

R 260. De termino Pasche Anno. V./Edwardi quarti./
Colla. i–viii.
Colo. ¶ Imprinted at Lon-/don in fletestrete within Temple/ Barre at the signe of the hande and starre,/by Richard Tottell. 1566./Cum priuilegio ad imprimendum solum./

R 261. ¶ De termino Pasche Anno V./regni Regis Edwardi quarti./
Colla. i–viii.
Colo. ¶ Imprinted at London in/Fleetestrete within Temple Barre at the signe/of the Hande and Starre, by Richard Tottill./ Anno. 1566./Cum priuilegio ad imprimendum solum./

R 262. ¶ De termino Pasche anno/v. regni Regis Edwardi quarti./
Colla. I–VIII.
Colo. ¶ Imprinted at London/in Fleetstrete, within Temple Barre/at the signe of the hand and starre, by/Rycharde Tottel./ 1584./Cum priuilegio.

YEAR 6

R 263. De ter° Mich. A° VI. E. iiii./ [Pynson, 1496.]
Colla. A 8, B 6.
Colo. ¶ Explicit annus Sextus Edwardi quarti./

R 264. ¶ De termino Michael'. Anno. vi° Edwardi. iiii./ [Pynson, 1502.]
Colla. A 6, B 8.
Colo. ¶ Explicit Annus sextus Edwardi quarti./

R 265. ¶ De termino Michael'. Anno vi. Edwardi iiii./ [Pynson, 1508.]
Colla. A 6, B 8 (last leaf blank).
Colo. ¶ Explicit Annus sextus Edwardi quarti./

R 266. ¶ De Termino Michaelis. Anno VI. Edwardi quarti./ [Redman.]
Colla. A 6, B 6.
Colo. ¶ Explicit Annus sextus Edwardi quarti./

R 267. ¶ De termino Michaelis. Anno. VI./Edwardi quarti./
Colla. i–xii.
Colo. ¶ Imprinted at London/in Fletestrete within Temple Barre, at the/signe of the hand & starre by Richard Tottle./ Anno. 1557./Cum priuilegio ad imprimendum solum./

R 268. ¶ De termino Michaelis. Anno. VI./Edwardi quarti./
Colla. i–xii.
Colo. ¶ Imprinted at Lon-/don in fletestrete within Temple/ Barre at the signe of the hande and starre/by Richard Tottell./ Anno. 1557./Cum priuilegio ad imprimendum solum./

R 269. ¶ De termino Michaelis Anno. VI./Edwardi quarti./
Colla. i–xii.
Colo. ¶ Imprinted at London/in Fletestrete within Temple Barre at/the signe of the Hand and Starre, by Rychard/Tottel in the yeare of our Lorde. 1572./Cum priuilegio.

R 270. ¶ De termino Michaelis anno/vj. Edwardi quarti./
Colla. i–xii.
Colo. ¶ Imprinted at London/in Fleetestrete, within Temple Barre/at the signe of the Hand and Starre,/by Rycharde Tottell./ 1556./Cum priuilegio.

YEAR 7

R 271. De termino pasche a° VII. Edwardi iiii./ [Pynson, 1496.]
Colla. a–d 8's (first leaf blank).
Colo. ¶ Explicit annus Septimus Edwardi quarti./

R 272. ¶ De termino Pasche anno vii° Edwardi iiii^{ti}/ [Pynson, 1510].
Colla. A–E 6's.
Colo. ¶ Explicit annus septimus Edwardi iiii./

R 273. De termino Pasche Anno. vii. Edwardi quarti./
Colla. A 6, B 4, C 6, D 4, E 6, F 4.
Colo. ℂ Imprinted at London in Fletestrete, by/Rycharde Pynson, prynter to the/kyng noble grace./

R 274. De termino Pasche Anno. vii. Edwardi quarti./
Colla. A 6, B 4, C 6, D 4, E 6, F 4.
Colo. ❧ Explicit annus septimus/Edwardi quarti. Imprinted at London in/Fletestrete, at the sygne of the George/by Robert Redman./

R 275. ℂ De termino Pasche anno./VII. Edwardi quarti./
Colla. [i]–xxxii.
Colo. ❧ Imprinted at London/in Fletestrete within Temple Barre, at the/signe of the hande & starre by Richard Tottyll./ the viii daye of Ianuary/Anno domini. 1556./ℂ Cum priuilegio.

R 276. ℂ De termino Pasche Anno/VII. Edwardi quarti./
Colla. i–xxxii.
Colo. ℂ Imprinted at Lon-/don in fletestrete within Temple/ Barre at the signe of the hand & starre, by/Richard Tottill, yͤ last day of A-/pril in the yeare of our lorde/M.1567./

R 277. ¶ De termino Pasche anno. VII./Edwardi quarti./
Colla. i–xxxii.
Colo. ¶ Imprinted at London in/Fleetestrete within Temple Barre at the signe/of the Hande and Starre, by Richard Tottill./ Anno. 1567./Cum priuilegio ad imprimendum solum./

R 278. ¶ De termino pasche anno/vij. Edwardi quarti./
Colla. i–xxxii.
Colo. ¶ Imprinted at London/in Fleetstrete, within Temple Barre/at the signe of the hand and starre, by/Rycharde Tottel./ 1584./Cum priuilegio./

Year 8

R 279. De termīo pasche A° viii. E. iiii./ [Pynson, 1496.]
Colla. a 8, b 6, c 8, d 8, e 6.
Colo. Explicit annus octauus Edwardi quarti./

R 280. Edwardi. iiii./ [Pynson, 15—.]
Colla. A–D 6's, E 8.
Colo. ℂ Explicit annus octaus Edwardi quarti.

R 281. Edwardi quarti./ [Pynson, 152–.]
Colla. A–D 6's, E 8.
Colo. None. [Device, McK. 44.]

R 282. De termino Pasche. Anno. viii. Edwardi quarti./
Colla. A 6, B 4, C 6, D 4, E 6, F 4.
Colo. ℂ Imprynted at London by Wyllyam Myddylton.

R 283. ¶ De termino Pasche anno/viii. regni regis Edwardi. iiii./
Colla. i–xxv+[1 bl.].

Colo. ℂ Imprinted at London/in Fletestrete within Temple Barre, at the/signe of the hand & starre by Richard Tottel,/ Anno. 1556./☙ Cum priuilegio ad imprimendum solum./

R 284. ℂ De termino Pasche anno/viii. regni Regis Edwardi quarti./
Colla. i–xxv+[1 bl.].
Colo. ℂ Imprinted at Lon-/don in fletestrete within Temple/ Barre at the signe of the hande and starre/by Richard Tottel,/ Anno. 1556./Cum priuilegio ad imprimendum solum./

R 285. De termino Pasche anno/viii. regni regis Eduardi quarti./
Colla. [i]–xxv+[1 bl.].
Colo.¶ Imprinted at London in/Fleetestrete within Temple Barre at the signe/of the Hande and Starre, by Richard Tottill./ Anno. 1556./Cum priuilegio ad imprimendum solum./

R 286. ℂ De termino Paschae anno/viij. regni Regis Edwardi quarti./
Colla. i–xxv+[1 bl.].
Colo. ¶ Imprinted at London/in Fleetestrete within Temple Barre/at the signe of the Hand and Starre,/by Rycharde Tottell./ 1582./Cum priuilegio.

Year 9

R 287. De termino Pasche Anno ix Edwardi iiii./
Colla. A–D 8's, E, F 6's, G 8, H 8 (last leaf blank).
Colo. Explicit Annnus. Nonus. Edwardi. quarti./Per me Ricardum. Pynson./ [McK. 3 a.]

R 288. De termino Pasche Anno. ix. Edwardi quarti./
Colla. A, B 6's, C 4, D–H 6's, I 4, K 6.
Colo. ℂ Imprinted at London in Fletestrete, by/Rycharde Pynson, prynter to the/kynge noble grace./

R 289. De termino Pasche Anno ix. Edwardi. iiii./
Colla. I–LVII+[1 bl.].
Colo. ℂ Imprynted at London withowt tem-/pull Barre in sent clementis/Paryshe By me Robert/Redman at syne of/ the George./

R 290. ¶ De termino Pasche anno/IX. regni regis Edwardi quarti./
Colla. i–liii+[1 bl.].
Colo. ℂ Imprinted at London/in Fletestrete within Temple Barre, at/the signe of the hand & starre, by Richard/Tottel, the xxv. daye of Ianuarye,/in the yere of oure/Lorde. 1556./ ☙ Cum priuilegio ad impri-/mendum solum./

R 291. ¶ De termino Pasche Anno/ix. regni regis Edwardi quarti./
Colla. I–LIII+[1 bl.].
Colo. ❧ Imprinted at Lon-/don in Fletestrete within Temple/ barre at the signe of the hande and/starre by Richard Tottell./ the. viii. daye of Februarie in the yere/of our Lord/1556./Cum priuilegio.

R 292. ¶ De termino Pasche Anno/ix. regni regis Edwardi quarti./
Colla. i–liii+[1 bl.].

Colo. ¶ Imprinted at London/in Fletestrete within Temple Barre at/the signe of the Hande and Starre, by Rychard/Tottel in the yeare of our Lorde. 1572./the. 24. of Iuly./Cum priuilegio./

R 293. ¶ De termino Paschae anno/ix. regni regis Edwardi quarti./
Colla. i–liii+[1 bl.].
Colo. ☙ Imprinted at London/in Fletestrete within Temple Barre,/at the signe of the Hand and Starre, by/Rychard Tottel, the vj. day/of Iune./1582./Cum priuilegio./

Year 10

R 294. ¶ De termino Pache. Anno. x. Edwardi. iiii./
Colla. i–xxii.
Colo. ¶ Explicit annus decimus Edwardi quarti. Et de ter-/mino Michaelis. Anno ab incohacione regni Hērici sexti. xlix. et reapcionis regie potestatis/primo. Impressum per Richar-/dum Pynsonum regium/impressorem./Cum priuilegio./

R 295. De termino Pach. Anuo decimo Edward' quarti./[Rastell 1515].
Colla. I–XX.
Colo. ¶ The price of thys boke is. iiii. d'. un bounde.

R 296. De termino Pasche Anno Decimo. E. iiii./[Pynson 1518].
Colla. Primo–xx.
Colo. None.

Year 11

R 297. ¶ De termino sancte Trinitatis Anno xi° Edwardi iiii./[Pynson 1500].
Colla. a 6, b 6, c 4.
Colo. None.

R 298. ¶ De termino sancte Trinitatis. An. xi. E. iiii./
Colla. I–XIV.
Colo. ¶ Imprynted at London by/me Robert Redman./Cum priuilegio/Regali./

R 299. ¶ De termino Trinitatis An. xi. E. iiii./[Powell].
Colla. i–xiii.
Colo. (lacking).

Year 12

R 300. ¶ De termino Pasche. Anno. xii. Edwardi. iiii./
Colla. i–xxi+[1 bl.].
Colo. ¶ Explicit annus. xii. Edwardi quarti./ ¶ Imprynted at London in Fletestrete, by Rycharde/Pynson, prynter to the kynges noble grace./

R 301. De termino Pashe Anno. xii. E. iiii./
Colla. i–XXI+[1 bl.].
Colo. ¶ Imprynted by me Robert Redman./ ¶ Cum priuilegio a rege indulto./

R 302. De termino Pashe Anno. xii. E. iiii./[Powell].
Colla. i–xx.
Colo. (lacking).

Years 10–12

R 303. ℂ De termino Pasche anno. X./regni regis Edwardi quarti./
Colla. i–xix+i–xi+i–xxi.
Colo. ℂ Imprinted at London in fletestrete with-/in temple barre, at the signe of the hande and/starre, by Richard Tottill./ ☞ */Cum priuilegio./

R 304. ℂ De termino Pasche anno/X. Edwardi quarti./
Colla. i–xix+i–xi+i–xxi+[1 bl.].
Colo. ℂ Imprinted at Lon-/don in fletestrete within Temple/ Barre at the signe of the hand & starre,/by Richard Tottell. 1566./Cum priuilegio ad imprimendum solum./

R 305. ¶ De termino Pasche anno/decimo Edwardi quarti./
Colla. i–xix+i–xi+i–xxi+[1 bl.].
Colo. ¶ Imprinted at London in/Fleetestrete within Temple Barre at the signe/of the Hande and Starre, by Richard Tottill./ Anno. 1566./Cum priuilegio ad imprimendum solum./

R 306. ¶ De termino Pasche anno/decimo Edwardi quarti./
Colla. i–xix+i–xi+i–xxi.
Colo. ❧ Imprinted at London/in Fleetestrete within Temple Barre,/at the signe of the Hand and starre by/Rychard Tottyl. Anno./1584./ ¶ Cum priuilegio ad imprimendum solum./

Year 13

R 307. ℂ De termīo Michaelis Anno. xiii. E. iiii./
Colla. i–x.
Colo. ℂ Explicit Annus Decimus tertius. Impressus per/ Richardum Pynson regium impressorum./Cum priuilegio a rege indulto./

R 308. De Termino Michaelis Anno. xiii. E. iiii./
Colla. j–x+[1 bl.].
Colo. ℂ Imprynted by me Robert Redman dwellynge/in Fletestrete in saynt Donstones/Parysshe at the signe of/the George./ ℂ Cum Gratia et priuilegio a Rege Indulto./

R 309. De termino Michaelis An. xiii. E. iiii./
Colla. i–x.
Colo. ℂ Imprinted at London in Fletestrete at/the signe of the George, nexte to saint Dunstones/churche by Wyllyam Powell./

R 310. ❧ De termino Michaelis anno/xiii. Edwardi quarti./
Colla. i–x.
Colo. ℂ Imprinted at London in fletestrete within/Temple barre, at the signe of the hande and starre,/by Richard Tottill, the. xvi. day of Marche/in the yeare of owr Lorde. M./v.C.lix./

R 311. ℭ De termino Michaelis anno. XIII./regni Regis Edwardi quarti./
Colla. i–x.
Colo. ℭ Imprinted at Lon-/don in fletestrete within Temple/ Barre at the signe of the hand & starre, by/Richard Tottill, y^e^. xvi. day of Au-/gust in the yeare of our lorde/M.1556./

R 312. ¶ De termino Michaelis Anno XIII./Regni Regis Edwardi quarti./
Colla. i–x.
Colo. ¶ Imprinted at London/in Fletestrete within Temple Barre at/the signe of the Hand and Starre, by Rychard/Tottel in the yeare of our Lorde. 1572./Cum priuilegio.

R 313. ¶ De termino Michaelis anno/ix. regni regis Edwardi quarti./
Colla. i–x.
Colo. ☙ Imprinted at London/in Fletestrete within Temple Barre,/at the signe of the Hand and Starre, by/Rychard Tottel, the xii. day/of Iune./1582./Cum priuilegio./

Year 14

R 314. De termĩo Michaelis Anno. xiiii. E. iiii./
Colla. I–VIII.
Colo. ℭ Explicit ann.' xiiii. E. quarti. Imprinted at London/ in Fletestrete by Rycharde Pynson, printer/to the kynges most noble grace./ℭ Cum priuilegio./

R 315. De termino Michaelis Anno. xiiii. E. iiii./
Colla. i–viii.
Colo. ℭ Imprinted by me Robert Redman./Cum priuilegio a rege indulto./

R 316. ☙ De termino Michaelis anno. XIIII./regni regis Edwardi quarti./
Colla. i–viii.
Colo. ℭ Imprinted at London/in Fletestrete within Temple Barre, at the/signe of the hand & starre, by Richard Tottel,/ Anno. 1556./☙ Cum priuilegio ad imprimendum solum./

R 317. ℭ De termino Michaelis Anno. XIIII./regni regis Edwardi quarti./
Colla. i–viii.
Colo. ❧ Imprinted at Lon-/don in Fletestrete within Temple/ barre at the signe of the hande and/starre by Richard Tottell./ Cum priuilegio.

R 318. ¶ De Termino Michaelis Anno. XIIII./regni regis Edwardi quarti./
Colla. i–viii.
Colo. ¶ Imprinted at London/in Fletestrete within Temple Barre at/the signe of the Hand and Starre, by Rychard/Tottel in the yeare of our Lorde. 1572./Cum priuilegio./

R 319. ¶ De termino Michaelis Anno./xiiii. regni regis Edwardi quarti./
Colla. i–viii.

Colo. ☞ Imprinted at London/in Fletestrete within Temple Barre,/at the signe of the Hand and Starre, by/Rychard Tottel, the xii. day/of Iune. 1582./Cum priuilegio./

YEAR 15

R 320. De termino Michaelis anno. xv. E. iiii./
Colla. A, B 6's, C 4, D 6, E 4, F 6.
Colo. ¶ Impress. per me Richardũ Pynsoñ,/regis impress. Cum priuilegio/a rege indulto./

R 321. De termino Michaelis Anno XV. E. iiii./
Colla. i–xxxii.
Colo. ¶ Imprynted at London witwout tempull/Barre in sent Clementis Paryshe/By me Robert Redman/at sygne of the/George/ ¶ Cum privilegio a Rege indulto./

R 322. ¶ De termino Michaelis anno/XV. regui regis Edwardi quarti./
Colla. I–XXXIII, 1 bl.
Colo. ¶ Imprinted at London/in Fletestrete within Temple Barre, at/the signe of the hand & starre, by Richard/Tottel, the ii. daye of February,/in the yere of oure/Lorde. 1556./(.·.)/☞ Cum privilegio ad impri-/mendum solum./

R 323. ¶ De termino Michaelis Anno/XV. regni regis Edwardi quarti./
Colla. I–XXXIII, 1 bl.
Colo. ¶ Imprinted at London/in fletestrete within Temple Barre, at/the signe of the hande and starre, by Richarde/Tottel, the. ii. daye of Februarye,/in the yere of oure/Lorde. 1556./(.·.)/Cum privilegio ad impri-/mendum solum./

R 324. ¶ De Termino Michaelis Anno. XV./regni regis Edwardi quarti.
Colla. i–xxxiii+1 bl.
Colo. ¶ Imprinted at London/in Fletestrete within Temple Barre at/the signe of the Hand and Starre, by Rychard/Tottel in the yeare of our Lorde. 1572./(.·.) Cum privilegio.

R 325. ¶ De termino Michaelis Anno/XV. regni regis Edwardi quarti./
Colla. I–XXXIII, 1 bl.
Colo. ☞ Imprinted at London/in Fletestrete within Temple Barre,/at the signe of the Hand and Starre, by/Rychard Tottel, the xij. day/of Iune. 1582./Cum privilegio./

YEAR 16

R 326. ¶ De termino Pasche. Anno xvi. Edwardi quarti./
Colla. A 6, B 6.
Colo. ¶ Explicit Annus decimus sextus Edwardi Quarti:/ Impressum per me Richardũ Pynsonum/regium impressorem. Cum pri-/uilegio rege indulto./ [McK. 44.]

R 327. De termino Pasche Anno. xvi. E. iiii./
Colla. I–XII.
Colo. ¶ Imprynted by me Robert Redman./ ¶ Cum privilegio a rege indulto./

R 328. ¶ De termino Pasche anno. XVI./Edwardi quarti./
Colla. I–XII.
Colo. ¶ Imprinted at London/in Fletestrete within Temple Barre, at the/signe of the hand and starre by Richard Tottle./ Anno. 1557./Cum privilegio ad imprimen-/dum solum.

R 329. De termino Pasche Anno. XVI./Edwardi quarti.
Colla. I–XII.
Colo. ¶ Imprinted at Lon-/don in fletestrete within Temple/ Barre at the signe of the hande and starre/by Richard Tottell./ Anno. 1556./Cum privilegio ad imprimendum solum./

R 330. De termino Pasche Anno/xvi. Eduardi quarti./
Colla. I–XII.
Colo. ¶ Imprinted at London in/Fleetestrete within Temple Barre at the signe/of the Hande and Starre, by Richard Tottill./ Anno. 1556./Cum privilegio ad imprimendum solum./

R 331. ¶ De termino paschae anno/xvi. Edwardi quarti./
Colla. i–xii.
Colo. ¶ Imprinted at London/in Fleetstrete, within Temple Barre/at the signe of the hand and starre, by/Rycharde Tottel./ 1583./Cum privilegio./

Year 17

R 332. ¶ De termino Pasche. Anno. xvii. E. iiii./
Colla. i–viii.
Colo. ¶ Explicit, annus. xvii. Edwardi quarti, nouiter/impressus, per me Robertum Redman,/cõmorantem in ꝑochia sancti Dun-/stani, ad signum diui Georgii./Cum privilegio./

R 333. ¶ De termino Pasche. Anno xvii. E. iiii. Fo. i.
Colla. i–viii.
Colo. Explicit annus. xvii. Eduardi quarti, nouiter/impressus per me Wilhelmum Powel, com-/morãtem in parochia sancti Dun-/stani ad signum diui/Georgii./Cum privilegio ad imprimendum solum./

R 334. ¶ De termino Pasche Anno. XVII./Edwardi quarti./
Colla. i–viii.
Colo. ¶ Imprinted at London/in Fletestrete within Temple Barre, at the/signe of the hande & starre by Richard Tottel./ Anno. 1557./Cum privilegio ad impri-/mendum solum./

R 335. De termino Pasche anno/xvij. Edwardi quarti./
Colla. i–viii.
Colo. Imprinted at London/in Fletestrete within Temple Barre, at the/signe of the hande & starre by Richard Tottel./ Anno. 1557./Cum privilegio ad impri-/mendum solum./

R 336. ¶ De termino Pasche Anno. XVII./Edwardi quarti./
Colla. i–viii.
Colo. ¶ Imprinted at Lon-/don in fletestrete within Temple/ Barre at the signe of the hande and starre/by Richard Tottel,/ Anno. 1557./Cum privilegio ad imprimendum solum./

R 337. ¶ De termino Pasche Anno. XVII./Edwardi quarti./
Colla. i–viii.
Colo. ¶ Imprinted at London/in Fletestrete within Temple Barre at/the signe of the Hand and Starre, by Rychard/Tottel in the yeare of our Lorde. 1572./(.˙.)/Cum privilegio./

R 338. ¶ De termino Paschae Anno/xvij. Edwardi quarti./
Colla. i–viii.
Colo. ¶ Imprinted at London/in Fleetstrete, within Temple Barre/at the signe of the hand and starre, by/Rycharde Tottel./ 1583./Cum priuilegio./

Year 18

R 339. ¶ De termino Pasche. Anno. xviii. Edwardi quarti./
Colla. A–B 6's, C 4, D 6, E 4, F 6.
Colo. Explicit Annus decimus octauus Edwardi quarti:/ impressum per Richardum Pynsonum/regium impressorem. Cum pri-/uilegio a rege indulto./

R 340. De Termino Pasche Anno. xviii. E. iiii.
Colla. i–xxxi.
Colo. ¶ Imprynted by me Robert Redman dwel-/lynge within Tempull barre in/Saynt Donstones/Paryshe./Cum gracia & priuilegio a Rege indulto./

R 341. ¶ De termino Pasche Anno/XVIII. regni regis Edwardi quarti./
Colla. i–xxix.
Colo. ¶ Imprinted at London/in Fletestrete within Temple Barre, at/the signe of the hand & starre, by Richard/Tottel, the xxv. daye of Ianuarye./in the yere of oure/Lorde. 1556./ (.˙.)/❧ Cum priuilegio ad impri-/mendum solum./

R 342. ¶ De termino Pasche anno/XVIII. regni regis Edwardi quarti./
Colla. i–xxix (error).
Colo. ❧ Imprinted at Lon-/don in Fletestrete within temple/ barre at the signe of the hande and/starre by Richard Tottell. /Cum priuilegio./

R 343. ¶ De termino Pasche anno/XVIII. regni regis Edwardi quarti./
Colla. i–xxx.
Colo. ¶ Imprinted at London/in Fletestrete within Temple Barre at/the signe of the Hand and Starre, by Rychard/Tottel in the yeare of our Lorde. 1572./ (.˙.) /Cum priuilegio.

R 344. ¶ De termino Paschae anno/xviij. regni Regis Edwardi quarti./
Colla. i–xxx.
Colo. ¶ Imprinted at London/in Fleetestrete, within Temple Barre/at the signe of the Hand and Starre,/by Rycharde Tottell./1582./Cum priuilegio./

Year 19

R 345. De termino Michaelis Anno. xix. E. iiii.
Colla. A 6, B 4.
Colo. ¶ Impress. per Richard' Pynsoñ.

R 346. De Termino Michaelis Anno xix. E. iiii.
Colla. i–xi+1 bl.
Colo. ℂ Imprynted by me Robert Redman dwellynge in flete/strete in Saynt Donstones Parysshe at the/signe of the George Anno M./CCCCC. & xxvii./ ℂ Cum gratie & priuilegio a Rege indulto.

R 347. ☞ De termino Michaelis Anno/xix. Edwardi quarti./
Colla. i–x.
Colo. ℂ Imprinted at London/in Fletestrete within Temple Barre at the/signe of the hand & starre by Richard Tottle,/ Anno. 1556./Cum priuilegio ad imprimendum solum./

R 348. De termino Michaelis anno/xix. Edwardi quarti./
Colla. i–x.
Colo. ℂ Imprinted at Lon-/don in fletestrete within Temple/ Barre at the signe of the hande and starre/ by Richarde Tottel,/ Anno. 1556./Cum priuilegio ad imprimendum solum./

R 349. De termino Michaelis anno/xix. Eduardi quarti./
Colla. i–x.
Colo. ¶ Imprinted at London in/Fleetestrete within Temple Barre at the signe/of the Hande and Starre, by Richard Tottill./ Anno. 1556./ Cum priuilegio ad imprimendum solum./

R 350. ¶ De termino Michaelis Anno/xix. Edwardi quarti./
Colla. i–x.
Colo. ¶ Imprinted at London/in Fleetestrete, within Temple Barre/at the signe of the Hand and Starre/by Rycharde Tottell./ 1556./Cum priuilegio./

Year 20

R 351. ℂ De termino Pasche. Anno. xx. Edwardi. iiii./
Colla. A–C 6's.
Colo. ℂ Explicit Annus vigesimus Edwardi quarti./Impressum per Richardum Pynsonum/regium impressorem. Cum pri-/uilegio a rege indulto./

R 352. De Termino Pasche Anno xx. Edwardi. iiii.
Colla. i–xviii.
Colo. ℂ Imprynted at London without tempull/Barre in sent Clementis Paryshe/By me Robert Redman/at syne of the/ George/Cum priuilegio a Rege indulto./

R 353. ¶ De termino Pasche Anno/XX. regni regis Edwardi. iiii./
Colla. i–xix.
Colo. ℂ Imprinted at London/in Fletestrete within Temple Barre, at the/signe of the hand & starre, by Richard Tottel,/ Anno. 1556./☞ Cum privilegio ad imprimendum solum./

R 354. ℂ De termino Pasche Anno/xx. regni regis Edwardi quarti./
Colla. i–xxix, 1 bl.
Colo. ☞ Imprinted at Lon-/don in Fletestrete within temple/ barre at the signe of the hande and/starre by Richard Tottell./ Cum priuilegio./

R 355. ¶ De Termino Pasche Anno. XX./regni Regis Edwardi quarti,/
Colla. i–xix.
Colo. ¶ Imprinted at London in/Fletestrete within Temple Barre at the signe/of the Hande and Starre, by Richard Tottill./ Anno. 1556./Cum priuilegio ad imprimendum solum./

R 356. ¶ De termino Paschae anno/XX. regni Regis Edwardi quarti./
Colla. I–XIX, 1 bl.
Colo. ¶ Imprinted at London/in Fleetestrete, within Temple Barre/at the signe of the Hand and Starre,/by Rycharde Tottyll./1582./

YEAR 21

R 357. De termino Pasche Anno. xxi. E. iiii./
Colla. i–ci.
Colo. Explicit Annus vigesimus primus Edwardi quarti secundum longū/reportum. Impressus per Richardum Pynson regium impressorem./Cum priuilegio a rege concesso./ [McK. 44.]

R 358. ℂ De Termino Pasche Anno Regis xxi. E. iiii.
Colla. i–ci.
Colo. ℂ Explicit Annus vigesimus primus Edwardi quarti/ secundum longum reportum. Impressus per/Robertum Redman commorante/sub intersignio diui/Georgii./

R 359. ℂ De termino pasche anno/xxi. Edwardi quarti./
Colla. i–lxxxiiii.
Colo. ℂ Imprinted at London in fletestrete with-/in Temple barre, at the sygne of the/hande and starre, by Ri-/charde Tottyll./ ℂ Cum priuilegio./

R 360. ℂ De termino Pasche anno/xxi. Edwardi quarti./
Colla. i–lxxxiiii.
Colo. ℂ Imprinted at Lon-/don in fletestrete within Temple/ Barre at the signe of the hande and starre,/by Richard Tottell. 1566./Cum priuilegio ad imprimendum solum./

R 361. ¶ De termino Pasche Anno/xxi. Edwardi quarti./
Colla. i–lxxxiiii.
Colo. ¶ Imprinted at London in/Fleetestrete within Temple Barre at the signe/of the Hande and Starre, by Richard Tottill./ Anno. 1566./Cum priuilegio ad imprimendum solum./

R 362. ¶ De termino Pasche anno/xxi. Edwardi quarti.
Colla. i–lxxxiii.
Colo. ¶ Imprinted at London/in Fleetstrete, within Temple Barre/at the signe of the hand and starre, by/Rycharde Tottel./ Anno 1584./ ¶ Cum priuilegio ad imprimendum solum./

YEAR 22

R 363. ℂ De termino Pasche. Anno. xxii. Edwardi quarti./
Colla. A–E 6's, F 4, G 6, H 4, I 6.

Colo. ¶ Explicit annus Vigesimus secūdus Edwardi quarti./ Impress. per Richardum Pynsonum regium/impressorem. Cum priuilegio a rege/indulto./

R 364. De termino pasche. Anno. E. iiii. xxii.
Colla. A–E 6, F 4, G 6, H 4, I 6.
Colo. ¶ Emprynted at London in Fletestrete at the signe of the George by/Richard Pynson, Prenter unto the Kynges noble grace dwellynge/besayde saynt Dunstones Chirche./ [McK. 32 b.]

R 365. ¶ De termino Pasche. Anno. xxii. Edwardi quarti. Fo. i./
Colla. i–l.
Colo. ¶ Explicit Annus. xxii. Edwardi quarti. Impryn-/ted at London in Fletestrete at the sygne of/the George nexte to saynt Dunstons/ Churche by Wyllyam/Myddylton. · ./

R 366. ❧ De termino Pasche. Anno. XXII./regni regis Edwardi quarti./
Colla. i–li.
Colo. Imprinted at London/in Fletestrete within Temple Barre, at/the signe of the hand & starre, by Richard/Tottel, the/ viii. daye of February,/in the yere of oure/Lorde. 1556./Cum priuilegio, etc.

R 367. ¶ De termino Pasche. anno. XXII./regni regis Edwardi quarti./
Colla. i–li+1 bl.
Colo. ❧ Imprinted at Lon-/don in Fletestrete within Temple/ barre at the signe of the hande and/starre by Richard Tottell./ the. viii. daye of Februarie in the yere/of our Lord/1556./Cum priuilegio./

R 368. De termino Pasche anno XXII./Regni Regis Edwardi quarti./
Colla. i–li. 1 bl.
Colo. Imprinted at London in Fleetestreate/within Temple Barre at the signe of the/Hande and Starre by Richard Tottle. /1572./

R 369. ¶ De termino Paschae anno XXII./Regni Regis Edwardi quarti./
Colla. i–li.
Colo. ❧ Imprinted at London/in Fletestrete within Temple barre/at the signe of the Hand and starre,/by Rycharde Tottel in the/yeare of our Lorde./1578./

Long Quint

R 370. ❧ Anno ❧/Quinto Edwar-/di quarti,/Nowe fyrste imprinted, a golden yere and/very fruitefull, &c. . . . / ¶ Imprinted at London in Fletestrete/by Wyllyam Powell./Anno. domini. 1552./Cum privilegio ad imprimendum solum./ [In border 31.]
Colla. T.p.+ii–iiii.+1 bl.+i–cxlii.
Colo. ¶ Imprinted at London in Fletestrete at/the signe of the George, nexte to saint Dunstones/churche by Wyllyam Powell./

R 371. ¶ En cest/volume est con-/teinus le longe Re-/port de Anno quinto Ed-/wardi quarti. Ore nouelment/imprimee & corrigee, &c. . . . /In aedibus Richardi/Tottelli./ ¶ Cum priuilegio./

Colla. T.p.+[3]+1–142.

Colo. ☙ Imprinted at London/in Fleetestrete within Temple Barre,/at the Signe of the Hand and Starre/by Richarde Tottyll./1587./

Years 1–22

R 372. Les ans/our Reports del raigne/du Roye Edward le quart,/&c. . . . Londini/in aedibus Thomae Wight & Bonhami Norton./ 1599./Cum priuilegio./

Colla. T.p. 557 leaves (each year numbered separately) A–F 6's, G 4 (table).

Colo. None.

EDWARD V.

Year 1

R 373. Incipit Annus Primus E. Quinti./ [Cuts 9 & 10.]

Colla. T.p.+ai–vii.

Colo. None.

R 374. De termino Trinitat' Anno primo E. quinti./

Colla. A–B 4's.

Colo. ¶ Explicit. Impress. p Ric' Pynsoñ. [In No. 39 enclosing McK. 3.]

R 375. ¶ De termino Trinitates Anno. I./regni regis Edwardi quinti./

Colla. A–B 4's.

Colo. ¶ Imprinted at London/in Fletestrete within Temple Barre, at/the signe of the Hande and Starre, by Rycharde/ Tottel, the. xii. daye of September, in the yere/of oure Lorde. 1555./☙ Cum priuilegio ad impri-/mendum solum./

R 376. ¶ De termino Trinitatis Anno I./regni regis Edwardi quinti./

Colla. I–VIII.

Colo. Imprinted at London in/Fleetestrete within Temple Barre at the signe/of the Hande and Starre, by Rychard Tottyll./ Anno 1558./Cum priuilegio ad imprimendum solum./

R 377. ¶ De termino Trinitatis Anno I./regni regis Edwardi quinti.

Colla. A–B 4's.

Colo. ☙ Imprinted at London/in Fletestrete within Temple Barre, at the/signe of the hande & starre by Richard Tottyll./ And finished the. 12. day of September./Anno domini. 1559./ ☙ Cum priuilegio ad impri-/mendum solum./

R 378. ¶ De termino Trinitatis anno. i./regni regis Edwardi quinti./

Colla. A–B 4's.

Colo. ❧ Imprinted at Lon-/don in Fletestrete within Temple/ barre at the signe of the hande and/starre by Richard Tottell./ the. xii. daye of September in the yere/of our Lord/1559./Cum priuilegio./

R 379. ℂ De termino Trinitatis Anno. I./regni regis Edwardi quinti./
Colla. i–viii./
Colo. ☙ Imprinted at Lon-/don in Fletestrete within Temple/ Barre at the signe of the hand and starre,/by Richard Tottill, in the/yeare of our lorde/1568./

R 380. ¶ De termino Trinitatis Anno. I./regni Regis Edwardi quinti.
Colla. i–viii.
Colo. ¶ Imprinted at London in/Fleetestrete within Temple Barre at the signe/of the Hande and Starre, by Richard Tottill./ Anno. 1558./Cum priuilegio ad imprimendum solum./

R 381. ¶ De termino Trinitatis Anno I./regni regis Edwardi quinti./
Colla. i–viii.
Colo. ¶ Imprinted at London in/Fleetestrete within Temple Barre at the signe/of the Hande and Starre, by Rychard Tottyll. /Anno 1579./Cum priuilegio ad imprimendum solum.

R 382. ¶ De termino Trinitatis anno/primo regni regis Edwardi quinti./
Colla. i–viii.
Colo. ¶ Imprinted at London in/Fleetestrete within Temple Barre at the signe/of the Hande and Starre, by Richard Tottyl./ Anno Dom̄. 1585./Cum priuilegio./

RICHARD III

Year i

R 383. ℂ Annus primus Richardi. iij. [Cut 7.]
Colla. i–v.
Colo. ℂ Explicit. Annus primus Richardi tercii, nouiter/ emendatus atqz impressus per me Robertum/Redman, cōmorantem in parochia sancti/Dunstani, sub signum diui Georgii./ Cum priuilegio./ [McK. 9 c.]

R 384. ℂ Incipit annus primus Richardi tertii./ ℂ De termino Michaelis anno/primo Richardi tertii./
Colla. I–IIII.
Colo. ☙ Imprinted at London/in Fletestrete within Temple Barre, at the/signe of the hande & starre by Richard Tottyll./ ℂ Cum priuilegio./

R 385. ℂ Incipit annus primus Richardi tertii./☙ De termino Michaelis anno/primo Richardi tertii./
Colla. i–iv.
Colo. ℂ Imprinted at London/in Fletestrete within Temple Barre, at/the signe of the Hand & Starre, by Richard Tottel./ ☙ Cum priuilegio ad impri-/mendum solum./

R 386. Incipit annus primus Richardi tertii./ ℂ De Termino Michaelis Anno/primo Richardi tertii./
Colla. i–iiii.
Colo. ❧ Imprinted at Lon-/don in Fletestrete within Temple/ barre at the signe of the hande and/starre by Richard Tottell./ Cum priuilegio/

R 387. ¶ De termino Michaelis Anno/primo Richardi tertii./
Colla. i–iiii.
Colo. ☞ Imprynted at Lon-/don in fletestrete within temple barre/at the signe of the Hand and starre, by/Rychard Tottel. Anno./1568./

R 388. ¶ De termino Michaelis anno/primo Richardi tertii./
Colla. i–iiii.
Colo. ☞ Imprinted at London/in Fletestrete within Temple barre/at the signe of the Hand and starre,/By Rychard Tottel the/vi. day of December in the/yere of our Lord./1574./

R 389. ¶ De termino Michaelis anno/primo Richardi tertij./
Colla. i–iiii.
Colo. ☞ Imprinted at London/in Fletestrete within Temple Barre,/at the signe of the Hand and Starre, by/Rychard Tottel, the xvi. day/of Marche./1581./

R 390. ¶ De termino Michaelis anno/primo Richardi tertij./
Colla. 1–4.
Colo. ¶ Explicit Annus primus Richardi Tertij.

Year 2

R 391. Anno secundo Richardi. iij./ [No. 7.]
Colla. T.p.+ii–xxii.
Colo. ¶ Imprynted by Richarde Pynson prynter/unto the kyngz noble grace./

R 392. Anno secundo Richardi iii./
Colla. A 8, B 6, C 8.
Colo. ¶ Imprynted by Richarde Pynson prynter unto the Kyngz noble grace.

R 393. ¶ Incipit annus secundus Richardi tertii./
Colla. i–xxii.
Colo. ☞ Imprinted at London/in Fletestrete within Temple Barre, at the/signe of the hande & starre by Richard Tottyll./ ¶ Cum priuilegio./

R 394. ¶ Incipit annus secundus Richardi tertii./
Colla. i–xxii.
Colo. ¶ Imprinted at London/in Fletestrete within Temple Barre, at/the signe of the Hand & Starre, by Richard Tottel./ ☞ Cum priuilegio ad impri-/mendum solum./

R 395. Incipit Annus secundus Richardi tertii./
Colla. i–xxii.
Colo. ☜ Imprinted at Lon-/don in Fletestrete within Temple/barre at the signe of the hande and/starre by Richard Tottell./ Cum priuilegio./

R 396. ¶ De termino Michaelis anno/secudo Richardi tertii./
Colla. i–xxii.
Colo. ☞ Imprynted at Lon-/don in fletestrete within temple barre/at the signe of the Hand and starre, by/Rychard Tottel, Anno./1568./

R 397. De termino Michaelis Anno/secundo Richardi tercii./
Colla. i–xxii.
Colo. ☙ Imprinted at London/in Fletestrete within Temple barre/at the signe of the Hand and starre,/By Rychard Tottel the/xvi. day of December in the/yere of our Lord./1574./

R 398. ¶ De termino Michaelis anno/secundo Richardi tertij./
Colla. i–xxi.
Colo. ☙ Imprinted at London/in Fletestrete within Temple Barre,/at the signe of the Hand and Starre, by/Rychard Tottel, the xvi. day/of Marche./1581./

R 399. ¶ De termino Michaelis, anno/secundo Richardi tercij./
Colla. 1–22.
Colo. ☙ Imprinted at London/in Fleetestrete within Temple Barre,/at the signe of the Hand and Starre/by Richarde Tottyll./ 1587./

HENRY VII

Years 1–8

R 400. Anno primo Henrico. vii.
Colla. A 6, a 6, b 4 (last leaf blank); B 6, c 6 (last leaf blank); C 4, d 6, D 6, E 6, F 4 (last leaf blank); G 6, g 6, h 6, H 6, I 6, k 6, I 6, K–P 6's.
Colo. None.

R 401. Hic sequntur omnes anni re-/gis Henrici septimi, a primo usqz ad annũ octauum/inclusiue nouiter impressi, cũ multis casib' in/predictis annis hucusqz deficientibus./
Colla. T.p. ii–xxi, i–xv, i–xvii, i–xix, i–xliii, i–xvi, i–xvi, i–xiiii,[1].
Colo. ¶ Explicit. Annus octauus Henrici septimi, nouiter/ emendatus atqz impressus per me Robertum/Redman, cõmorantem in parochia sancti/Dunstani, ad signum diui Georgii./ Cum priuilegio./ [McK. 9 c.]

Year 9

R 402. De termĩo Trinitatis an. ix H. vii./
Colla. i–xxvi.
Colo. ¶ Imprinted by Richarde Pynson, pri-/ter to the Kynges moost/noble grace./

Year 12

R 403. ¶ De termino Michaelis. Anno. xii. Hẽrici. vii./
Colla. i–xxviii.
Colo. ¶ Explicit Annus duodecimus Henrici septimi: Im-/ pressum per me Richardum Pynsonum/regium impressorem. Cum pri-/uilegio a rege indulto./

Year 14

R 404. De termino Michaelis. Anno regni regis/Henrici Septimi, decimo quarto.

Colla. i–xxxiiii.

Colo. Si non adhuc, nihilominus spero me olim satisfacturum delicatissimo palto. Scio/per Iouem non omnino displiciturum hunc libellum. Londini in edibus Thome/Bertheleti prope aquagiū sitis in Vico Fletestrete sub intersignio Lucrecie Romane/ excusus. Anno domini. 1529. mensis Decembris die. vii./Cum priuilegio &c.

YEAR 15

R 405. De termino Hillarii. Anno regni regis/Henrici septimi, decimo quinto./

Colla. i–xviii.

Colo. Explicitus est hic annus. xv. Henrici septimi, diligēter castigatus,/et excusus Londini in vico Fletestrete, in edibus Thome Berthe-/leti, prope aquagium sitis, sub intersignio Lucrecie romane./Hunc eme et lege, et disperiam si non placebit./ Cum priuilegio.

YEAR 21

R 406. ¶ De termino Hillarii Anno. xxi. Henrici. vii.

Colla. i–xliii.

Colo. Here endeth the. xxi. yere of Henry the. vii./newely imprynted by me Robert Redman,/dwellynge in sannt Dunstons parische/at the sygne of the George./Cum priuilegio./

YEARS 1–21

R 407. ¶ Anni regis Henri-/ci septimi./ ¶ Quibus accesserunt/Annus Primus et secundus . . . &c./Anno Domini./1555./ ¶ Londini in aedibus Ri-/chardi Totteli./ ¶ Cum priuilegio./ [In McK. 110.]

Colla. [As in R 408.]

Colo. ¶ Imprinted at London/in Fletestrete within Temple Barre at/the signe of the Hand and Starre, by Rychard/Tottyl, the. xii. daye of September, in the/yere of our Lorde. 1555./ ☙ Cum priuilegio ad impri-/mendum solum./

R 408. ¶ Anni Regis Henri-/ci Septimi./Quibus accesserunt . . . 1555./ Londini in aedibus Ri-/chardi Totteli. ¶ Cum priuilegio./ [In McK. 110.]

Colla. T.p., ii–xxxi, i–xix, i–xv, i–xviii, l–xli, ii–xvi, ii–xvi, i–xiii, ii–xxvi, ii–xxx, ii–xxix, ii–xxviii, i–xxxii, i–xvii, i–xvii, i–xiii, i–xli.

Colo. ¶ Imprinted at London/in Fletestrete within Temple Barre at/the signe of the Hande and Starre, by Rychard/ Tottyl, the. xii. daye of September, in the/yere of our Lorde. 1555./ (. ˙ .)/☙ Cum priuilegio ad impri/mendi solum.

R 409. ☙ Anni Regis Hen-/rici septimi./ ¶ Quibus accesserunt/Annus Primus & secundus de noua &/valde bona collatione . . . &c./ An. Do./1555./☙ Londini in aedibus Ri-/chardi Totteli./ ¶ Cum priuilegio ad im-/primendum solum./ [In McK. 110.]

Colla. [As in R 408.]

Colo. ℂ Imprinted at London/in Fletestrete within Temple Barre, at/the signe of the Hande and Starre, by Rycharde/ Tottel, the. xii. daye of September, in the yere/of oure Lorde. 1555./(❧❧)/❧ Cum priuilegio ad impri-/mendum solum./

R 410. ¶ Anni Regis Henri-/ci septimi./ ¶ Quibus Accesserunt . . . &c./ Anno Domini./1555./ ℂLondini in aedibus Ri-/chardi Totteli./ ¶ Cum priuilegio. [In McK. 110.]

Colla. [as in R 408.]

Colo. ❧ Imprinted at Lon-/don in Fletestrete, within Temple/ barre at the signe of the hande and/starre by Richard Tottell./ the. xii. daye of September in the yere/1555./Cum priuilegio./

R 411. ℂ Anni regis Henri-/ci septimi./ ℂ Quibus accesserunt/Annus Primus et secundus de nona et/valde bona collatione . . ./ Anno Domini./1555/ ℂ Londini in aedibus Ri-/chardi Totteli./ ¶ Cum priuilegio./ [In McK. 110.]

Colla. [as in R 408.]

Colo. ❧ Imprinted at Lon-/don in fletestrete within Temple/ Barre at the signe of the hand & starre,/by Richard Tottill, in the/yeare of our lorde/1567./

R 412. ¶ Anni Regis Henrici/Septimi./Quibus accesserunt/Annus Primus, &c. . . . nunquam ante/hac aediti./Anno Domini./ 1555./ ¶ Londini in aedibus Ri-/chardi Totteli./ ¶ Cum priuilegio./ [In McK. 110.]

Colla. [as in R 408.]

Colo. ¶ Imprinted at London in/Fleetestrete within Temple Barre at the signe/of the Hande and Starre, by Richard Tottill./ Anno. 1567./

R 413. ¶ In hoc volu-/mine continentur omnes/Anni Regis Henrici Sep-/timi, ab anno primo, usque ad/Annum vicesimum secundum eius-/dem Regis, . . . ¶ Londini in Aedibus Ri-/chardi Tottelli. 1580./ ¶ Cum priuilegio./

Colla. [as in R 408.]

Colo. ¶ Imprinted at London in/Fleetestrete within Temple Barre at the signe/of the Hande and Starre, by Rychard Tottle./ Anno 1580./

R 414. ¶ In hoc volu-/mine continentur omnes/Anni Regis Henrici Sep-/timi, ab anno primo, usque ad/Annum vicesimum secundum, . . . / ¶ Londini, in Aedibus Richardi/Tottelli. 1585./ ¶ Cum priuilegio./

Colla. [as in R 408.]

Colo. ¶ Imprinted at London in/Fleetestrete within Temple Barre at the signe/of the Hande and Starre, by Richard Tottel./ Anno 1583./

HENRY VIII

YEARS 12–13

R 415. ℂ De Termino Trinitatis Anno. xii. Henrici. viii./

Colla. i–xv, 1 bl.

Colo. ℂ Eplicit Ann'. xii. et. xiii. Henrici Octaui./Impressū p me Robertum Redman./Cum gracia et priuilegio a/Rege indulto./

R 416. De Termino Trinitatis An. xii. Hen. viii./
Colla. i–xvii.
Colo. ℂ Explicit Annus. xii. et. xiii./Henrici Octaui./Imprinted at London in Fletestrete at the/sygne of the George next to sayncte Dunstons/churche by Wyllyam Powell./Anno. M.D. XLVIII./Cum priuilegio ad imprimendum solum./

R 417. De termino trinitatis. Anno. xii. Hen. viii.
Colla. i–xviii.
Colo. ℂ Hic explicit Annus. xii. et. xiii. Henrici octaui./ Imprinted at London in Fletestrete within/Temple barre at the signe of the hande and starre/by Richarde Tottel./Cum priuilegio ad imprimendum solum./

Year 14

R 418. De termino Michaelis anno. xiiii H. viii.
Colla. A–D 8's, E.F. 4's.
Colo. ℂ Impressū p Richardū Pynsoñ.

R 419. Anno. XIIII. Henrici. VIII./ ℂ De Termino Mi-/chaelis./
Colla. A 6, B 4, C 6, D–H 4's.
Colo. Explicit Annus/quartusdecimus Henrici. VIII./Impres. Londini per Robertum/Redmañ commorantem in parochia sancti Dun-/stani ad intersignium sancti Georgii./An. Do. M.CCCCC. XL./

R 420. Anno. xiiii. Henrici. viii./De termino Mi-/chaelis./
Colla. i–xxxvi.
Colo. ℂ Explicit Annus. xiiii. Henrici viii./Imprinted at London in Fletestrete within/Temple barre at the signe of the hande and starre,/by Richard Tottel./Cum priuilegio ad imprimendum solum./

Years 12–14

R 420a. ¶ De termino Trinitatis Anno/regni Regis Henrici octaui XII./
Colla. I–XVI, I–XXXI, 1 bl.
Colo. ¶ Imprinted at London/in Fleetstrete, within Temple Barre/at the signe of the hand and starre, by/ Rycharde Tottel./1556./Cum priuilegio./

R 421. De termino Trinitatis anno/regni regis Henrici octaui. XII./
Colla. i–xvi, i–xxxi, 1 bl.
Colo. ¶ Imprinted at London in Fletestrete/within Temple barre at the signe of the/hande and Starre, by Ry-/charde Tottyll./An. Do. 1560./Cum priuilegio./

R 422. De termino Trinitatis./Anno. xii. Henrici. Viii./
Colla. I–XVI, I–XXXI.

Colo. ℭ Imprinted at London in Fletestrete/within Temple barre at the signe of the/hande and Starre, by Ry-/charde Tottyll./An. Do. 1560./Cum priuilegio.

R 423. ℭ De termino Trinitatis Anno/regni regis Henrici octaui. XII./
Colla. i–xvi, i–xxxi.
Colo. ℭ Imprinted at Lon-/don in fletestrete within Temple/ Barre at the signe of the hand & starre,/by Richard Tottell. 1566./Cum priuilegio ad imprimendum solum./

R 424. ¶ De termino Trinitatis Anno/regni Regis Henrici octaui. XII./
Colla. i–xvi, i–xxxi, 1 bl.
Colo. ¶ Imprinted at London in/Fleetestrete within Temple Barre at the signe/of the Hande and Starre, by Richard Tottill./ Anno. 1567/Cum priuilegio./

R 425. ¶ De termino Trinitatis Anno/regni regis Henrici octaui. XII./
Colla. i–xvi, i–xxxi, 1 bl.
Colo. ❧ Imprynted at Lon-/don in Fletestrete within Temple barre/at the signe of the Hand and starre, by Rychard Tottel. Anno./1569./Cum priuilegio.

R 426. ¶ De termino Trinitatis Anno/regni regis Henrici octaui. XII./
Colla. i–xvi, i–xxxi, 1 bl.
Colo. ❧ Imprinted at London/in Fletestrete within Temple barre/at the signe of the Hand and starre, by/Rycharde Tottel. Anno./1579./Cum priuilegio./

Years 18–19

R 427. ℭ De Termino Michaelis/Anno XVIII regni regis Henrici octaui./
Colla. i–xiiii.
Colo. ℭ Imprynted at London in Fletestrete at the sygne/ of the George nexte to saynt Dunstons/ Churcheby Wyllyam/ Myddylton . ˙ ./ */

R 428. ¶ De termino Michaelis Anno/regni Regis Henrici octaui XIIII (should be XVIII).
Colla. i–xiiii.
Colo. ¶ Imprinted at London/in Fleetstrete, within Temple Barre/at the signe of the hand and starre, by/Rycharde Tottel./ 1556./Cum priuilegio./

R 429. De termino/Michaelis. Anno. xviii/regni regis Henrici octavi./
Colla. i–xiiii.
Colo. ℭ Imprinted at London in fletestrete with-/in Temple barre, at the signe of the hāde and/starre, by Richard Tottill. /☞ */Cum priuilegio./

R 430. ℭ De Termino/Michaelis. Anno. xviii./regni regis Henrici octaui.
Colla. [i]–xiiii.
Colo. ℭ Explicit Annus. xix. Henrici. viii./Imprinted at London in Fletestrete within/Temple barre at the signe of the

hande and starre,/by Richard Tottel./Cum priuilegio ad imprimendum solum./

R 431. De termino Michaelis/Anno. xviii. regni regis Henrici octaui./
Colla. i–xiiii.
Colo. ℭ Imprinted at London in Fletestrete with-/in Temple barre, at the signe of the hand and/starre, by Richard Tottil./(. ˙ .)/Cum priuilegio./

R 432. De termino Michaelis/Anno. xviii. regni regis Henrici octaui./
Colla. i–xiiii.
Colo. ℭ Imprinted at Lon-/don in fletestrete within Temple/Barre at the signe of the hand & starre,/by Richard Tottell. 1566./Cum priuilegio ad imprimendum solum./

R 433. ¶ De termino Michaelis Anno/regni Regis Henrici octaui XVIII./
Colla. i–xiii.
Colo. ¶ Imprinted at London in/Fletestrete within Temple barre/at the signe of the Hand and starre,/By Rychard Tottel. Anno./1567./Cum priuilegio./

R 434. ¶ De termino Michaelis. Anno/regni regis Henrici octaui· XVIII./
Colla. i–xiiii.
Colo. ☙ Imprynted at Lon-/don in Fletestrete within Temple barre/at the signe of the Hand and starre, by/Rychard Tottel. Anno./1569./Cum priuilegio./

R 435. ¶ De termino Michaelis Anno/regni regis Henrici octaui. XVIII.
Colla. i–xiiii.
Colo. ☙ Imprinted at London/in Fletestrete within Temple barre/at the signe of the Hand and starre, by/Rycharde Tottel. Anno./1579./Cum priuilegio./

Year 26

R 436. ℭ De Termino Pasche Anno./XXVI. regni regis Henrici octaui./
Colla. i–xii.
Colo. ℭ Explicit Annus XXVI. Regni/Regis Henrici Octaui noviter impressus./ ℭ Imprynted at London in Fletestrete at the sygne/of the George nexte to saynt Dunstons/Churche by Wyllyam Myddylton . ˙ ./

R 437. ℭ De termino Pasche. Anno. XXVI./regni regis Henrici octaui./
Colla. i–x.
Colo. ☙ Imprinted at Lon-/don in Fletestrete, within Temple/barre at the signe of the hande and/starre by Richard Tottell./the. iiii. daye of February in the yere/of our Lord/1556./Cum priuilegio./

R 438. ¶ De termino Paschae Anno/XXVI. regni Regis Henrici octaui./
Colla. i–x.
Colo. ¶ Imprinted at London/in Fleetstrete, within Temple Barre/at the signe of the hand and starre, by/Rycharde Tottel./1556./Cum priuilegio./

R 439. De termino pasche anno. XXVI./regni regis Henrici octaui./
Colla. i–x.
Colo. Imprinted at London/in Fletestrete within Temple Barre, at/the signe of the hand & starre, by Richard/Tottel, the. iiii. daye of February,/in the yere of oure/Lorde. 1556./(.˙.)/ ☙ cum priuilegio ad impri-/mendum solum./

R 440. De termino Pasche. Anno. XXVI/regni regis Henrici octaui./
Colla. i–x.
Colo. ☙ Imprinted at London/in Fletestrete within Temple Barre, at the/signe of the hande & starre by Richard Tottyll./ the. iiii. daye of February./Anno Domini. 1559./Cum priuilegio./

R 441. ¶ De termino Paschae Anno/XXVI. regni regis Henrici octaui./
Colla. i–x.
Colo. ¶ Imprinted at Lon-/don in fletestrete within Temple/ Barre at the signe of the hand & starre,/by Richard Tottell. 1566./Cum priuilegio ad imprimendum solum./

R 442. De termino Pasche anno/XXVI. Regni Regis Henrici octaui./
Colla. i–x.
Colo. ¶ Imprinted at London in/Fletestrete within Temple barre/at the signe of the Hand and starre,/By Rychard Tottel. Anno./1567./Cum priuilegio./

R 443. ¶ De termino Pasche Anno/XXVI. regni regis Henrici octaui./
Colla. i–x.
Colo. ☙ Imprynted at Lon-/don in Fletestrete within Temple barre/at the signe of the Hand and starre, by/Rychard Tottel. Anno./1569./Cum priuilegio./

R 444. ¶ De termino Paschae Anno/XXVI. regni regis Henrici octaua./
Colla. i–x.
Colo. ☙ Imprinted at London/in Fletestrete within Temple barre/at the signe of the Hand and starre, by/Rycharde Tottel. Anno./1579./Cum priuilegio./

Year 27

R 445. Anno. xxvii. Henrici. viii./ ¶ De termino Pasche Anno. xxvii. regni/regis Henrici. viii./
Colla. i–xxxvi.
Colo. ¶ Explicit annus xxvii. Regni/Regis Henrici octaui nouiter impressus./ ¶ Imprynted at London in Fletestrete at the sygne/of the George nexte to saynt Dunstons/Churche by Wyllyam/Myddylton/.˙./

R 446. ☙ De termino Pasche anno/regni regis Henrici octaui. XXVII./
Colla. i–xxx.
Colo. ☙ Imprinted at London/In Fletestrete within Temple Barre, at the/signe of the hande & starre by Richard Tottyll./ the. viii. daye of February./Anno domini. 1556./ ¶ Cum priuilegio./

R 447. De termino pasche anno. XXVII./regni regis Henrici octaui.
Colla. i–xxx.
Colo. Imprinted at London/in Fletestrete within Temple Barre, at/the signe of the hand & starre, by Richard/Tottel, the. viii. daye of February,/in the yere of oure/Lorde. 1556./ ☙ Cum priuilegio ad impri-/mendum solum./

R 448. ¶ De termino Pasche. anno/regni regis Henrici octaui. XXVII./
Colla. i–xxx.
Colo. ☙ Imprinted at Lon-/don in Fletestrete, within Temple/ barre at the signe of the hande and/starre by Richard Tottell./ the. viii. daye of February in the yere/of our Lord/1556./Cum priuilegio./

R 449. ¶ De termino pasche anno/XXVII. regni regis Henrici octaui./
Colla. i–xxx.
Colo. ¶ Imprinted at Lon-/don in fletestrete within Temple/ Barre at the signe of the hand & starre, by/Richard Tottill, y[e] viii. day of Au-/gust in the yeare of our lorde/M.1566./

R 450. ¶ De termino Pasche anno/XXVII. regni regis Henrici octaui.
Colla. i–xxx.
Colo. ¶ Imprinted at London in/Fletestrete within Temple barre/at the signe of the Hand and starre,/By Rychard Tottel. Anno./1569./Cum priuilegio./

R 451. ¶ De termino Pasche anno/XXVII. regni regis Henrici octaui./
Colla. i–xxx.
Colo. ☙ Imprynted at Lon-/don in Fletestrete within Temple barre/at the signe of the Hand and starre,/by Rychard Tottel. Anno./1569./Cum priuilegio./

R 452. ¶ De termino Paschae anno/XXVII. regni regis Henrici octaui./
Colla. i–xxx.
Colo. ☙ Imprinted at London/in Fletestrete within Temple barre/at the signe of the Hand and starre, by/Rycharde Tottel. Anno./1579./Cum priuilegio./

R 453. ¶ De termino Paschae Anno/XXVII. regni Regis Henrici octaui./
Colla. i–xxx.
Colo. ¶ Imprinted at London/in Fleetstrete, within Temple Barre/at the signe of the hand and starre, by/Rycharde Tottel./ 1583./Cum priuilegio./

YEARS 12–27

R 454. Cy ensuist le Re-/port de tout ceux/cases, queux fueront col-/lect . . . /1591./In Aedibus Ri-/chardi Tottelli./ ¶ Cum priuilegio./ [In border, McK. 196.]
Colla. T.p. 1–16, 1–31, 1–14, 1–10, 1–30.
Colo. ☙ Imprinted at London/in Fleetestrete within Temple Barre,/at the Signe of the Hand and Starre/by Richarde Tottyll./1591./

SECTION 2. ABRIDGMENTS

R 455. No title-page (Statham's Abridgment). [Cut 2.]
Colla. 2, A–Y 8's, Z 6 6's.
Colo. (at end of table) Per me. R. pynson.

R 456. Prima pars huius libri./ [Cut 7.]
Colla. T.p.+i–CClxxxvii.
Colo. None.

R 457. ¶ Sequitur Secunda pars./ [Cut 8.] Table on rev. in same type as body.
Colla. T.p.+i–CClxxiiii.
Colo. None.

R 458. ¶ Sequitur Secunda pars./ [Cut 8a.]
Colla. T.p.+i–cclxxiiii.
Colo. None.

R 459. ❧ : Ultima pars huius libri./❧ The pryse of the whole boke (.xl.s.) whiche boke conteynyth. iii. grete volumes./ [Cut 8.]
Colla. (Title-page only.)
Colo. lacking.

R 460. ¶ Ultima pars huius libri./ ¶ The pryse of the whole boke (.xl.s.) whiche boke conteynyth. iii. great volumes./ [Cut 8 a.]
Colla. T.p. II–CCXXXI.
Colo. ¶ Finis tocius istius opis finit. XXI. die. Diecembr̄/ A dn̄i Millecimo quīgētesimo sextodecimo./

R 461. ¶ Ultima pars huius libri./ ¶ The price of the whole boke. (.xl.s.) whych. boke conteynyth. iii. grete volumes./ [Cut 8.]
Colla. T.p.+ii–ccxxxi.
Colo. ¶ Finis tocius istius opis finit. xxi die Dicembr̄/A° dn̄i Millecimo quīgētesimo sextodecimo/

R 462. Tabula prima partis magni abbreuiamēti librorū legū anglorū.
Colla. a–n 8's, o 6, p 4.
Colo. None.

R 462a. Tabula secunde ptis magni/abbreuiamenti librorū legū anglorū/ [Cut 13.]

R 463. 1565./La graunde/abridgement collect/par le iudge tresreuerend/ monsieur Anthony Fitz-/herbert, etc. . . . In aedibus Richard/ Tottell duodecimo/Nouembris./(1565)/Cum privilegio./ [In McK. 196.]
Colla. T.p.+1–379.
Colo. None.

R 464. 1565./La secounde/part du graund abrid-/gement collect par ler iudge/tresreuerend monsieur An-/thonie Fitzherbert, . . . In Aedibus Richardi/Tottell duodecimo/Nouembris./(1565)/ [In McK. 196.]
Colla. T.p.+1–207.
Colo. In aedibus Richardi Tottell./Cum priuilegio./Anno Salutis. 1565. 12 Nouembris./

R 465. La table cōtey-/nant en sommarie les cho-/ses notables en la graunde/Abridgement, composee par/le Iudge tresreuerend monsieur An-/thony Fytzherbert, . . . ¶ In aedibus Richardi Tottell/decimo Nouembris./(1565)/ [In McK. 110.]
Colla. T.p.+1–210.
Colo. In aedibus Richardi Tottell/Cum priuilegio/Anno saultis 1565. decimo Nouebris/.

R 466. 1577./ ¶ La Graunde/Abridgement,/Collecte par le Iudge/tres-reurend mōsieur Anthony/Fitzherbert,/ . . . In aedibus Richardi Tottelli/uicesimo die Augusti./1577./ [In McK. 196.]
Colla. T.p. 1–342.
Colo. None.

R 467. 1577./ ¶ La Secounde/Part du Graund/Abridgement, Col-/lect par le Iudge tres-/reuerend monsieur Anthonye/Fitzherbert, . . ./ In aedibus Richardi Tottell/uicesimo die Augusti./1577./ [In McK. 196.]
Colla. T.p. 1–265.
Colo. ☞ Imprinted at London/in Fletestrete within Temple barre/at the signe of the Hand and starre,/by Rycharde Tottel the. 20./day of August. Anno/1577./

R 468. Tabula./ ¶ Cy ensuit la Table pur trouer les titles, etc.
Colla. 1–66.
Colo. ☞ Imprinted at London/in Fletestrete within Temple barre/at the signe of the Hand and starre,/by Rycharde Tottel the. 20./day of August. Anno/1577./

R 469. 1573./La Graunde/Abridgement, Collect/& escrie per le Iudge tres-/reuerend Syr Robert Brooke/ . . ./In aedibus Richardi/Tottell Vicesimo/quinto Ianuarii./1573./ [In McK. 196.]
Colla. T.p., II–IV, 1–360.
Colo. None.

R 470. 1573./La Secounde/part du Graund Abrid-/gement Collect & escrie/per le Iudge tresreuerend/Syr Robert Brooke, . . ./ In aedibus Richardi/Tottell Vicesimo/quinto Ianuarii./(1573.)/ [In McK. 196.]
Colla. T.p., 2–338.
Colo. Imprynted at London in/Fletestrete within Temple barre, at the signe/of the hande and starre, by Rychard Tottyl./ the xxv. day of Ianuary. Anno/domini. 1573./

R 471. 1576./La Graunde/Abridgement,/Collect & escrie per/le Iudge tresreverend/Syr Robert Brooke Chiua-/lier, . . . ¶ In aedibus Richardi/Tottell Duodecimo/die Octobris./1576./ [In McK. 196.]
Colla. T.p.+ii–iv+1–351.
Colo. None.

R 472. 1576./La Secounde/part du Graunde/Abridgement,/Collecte & escrie per/le Iudge tresreuerend/Syr Robert Brooke . . ./ ¶ In aedibus Richardi/Tottell Duodecimo/die Octobris./1576./ [In McK. 196.]

Colla. T.p.+2–328.

Colo. Imprinted at Lon-/don in Fletestrete, within Temple/ Barre at the signe of the hande and/starre by Richarde Tottyl the/XII. of October. Anno./domini. 1576./

R 473. La Graunde/Abridgement,/Collect & escrie, per le/Iudge tresreuerend Sir/Robert Brooke Chiualer,/nadgairs chiefe Iu-/ stice del common/Banke./ ¶ In aedibus Richardi/Tottelli, uicesimo nono/die Septembris./1586./ [In McK. 196.]

Colla. T.p.+ii–iv+1–351+[1 bl.]

Colo. None.

R 474. 1586./La Secounde/part du Graunde/Abridgement,/Collecte & escrie per le/Iudge tresreuerend, Sir/Robert Brooke Chiualer,/ nadgairs chiefe Ius-/tice del common/Banke,/ ¶ In aedibus Richardi/Tottelli, uicesimo nono/die Septemb./1586./

Colla. T.p.+2–328.

Colo. None.

R 475. 1586. La Graunde/Abridgement,/Collect & escrie, per le/Iudge tresreuerend Sir/Robert Brooke, etc. . . . ¶ In aedibus Richardi/Tottelli, uicesimo nono/die Septemb. 1586./ [In McK. 196.]

Colla. T.p.+ii–iv+1–351.

Colo. None.

R 476. 1586./La secounde/part du Graunde/Abridgement,/Collect & escrie per le/Iudge tresreuerend, Sir/Robert Brooke, . . ./ ¶ In aedibus Richardi/Tottelli, vicesimo nono/die Septemb./ 1586./ [In McK. 196.]

Colla. T.p.+2–328.

Colo. ¶ Imprinted at London in/Fleetestrete within Temple Barre at the signe/of the Hande and starre, by Richard Tottyl./ Anno Dom. 1586./

R 477. L'abridgement/des cases con-/cernants les Titles plus ma-/ teriall pur les Estudients, . . ./ Londini,/In aedibus Thomae Wight &/Bonhami Norton./Anno Domini/1599./Cum gratia & priuilegio/etc. . . .

Colla. A–C 8's, D 2, 1–370, 1–35.

Section 3. Reports

R 478. Les/ans du roy/Richard le second/collect' ensembl'/hors de les Abridgments de Sta-/tham, Fitzherbert et Brooke per/Richard Bellewe/ . . . /At London,/Imprinted by/Robert Robinson dwelling/in Fewter lane neere/Holborne./

Colla. T.p.+[4]+[1]–320+[4].

Colo. ☙ Imprinted at London/by R. Robinson, T. Dunne, Th./Hanylande, Ia. Bowring,/and Th. Moris./The 17. of Ianuary./1585./

R 479. ¶ Ascun/Nouell cases de/les ans et temps le Roy,/H.8.Ed. 6. et la Roygne Mary/ . . . Anno. Do. 1578./ ¶ In aedibus Richardi Tottelli./☞ Cum Priuilegio./ [In border 46.]

Colla. T.p.+1–116+[2].
Colo. Imprinted at London/in Fleetstreete within Temple/Barre at the signe of the Hand/and Starre by Ry-/chard Tottyl./the xv. of October./1578./

R 480. ¶ Ascuns/Nouell cases de les/ans & temps le Roy, H.8./Ed. 6 & la Roygne Mary. . . . / ¶ In aedibus Richardi/Tottelli./¶ Cum priuilegio./
Colla. T.p.+1–116+[3].
Colo. ¶ Imprinted at London/in Fleetestrete within Temple/Barre at the signe of the Hande and/Starre by Richard/Tottill./Anno Domini. 1587./

R 480a. Ascuns/novel cases de/les ans & temps le Roy,/H.8 . . . . / Londini/In aedibus Ianae Yetsweirt./An. Dom. 1597./Cum priuilegio./
Colla. T.p.+1–116+[3].
Colo. London/In aedibus Ianae Yetsweirt/Cum Priuilegio./

R 481. ¶ Cy ensount/ascuns nouel cases,/Collectes per le iades/tresreuerend Iudge, Moun-/sieur Iasques Dyer, . . . /Londini, in Aedibus Ri-/chardi Tottelli, Ianuarii/primo. 1585. ¶ Cum priuilegio./ [In McK. 196.]
Colla. T.p.+ii–iiii+1–377+[1].
Colo. ❧ Imprinted at London in Fleetestrete/at the Signe of the Hande and Starre, by/Richarde Tottyll. An. Do. 1585./¶ Cum priuilegio.

R 482. ¶ Cy ensount/ascuns nouel cases,/Collectes per le iades/tresreurend Iudge, Moun-/sieur Iasques Dyer, . . . Londini, in aedibus Ri-/chardi Tottelli, Ianua-/rii primo. 1592./ ¶ Cum priuilegio./ [In McK. 196.]
Colla. T.p.+ii–iv+1–377.
Colo. ❧ Imprinted at London/in Fleetestrete within Temple, Barre,/at the Signe of the Hand and Starre/by Richarde Tottyll./1591/

R 483. ¶ La Table al lieur des/Reports del tresreuerend/Iudge Sir Iames Dyer . . . /Anno Domini 1588/ . . . /In Aedibus Richardi/Tottelli./
Colla. T.p.+[7]+[1]–167.
Colo. None?

R 483a. Le/Table al/lieur des Re-/portes del tresreue-/rend Iudge Sir Ia. Dyer/ . . . /Londini/In aedibus Thomae Wight./Anno Domini. 1600./Cum Priuilegio./
Colla. T.p.+[7]+1–167.
Colo. None.

R 484. 1571. Les Comen-/taries, ou les Reportes de/Edmunde Plowden un appren-/tice de le comen Ley, de dyuers/cases esteantes matters en ley, &/de les Argumentes sur yceux, en/les temps des Raygnes le Roye/Edwarde le size, le Roigne/Mary, le Roy & Roigne/Phillipp & Mary, &/le Roigne Eli-/zabeth./In

Ædibus Richardi/Tottelli./Octobris. 24./Cum priuilegio./ [In McK. 147a, without motto on sill.]
Colla. [6]+1–401+[1 bl.]
Colo. ☞ Imprinted at London/in Fleetstrete within Temple Barre at/the signe of the Hand and Starre, by Rychard/Tottyl in the yeare of our Lorde. 1571./the. 24. of October,/Cum priuilegio./

R 485. 1578./Les Commentaries,/ou Reportes de Edmunde/Plowden, . . ./ In aedibus Richardi/Tottelli./Octobris 20./Cum priuilegio./ [In McK. 196.]
Colla. T.p.+ii–vi,+A–C 4's+1–401.
Colo. ☞ Imprinted at London/in Fleetstrete within Temple Barre at/the signe of the Hande and Starre, by Richard/Tottell in the yere of our Lorde. 1578./the 20. of October./Cum priuilegio.

R 486. ¶ Un report fait per un uncerteine/authour del part de un argument del Edmond Plowden, etc.
Colla. 1–15.
Colo. ¶ In aedibus Richardi Tottelli./1579.

R 486a. ¶ Un Report fait per un uncertein/authour del part de un argument del Edmoūd Plowden . . . /
Colla. 1–15.
Colo. ¶ In Aedibus Richardi Tottelli./1584./Cum Priuilegio./

R 487. Cy ensu-/ont certeyne ca-/ses reportes, per/Edmunde Plowden' . . . Anno. 1584.
Colla. T.p.+403–565+4.
Colo. In aedibus Richardi Tottelli,/15. die Februarii./1584./

R 488. ¶ The table for the seconde parte of the Commentaries,/deuised by William Fleetewoode Re-/corder of London./
Colla. A 6, last leaf blank.
Colo. None.

R 489. 1571./Les Comen-/taries, ou les Reportes de/Edmunde Plowden, . . ./ In aedibus Richardi/Tottelli./Octobris. 22./Cum priuilegio./ . . .
Colla. A 6+B–C 4's+D 6+1–401.
Colo. ☞ Imprinted at London/in Fleetestrete within Temple barre,/at the signe of the hand and starre/by Richarde Tottyll./ 1588./

R 489a. 1594/La/second part de les/Reports, . . . /Londini/In aedibus Caroli Yetsweirti/Armigeri./Cum priuilegio Regiae/Maiestatis.
Colla. T.p.+403–565+[Table to First Part, TTii–[iv], VVI].
Colo. In aedibus Caroli Yetsweirti, Armigeri./1594./Cum priuilegio Regiae Maiestatis./

489b. Un Report fait per un uncerteine authour/ . . . .
Colla. 1–15.
Colo. In Aedibus Caroli Yetsweirti./1594./Cum Priuilegio Regiae Maiestatis./

489c. ¶ The Table for the Second part of the Commentaries./
Colla. A4.
Colo. None.

R 490. Les/Commentaries,/Ou Reportes de Edmund/Plowden, . . ./ Londini,/In aedibus Thomae Wight, &/Bonhami Norton./1599./ Cum Priuilegio./ [In McK. 168 b.]
Colla. A–C 4's + D 6's+1–401.
Colo. None.

R 491. Abridgement/des touts les cases/reportez alarge per Monsieur/ Plowden. . . . /Composee & digest p T.A./Londini,/In aedibus Ianae Yetsweirt/Cum Priuilegio./
Colla. T.p.+[3]+1–91+[1].
Colo. None.

CHAPTER III

Treatises

SECTION 1. TRACTS IN RASTELL'S COLLECTION

a. Collected Editions

T 1. Natura breuium./The olde tenures./Lyttylton tenures./The new talys./The articles uppon the new talys./Diuersyte of courtes./Iustyce of peace./The chartuary./Court baron./Court of hundrede./Returna breuium./The ordynaunce for takynge of fees in the escheker./And fyrste a table to all these. xii. bokes./Cum priuilegio./

Colla. T.p.+[11]+[1]–423.(text in double column).

Colo. Prentyd/by W. Rastell/in Fletestreete in/saynt Brydys chyrche/yarde, the yere of/oure lorde/1534/.

T 2. Natura breuium./ [Separate title for each tract.]

Colla. T.p.+1–635+[1] (text in single column).

Colo. Prentyd/by W. Rastell/in Fletestreete in/saynt Brydys chyrche/yarde, the yere of/oure lorde/1534/

[Printed from the same type as the preceding, rearranged in single column, and the Table distributed to the several tracts.]

b. Littleton's Tenures : in French

T 3. No title-page.

Colla. A–H 8, I 6.

Colo. ¶ Expliciūt Tenores nouelli Impssi p nos Johez lettou & Willz/de machlinia ī Cītate Londoniaꝝ iuxta eccāz omi s'coꝝ/.

T 4. No title-page.

Colla. A–G 8, H, I 6.

Colo. ¶ Expliciunt Tenores nouelli Impressi/per me Wilhelmū de machlinia in opulen/tissima Civitate Londoniaꝝ iuxta pontē/qui vulgariter dicitur Fletebrigge./

T 5. No title-page (On the first [blank] page Tailleur's mark No. 2. is on the obverse; in the British Museum copy Pynson's device, McK. 3a, is on the reverse).

Colo. Expliciunt Tenores nouelli. Impressi per me/Wilhelmū le tailleur in opulentissima civitate/rothomagensi iuxta prioratum sancti laudi ad/instantiam Richardi pynson./

T 6. No title. [Cut 7.]

Colla. A–B 8, C–D 6, E–F 8, G–I 6.

Colo. None. [McK. 9 a on last leaf.]

T 7. ¶ No. title page. [Cut 7.]

Colla. T.p.+i–lvii.

Colo. ¶ Tenorum Lyttylton Lector iam cernito Finem./ [On reverse, McK. 9 b.]

T 8. ¶ Leteltun tenuris new correcte. [Cut 7 below; cut 8 on reverse.
Colla. A 8, B–H 6, I 8.
Colo. ¶ Impressum per me Richardū Pynson./Anno dñi. M.CCCCC.xvi./ [McK. 9 c.]

T 9. ¶ Lytylton tenures/newly and moost/truly correctyd/& amendyd./ [Over No. 11.]
Colla. A–Y 8's.
Colo. Londini in edibus Ri-/chardi Pynsoni regii impres-/soris. Anno a Christi natu./1525. quarto idus/Octobris./

T 10. ¶ Lytylton tenures/newly and most/truly corrected/& amended./ [Over 11.]
Colla. A–U 8's, X 6.
Colo. ¶ Expliciunt tenores Litil-/tone cum alterationibus eorun-/dem et additionibus nouis/necnon cum aliis non/min' utilioribus,/Lōdini in edi/bus Ri-/chardi Pynsonis. Anno./dñi. M.CCCCC./xxviii. die vero/xviii. Iunii./ ¶ Cum priuilegio./ [McK. 3 on reverse.]

T 11. ❧ Les tenures/de Lyttelton novelment impri-/mes. . . ./❦/ [Cut 44.]
Colla. T.p.+1–50+[1]:Folio.
Colo. ¶ Imprynted at London/by me Robert/Redman./ ¶ Cum gratia et priuilegio/Regali./

T 12. ¶ Lytylton tenures/newly and most/truly correctyd/& amendyd./ [Over No. 12.]
Colla. T.p.+A–X 8's.
Colo. ¶ Expliciūt Tenores Litiltoni cum al-/terationibus eorundem et additi-/nib' nouis necnon cū aliis non/min' utiliorib', Londini in/edibus Roberti Red/man anno salut' nostre M./ ccccc.xxviii, die vero vi. aprilis./ ¶ Cum gratia & priuilegio./

T 13. [Littleton Tenures] lacking.
Colla. A–U 8's, X 6.
Colo. None.

T 14. Lyttyltō te-/nures new-/ly imprin-/ted./
Colla. A–R 8's.
Colo. ¶ Londini in edibus Thome Berthe-/leti Reg. impressoris, in Fletestrete/prope aquagium sitis, sub signo/Lucrecie Romane. Anno/domini. M.D.xxx./

T 15. ❧ Lit/telton te-/nures neu-/ly imprin/ted./In the yere of our Lord/God. M.CCCCC./XXXIX./
Colla. T.p.+2–155+[2].
Colo. ¶ Imprynted at Lon-/don by me Robert/Redman./ ☞ Cum gracia et priui-/legio Regali./ [Over McK. 3.].

T 16. ❧ Lyttyl-/ton/Tenures/&c. M.D.XL.I.
Colla.
Colo.

T 17. Lytyl-/ton/Tenures/neulye im-/prynted./An. M.D.XLV./ [In border 31.]

Colla. T.p.+2–151+[1].

Colo. ℂ Prynted at London by Henry Smyth/dwellynge wythout Temple barre/at the signe of the Trinitie./Cum priuilegio ad imprimen-/dum solum./

T 18. ❧ Lytyl-/ton Tenures/newly revised,/etc. . . . / ℂ Cum priuilegio/ad imprimendum solum per sep-/tennium./

Colla. T.p.+16 (table and one bl.)+1–251+[1].

Colo. ❧ Imprinted at London in Fletestrete/at the sygne of the George by Wyllyam/Myddylton. In the yere of our Lorde/M. CCCCC. XLV. The/xxvi. day of Marche./ ℂ Cum priuilegio ad/imprimendum/solum./

T 19. ❧ Lytyl-/ton tenures/newly revised,/and truly corrected, etc. . . . / ℂ Cum priuilegio./ad imprimendum/solum per sep-/tennium./

Colla. T.p.+[16]+i–cli+[1].

Colo. ℂ Imprinted at/London in Fletestrete at the sygne of/the George by Wyllyam Powel./In the yere of our Lorde/1553./ Cum priuilegio/ad imprimendum/solum./

T 20. ❧ Lyttyl-/ton tenures newly revised,/and truly corrected etc./ ℂ Imprinted at London in Fletestrete within/Temple barre, at the signe of the hand/and starre by Richard Tottel./☞ */Anno domini./1554./Cum priuilegio, &c.

Colla. T.p.+14+1 bl.+[1]–148.

Colo. Imprinted at London/in Fletestrete within Tem-/ple barre, at the signe of the hande/and starre by Richard Tottel./ ☞ */Anno domini./1554./ ¶ Cum priuilegio, &c.

T 21. ¶ Litletons/Tenures./Apud Richardum Tottele/Cum priuilegio./ 1557./

Colla. T.p.+1–173+[1].

Colo. ℂ Imprin-/ted at London in Fletestret/within Temple barre, at the/sygne of the hand and/Starre, by Rychard/Tottil, y^e^. xxviii./daie of Octo-/ber./Anno domini. 1557./Cum privilegio ad impri-/mendum solum./

T 22. ¶ Litletons/Tenures./Apud Richardum Tottel./Cum priuilegio./ 1557./

Colla. T.p.+1–173+[1].

Colo. ℂ Imprin-/ted at London in Fletestrete/within Temple barre, at the sygne of the hand and/starre, by Richard/Tottil, ye xxviii./daie of Octo-/ber./Anno domini. 1557./Cum priuilegio ad impri-/mendum solum./

T 23. ¶ Litletons/Tenures./Conferred with divers true wrytten/copies, and purged of sondry cases/hauing in some places more then ye au-/tour wrote, and less in other some./Apud Richardum Tottel./ Cum priuilegio./1557./

Colla. T.p.+1-173+[1].

Colo. ❧ Imprin-/ted at Lōdō in Flete-/strete within Temple/ barre, at the sygne of/the hand & starre,/by Richard Tot-/till, the. xxviii./daie of Oc-/tober./Anno domini. 1557./Cum priuilegio ad impri-/mendum solum./

T 24. ¶ Les/Tenures du Mon-/sieur Littleton, ovesque cer-/tein cases, etc./Cum priuilegio./1567./
Colla. T.p.+[1]–170+[1].
Colo. ¶ Imprin-/ted at London in Fletestret/within Temple barre, at the/sygne of the hand and/starre, by Rychard/Tottil, y^e^. xvii./of Maye./Anno domini. 1567/ ¶ Cum priuilegio.

T 25. ¶ Les/Tenures du Mon-/sieur Littletō,/1569./
Colla. T.p.+1–170+[1].
Colo. ¶ Imprin-/ted at London in Fletestret/within Temple barre, at the/sygne of the hand &/Starre, by Rycharde/Tottill. 1569./Cum priuilegio./

T 26. ¶ Les/Tenures du Mon-/sieur Littleton, ovesque/certein cases etc./ ¶ Cum priuilegio./1572./
Colla. T.p.+1–170+[1].
Colo. ¶ Imprinted at Lon-/don in Fletestrete with-/in Temple barre, at the signe/of the hand and starre/by Rychard Tottill./ 1572./Cum priuilegio./

T 27. ¶ Les/Tenures du mon-/sier Littleton oves-/q̄ certein cases, . . . /¶ Cum priuilegio./1572./
Colla. T.p.+1–170+[1].
Colo. Imprinted at Lon-/don in Fletestre with-/in Temple barre, at the signe/of the hand and starre/by Richard Tottyl./ 1574./Cum priuilegio./

T 28. ¶ Les/Tenures du mon-/sier Littleton, . . . / ¶ Cum priuilegio./ 1577./
Colla. T.p.+1–170+[1].
Colo. Imprinted at Lon/don in Fletestrete with-/in Temple barre, at the signe/of the hande and starre/by Rychard Tyttyl./ 1577./Cum priuilegio./

T 29. ¶ Les/Tenures du mon-/sieur Littleton. . . . &c./ ¶ Cum priuilegio./1579./
Colla. T.p.+1–170+[1].
Colo. ¶ Imprinted at Lon-/don in Fletestrete with-/in Temple barre, at the sygne/of the hande and starre/by Rychard Tottyl,/ 1579./Cum Priuilegio./

T 30. ¶ Les/Tenures du mon-/sieur Littleton, . . / ¶ Cum priuilegio/ 1581./
Colla. T.p.+1–170+[1].
Colo. Imprinted at Lon-/don in Fletestrete within/Temple barre, at the signe of the/Hande and Starre by Ry-/chard Tottel./ 1581./ ¶ Cum priuilegio./

T 31. ¶ Les/Tenures du mon-/sieur Littleton, . . . / ¶ Cum priuilegio./1583./
Colla. T.p.+1–171+[1].

Colo. Imprinted at Lon-/don in Fleestrete within/Temple Barre, at the signe of/the Hand and Starre, by/Rychard Tottill./ 1583./Cum priuilegio./

T 32. ¶ Les/Tenures de Mon-/sieur Littleton, &c./ ¶ Cum priuilegio./ 1585./
Colla. T.p.+1–171+[1].
Colo. Imprinted at Lon-/don in Fletestrete with-/in Temple Barre, at the signe/of the Hand and Starre,/by Rychard Tottill./ 1585/Cum priuilegio./

T 33. ¶ Les/Tenures du mon-/sieur Littleton, &c./Cum Priuilegio./ 1588./
Colla. T.p.+1–171+[1].
Colo. ¶ Imprinted at Lon-/don, in Fleetestrete within/Temple Barre, at the Signe of/the Hand and Starre/by Richarde/Tottell./ ¶ Cum priuilegio./

T 34. Les/Tenures de Monsieur/Littleton/ . . . /1591./
Colla. T.p.+1–171+P–R 12's.
Last 32 Leaves are Index Littleton.
Colo. None.

T 35. ¶ Les/Tenures de Mon-/sieur Littleton, . . ./Cum Priuilegio./ 1591./
Colla. T.p.+1–171+[1].
Colo. ¶ Imprinted at Lon-/don, in Fleetestrete within/Temple Barre, at the Signe of/the Hand and Starre/by Richarde/Tottell./ ¶ Cum priuilegio./

T 36. Les/Tenures de Monsieur/Littleton, &c./Londini/In aedibus Caroli Yetswerti/Armigeri. 1594./Cum priuilegio./
Colla. T.p.+1–170, P 4–12, Q 12, R 6.
Colo. None.

T 37. Les/Tenures de Monsieur/Littleton, &c. . . . /Londini/In aedibus Ianae Yetsweirt/relictae Caroli Yetsweirt/Ar̄ nuper defuncti./ Cum priuilegio./
Colla. T.p.+1–170+P 4–12, Q 12.
Colo. None.

T 38. Les/Tenures de/Monsieur Little-/ton, etc./Londini/In aedibus Thomae Wight,/& Bonhami Norton./Cum Priuilegio./1599./
Colla. T.p.+1–170+P 4, Q 12.
Colo. None.

c. Littleton's Tenures in English

T 39. ¶ : Lyttelton/tenures in/Englysshe./ [Over No. 11.]
Colla. T.p.+1–CC+[1]+[1 bl.].
Colo. ¶ Imprynted at London/in Fletestrete, by me Roberte/ Redman, dwellynge at the/sygne of the George,/nexte to Saynt/ Dunstones/Churche./ [McK. 3 on reverse of last leaf.]

T 40. [Littleton in English: Wyer, n.d. Herbert.]

T 41. [Littleton in English: Berthelet, 1538.]

T 42. ☙ Lyttelton/tenures in/Englysshe/[over No. 8]
Colla. T.p.+1–clxii+[1].
Colo. ¶: Imprynted/at London in Fletestrete/at the sygne of the George/next to saynt Dūstones church/by Wyllyam Myddylton./In the year of our Lorde./1544. The fourth/day of May.

T 43. Lyt-/tilton/tenures/truely tran-/slated in/to englyshe./❦/An. M.D. XL. V./ [In border 30.]
Colla. T.p.+1–162+[1].
Colo. None.

T 44. Lyt-/tilton/tenures/truely tran-/slated in/to/englyshe./❦/An. M.D.XLVIII./ [In McK. 106.]
Colla. T.p.+ii–clxxx+[2].
Colo. ¶ Imprynted/at Lōdon in Fletestrete/at the Sygne of the George/next to saynte Dunstones/churche by Wylly-/am Powell./In the yere of our Lorde God./M.D.xlviii. the syxte/daye of Iulye./ [Over No. 22.]

T 45. Lyt-/tilton/tenures/truely trans-/lated in-/to/Englyshe./❦/ Anno. Do. M.D.L.I./[In McK. 106.]
Colla. [i]–c.lxxx+2.
Colo. ¶ Imprinted/at Lōdon in Fletestrete/at the Sygne of the George/next to saynt Dunstones/Churche by Wylly-/am Powell./ In the yere of our Lorde God/M. D. L. I. the syxte/daye of Septēber./ [Over No. 22.]

T 46. ☙ Lyttelton/tenures in En/glysshe./ [Cut 32.]
Colla. T.p.+1–CC+[1]. Numbering irregular.
Colo. ¶ Prynted at london in/paules churche yearde at/the sygne of the may-/dens heed, by Tho-/mas Petyt./

T 47. Lyt-/tilton te-/nures/truelye translated into/Englishe./Anno domini./M.D.L.V.I./ [In made-up border.]
Colla. T.p.+ii–clxxx+[2].
Colo. ¶ Imprinted at Londō/in Fletestrete nere to. S./Dunstones church, by/Thomas Marshe./Anno/M.D.L.VI./

T 48. Lyt-/tilton te-/nures./truly translated into/Englishe./Anno domini./M.D.L.VI./ [In made-up border.]
Colla. T.p.+ii–clxxx+[1].
Colo. None.

T 49. ❧ Little-/ton tenures/in Englishe./❦/❧ Cum priuilegio ad im-/primendum solum./
Colla. T.p.+2–145+[1].
Colo. ¶ Imprinted at London/in Fletestrete within Temple barre,/at the signe of the hande and/Starre, by Richard Tot-/tle, the. xvi. daye of April/the yere of our lord./M.D.LVI./❦/❧ Cum priuilegio ad im-/primendum solum./

T 50. Little-/ton tenures/in Englishe./ ¶ Cum priuilegio ad im-/primendum solum./

Colla. T.p.+2–145+[1].

Colo. ℂ Imprinted at London/in Fletestrete within Temple barre/at the sygne of the hande and/starre, by Richard Tot-/tell the. xvi. daye of/April. Anno./do. 1556./ ℂ Cum priuilegio./

T 51. Little-/ton tenures/in englishe./ ¶ Cum privilegio.

Colla. T.p.+2–142+[2].

Collo. ¶ Imprinted at London/in Fletestrete within Temple/Barre, at the signe of the/hand and starre, by/Rychard Tottill,/1568./ ℂ Cum priuilegio.

T 52. Little/ton tenures/in Englishe./ ℂ Cum priuilegio ad im-/primendum solum./

Colla. T.p.+2–142.

Colo. lacking.

T 53. ¶ Little-/ton tenures/in Englishe./ ¶ Cum priuilegio./

Colla. T.p.+2–142+[2].

Colo. Imprinted at London/in Fletestrete within Temple/Barre at the signe of the hand/and Starre by Ry-/chard Tottyl./1574./Cum priuilegio./

T 54. ¶ Little-/ton tenures/in Englishe./ ¶ Cum priuilegio./

Colla. T.p.+2–142+[2].

Colo. Imprinted at London/in Fleetstreete within Temple/Barre at the signe of the Hand/and Starre by Ry-/chard Tottyl./1576./ ¶ Cum priuilegio./

T 55. ¶ Little-/tons Tenures/in Englishe./ ¶Cum priuilegio./

Colla. T.p.+2–142+[2].

Colo. Imprinted at London/in Fletestrete within Tem-/ple Barre at the signe of the hand/and Starre by Ry-/chard Tottel./1581./Cum priuilegio./

T 56. ¶ Little/tons tenures/in English./Cum priuilegio./

Colla. T.p.+2–142+[2].

Colo. Imprinted at Lon-/don in Fleestrete within/Temple Barre, at the signe of/the Hand and Starre, by/Rychard Tottill./1583./Cum priuilegio./

T 57. ¶ Little/tons tenures/in English./Cum priuilegio./

Colla. T.p.+2–142+[2].

Colo. ❧ Imprinted at London/in Fletestrete within Temple/Barre, at the signe of the Hand/and Starre by Rycharde/Tottill./1586./Cum priuilegio./

T 58. ¶ Little-/tons tenures/in English./Imprinted at London within Tem-/ple Barre, at the Signe of the Hand/and Starre, by Richard/Tottell./1592./ ¶Cum Priuilegio./

Colla. T.p.+2–142+[2].

Colo. ¶ Imprinted at London/in Fleetestrete within Temple/Barre, at the signe of the Hand/and Starre by Richard/Tottill./1593./ ¶ Cum Priuilegio./

T 59. Little-/tons tenures/in English./Lately perused and/amended./Imprinted at London by Charles/Yetsweirt Esq. and are to be sold/at his house within Temple Bar/neere to the middle/Temple./ 1594./Cum priuilegio Regiae Maiestatis./

Colla. T.p.+2–142+[2].

Colo. ¶ Imprinted at London by Charles/Yetsweirt Esq. at his house within Temple/Barre, neere to the middle/Temple./ 1594./Cum priuilegio Regiae/Maiestatis./

T 60. Little-/tons tenures/in English./Lately perused and/amended./ ¶ Imprinted at London by/Iane Yetsweirt./1597./Cum priuilegio Regiae/Maiestatis./

Colla. T.p.+2–142+[2].

Colo. None.

T 61. Little-/tons te-/nures in English./ . . . / ¶Imprinted at London by/Thomas Wight./1600./Cum priuilegio Regaie/Maiestatis./

Colla. T.p.+2–142+[2].

Colo. None.

d. West's Index to Littleton's Tenures

T 62. ¶ Index Littleton.

Colla. 24 leaves.

Colo. . . . ex interiori Templo,/duodecimo calendas Iulii anno resti-/tutae salutis 1581./

T 63. Littleton.

Colla. A–C 8.

Colo. . . . Ex in-/teriori Templo duodecimo ca-/lendas Iulij anno re-/stitutae salutis./1581./

T 64. Index Littleton.

Colla. A–C 8.

Colo. . . . Ex Interiori Templo, duo-/decimo Calendas Martij, Anno/restitutae salutis/1585/.

T 65. Index.

Colla. A–C 8.

Colo. . . . Ex interiori Templo 12 ca-/lendas Martij anñ restitute salutis./1585/.

T 66. Index Littleton.

Colla. A–C 8.

Colo. . . . Ex interiori Templo./12. Calendas Martij Anñ restitute salutis./1581./

T 67. Index Littleton.

Colla. A–C 8.

Colo. . . . Ex interiori/Templo 12. Calendas Martij. Anñ/ restitute salutis. 1581./

e. The Old Tenures

T 68. No title-page. No. 4 on reverse.

Colla. A 8 Folio.

Colo. ¶ Impressum per Richardum Pynson.

T 69. No title-page.

Colla. A 8 folio. 5-line initial.

Colo. This Booke with the Natura Breuium/was Emprynttyd by me Rychard Pynson/at the instaunce of my maistres of the cō/pany of stronde Inne with oute tempyll/Barre. off Londoñ/.

T 70. No title-page.
Colla. A 6. 8-line initial at beginning. Folio.
Colo. ¶ Finis.

T 71. The Tenuris.
Colla. A 6, B 4: double column, in French and English. Folio.
Colo. None. [McK. 37 on reverse.]

T 72. ¶ Olde teners new-/ly corrected. [Over No. 11.]
Colla. A, B 8's.
Colo. Londini in edibus Ri-/chardi Pynsoni regii impres-/soris. Anno a Christi natu./1525. quarto idus Oc-/tobris. Cum pri-/uilegio a rege/indulto. [Over McK. 3.]

T 73. ¶ Olde teners newly/corrected./ [Over No. 12.]
Colla. A–B 8's.
Colo. ¶ Finis vetusta tenurarum cum/additionibus nouis necnon cū/aliis non min' utili-/orib', Lōdini/in edib'/Roberti Redmā/Anno salut' nostre M./ccccc.xxviii. die vero xx. Ianuarii./ ¶ Cum gratia & priuilegio./ [Over No. 43.]

T 74. ¶ The olde./Tenures./ [Over No. 12.]
Colla. A–B 8's.
Colo. ¶ Imprynted by me Robert Redman,/dwellynge in the Fletestrete in/saynt Dunstones parysshe,/at the sygne of the/George./In the yere of our lorde god. M./CCCCC.xxxii./ [McK. 3 on reverse.]

T 75. ¶ The olde tenures.
Colla. A 8, B 4.
Colo. Hunc libellum excudebat/Thomas Ber/theletus re-/gius impressor. Anno do-/mine millesimo quingen-/tesimo tricesimo./

T 76. Olde/tenures./Londini in aedi-/bus Thomae Bert./regii impres-/soris./Anno. M.D.xxxviii./ [In border 30.]
Colla. A, B 8's.
Colo. None.

T 77. The olde./Tenures./ [Over No. 25.]
Colla. A–B 8's.
Colo. ¶ Imprinted at London in/Fletestrete: by Wyllyam Myd-/dylton, dwellynge at the/sygne of the George,/next to sainct Dū-/stones Chur-/che./

T 78. The Olde tenures.
Colla. A 8, B 4.
Colo. None.

f. Natura Brevium in French

T 79. Title-page lacking.
Colla. A–C 8's, D, E 6's, F 8, G, H 6's, I 4. Folio.
Colo. ¶ Here endith the boke of Natura/breuium. Emprynted by Richard/Pynson. [On reverse, McK. 3.]

T 80. No title-page.
Colla. A, B 8's, C–I 6's, 38 lines on page. Folio.
Colo. ¶ Here endeth the boke of Natura/breuium. Emprynted by Richard/Pynson. [On reverse, McK 9 a.]

T 81. Natura Breviū.
Colla. A–H 6's, I 4. 40 lines on page. Folio.
Colo. ¶ Here endeth the boke of Natura/breuium. Emprinted by Richarde/Pynson./ [McK. 9 b.]

T 82. ¶ Natura breuiū newly corrected, with diuers addiciōs of/ statutis: boke casis: plees in abatementz of the sayd writtes/ and theyr declaracions: and barris to the same: added and/put in theyr places moste conuenient./ [Over No. 7, No. 8 on reverse.]
Colla. [i]–lxxii+[2]. Folio.
Colo. ¶ Libri de Natura breuium finis. Impressus p Richardum Pynson/regium Impressorem cum priuilegio a reges indulto: in quo multa erra-/ta fuerunt: sed nūc (non parua solicitudine) emendata, castigataqz a viro/in legum multum solerti studio: qui multa insuper utilissima addidit, is/nil aliud nimirum cupiens: q̄z qz pre ceteris rebus uiros studiorū legum/Anglorꝫ luculentissimos esse. Hunc librum iam lector quisquis is eme,/lege, et gaudebis./ [McK. 44 on reverse.]

T 83. ¶ Natura breuiū new-/ly and moost trewly/corrected . . . [On reverse, No. 11.]
Colla. T.p.+i–ccxiii+[14].
Colo. Londini in edibus Ri-/chardi Pynsoni regii impres-/soris. Anno a Christi natu./M.D.xxv. Cum priui/legio a rege in/dulto. [Over McK. 3.]

T 84. ¶ Natura breuiū/newly and moost trewly/corrected. . . . &c./ [In made-up border; No. 11 on reverse.]
Colla. T.p.+i–CC.xx.+[4].
Colo. Londini in edibus/Richardi Pynsoni re-/gii impressoris./ Anno a/Christi natu./M.D.xxviii. Cum/priuilegio a rege indulto./ [McK. 3 on reverse.]

T 85. [Redman, 1525. Ames.]

T 86. [Redman, 1528, Dec. 16. Ames.]

T 87. ¶ Natura breuium/newly and moost trewly corre/cted, . . . Imprē/tyd the yere of our lorde. 1529/ ¶ Cum gratia & p̄uilegio/ a Rege Indulto./ [In made-up border; on reverse No. 12.]
Colla. T.p.+1–ccxix+[8].
Colo. ¶ Explicit Breuiū natura una cum/addicionibus nouis necnon cum aliis non minus utiliorib'/in edibus Roberti/Redman/in pochia sancti/Dunstani sub intersig-/no sancti Georgii nuperime/exarata./Anno salutis nostre. Millesimo quin-/gentesimo. xxix. die vero. xxiii. Martii./ [On reverse, No. 23.]

T 88. Natura/breui-/um,/❦/
Colla. T.p.+2–179+[3].
Colo. Impressus est hic libel-/lus Londini in aedibus/Thome/

Bertheleti Regii Impresso-/ris, in Fletestrete prope/Aquagiū sitis sub in-/tersignio Lucrecie/Romane. Anno/uerbi incar-/nati mille-/lesimo/quingentesimo tricesi-/mo primo. Kalendis Octobr̄./

T 89. Title-page lacking.
Colla. 1–306.
Colo. Londini in aedibus Tho-/mae Bertheleti regii/impressoris. Anno/DO. M.D.xxxiiii./mense Sept./Cum priuilegio./

T 90. Natura breuium./
Colla. i–lxxxix+[1]; folio.
Colo. ¶ Here endeth the Natures of writtes in Frenche./ Imprynted by me Robert Redman, at London dwel-/lynge in the Fletestrete by saint Dunstones/churche at the sygne of the/ George./ ¶ Cū Priuilegio a rege/Indulto./ [McK. 44 on reverse.]

T 91. ¶ Natura bre-/uium, newly & moost/trewly corrected &c. [In made-up border. No. 25 on reverse.]
Colla. T.p.+i–C.lxxiiii.+[5].
Colo. ¶ Imprinted at London in/Fletestrete: by Wyllyam Myd-/dylton, dwellynge at the/sygne of the George,/next to sainct Dū-/stones Chur-/che./

T 92. ☞ Natura bre/vium, newly and/moost treuly corrected. . . . / ¶ Imprynted in the yeare of our/Lorde God/M.CCCCC.XLV./ ¶ Cum priuilegio ad impri-/mendum solum./
Colla. T.p.+2–179+[5].
Colo. ¶ Imprynted at London Wythout/Temple barre in saint Cle/mentes paryshe by/me Henry/Smyth./

T 93. ¶ Natura Brevi-/um in frenche./In aedibus Richardi Tot-/tell. 1557./Cum priuilegio ad impri-/mendum solum./
Colla. T.p.+2–181+[5].
Colo. ☞ Imprin-/ted at Lōdō in Flete-/strete within Temple barre, at/the sygne of the hand &/starre, by Richard/Tottill./ Anno domini. 1557./Cum priuilegio ad impri-/mendum solum./

T 94. ¶ Natura Brevi-/um in French./In aedibus Richardi Tottell./ 1566./Cum priuilegio ad imprimen-/dum solum./
Colla. T.p.+2–180+[4].
Colo. ¶ Imprinted at London/in Fletestrete within Tem-/ple barre at the signe of the/hand & starre, by Ri-/chard Tottil./ 1567/Ianuarii vicesimo primo./Cum priuilegio./

T 95. ☞ La Vieux/Natura breuium, der-/nierment corrigee &/amend', & cy nouel-/ment imprimee./Londini./In aedibus Richardi Tottill./1572./Cum priuilegio ad impri-/mendum solum./
Colla. T.p.+2–180+[4].
Colo. ¶ Imprinted at London in Flete/strete within Temple barre at the/signe of the Hand and Starre/by Richarde Tottle./ 1572./Cum priuilegio ad impri-/mendum solum./

T 96. ☞ La Vieux/Natura breuium, der-/nierment corrigee et/amend', & cy nouel-/ment imprimee./Londini./In aedibus Richardi Tottelli./1580./Cum priuilegio ad impri-/mendum solum./

Colla. T.p.+2–180+[4].

Colo. ¶ Imprinted at London in Flete-/strete within Temple barre at the/signe of the Hande and Starre/by Richarde Tottle, the/first of Iune/1580./Cum priuilegio ad impri-/mendum solum,/

T 97. ☞ La Vieux/Natura breuium, der-/nierment corrigee et/amend', & cy nouel-/ment imprimee./Londini./In aedibus Richardi Tottelli./1584./Cum priuilegio ad impri-/mendum solum./

Colla. T.p.+2–180+[4].

Colo. Imprinted at London/in Fletestrete within Tem-/ple Barre, at the signe of the Hand/and Starre, by Rycharde/Tottle, the first of/Aprill 1584./ ¶ Cum Priuilegio ad imprimen-/dum solum./

g. Natura Brevium in English

T 98. Natura breuiū/newly corrected in Englisshe:/&c. [Over No. 12. No. 11 on reverse.]

Colla. T.p.+2–251+[4].

Colo. ℭ Here endeth the Natu/res of writtes ī Englissche. Impryn/ted at Lōdon in the Fletestrete/by me Robert Redman,/ dwellynge in saynt Dun/stones parysshe at the/signe of the George./In the yere of/our Lorde/God/1532./☞ Cum priu-ilegio/a rege indulto./ [McK. 3 on reverse of last leaf.]

T 99. Natura breuiū/newly corrected in Englisshe:/&c. [Over No. 12; No. 11 on reverse.]

Colla. T.p.+2–243+[3].

Colo. ℭ Here endeth the Natu/res of writtes in Englisshe. Imprin/ted at London in Fletestrete by me/Robert Redman, dwellyng in saynt/Dunstones parysshe at the/signe of George In/the yere of our/Lord God./1535./ [Over McK. 3.]

T 100. ℭ Natura Bre/uium newly corrected in En-/glysshe . . . &c. [Over No. 25.]

Colla. T.p.+2–243+[3].

Colo. ℭ Here endeth the Natu/res of wryttes in Englisshe. Imprin/ted at London in Fletestrete, by me/Robert Redman, dwellyng in saynt/Dunstones paryshe, at the/syng of the George In/the yere of our/Lorde God/1540./ [Over McK. 3.]

T 101. Natura breuiū/newly corrected in Englyshe,/with dyuers ad-dycyons of statutes/&c. . . . [Over No. 11].

Colla. T.p.+ii–clxxxviii+[2].

Colo. ℭ Imprynted at Londō in Paules church/yarde at the sygne of the maydens heed/by Thomas petit. An. M.D.xliiii./

T 102. Natura breuiū/newly corrected in Englyshe,/ . . . &c. [Over No. 11.]

Colla. T.p.+ii–lxxx [for clxxx]+[3].

Colo. ℭ Imprynted at London,/in Paules Churche yarde at/the signe of the maydēs/heed by Thomas/petit./

T 103. Natura breuiũ/newly corrected in Englisshe:/ . . . &c. [Over No. 25].
Colla. T.p.+ii–clxxxviii+[2].
Colo. ❧ Imprynted at London in Fletestrete/by Wyllyam Myddylton. An. 1544.

T 104. ¶ Natura/Brevium/Newely corrected in/Englysshe: . . . /&c. [In border, McK. 106.]
Colla. T.p.+ii–clxxxiii+[3].
Colo. ¶ Imprynted at Lon-/don in Fletestrete at the sygne of/the george nexte to saynt Dun-/stones Churche by Wyllyam/ Powell. In the yere of/our Lorde God. M./D.L.III. The/syxt daye of/May./ ¶ Cum priuilegio ad im-/primendum solum./

T 105. Natura/breuium newly corrected, in Eng-/lishe &c. . . . / ¶ Cum priuilegio ad im-/primendum solum./
Colla. T.p.+2–180+[3].
Colo. ❧ Imprinted/at London in Flete strete,/within Temple barre, at the/sygne of the hande and/starre, by Rycharde/ Tottell, the. xxvii./daie of Febru-/arye./Anno domini. 1557./ Cum priuilegio ad impri-/mendum solum./

T 105a. Natura/breuium in Englishe newelye cor-/rected.
Colla. T.p.+2–179+[3].
Colo. ❧ Imprin-/ted at London in Flete stret/ within Temple barre, at the/sygne of the hand and/starre, by Rychard/Tottil, y^e^. xxvii. daie of Febru-/arye./Anno domini, 1557.

T 106. Natura/Breuium in English new/lye corrected: . . . / ¶ Cum Priuilegio ad im-/primendum solum./
Colla. T.p.+2–173+[3].
Colo. ¶ Imprinted at Lon-/don in Fleetestreete within/ Temple Barre, at the signe of/the Hande and Starre,/by Rych-arde Tottill/the. 22. day of Fe-/bruarye./Anno domino. 1576./ ¶ Cum priuilegio ad impri-/mendum solum./

T 107. Natura Breuium in/Englishe newly corrected:/&c.
Colla. T.p.+2–164+[3].
Colo. ¶ Imprinted at London/in Fleetestrete within Temple/ Barre at the signe of the Hande and/Starre by Richard/Tottill./ Cum Priuilegio ad/imprimendum solum./

h. Novae Narrationes

T 108. Title-page lacking.
Colla. [2]+A–F 6's. Folio.
Colo. None. [McK. 9 on reverse of last leaf.]

T 109. [Nove Narrationes. Redman, n. d., folio. Herbert.]

T 110. ¶ Herein is con-/teined the booke called Nouae/Narrationes, the booke cal-/led Articuli ad Nouas/Narrationes, and the/ booke of diuersi-/tees of cour-/tes./Newly imprinted./1561./ ¶ In aedibus Richar-/di Tottell./Cum priuilegio./

Colla. T.p.+2–120.
Colo. ℭ Imprinted at Lon-/don in Fletestrete within/ Tēple barre, at the signe/of the hande & Starre,/by Richarde Tottil,/the firste daye of/Aprill./An. do. 1561./ ¶ Cum priuilegio./

i. Articuli ad Novas Narrationes

T 111. ℭ Articuli ad narratio-/nes nouas pertiñ/formati./ [Over No. 12.]
Colla. A–D 8's.
Colo. Londini in edibus/Richardi Pynsoni re-/gii impressoris./ Cum priuile-/gio a rege/indulto./ [Over McK. 3.]

T 112. [Articuli ad narrationes novas. Redman, 1525. Ames.]

T 113. Articuli ad narra/tiones nouas ꝑtiñ/formati. [Over No. 12.]
Colla. A–C 8's, D 4.
Colo. ℭ Apud Robertū Redman./Anno dñi. 1528. die/uero. 18. mensis/Decembris./ℭ Cum gratia &c.

T 114. Articuli ad/narrationes/nouas per'/tiñ for-/mati./
Colla. A–C 8's, D 2. Begins with 8-line initial.
Colo. Hunc libellum excudebat/Thomas Bertheletus re-/gius impressor. Anno do-/mini millesimo quingen-/tesimo tricesimo./

T 115. Articuli ad/narrationes/nouas per-/tiñ for-/mati./
Colla. A–C 8's [D 2 lacking]. Begins with 9-line initial.
Colo. lacking.

T 116. Arti-/culi ad/narrationes/nouas pertin./formati./Londini in aedi-/bus Thomae Bert./regii impres-/soris./Anno. M.D.xxxviii./ [In border 30.]
Colla. A–C 8, D 4.
Colo. None.

T 117. ❧ Arti-/culi ad Nar-/rationes No-/vas pertim./formati./❦/ Londini in ae-/dibus Roberti/Redman./Anno. M.D.xxxix./
Colla. A–D 8's. Roman letter.
Colo. None.

T 118. Articuli ad/narrationes/nouas per-/tiñ for-/mati.
Colla. A–C 8's.
Colo. None.

T 119. ❧ Arti-/culi ad Nar-/rationes no-/uas pfrtim/forma/ti./❦/ Londini in ae-/dibus Wilhel-/mi Powel./Anno. M.D.XLVII.
Colla. A–D 8's. Roman letter.
Colo. None.

k. Diversity of Courts

T 120. ℭ Diuersite/de courtz et lour iu-/risdictions, et alia/necessaria et uti-/lia.☞/ [Over No. 11.]
Colla. A–C 8's.

Colo. ¶ Impressum Londini. Anno./M.D.xxiii. Per me Ro-/bertum Redman. [Qu. 1532?]

T 121. [Diversity of Courts. Pynson, 1525. Ames.]

T 122. ¶ Diuersite de Courtz/et lour iurisdictions/et alia necessaria/et utilia./ [Over No. 11].
Colla. A–C 8's (last leaf blank).
Colo. Londini in ędibus Ri-/chardi Pynsonis Regii im-/pressoris. Anno a Christi/natu. 1526. vigesimo/idus Iunii. Cum/preuilegio a/Rege in-/dulto./ [Over McK. 3.]

T 123. ¶ Diuersite de Courtes/et lour iurisdiccions/et alia necessaria/& utilia./ [Over No. 12.]
Colla. A–C 8's (last leaf blank).
Colo. . . . Londini/in edibus/Roberti Redmā/Anno salut' nostre M./ccccc.xxviiii. die vero v. Ianuarii/ ¶ Cum gratia & priuilegio./

T 124. ¶ Diuersite/de courtz et/lour iurisdi/ctions, et a-/lia necessa-/ria & uti-/lia.
Colla. A, B 8's, C 4.
Colo. Thomas Bertheletus regius impressor/excudebat. Anno dñi. M.D.xxx.

T 125. ¶ : Diuersite/de courtz et lour iu-/risdictions, et alia/necessaria et uti-/lia./ [Over cut 11.]
Colla. A–B 8's, C 4.
Colo. ¶ Impressum Londini. Anno. M.D./xxxiii. Per me Robertum/Redman./ [McK. 3 on reverse.]

T 126. Diuersite/de courtes/lour iuris-/dictions/et alia/neces-/saria/et/utilia./ [In border 30.]
Colla. A, B 8's, C 4.
Colo. Londini in aedibus/Tho. Bertheleti./An. M.D.xxxv./Cum priuilegio./

T 127. ¶ Diuersite/de courtz et lour iu-/risdiccions, et alia/necessaria et uti-/lia.☞/ [Over No. 25.]
Colla. A–B 8's, C 4.
Colo. ¶ Impressum Londini. Anno/Dñi. M.CCCCC.xliii./Per me Wyllyam/Myddylton./

T 128. [Diversity of Courts. Middleton, n. d. B.]

T 129. Diversi-/te de/courtes/lour iurisdictions/et alia necessa-/ria et/utilia./ [In border 31.]
Colla. A 4, B, C 8's.
Colo. None.

l. Book for a Justice of Peace

T 130. ¶ The boke of Iustices of peas the charge with all/the processe of the cessions warrantes supersedias &/all that longeth to ony Iustyce to make endytemen-/tes of haute treason petyt treason felonyes appeles/trespas upon Statutes trespas contra Regis pacem/Nocumentis with dyuers thynges more as it apper/eth in the Kalendar of the same boke./[Over 5 altered, 12]

Colla. A, B 6's, C 8, D 4, E 8, F 4, G 8, H 4, I 8, K 6.

Colo. ¶ Thus endeth the boke of Iustices of peas. Enpryn/ted at London in Fletestrete in the sygne of the Geor/ge By Richard Pynson./[Mck. 9b on reverse]

T 131. ¶ the boke of Iustyces of peas the charge with all/the processe of the cessyons, warrantes supersedias &/all that longeth to ony Iustyce . . . /.

Colla. A, B 6's, C 8, D 4, E 8, F 4, G 8, H 4, I 8, K 6.

Colo. Enpryn/ted at London in Fletestrete in the sygne of the sonne/By Wynkyn de Worde. In the yere of our lorde god/ M.CCCCC.vi./

T 132. ¶ The Iustyces of paes./ ¶ The boke of iustyces of peas the charge with all/the processe of the cessyons, warrantes supersedias/and all that longeth to ony Iustyce to make endy-/temētes of haute treason petyt treason felonyes ap/peles trespas upon statutes, trespas contra Regis/pacem Nocumētis with dyuers thynges more as/it appereth in the kalender of the same boke./

Colla. A 8, B 4, C 8, D 4, E 8, F 4, G 8, H 4, I 8.

Colo. ¶ Thus endeth the boke of Iustyces of peas. En-/prynted at Londō in Fletestrete at the sygne of the/sonne. By Wynkyn de Worde. In the yere of our/lorde god. M.CCCCC. &x./ [On reverse, device McK. 23 a.]

T 133. ¶ The Iustices of Peas.

Colla. A 8, B 4, C 8, D 4, E 8, H 4. I 8.

Colo. ¶ Thus endeth the boke of Iustyces of peas. Enprӯted at London in Fletestrete at the synge of the sonne. By wynkyn de worde. In the yere of our lorde god. M.CCCCC.&.XV.

T 134. ¶ The Iustices of peas./(in label, over King & Council). ¶ The boke of iustyces of peas the charge with all the/processe of the cessions. . . . &c.

Colla. A 8, B 4, C 8, D 4, E 8, F 4, G 8, H 4, I 8.

Colo. ¶ Thus endeth the boke of Iustyces of peas. Emprӯ-/ted at London in Fletestrete at the sygne of the Rose/garlande by Robert Coplande In the yere of our lorde/M.CCCCC.&xv./ [On reverse Copland's device, McK. 71.]

T 135. ¶ The boke of Iustices of peas, the char-/ge with all the proces of the cessions war-/rantes &c. [Over 11.]

Colla. A–D 8, E 6, F 4.

Colo. ¶ Thus endeth the boke of Iustyces of peas. Emprynted at/London in Fletestrete at the signe of the George. By Rychard/Pynson. Anno of our lorde god. M.CCCCC.xxi./

T 136. ¶ The boke of Iustices of peas the charge with all the processe of cessyons, &c.

Colla. (?)

Colo. John Skot. 3 October 1521 [Description from Miss Putnam's bibliography.]

T 137. The boke of the Iustyce of/peas, the charge with all the/proces of the cessyons neuly/correctyd and amendyd with/dyuers new addycyons put/to the same./ [Over J. Rastell's cut of angels supporting arms.]
Colla. A–K 8.
Colo. None.

T 138. [The boke of the Iustices of peace.]
Colophon only. Redman, 1527.

T 139. ℭ The boke of iustices of/peace, the charge, with all the/processe. . . . &c./ [In made-up border.]
Colla. i–lxxi.
Colo. ℭ Thus endeth the boke of Iustices/of peace. Imprynted at London in Flete/strete at the George, by me Robert/Redman dwellyng ī saint Dun-/stones pysshe: nere to tem-/ple barre./ [McK. 3 on reverse of last leaf.]

T 140. ℭ The boke of/Iustices of peas: the charge with all the proces of the cessyōs/ . . . &c.
Colla. T.p.+ii–lxxiiii [for 79].
Colo. None.

T 140a. ℭ The Boke of Iustices of peas.
Colla. A–K 8.
Colo. ℭ Robertus Redman me excudebat habitans in parochia sancti Donstani sub intersigno scti Georgii.

T 141. Justice/of/Peace./❧/ [In border 30.]
Colla. T.p.+2–73+[3].
Colo. ❧ Londini in edibus Thome Ber-/theleti, prope aquagium sitis/sub intersigno Lucre-/cie Romane/excus./Cum priuilegio./

T 142. The Boke/for/a/iustyce of/Peace. . . ./Londini in aedibus Tho./Berthel. regii im-/press. excus./Cum privilegio./[in border 30.]
Colla. T.p.+2–28+1–52+[4].
Colo. None.

T 143. The boke/for/a/Iustyce of Peace/neuer so wel and/dylygently/set/forthe./Londoni in edibus/Roberti Red-/man./ [In border 29.]
Colla. T.p.+2–28+i–clxix+table.
Colo. None.

T 144. The Boke/for a iustice/of peace. . . . &c./
Colla. T.p.+2–111.
Colo. ¶ Londini in aedibus Thomae/Bertheleti typis impress. Cum/priuilegio ad imprimen-/dum solum/Anno. M.D.XXXIX./

T 145. The conten-/tes of this boke./Fyrste the boke for a Iustice of/peace. . . . &c.
Colla. T.p.+2–83+[5].
Colo. Londini in aedibus Thomae/Bertheleti typis impress./Cum priuilegio ad/imprimendum/solum./Anno. M.D.XLIIII./

T 146. The Boke/for/a/Iustyce of Peace/neuer so well and/dylygently

set/forthe./Londini in/edibus Wilhelmum/Middilton./ [In border 29.]
Colla. T.p.+2–28+1–51+[5].
Colo. None.

T 147. The Boke/for/a/Iustyce of pea-/ce . . . &c./ ℂ Londini in edibus/Nicholai Hyll./Anno. 1546./ [In border 30, without date in label.]
Colla. T.p.+ii–xxviii+i–li+[5].
Colo. None. No. 33.

T 148. [The same except on title-page: ℂ Londini in edibus/Henrici Smyth./Anno. 1546.]

T 149. The same except on title-page. ℂ Londini in edibus/Johñ Waley. Anno 1546./

T 150. The same except on title-page: ℂ Londini in edibus/Roberti Toye./Anno 1546./

T 151. The con/tentes of/this boke./Fyrst the booke for a Iustyce of/ peace. &c./
Colla. T.p.+2–83+[5].
Colo. Londini in edibus Wil-/helmi Powell typis impress./ Cum priuilegio ad/imprimendum/solum./Anno. M.D.L./

T 152. The con/tentes of this/boke./Fyrst the booke for a Iu-/stice of peace . . . &c. [Containing also Court Baron, Hundred Court, Natura Brevium, Carta Feodi, Ordinance of the Exchequer, Articuli ad Narrationes Novas.]
Colla. T.p.+2–234+[12].
Colo. ☞ Imprin/ted at London in flete-/strete within/ Temple barre at the signe/of the hande & Starre, by/Richard Tottle, the/xiii. daye of Maye./An. 1556./☞ Cum priuilegio ad im/primendum solum./

T 153. The Con-/tentes of this/boke./Fyrst the booke for a Iu-/stice of peace . . . &c.
Colla. T.p.+2–195+[11].
Colo. ℂ Imprin-/ted at London in Fletestrete/within Temple barre, at the/sygne of the hand and/starre, by Richard/Tottil, the. xiii/day of Maye Anno domini. 1559./Cum priuilegio ad impri-/mendum solum./

T 154. The con-/tentes of this/booke./Fyrste the Booke for a Iustice of/peace . . . &c.
Colla. T.p.+2–195+[11].
Colo. ℂ Imprin-/ted at London in Fletestreete/within Temple barre, at the/signe of the hande and/starre, by Richard/Tottil, the. xiii./day of Maye./Anno domini 1559./Cum priuilegio ad impri-/mendum solum./

T 155. The Con-/tentes of this/booke./Fyrste the booke for a Ius-/ tice of peace. . . . &c. . . .
Colla. T.p.+2–195+[11].
Colo. Imprinted at London/in Fletestrete within Temple/

Barre at the signe of the hand/and Starre by Ry-/charde Tottel/1569./ ¶ Cum priuilegio ad impri-/mendum solum./

T 156. Title-page lacking.
Colla. T.p.+2–195+[11].
Colo. . . . Rycharde Tottyl. 1569.

T 157. The Con-/tentes of this/booke./First the booke for a Ius-/tice of peace. . . . &c.
Colla. T.p.+2–195+[11].
Colo. ¶ Imprinted at Lon-/dō in Fletestrete, within/Temple Barre at the signe/of the hand & Starre/by Richarde/Tottyl./ 1574/¶ Cum priuilegio ad impri-/mendum solum./

m. Carta Feodi

T 158. ℂ Crata feodi simplicis cū/littera atturnatoria. [Cut no. 12.l
Colla. A–E 6, F 4.
Colo. ℂ Impressa Londoñ per/Richardū Pynson in vico/the Fletestrete cōmorantem in singo Georgii./[Mck. 9b on reverse of last leaf.]

T 159. ℂ Carta feodi simplicis cum/littera atturnatoria./ [In ribbon.] (Initial "S" inverted).
Colla. A 8, B 4, C 8, D 4, E 6.
Colo. ℂ Impressa Londoñ per Winandum de Worde in/vico the Fletestrete cōmorantē in signo solis./ [On reverse, McK. 23 a.]

T 160. ℂ Carta feodi simplicis/cū littera atturnatoria./ [No ribbon.] (Initial "S" pasted over misprinted initial "A.")
Colla. A–G 6's, F 4.
Colo. ℂ Impressa Londoñ per Winandum de Worde in/vico the Fletestrete cōmorantē in signo solis./

T 161. ℂ Carta feodi simplicis cum/littora atturnatoria./ [In ribbon.]
Colla. A 8, B 4, C 6, D 4, E 6.
Colo. ℂ Impressa Londoñ per Wynandum de Worde in vico/ the fletestrete in signo solis commorantem./

T 162. ℂ Carta feodi simplicis cum/littera atturnatoria./ [In ribbon].
Colla. A 8, B 4, C 6, D 4, E 6.
Colo. ℂ Impressa Londoñ per Wynandum de Worde/in vico the fletestrete in signo solis cōmorātem.

T 163. ℂ Carta feodi simplicis cum/littera atturnatoria./ [In ribbon.]
Colla. A 8, B 4, C 6, D 4, E 6.
Colo. ℂ Impressum Londoñ per Iohannem Skot in parro-/chia sancti Sepulcri iuxta portā commorantem./

T 164. Paruus libellus/continens formam multarum rerū/prout patet in Calenda-/rio in fine inde/contento./ [Over No. 15]/ ℂ Carta feodi simplicis/cum littera attur-/natoria./
Colla. A–H 4.
Colo. None. [Cut 15.]

T 165. ℂ Paruus libellus continens formam multarū/rerum prout

patet in kalēdario in fine in contento./ ¶ Carta feodi simplicis cum/littera atturnatoria./
Colla. T.p.+ii–xl+[4].
Colo. None.

T 166. [Carta Feodi. Redman, 1527.]

T 167. ¶ Paruus libellus continens/formam multarum rerum/&c. [Over No. 11.]
Colla. T.p.+ii–xl+[3].
Colo. ¶ Impressum per me Robertum Redman./Anno domini millesimo quingenti-/simo. xxx./ [McK. 3 on reverse.]

T 167a. Carta/feo-/di./❦/ [In border 27.]
Colla. T.p.+ii–xl+[3].
Colo. ☙ Londini in edibus Thome Ber-/theleti, prope aquagium sitis/sub intersigno Lucre-/cie Romane/excus./Cum priuilegio.

T 168. ¶ Paruus libellus conti-/nens forman multarū rerum/&c. [Over No. 12.]
Colla. T.p.+ii–xl+[4].
Colo. ¶ Explicit Carta feodi. Impressum/Londini in vico qui vocatur/Fletestrete per me Rober-/tum Redman. Anno/Dn̄i. M.CCCCC./XXX.III./ [McK. 3.]

T 169. ¶ Paruus li-/bellus continens formam/multarum rerum, prout patet/in Kalendario in fine/in contento./ [Over No. 11.]
Colla. T.p.+ii–xl+[4].
Colo. ¶ Explicit Carta feodi. Impressum/Londini in vico qui vocatur/Fletestrete per me Rober-/tum Redman. Anno/ Dn̄i M.CCCCC./xxx.viii./ [Over McK. 3.]

T 170. ☙ Par-/uus libellus conti-/nens formaz mul-/tarum rerum, pro-/ut patet in ka-/lendario in/fine in/contento./
Colla. T.p.+ii–xxxix+[1].
Colo. ¶ Explicit Car/ta Eeodi./Impres-/sum Londini, in vico qui vocatur/Eletestrete, per me Robertum/Redman. Anno Dn̄i./M.CCCCC./XXX./viii./ [Over McK. 3.]

T 170a. Carta Feodi.
Colla. A–D 8, E 10.
Colo. Londoni in aedibus Thomae Bertheleti . . .

T 171. Car-/ta/Feodi./❦/An. M.D.XXXIX./ [In border 28.]
Colla. T.p.+2–40+[2].
Colo. Londini in aedibus Thomae Ber-/theleti typis impress./Cum priuilegio ad imprimen-/dum solum./Anno. M.D. xxxix./

T 172. ☙ Par-/uus libellus conti-/nens formaz mul-/tarum rerum, pro-/ut patet in ka-/lendario in fine in/contento./ [In border 29; No. 11 on reverse.]
Colla. T.p.+2–42+[2].
Colo. ¶ Explicit Car/ta feodi. Impres-/sum Londini, in vico qui vocatur/Fletestrete, per me Robertum/Redman. Anno Dn̄i./M.CCCCC./XLI./ [Over McK. 3.]

T 172a. Car-/ta feodi./Londini in aedibus Tho-/mae Bertheleti regii/ impress./Cum priuilegio./ [In border 28.]
Colla. T.p.+[2]-40+[2.]
Colo. None.

T 173. Car-/ta fe-/odi./❦/Londini in aedibus Tho./Berth. typis impress./Cum priuilegio/ad imprimen-/dum solū./1543./ [In border 38.]
Colla. T.p.+[2]-36+[2].
Colo. None.

T 174. ❧: Par/uus libellus conti-/nens formaz mul-/tarum rerum, prout/patet in kalenda/rio in fine in/cōtento./ ¶ Cum priuile/gio ad impri/mendum/solum. [In border 28.]
Colla. T.p.+ii-xlii+[2].
Colo. ¶ Explicit Car/ta Feodi. Impres-/sum Londini in vico qui vocatur/Fletestrete, per me Wilhel/mum Myddylton./ Anno Dñi./M.CCCCC./XLIII./

T 175. ❧ Par/uus libellus conti-/nens formaz mul-/tarum rerum, pro-/ut patet in Ka-/landario in/fine in/contento./❦/ [In border 29: 22 on reverse.]
Colla. T.p.+2-42+[2].
Colo. ¶ Explicit Car-/ta feodi. Impres-/sum Londini in vico qui vocatur/Fletestrete, per me Wilhel-/mum Myddylton./ Anno Dñi. M./CCCCC./XLV./ ¶ Cum priuilegio ad/imprimen-dum/solum./ [Over No. 22.]

T 176. ¶ Paruus li-/bellus continens/formam multaruz/rerum, prout pa-/tet in kalenda-/rio in fine/in/contento./Anno. 1546./ [In border 30 without date.]
Colla. T.p.+ii-xlvii+[2].
Colo. ¶ Explicit carta feodi./Impressum Londini per/Nicholaum Hyll/An. dñi M./CCCCC./xLvi./ ¶ Cum priuilegio ad impri-/mendum.

T 177. The same, except that in place of "Nicholaum Hyll" in colophon is/Iohñ Waley./

T 178. The same, except that in place of "Nicholaum Hyll" in colophon is/Henricum Smyth./

T 179. [The same, except in place of "Nicholaum Hyll" in colophon is/Robertum Toye./]

n. Court Baron

T 180. Modus tenend' Cur̄ Baroñ cum/visu franc̄ plegii./ [Over No. 5 altered.]
Colla. A, B 6's, C 4.
Colo. None. [McK. 9 b.]

T 181. ¶ Modus tenend' Cur̄ Baroñ cum visu/franem plegii./ [Cut 6 on reverse.]
Colla. A 6, B 4, C 4.
Colo. ¶ Enprynted at London in Fletestrete at ye sygne/ of the sonne. By me Wynkyn de Worde./ [On rev., McK. 23 a.[

T 182. ¶ Modus tenend cur baroñ/cum visu franem plegii./
Colla. A 6, B 4, C 4.
Colo. ¶ Enprynted at london in Fletestrete at the sygne of/ the sone. By Robart Copelande./ [On rev., device McK. 71.]

T 183. T.p. lacking [probably No. 7]. ¶ Modus tenend cur̄ baroñ cum/ visu Franc' plegii./ [Over 15?]
Colla. A 6, B 4, C 4.
Colo. ¶ Impressum per Richardum Pynson/Regis impressorem./

T 183a. Modus tenend Cur̄ Baroñ cum/visu franc' plegii./ [Rastell's cut of angels supporting arms below.]
Colla. A 8, B 8, C 4.
Colo. None.

T 184. T.p. lacking.
Colla. Unknown.
Colo. ¶ Imprynted at London in Poules chyrchyarde at/ the sygne of the Trynyte. By Henry Pepwell./ [Device, McK. 47 beneath; on reverse, McK. 52.]

T 185. ¶ Modus obseruandi cur cū leta siue visu franci ple/gii secuntur hoc modo./
Colla. A 4, B 6, C 4, D 6.
Colo. ¶ Imprynted at London in Poules/chyrcheyarde by Iohn Skot./ [On reverse, McK. 59 b.]

T 185a. ¶ Modus tenend' Cūr Baroñ cum visu franc'plegii.
Colla. A 6, B 4, C 4.
Colo. ¶ Imprynted in Poules chyrche yarde by Iohñ Skot. (McK. 59b).

T 187. [Carta Feodi. Redman, 1527.]

T 188. ¶ Modus obseruandi cur̄ cum leta/siue visu franci plegii sequntur/hoc modo./ [Over No. 11.]
Colla. A–E 8.
Colo. ¶ Explicit Mod' obseruandi Cur/cū nouis addicionibus. Impressū Londini/in vico qui vocatur Fletestrete p me/Robertū Redmā. Anno dñi/M.CCCCC.xxx/Cum priuilegio./[McK. 3 on reverse.]

T 189. Modus Tenen-/di curiam/baro-/nis. [No. 11.]
Colla. T.p.+ii–xl.
Colo. ¶ Explicit modus obseruandi Cu-/riam cum nouis additionibus. Im-/pressnm Londini in vico qui voca-/tur Fletestrete, per me Ro-/bertum Redmam./Anno Dñi. M.D. xxxiii./Cum priuilegio./ [McK. 3 on reverse.]

T 190. The ma-/ner of kepynge a/courte Baron and a/Lete &c. [In border 29; No. 25 on reverse.]
Colla. T.p.+ii–xxxviii.
Colo. ¶ Explicit modus obseruandi Curi-/am novis addicionibus. Im-/pressum Londini in vico qui/vocatur Fletstret, per me/Robertum Redman./Cum priuilegio.

T 191. Modus te-/nendi/curiam/baro-/nis./ An.M.D.XXXVI./ [In border 30.]
Colla. T.p.+2–31+1 [Including Hundred Court.]
Colo. ¶ Londini in edibus Thome Ber-/theleti, prope aquagium sitis/sub intersignio Lucre-/cie Romane/excus./ Cum priuilegio./

T 192. [Court Baron. Berthelet 1539. Herbert.]

T 193. ❧ Modus/te-/nendi curi-/am baro-/nis./❧/Anno. M.D.XL./ [In border 28.]
Colla. T.p.+2–31+[1].
Colo. Londini in aedibus Thomae/Bertheleti typis impress./ Cum priuilegio ad imprimen-/dum solum./Anno. M.D.XL./

T 194. ❧ Modus/te-/nendi curi-/am baro-/nis./❧/Anno. M.D./ XLIIII./ [In border 28.]
Colla. A–D 8's.
Colo. Londini in aedibus Thomae Bertheliti typis impress./ Cum priuilegio ad imprimen-/dum solum./Anno. M.D.XLIIII./

T 195. The ma-/ner of kepynge/a Court Baron & a/Leet . . . &c./ Anno. 1544./
Colla. A–D 8's, E 4.
Colo. ¶ Explicit Modus obser-/uandi Curiam Baroñ. Cum Nouis ad/dicionibus. Impress. Londini in vico/qui vocatur Fletstrete per me Wil-/helmum Middiltō cōmorantem/in parochia sancti Dunstani/ad iutersigniū sancti/Georgii./

T 196. ¶ The maner/of kepynge a court/Baron and a Lete/&c./Anno. 1546./ [In border 30, without date.]
Colla. A–D 8, E 4.
Colo. ¶ Explicit Modus obseruandi Cu-/riam Baroñ, Cum Nouis additioni-/bus. Impres. Londini per me./Nicholaum Hyll./

T 197. Same, except last line/Johñ Waley./

T 198. Same, except last line/Henricum Smyth./

T 199. Same, except last line/Robertum Toye./

T 200. The ma-/ner of kepynge/a court Baron & a/Lete &c . . . / Anno. 1547./ [In border, McK. 106.]
Colla. A–D 8's, E 4.
Colo. ¶ Explicit Modus obser-/uandi Curiam Baroñ, cum Nouis ad-/dicionibus. Impress. Londini in vico/qui vocatur Fletestrete per me Wil-/helmum Midditoñ cōmorantem/in parochia sancti Dunstani/ad intersignū sancti/Georgij./ [Over No. 25.]

T 201. The Ma/ner of keping/a courte Baron & a/Lete &c./Anno. 1552./ [In McK. 106.]
Colla. A–D 8's, E 4.
Colo. ☞ Explicit Modus obser-/uandi Curiam Baroñ, cum Nouis ad-/dicionibus. Impress. Londini in vico/qui vocatur Fletestrete per me Wil-/helmum Powell commorantem/in parochia sancti Dunstani/ad intersigniū sancti/Georgii./ [Over No. 22.]

o. Hundred Court

T 202. [Hundred Court. de Worde, 1510. Dibdin.]

T 203. ¶ Modus tenendi unum hun/dredū siue curiam de/Recordo./ [Over No. 11.]

Colla. A 6, B 4.
Colo. ¶ Impressum per Richardum Pyn-/son Regis impressorem./ [On reverse, McK. 44.]

T 204. Modus tenendi unum Hundredū.
Colla. A 6, B 4.
Colo. ¶ Imprynted at London in Poules chyrchyarde by Iohn̄ Skot.

T 205. ¶ Modus tenendi unum Hundre-/dū siue curiam de Recordo./ [Rastell's cut.]
Colla. A 8, B 8.
Colo. None.

T 206. [Hundred Court. Redman 1527.]

T 207. ¶ Modus tenendi unum Hū/dredum siue curiam de/recordo./ [Over No. 11.]
Colla. A, B 8's.
Colo. None.

T 208. ¶ Modus tenēdi unum Hū/dredum siue curiam de/recordo./ [Over No. 11.]
Colla. A 8, B 6.
Colo. ¶ Explicit Modus tenendi unū hū/dredum Impressum Londini in/vico qui vocatur Fletestrete/per me Robertū Redman./An. Dn̄i. M.CCCCC./xxx.viii./

T 209. ¶ : Modus tenendi unum/Hundredum siue Cu-/riam de recordo./
Colla. A 8, B 6.
Colo. ¶ Explicit Modus tenendi unū hū-/dredum Impressum Londini in/vico qui vocatur Fletestrete/per me Robertū Redman/An-Dn̄i M.CCCCC./xxx.viii./

T 210. [Hundred Court. Redman n. d.]

T 211. ¶ : Modus tenendi unum/Hundredum siue Cu-/riam de recordo./
Colla. A 8, B 6.
Colo. ¶ Explicit Modus tenēdi unū hū-/dredum Impressum Londini in/vico qui vocatur Fletestrete/per Wilhelmū Myddyl-/ton. Anno Dn̄i. M./CCCCC.xliiii./

T 212. Modus tenen/di unum Hundre-/dum siue Curi-/am de re-/cordo./ ¶ Londini in edibus/Nicholai Hyll.
Colla. A 8, B 6.
Colo. ¶ Explicit Modus tenendi/unum hundredum. Im-/pressum Londini per/Nicholaum Hyll/An. dn̄i/1546./

T 213. The same, substituting "Iohn̄ Waley" for N. Hyll in title and colophon.

T 214. The same, substituting "Roberti Toye" for "Iohn Waley" in title and colophon:
Robertum/Toye. An./1546./

T 215. The same as 11, substituting "Richardi Kele" and "Richardum/Kele. An./" in title and colophon.

T 216. ℭ Modus tenendi unum/Hundredum siue Cu-/riam de Recordo./ [Over No. 25.]
Colla. A 8, B 6.
Colo. ℭ Explicit Modus tenēdi unū hun-/dredum Impressum Londini in/vico qui vocatur Fletestrete/per Wilhelmū Myddyl-/ton. Anno Dñi. M./CCCC.xlvii./

p. Returna Brevium

T 217. ℭ Returna Br̄m./ [No. 12.]
Colla. A 8, B 4.
Colo. ℭ Emprynted at Lōdon in Fletestrete by Rychard/Pynson. The yere of oure lord god. M.CCCCC./xvi./ [McK. 9 c.]

T 218. ℭ Returna Br̄m/
Colla. A 8, B 4.
Colo. ℭ Emprynted at Lōdō in Fletestrete by Wynkyn/de Worde dwellynge at the sygne of y[e] sonne. The/yere of our lorde god M.CCCCC. &. xix./ [McK. 23 a.]

T 219. ℭ Returna Br̄m. [No. 12.]
Colla. A 8, B 4.
Colo. ℭ Emprynted at Lōdon in Fletestrete by Rychard/Pynson. The yere of oure lord god. M.CCCC./xxi/ [McK. 9 c.]

T 220. ℭ Returna breuium./ [Over Rastell's cut of angels supporting royal arms.]
Colla. A 8, B 4.
Colo. None.

T 221. [Returna Breuium. Redman 1527. Dibdin.]

T 222. ℭ Returna breuium: vel/si mavis, Rescripta Viceco-/mitum cum aliis scitu/dignioribus./ [Over cut 11.]
Colla. T.p.+ii–xxii[xxiv] [including the Hundred Court].
Colo. ℭ Robertus Redman/me fecit./ ℭ Cum priuilegio/Regali./ [On reverse, McK. 3 c.]

T 223. ℭ Returna breuium/ [Over No. 11.]
Colla. T.p.+ii–xii.
Colo. ℭ Explicit Returna Breuiū, noviter/castigatum, Impressum Londini per me/Robertum Redman. Anno domini/M.CCCCC.xxxii die vero/mensis Februarii./xviii./ [McK. 3 on reverse.]

T 224. ℭ Returna Brevium./ [Over No. 11.]
Colla. T.p.+ii–xii.
Colo. ℭ Explicit Returna Breuium, no/uiter castigatum, Impressum Londini per/me Robertum Redman. Anno domini/M.CCCCC.xxxvii. die vero/mensis. Augustii./xxxi./ [McK. 3 on reverse.]

T 225. ¶ Returna Brf-/uium./ [Over No. 25.]
Colla. A 8, B 4.
Colo. ¶ Explicit retur-/na breuium, nouiter castigatum, Im/pressum Londinii per me Ro-/bertum Redman. An. domi/ni M.CCCCC.xli. die/vero mensis Maii./vi./ [McK. 3 c on reverse.]

T 226. ☞ Re-/turna breui-/um./Londini in aedibus Thomae Bertheleti regii impress./Cum priuilegio ad/imprimendum/solum./ [In border 28.]
Colla. A 8, B 4.
Colo. None.

T 227. ☜ Re-/turna brevi-/um./Londini in aedibus Thomae/Bertheleti regii impress./Cum priuilegio./ [In border 28.]
Colla. T.p.+2–12.
Colo. None.

T 228. ☞ Re-/turna/breui-/um./Londini in aedibus Thomae/ Bertheleti regii impress./Cum priuilegio ad/imprimendum/solum./ [In border 30.]
Colla. T.p.+2–12.
Colo. None.

T 229. ¶ Returna Bre-/uium./ [Over 11.]
Colla. A 8, B 4.
Colo. ¶ Explicit Retur-/na Breuium, nouiter castigatum, Im-/pressum Londinii per me Wil-/helmũ Myddylton. An. do-/mini M.CCCCC.xliii./die vero. mensis/Octobris./

T 230a. Retur-/na breuium./An. M.D.XLVI./ [In border 30, without date.]
Colla. A 8, B 4.
Colo. None. [Bound with Smyth's edition.]

T 230b. The same, bound with Toye's edition.

T 230c. The same, bound with Waley's edition.

T 231. ☞ Re-/turna/breui-/um./Londini in edibus Wil-/helmi Powel/ Cum priuilegio/ad imprimen/dum so-/lum./ [In McK. 106.]
Colla. A 8, B 4.
Colo. None.

q. Ordinance of the Exchequer

T 232. ¶ This is a true Copy of thordinaũce made in/the tyme of the reygne of Kynge Henri the. vi. to/be obseruyd in the kynges Eschequier &c. [Over J. Rastell's cut of angels supporting royal arms.]
Colla. A 8.
Colo. None.

T 233. ¶ This is a true copy of the or-/dynaũce made in the tyme of the reygne of kynge/&c. [Over No. 11.]
Colla. A 8.
Colo. None. [McK. 3 on reverse of last leaf.]

T 234. ¶: This is a/true copy of the ordynaunce/made in the tyme of the reygne of/kynge Henry the. vi. to be obserued in/the kynges Eschequier &c.

Colla. T.p.+II–VIII.

Colo. ¶ Imprynted at London./by me Roberte/Redman./ [On reverse, McK. 3.]

T 235. ❧: This is a/true copy of the ordynaunce/made in the tyme of the reygne of/Kynge Henry the. VI. to be obserued in the/ kynges eschequier &c. [Over No. 11.]

Colla. A 8.

Colo. ¶ Imprynted at London/by me Roberte/Redman./

T 236. ¶: This is a/true copy of the ordinaunce/made in the tyme of the reygne of/kynge Henry the. vi. to be obserued in/the kynges Eschequier &c. [Over 11.]

Colla. A 8.

Colo. ¶ Imprinted at London,/by me Robert/Redman./ [McK. 3 on reverse.]

T 236a. A true/copy of/the ordi-/nance made in the tyme of/Kynge Henry the. vi . . -/❦/ [In border 28.]

Colla. A 8.

Colo. None.

T 237. A true/copy of/the ordi-/nance made in the tyme of/kynge Henry the. VI. to be/obserued in the kynges/Escheker . . . &c./ [In border 30.]

Colla. A 8.

Colo. Londini in aedibus/Thomae Bertheleti/an. M.D.XXX-VII./Mense Augusti./

T 238. ❧ A true/copy of/the or-/dinance/made in/the/tyme of king Henry the. VI./to be obserued in the kinges/Escheker &c./ [In border 30.]

Colla. A 8.

Colo. Londini in aedibus Tho-/mae Bertheleti typis/impress./ Cum priuilegio./Ad imprimendum/solum./Anno. M.D.XL./

T 239. ❧ A true/copy of/the or-/dinance/made in/the/tyme of king Henry the. VI./to be obserued in the kinges/Escheker, . . . &c./❧ Londini/An. 1544./ [In border 28.]

Colla. A 8.

Colo. Londini in aedibus Tho-/mae Bertheleti typis/impress./ Cum priuilegio/Ad imprimendum/solum./Anno. M.D.XLIIII./

T 240. ❧: This is a/true copy of the ordynaũce/made in the tyme of yᵉ reygne of/kynge Henry the. VI. to be obserued in the/kynges Eschequier . . . &c. [Over No. 11.]

Colla. A 8.

Colo. ¶ Imprynted at London in Fletestrete/at the sygne of the George by/Wyllyam Myddylton./

T 241. ¶ Thys is a/true copy of the ordynaũce/made in the tyme of the reygne of/Kynge Henry the. vi. to be obser-/ued in the kynges eschequier . . . &c. [Over No. 35.]

Colla. A 8.
Colo. ℂ Imprynted at London by/Nicolas Hyll./

T 242. The same, except last line of colophon,/Robert Toye./

T 243. The same, except last line of colophon,/Henry Smythe./

T 244. The same, except last line of colophon,/Iohñ Waley./

T 245. The same, except last line of colophon/Rycharde Kele./

T 246. ❧ A true/copy of/the ordi-/nance/made in/the/time of king Henry the. vi./to be obserued in yᵉ kinges/Escheker . . . &c./Londini./Anno. 1552./ [In McK. 106.]
Colla. A 8.
Colo. ❧ Imprinted at Lon/don in Fletestrete at the sygne/ of the George nexte to saynt/Dunstones Churche/by Wyllyam/ Powell./ ℂ Cum priuilegio ad impri-/mendum solum./Anno. M.D.L.II./

SECTION 2. ANONYMOUS TREATISES

T 247. ℂ An admonicion or warnyng, to/all the Kynges Maiesties Iustices of Peace,/in the name of the Lorde Protector &c.
Colla. ai, (aii) aiii, 1 bl.
Colo. Excusum Londini, in aedibus Richardi Graftoni,/ Regii Impressoris./Cum Privilegio ad Impri-/mendum solum./

T 248. The/ancient state,/authoritie, and/proceedings of/the Court of/Requests./2. Octob. 1596./Anno 1597.
Colla. Ai+t.p.+[6]+1–162.
Colo. None.

T 249. An Apologie/for sundrie proceedings/by Iurisdiction Ecclesiasticall, of late/times by some chalenged . . . &c./Imprinted at London by the Depu-/ties of Christopher Bar-/ker, Printer to the Queenes most/excellent Maiestie./1593./
Colla. T.p.+[14]+1–130. The Second Part, T.p.+[4]+1–140+[1 bl.]. The Third Part, T.p.+1–255.
Colo. None.

T 250. Articles to/be enquyred in the visi-/tation, in the fyrste yeare of/the raygne of our moost/drad soveraygne la-/dy, Elizabeth, &c. . . . /Anno. 1559./ [In border 42.]
Colla. A 4, B 3, 1 bl.
Colo. ❧ Imprin-/ted at London in Pou-/les Churcheyarde by Richard Iugge, and/Iohn Cawood, Printers to the/Quenes Ma-/iestie./Anno. M.D.LIX./Cum priuilegio Regiae/Maiestatis./

T 250a. ❧ Articles to/be enquired in the visita-/tion, in the fyrst yeere of the/raigne. . . . /Anno domini. 1559./[In border McK. 181.]
Colla. A, B 4's, last leaf blank.
Colo. Imprinted at Lon-/don by Richard Iugge, Prin-/ter to the Queenes Maiestie./¶ Cum priuilegio Regiae Maiestatis.

T 250b. ¶ Articles to/be enquired in the vi-/sitation, in the first yere of/ . . . /Anno dominio/1559./

Colla. A, B 4's.
Colo. ¶ Imprinted at Lon-/don by Iohn Kyngston, by the/ assent of Christopher Barker, Printer to the Queenes moste/ excellent Maiestie./Cum priuilegio Regiae Maiestatis./

T 250c. Articles/to be enquired in the/visitation, in the first yeere/. . . ./ Anno domini, 1583/[In border McK. 221.]
Colla. A, B 4's, last leaf blank.
Colo. Imprinted at/London, by Christopher Bar-/kar, Printer to the Queenes/Maiestie./Cum priuilegio Regiae Maiestatis./

T 250d. Articles to/be enquired of in the vi-/sitation, in the first yeare. . . . /Anno domini. 1559./[In border McK. 221.]
Colla. A, B 4's, last leaf blank.
Colo. Imprinted at London/by the Deputies of Christopher/ Barker, printer to the Queenes/Maiestie./Cum priuilegio Regiae Maiestatis./1591./

T 250e. Articles to/be enquired of in the vi-/sitation, in the first yeare . . . . /Anno domini. 1559./
Colla. A, B 4's, last leaf blank.
Colo. Imprinted at London/by the Deputies of Christopher/ Barker, printer to the Queenes/Maiestie./Cum priuilegio Regiae Maiestatis./An. Dom./1595/.

T 251. Articles to be en/quired of in the visitatiō, in/the First yeere of the Raign/of our most dread Soue-/raign Ladie Elizabeth, &c. . . . Anno. Dom. 1559./ [In border, McK. 221.]
Colla. A 4, B 3, 1 bl.
Colo. ❧ Imprinted at London by the/Assignement of Robert Barker/Printer to the Queenes most/excellent Maiestie./Cum Priuilegio Regiae Maiestatis./Anno Dom. 1600./

T 251a. Articuli, de quibus conve-/nit inter Archiepiscopos, &/Episcopos utriusque provinciae,/& Clerum uniuersum in Synodo, Lon-/ dini. An. 1562. . . . /Londini, apud Iohannem Dayum/Typo-graphum./Anno Domini./1575./
Colla. T.p.+3–24 (paged).
Colo. None.

T 252. [The assise of bread and ale. Bankes (c. 1530)].

T 253. The assyse of/breadde/and ale, and/other/thynges, as/appereth/ on/the other syde/of the leafe./
Colla. T.p.+2–32.
Colo. Imprinted at/London in Fletestrete, in the/house of Thomas/Berthelet./Cum privilegio ad impri-/mendum solum./

T 253a. ¶ The assise of bread/and ale, and dyvers other/thynges, as appereth/on the other syde/of the leafe./❦/
Colla. A–E 4's.
Colo. Im-/prynted at London in Fletestrete, in the/house of Thomas Berthelet,/nere the Cundite, at/the signe of Lu-/crece./ Cum priuilegio a rege indulto./

T 254. ¶ Here begynneth the Boke/named the Assyse of breade, what it ought to weye./ ¶ Imprynted by me Robert Wyer./ [Nos. 14 & 14 a.]
Colla. A–D 4.
Colo. ¶ Imprynted by me Robert Wyer: dwellynge/in saynct martyns paryshe, besyde Cha-/rynge Crosse, at the sygne of sayncte/Iohñ Euangelyst, besyde the/Duke of Suffolkes /place./ [Device, McK. 69.]

T 255. ¶ Here begynneth the boke/named the Assyse of Bread, what it ought to/weye, after the Pryce of a quarter of wheete./And also the Assyse of Ale, with all maner/of woode and cole, lath, bourde, and Chese./ ¶ Imprynted by me Robert Wyer./ [Nos. 14 & 14 a.]
Colla. A–D 4's.
Colo. Imprynted by me Robert Wyer,/Dwellynge in seynt Martyns/parysshe at Charynge crosse,/at the Sygne of seynt/ Iohñ Euangelyst./ [McK. 68 & 69.]

T 256. Here begynneth the booke/named the Assize of bread . . . [Nos. 14 & 14 a.]
Colla. A–D 4's.
Colo. Imprynted by me Robert Wyer, dwellyng/in saynt Martyns parysshe besyde cha-/rynge Crosse at the sygne of saynt/Iohñ Euangelyst./ [Over McK. 67, without name below.]

T 256a. ☙ Here begynneth the boke/named the Assise of bread, what it ought to wey/after the pryse of a quarter of Wheet . . . /
Colla. A–D 4's.
Colo. ¶ Imprynted by me Thomas Colwell, Dwel-/lynge in the house of Robert Wyer: at the/sygne of seynt Iohñ Euangelyst:/in seynt Martyns Parysshe/besyde Charynge/Crosse./

T 257. ¶ Here beginneth the Booke, named/the Assise of Breade, what it ought to/weygh, after the price of a Quarter of Wheate,/ . . .
Colla. A–D 4.
Colo. ¶ Imprinted at London,/by H. Jackson./

T 258. The assise of/bread,/&c. . . . London/Printed by Iohn Windet, dwelling at Powles/Wharfe, at the signe of the Crosse Keyes, 1600./
Colla. A–F 4's.
Colo. None.

T 259. ¶ A Booke/of certaine Canons,/concernyng some parte/of the discipline of/the Church of/England./In the yeare of our Lord./ 1571./At London/Printed by Iohn Daye,/dwellyng ouer Al-/ dersgate./ ¶ Cum gratia & Priuilegio/Regiae Maiestatis./
Colla. A–D 4's.
Colo. None.

T 260. A Breefe/Discourse, declaring/and approving the necessarie/ and inviolable maintenance/of the laudable customes/of London:/&c. . . . /At London/Printed by Henrie/Midleton for Rafe/Newberie./1584./

Colla. T.p.+[2]+4–48.
Colo. None.

T 261. A briefe treatise of Oathes exacted/by Ordinaries and Ecclesiasticall Iudges/ . . . &c.
Colla. T.p.+3–58.
Colo. None.

T 262. Capitula sive/constitutiones/Ecclesiasticae . . . /Londini/Excudebant Deputati Christo-/pheri Barker, Regiae Maiestatis/ Typographi./Anno Domini 1597./
Colla. T.p.+1–23.
Colo. None.

T 262a. Capitula sive/Constitutiones/Ecclesiasticae. . . . /Londini/Excudebant Deputati Christo-/pheri Barker, Regiae Maiestatis/ Typographi./Anno Domini 1599./
Colla. T.p.+1–21.
Colo. None.

T 262b. ¶ A Defence/of priestes mariages stablysshed/by the imperiall lawes of the/Realme of Englande . . . /
Colla. T.p.+[5]+[21]+22–274.
Colo. Imprinted at London by Iohn/Kinston, for Richarde Iugge/Printer to the Queenes Maiestie./Cum priuilegio ad imprimendum solum.

T 263. ¶ A defence/of priestes mariages, stablysshed/by the imperiall lawes of the/Realme of Englande, agaynst/a Ciuilian, namyng hym/selfe Thomas Mar-/tin &c.
Colla. T.p.+[5]+1–359+[4].
Colo. ¶ Imprinted at London by/Richarde Iugge, printer to the Queenes/Maiestie./Cum priuilegio Regiae Maiestatis./

T 263a. A Treatise coucer-/nynge the diuisi-/on betwene/the spi-/ritu-/alitie and tem-/poralitie./ / [In border 29.]
Colla. T.p.+2–46+[1].
Colo. Londini in edibus Thome Ber-/theleti, prope aquagium sitis/sub intersignio Lucre/cie Romane/excus./Cum priuilegio.

T 264. [Exhortation . . . to the Justices of Peace. Grafton 1548. Dibdin.]

T 265. The Tenours & fourme of Indentures . . . &c.
Colla.
Colo. Imprinted in Knight Riders strete by John Tysdale the xxxix. daye of December. [From Herbert.] (See also T 285.)

T 266. Iniuncci-/ons gevē by the moste ex-/cellent prince, Edward the/ sixte. . . . To all and/singuler his lo-/uyng subiec-/tes, as well/ of the/Clergie, as of the/Laietie./[In border.]
Colla. A–C 4, D 2.
Colo. ¶ Imprinted at London, the/laste daie of Iulii, in the/ first yere of the reigne/of our sovereigne Lord/Kyng Edward the. VI./by Richard Grafton/printer to his/moste royall/Maiestie./

Anno. 1547./Cum priuilegio ad impri-/mendum solum./[McK. 104 on reverse.]

T 267. Injunctions given by the Queen's Majesty. Jugge & Cawood, 1559.

T 267a. Injunctions given by the Queen's Majesty Jugge. 157.

T 267b. Iniunctions/given by the Quee-/nes Maiestie./The first yere of the/raigne of our soue-/raigne Lady Queene/Elizabeth./¶ Cum priuilegio Regiae/Maiestatis./Anno domini./1559./[In border, minstrels at sides, satyrs in corner of sill-piece.]
Colla. A–D 4's.
Colo. None.

T 267c. Iniunctions given by/the Queens Maiesty./Anno domini. 1559./ The first yere of the raign/. . . . /¶ Cum priuilegio Regiae/ Maiestatis./[In border McK. 221.]
Colla. A–D 4's.
Colo. None.

T 267d. Iniunctions given by/the Queenes Maiestie./Anno domini. 1559./ The first yere of the raign/ . . . /¶ Cum priuilegio Regiae/ Maiestatis./[In border McK. 221.]
Colla. A–D 4's.
Colo. None.

T 267e. Injunctions given/by the Queenes/Maiestie./Anno Dom. 1559./ &c. . . . / [In border, McK. 221.]
Colla. A–D 4's.
Colo. None.

T 267f. Iniunctions geuen by the Queenes/Maiestie./Anno Domini. 1559. The fyrst yere of the raigne/ . . . /
Colla. A–D 4's.
Colo. None.

T 268. Insti-/tutions in/the lawes/of Eng-/lande,/Cum priuilegio. [In McK. 94.]
Colla. A–G 8 (last leaf wanting, blank or colo.).
Colo. None.

T 269. The prin-/cipal lawes customes and estatutes/of England, . . ./ ❦/Londini./M.D.XL./❧/Cum priuilegio ad imprimen-/dum solum./
Colla. T.p.+[3]+1–96.
Colo. Ex aedibus Richar/di Taverneri, per/Richardum Ban-/kes typogra-/phum./Cū priuilegio ad imprimendum./solum./

T 270. The prin-/cipall lawes and sta-/tutes of Englande,/ . . . &c./ Londini./M.D.XLII./Cum priuilegio ad impri-/mendum solum./ [In McK. 91.]
Colla. T.p.+[1]+iii–lxxxv+[2].
Colo. ¶ Imprynted at Lon[don by Ri/charde Ban[kes]/ ¶ Cum priuilegio [ad imprimen-]/dum solum.

T 271. ☙ Insti-/tutions, or princi-/pall groundes of the lawes & statuts of Englā-/de . . . . /❧ Londini./M.V.XLIII./
Colla. [i]–lxvi+[2].
Colo. ☙ Imprynted at/London in Fletestrete at the sygne/ of the George nexte to saynt Dun-/stones churche by me Wyl-/ lyam Myddylton. In/the yere of our Lorde/God a M.D.xliii./ The xxv. day/of Iune./¶ Cum Priuilegio Ad Imprimen-/dum Solum./

T 272. ☙ Insty-/tutions or, princi-/pall groundes of the/lawes and statutes of En-/glande &c./ [In border 29.]
Colla. T.p.+ii–lxvi+[2].
Colo. ☙ Imprynted at/London in Fletestrete at the/sygne of the George next to saynt/Dunstones Churche by Wyllyam/ Myddylton. In the yere of/our Lorde God a M.D./xliiii. The fyrst day/of Marche./Cum priuilegio. [Device, McK. 102, on reverse.]

T 273. ☙ Insty-/tutions or, princi-/pall groundes of the/lawes and statutes of En-/glande &c./ [In border 29.]
Colla. T.p.+[2]+iiii–lxvi+[2].
Colo. ☙ Imprynted at/Lōdon in Fletestrete at the sygne/ of the George next to saynt Dunstones/churche by Wyllyam Myddylton./In the yere of our Lorde god./M.D.xlv. The. xxi. day/of Auguste./☞ Cum Priuilegio/ad imprimen-/dum solum./

T 274. [Institutions or principal grounds. Hyll for Toye, 1546. Dibdin.]

T 275. ¶ Insti-/tutiōs or princi-/pal groūdes of the/lawes and statutes of/Englande, newly and/etc./An. D. 1547./ [In McK. 106.]
Colla. +i–lxvi+[2].
Colo. ☙ Imprynted at/London in Fletestrete at the signe/of the George next to saynt Dunstones/churche by Wyllyam Myddylton./In the yere of our Lorde god./M.D.xlvii. The. xix. day of Marche./ [McK. 102 on reverse.]

T 276. ❧ Insti-/tuti-/ons,/or pryncypall groundes/of the lawes and Statutes/of Englande, newelye and/verye truelye corrected, &c. . . . /An. D. 1551./ [In border, McK. 106.]
Colla. T.p.+[1]+3–66+[2].
Colo. ❧ Imprynted at/London in Fletestrte at the/signe of the George next to saynte dun-/stones churche by Wyllyam Powell./In the yere of our Lorde God./M.D.L.I. The xix./daye of Marche./

T 277. Institu/tions or princypal/groundes of the lawes and/statutes of Englande, new-/ly and very truely correc-/ted and amended with/many newe, &c. . . . /1555. [In border 43.]
Colla. T.p.+ii–lxvi+[2].
Colo. ¶ Imprynted at London in/Fletestrete at the sygne of/the Prynces armes/by Thomas/Marshe./Anno. M.D.L.V./

T 277a. Institu-/tions or princypal/groundes of the lawes and/statutes of England. . . ./1556./ [In border McK. 106.]

Colla. T.p.+[ii]-lxvi+[2].
Colo. ¶ Imprynted at London in/Fletestrete at the sygne of/the Prynces armes/by Thomas/Marshe./Anno. M.D.L.V./

T 278. ☞ Instituti-/ons or princi-/pall groundes of the lawes and/statutes of England, newly and/very truely corrected and amended,/with many new . . . /☞ Imprinted at London in/Fletestrete within Temple/barre, at the sygne of the/hande and starre, by/Richard Tottel./Anno Domini./1567./
Colla. T.p.+[2]+iiii–lxvi+[2].
Colo. None.

T 279. ☞ Institutions/or principall groundes of the/Lawes and statutes of England,/newly and very truely corrected and amended,/&c. . . . /Imprinted at London/in Fletestrete within Temple/Barre at the signe of the hand/and Starre by Ry-/charde Tottyl/1570./
Colla. T.p.+[1 bl.]+2–66+[2].
Colo. None.

T 280. Institutions/or principall groundes/of the lawes, &c./(. · .)/Anno. 1574./
Colla. T.p.+[ii]–lxxxv+[3].
Colo. ¶ Imprynted at London by Ry-/charde Bankes./ ¶ Cum privilegio ad imprimen-/dum solum./

T 281. ☞ Instituti-/ons or princi-/pall groundes of the Lawes. . . &c./Imprinted at London in/Fleetestrete within Temple/Barre at the signe of the/Hand and Starre, by/Richard Tottell./
Colla. T.p.+ii–lxvi+[2].
Colo. None.

T 282. Institutions/or principall groundes of/the Lawes and statuts of Eng-/land, newly & very truely corrected & amen-/ded, with many newe, etc./Imprinted at London in/Fleetestrete within Temple/Barre at the signe of the/Hand and Starre by/Rychard Tottell./1580./
Colla. T.p.+[2]–66+[2].
Colo. None.

T 283. Intrationū excellentissimus liber per q. necessarius oībus legz ho/minib': . . . &c.
Colla. Aa 6, Bb 4 [20 ll.], I–CLXXXV.
Colo. ¶ Explicit opus excellentissimū & perutile in se conti-/nens multas materias oībus legz hoīb' p q̄ necessa/rias nouiter Impressum, correctum, emendatum, &/nō minimo labore reuisum London̄ in vico vulga-/riter nūcupato Fletstrete in officina ere ac impensis/honesti viri Richardi Pynson Regis Impressoris/moram suam trahentis sub Signo diui Georgii An-/no nr̄e redemptionis. M.CCCCC.x. Die vero ul-/tima mensis Februarii./

T 284. ¶ Intrationum/liber omnibus legum Anglie/studiosis apprime necessarius/&c. . . . /¶ Excudebat Henricus/Smythe cōmo-rans extra Tem/ple barre in parochia sancti/Clementi ad inter signū/sancti Trinitatis. An./restituete salutis/ M.D.XLVI./ [In border, McK. 62.]

Colla. T.p.+aii–vi, B–D 6's, I–CC.XLIIII.

Colo. . . . Impressum, correctum, emendatum, et non minime labo-/re reuisum Londoñ in parochia sancti Clemētis/ extra Temple barre impensis honesti vi-/ri Henrici Smyth moram suam tra-/hentis sub signo sancti Trini-/tatis. Anno nr̄e redemptio-/nis. M.CCCCC.XLV./die vero primo men-/sis Novembris./

T 285. An Intro/duction to the Know/lege and understandyng/aswel to make as also to/perceyue the tenour and/forme of indentures, etc.

Colla. T.p. ii–xxxii.

Colo. ¶ Imprinted at London by John/Waylye. [See also T 265.]

T 286. A Collection/of the Lawes & statutes/of this Realme concer-/ning Liueries of com-/panies and Retey-/nours./ . . . /In aedibus Richardi Totelli./Anno. 1571./Februarij. 17./Cum priuilegio./

Colla. [2]+1–39+[5].

Colo. None.

T 287. The/Lawes/and Statutes of the/Staunarie of/Deuon./ ¶ Printed at London by Va-/lentine Simmes./1600./ [In McK., 168.]

Colla. A–D 6's, E 8, Aa 6, Bb 4./Folio.

Colo. None.

T 288. In This/Booke is contay-/ned ye offices of She-/ryffes, Bailliffes of li/berties, Escheatours/Cōstables and Coro-/ners, & sheweth what/euery one of thē maye/do by vertue of theyr/offices, drawen out of/bokes of the comon lawe/& of the Statutes./ Cum priuilegio./ [In border 29. 25 on reverse.]

Colla. A–K 8's.

Colo. ¶ Imprynted/at London in Fletestrete,/by me Robert Redman, dwelling/at the sygne of the George,/nexte to S. Dunsto-/nes churche./ ¶ Cum pri-/uilegio Re-/gali./

T 289. In This/boke is conteyned/the offyce of Shy-/reffes, Bailliffes of li-/berties, Escheatours/Cōstables and Coro-/ners, & sheweth what every one of thē maye/do by vertue of theyr/offyces, drawen out of/bokes of the comon/lawe & of the statutes./Cum priuilegio./

Colla. A–K 8's.

Colo. Imprynted at/London in Fletestrete by/me Elyzabeth Pykerynge/wydo to Robert Red-/man dwellynge at/the sygne of the/Gorge nexte/to saynt Dunstones Churche./Cum priuilegio.

T 290. [Office of Sheriffs. Petyt, 1543.]

T 291. In Thys/boke is conteyned/the offyce of Shy-/ryffes, Bailliffes of li-/berties, Escheatours/Cōstables Coro-/ners, & sheweth what/euery one of them maye/do by vertue of theyr/offyces drawen out of/bokes of the comen/lawe & of the statutes./

Colla. A–k 8.

Colo. ¶ Imprynted at/London in Fletestrete, at the/sygne of the George nexte/to saynt Dunstones/Church by Wyl-/lyam Myd-/dylton./In the yere of our Lorde/M.CCCCC.XLV./The. x. daye of/Ianuary./ [McK. 102 on reverse.]

T 292. ¶ In this/boke is/contey/ned yᵉ office of Shy-/ryffes, Bayylffes of ly-/bertyes. . . . &c./ [In McK. 106. 22 on reverse.]

Colla. A–K 8's.

Colo. ❧ Imprynted/at London in Fletestrete/at the sygne of the George/nexte to saynte Dunstones/Churche by Wylly-/am Powell./In the yere of our Lorde God. M./CCCCC.XLIX./ The. IX. daye of/Marche./ [Cut 25.]

T 293. First two pages lacking.

Colla. A–G 4 in 8's; last leaf blank.

Colo. ☞ Imprynted at London by Ry-/charde Kele, dwel-lynge in Lum-/berde streate at the signe of/the Egle./Anno. M.D.LII./

T 294. ❧ In this/booke is/conteined/the office of shiriffes/&c. . . ./ [In McK. 106.]

Colla. A–K 8's.

Colo. ❧ Imprynted/at London in Fletestrete/nere to Saynte Dun-/stones Churche/by Thomas/Marche./

T 295. In this booke/is contained the office of Shiriffes,/&c. . . ./Anno domini/❧ Imprinted at London in fleete-/strete neare to saynct Dunstanes/Churche, by Thomas/Marshe./

Colla. A–I 8's, K 7.

Colo. None.

T 296. In this booke/is contained the office of Shiriffes,/&c. Anno domini./Imprinted at London in fleete-/strete nere to saynct Dunstons/church by Thomas/Marshe./

Colla. A–I 8's, K 7.

Colo. None.

T 297. In this bo-/ke is conteyned the of-/fices of Shyriffes . . . &c./ Anno salutis. 1556./ [In No. 43.]

Colla. A–E 8's, F & G 6's.

Colo. ¶ Imprynted/at London by Iohn/Wight, dwelling in/ pouls churchyard/at the sine of the/Roose./Anno. M.D.LII.

T 298. [Office of Sheriffs, W. Powell, 1552. Dibdin.]

T 299. In this/Booke is conteyned/the offyce of Shyryffes,/ . . . , [In made-up border]

Colla. A–K 8's.

Colo. ¶ Imprinted at/London, in Crede Lane,/by Iohn King./

T 300. [Office of Sheriffs, Tottel, 1562. Dibdin.]

T 301. In this booke/is contayned the office of/Shiriffes, &c. . . ./

Anno domini./1562./☞ Imprinted at London in Flete-/strete nere to saynct Dunstons/Churche by Thomas/Marshe./

Colla. A–K 8's.

Colo. ¶ Imprynted/at London in Fletestrete/nere to Saynte Dun/stones Churche/by Thomas/Marche./

T 302. ¶ In this booke/is contayned the office of/Shiriffes, &c. . . ./ Anno domini./1570./Imprinted at London/in Fletestrete within Temple/Barre at the signe of the hand/and Starre by Ry-/charde Tottyl./

Colla. T.p.+2–57.

Colo. Imprinted at London/in Fletestrete within Temple/ Barre at the signe of the hand/and Starre by Ry-/chard Tottyl./

T 303. ¶ In this booke/is contayned the office of/Shiriffes, &c. . . . 1570/Imprinted at London/in Fletestrete within Temple/Barre at the signe of the hand/and Starre by Ry-/charde Tottyl./

Colla. T.p.+2–57.

Colo. Imprinted at London/in Fletestrete within Temple/ Barre at the signe of the hand/and Starre by Ry-/charde Tottyl./

T 304. In this book/is contained the offices of Shi-/riffes, Bayliffes of liberties, Es-/cheatours, Constables and Co-/roners, and sheweth what e-/ueryone of thē may doo by/ vertue of their offices, dra-/ wen out of books of the/common Law and/of the Statutes./ ¶ Imprinted at London by/Iohn Allde, for Iohn/Waley./

Colla. A–G 8's.

Colo. ¶ Imprinted at London, by/Iohn Allde./1573./

T 304a. ¶ Orders deuised by/the especiall commandement of/the Queenes Maiestie, for the/reliefe and stay of the present/ dearth of Graine within/the Realme . . . /Imprinted at London by Christopher/Barker. Printer to the Queenes most/ excellent Maiestie./1586./

Colla. T.p.+1–20 (paged).

Colo. ¶ Imprinted at Lon-/don, by Christopher Barker,/ Printer to the Queenes most/excellent Maiestie./

T 305. The Ordynal/or statuts concernynge Arty-/fycers, serrauntes, & labou-/rers' newly prynted/with dyuers other/thynge thereunto/added. [McK. 70.]

Colla. T.p.+[3]+i–xxxxvi.

Colo. ¶ Imprinted by me Robert/Wyer, for Rycharde/ Bankes./¶ Cum privilegio regali,/ad imprimendū solum.

T 306. [Same: by Richard Banks, n.d.]

T 307. [Same: Hyll, n. d: Dibdin.]

T 307a. [Same: Tysdale, 1562: Dibdin.]

T 307b. ☞All suche Proclamacions, as have/been sette furthe by the Kynges/Maiestie (and passed the Print) from/the last daie of Ianunrii, in the firste/yere of his highnes reigne, unto the/ last daie of Ianuarii, beeyng in/the.iiii. yere of his said moste/ prosperous reigne, that/is to saie, by the/space of. iiii./whole/ ye-/res./Anno. 1550./

Colla. T.p.+ii–c+[2].

Colo. Imprinted/at London, by Richard/Grafton, Printer/ to the kynges/maiestie./Anno 1550./Cum privilegio ad impri-/mendum solum./ [McK. 122 on reverse].

T 308. Reformatio/legum ecclesiasti-/carum, ex authorita-/te primum Regis Henrici. 8. in-/choata: &c. . . . [McK. 83 b.]/Londini/ Ex officina Johannis Daii Anno/salutis humanae, 1571./Mense Aprili./

Colla. T.p.+[10]+2–149+[3].

Colo. None.

T 309a. ¶ Registrum/omniū brevium/tam originaliū/q̄ iudicia-/lium./ Londini/☞ Apud Gulielmum Rastell./1531/❧ Cum priui-legio./ [In border, McK. 62.]

Colla. T.p.+ii–vi, i–vi, i–iii+1–321+1 bl.

Colo. Londini/ex aedibus Guilielmi Rastell./1531./❧ Cum privilegio./

T 309b ¶ Registrum/omniū brevium/iudicialium./Londini./☞ Apud Guilelmum Rastell./1531./❧ Cum priuilegio./ [In border, McK. 62.]

Colla. T.p.+[10]+1–85.

Colo. ¶ Thus endyth thys boke callyd the Register of the wryttys/orygynall and iudiciall, prentyd at London by Wyl-lyam/Rastell, and it is to sell in Fletestrete at the/house of the sayd Wyllyam, or in Poulys/chyrch yarde, or els at temple barre/ at the house of Robert/Redman./❧ Cum priuilegio./

T 310. ¶ Registrum/omnium breuium tam origi-/nalium quam iudi-cialium . . . / ¶ Excusum Londini, apud Ri-/chardum Tot-/ telum./Anno Domini./1553./☞/Cum priuilegio ad imprimen-/ dum solum./ [In border 40]. [The body of this is the same as the preceding.]

Colla. T.p.+[7]+1–321+[4]+1–85+[1].

Colo. (at end of first part) Londini/Ex aedibus Guellelmi Rastell./1531/❧ Cum priuilegio.

Colo. (on last leaf; printed by Tottel? The original colophon left uninked, but the impression visible in one copy) ¶ Thus endyth thys booke callyd the/Regyster of the wryttes orygynall &/iudycyall, pryntyd at London by/Wyllyam Rastell, & fyn-ysshed/the. xxviii. day of Septēber/in the yere of our lorde/ 1531 and in the. xxiii./yere of ye rayne of/our souerayn/lord kyng/Henry/the eyght/with the pryuy/lege of our sayd so-/ uerayn lord grauntyd/to the sayde wyllyam, that/no person imprynt the/same in thys realme/within the space/of. vii. yere/ nexte en-/suyng./

(The original last leaf in the preceding is blank.)

T 311. 1595/Registrum/omnium brevium,/&c. . . . /Londini/In aedi-bus Ianae Yetsweirt relictae/Caroli Yetsweirt Ar. nuper/de-functi./Cum priuilegio Regiae/Maiestatis./ [In McK. 168.]

Colla. T.p.+[8]+[1]–321+1–85.

Colo. None.

T 312. [Graunts ordinances &c. . . . of Romney Marsh. Berthelet, 1543. Herbert.]

T 313. The/Charter/of/Romney/Marsh./London,/Printed by Iohn Wolfe,/1597./
Colla. 1–40.
Colo. None.

T 314. The statutes/whiche the ivsti-/ces of peace, Mayres, Shy-/ryffes, Baylyffes, Consta-/bles & other officers were/of late commaunded by the/kynges maiestye to put in/execution, on peyne of/his graces moste/hyghe indi-/gna-/tion and displea-/sure./ [In border 30.]
Colla. A–D 8's, E 6.
Colo. Londini in aedibvs/Thomae Berthe-/leti regii im-/pres-/soris. excus./Anno. M.D. XXXVIII./Cum priuilegio./

T 315. The Sta-/tutes whi-/che the Iustices of peace,/Mayres, Shyreffes,/Bailiffes, Constables,/and other offycers/were of late/com-/maunded by the kynges/maiesty to put in execu-/tion, on peyne of his/most hygh indig-/nation and dis-/pleasure. [In border 30.]
Colla. A–C 8, D 10.
Colo. Londini in aedibus Thomae Berthe-/leti typis impress./Cum priuilegio ad imprimen-/dum solum./Anno. M.D. XL./

T 316. [Statutes for a Justice. Berthelet, 1543.].

T 317. ¶ Hereafter Ensue certayne Statuts/and ordenaũces of warre made ordey-/ned enacted & establysshed by the most/noble victoryous, and moste Christed/Prynce our moste drade Soueraygne/lorde Kynge Henry the viij./
Colla. A–B 6's, C 4.
Colo. By Rycharde/Pynson, prynter unto his noble grace /The yere of oure lorde. M.CCCCC./and.xiij./

T 318. [Statutes for war. Berthelet, 1544].

T 319. The order for Swannes/both by the Statutes, and by/the auncient Orders and Customes vsed/within the Realme of England./
Colla. [2]+1–5.
Colo. None.

T 320. A true and Sum-/marie reporte of the declaration of/some part of the Earle of Nor-/thumberlands Treasons, &c./ [McK. 193 without initials.] In aedibus C. Barker.
Colla. T.p.+[2]+1–18.
Colo. None.

T 321. ❧ A true report of the/Disputation or rather priuate Confe-/rence had in the Tower of London, with/Ed. Campion Iesuite . . . &c./Imprinted at London/by Christopher Barker, Printer to the/Queenes most excellent Maiestie./Ianuarij. 1. 1583./
Colla. A 2, C–Ff 4's, G 2.
Colo. Imprinted at London/by Christopher Barker, Printer/to the Queenes most excel-/lent Maiestie./Anno 1583./

SECTION 3. OTHER TREATISES

T 322. The/Order of Keeping a/Court Leete, and Court Ba-/ron: &c./By Ionas Adames./ [McK. 273.] Imprinted at London by Thomas Orwin & William Kirckham,/& are to be sold at the little North doore of Saint Paules/Church, at the signe of the Blacke-boy. 1593./

Colla. A–E 4's.
Colo. None.

T 323. Henrici de Bracton de/legibus & consuetudinibus Angliae Libri/ quinq; &c. . . . Londini./Apud Richardum Tottellum/An. do. 1569./Cum priuilegio./

Colla. T.p.+[12]+1–444.
Colo. None.

T 324. ¶ Britton./[No. 11]/Cum priuile-/gio Regali./

Colla. T.p.+[6]+i–CC.lxxxvii.+[1].
Colo. ¶ Imprynted at London in Flete/strete by me Robert Redman dwel/lyng in saynt Dunstones pa-/rysshe at the signe of the/George./ [McK. 3.]

T 325. The Execution of/Iustice in England for maintenance/of pub-, lique and Christian peace,/against certeine stirrers of sedition and adhe-/rents to the traytors and enemies of the/Realme, without any persecution of them/for questions of Religion, as is falsely/reported and published by the/fautors and fosterers of/ their treasons./xvii Decemb./1583./Imprinted at/London. 1583./

Colla. A–E 4.
Colo. None.

T 326. The execution of/Iustice in England for maintenaunce/ of publique and Christian peace,/. . . Secondly/Imprinted at London mense Ian./1583. An. Reg. Eliz. 26./ . . . /[McK. 193 without initials.]

Colla. A–E 4's.
Colo. None.

T 327. The triall of Bastardie/That part of the/second part of Policie, or maner of Gouerne-/ment of the Realme of England: so termed, Spiri-/tuall, or Ecclesiasticall./ . . . /By William Clerke/ . . . London,/Printed by Adam Islip./1594./ [McK. 226.]

Colla. ⁂ 4's, A–O 4's + table.
Colo. None.

T 328. L'authoritie/et iurisdiction des/courts de la maiestie de la/ Roygne: Nouelment collect & compose, per/R. Crompton, . . ./Londini./In aedibus Caroli Yetsweirti Armig./Cum Priuilegio Regiae Maiestatis./Anno Dom̄ 1594./

Colla. T.p.+[3]+1–232.
Colo. Imprinted at London in Fleetestreet, by/Charles Yetsweirt Esq. and are to be sold at his house/within Temple Barre,

neare to the Middle Tem-/ple gate, Anno. Domini 1594./Cum priuilegio Regiae Maiestatis./

T 329. Loffice/et aucthoritie de Iustices/de peace, in part collect per le iades/tresreuerend Iudge, Mounsieur A. Fitzherbert./et ore enlarge per Richard Crompton,/ . . . /1583./. . . / ¶ Imprinted at London by/Richarde Tottill./Cum priuilegio./
Colla. T.p.+[24]+1–206.
Colo. None.

T 330. Loffice/et aucthoritie de Iustices de/peace, in part collect per le tresrueue-/rende Monsier Antho. Fitzherbert, . . . 1584./ At London by/Richard Tottell./
Colla. T.p.+[11]+1–227+[1].
Colo. ¶ Imprinted at London in Fleete-/strete within Temple Barre, at the signe/of the Hand & Starre, by Rychard/Tottel. An. 1584./

T 331. Loffice/& aucthoritie de Iustices de Peace,/in part collect per Sir Anthonie/Fitzherbert Chiualer, iades vn de les Iustices/ . . . 1587./At London by/Richard Tottell.
Colla. T.p.+[11]+1–268.
Colo. None.

T 332. Loffice/& aucthority de Iustices de Peace,/in part collect per Sir Anthonie Fitzherbert/ . . . /Et ore le quart fois inlarge & corrigee per/Richard Crompton un Apprentice/de la Common ley: Et imprimee/lan du grace 1593./ . . . /Imprinted at London by/Richard Tottell./
Colla. T.p.+[9]+1–252.
Colo. None.

T 333. A short declaration of/the ende of Traytors, and false/Conspirators against the state, &/of the duties of Subiectes to theyr/ soueraigne Gouernour . . . /Published by Richard Crompton, an/Apprentice of the common Lawes./. . . /At London,/ Printed by I. Charlewood, for Tho-/mas Gubbin, and Thomas/ Newman. 1587./
Colla. A–F 4.
Colo. None.

T 334. Loffice et/auctoryte des/Iustyces de peas cō-/pyle et extrayte hors/des aunciēt liures si-/bien del comen ley cōe/des estatutz &c./1538./¶ Cum priuilegio regali./ [In border 29. At end of Table, No. 22.]
Colla. T.p.+8+i–cc.vij.+[1].
Colo. ¶ Imprynted/at Lōdon in Fletestrete:/by me Robert Redman, dwel-/lynge at the sygne of the/George, nexte to S./ Dunstones/churche./ ¶ Cum pri-/uilegio Re-/gali./ [McK. 3.]

T 335. The newe/Boke of Iusti-/ces of the peas, by/A.F.K. lately transla/ted out of Fren-/che into En-/glyshe./The yere of our Lord/God. M.D. xxx/viii. The. xxix/day of De-/cembre./Cum priuilegio./ [In border 29.]

Colla. T.p.+[3]+i–lxix (for clxix)+[1].
Colo. ¶ Imprynted/at London in Fletestrete/at the sygne of the George next/to Saynt Dūstones Chur-/che, by me Robert/ Redman./❧/ ¶ Cum Pri-/uilegio re-/gali./ [On reverse, McK. 3.]

T 336. [The newe/Boke of Justi-/ces of peas &c.
Colla.
Colo. . . . by Elizabeth Redman, 31 Jan. 1540/1.]
[The title-page only in British Museum. See Putnam, *op. cit.*, p. 233, who makes two editions: Redman 1540, Elizabeth (Redman) Pickering 1541.]

T 337. ¶ The newe/booke of Iustyces of/Peas, made by Anthony/ Fitzherbard Judge, lately/trāslated out of Fren-/che into Englyshe/The yere of/our Lord/God/M.D.XLI./Cum priuilegio./Ad Imprimendum solum./ [In McK. 86; No. 32 on reverse.]
Colla. T.p.+i–cxc+[4].
Colo. ❧ Imprinted at/Lōdō in Paules church yearde/at the sygne of the maydens/heede by Thomas/Petyt/The yere of our lorde God/M.D.XLI./❧ Cum priuilegio/Ad Imprimendum solum./ [Over portcullis.]

T 338. The new/Booke of Iustices/of Peace, made by An-/thony Fitzherbard Judge/lately translated out of/Frēche into Englyshe/ and newly corrected/The yere of our/Lorde God./M.D. xlviii/ Cum priuile-/gio. ad impri-/mendum solum./ [In border 29.]
Colla. T.p.+[3]+i–Cxxxix.
Colo. ❧ Imprynted/at London in Fletestrete/at the sygne of the George/nexte to saynt Dunstones/Churche by my Wyl-/ lyam Myddylton./ ¶ Cum priuilegio ad/imprimendum solum./ [Over No. 24.]

T 339. ❧ The/new booke of/Iustices of peace,/made by Anthony Fitz/ herbarde Iudge late-/ly translated out of/Frenche into En-/ glyshe, etc./M.D.xlvii./ [In McK. 106.]
Colla. T.p.+[3]+i–C.lxxix.
Colo.❧ Imprynted/at London in Fletestrete/at the sygne of the George/nexte to saynt Dunstones/Churche by me Wyl-/ lyam Powell./ [Over No. 22.]
[Except for the colophon, this seems to be the same as the preceding.]

T 340. The new/bokf of iu-/stices/of peace,/made by Anthony Fitz/ herbarde Iudge lately/trāslated out of French/into Englyshe, and/newly corrected./The yere of/our Lorde/God./M.D.L.I./ [In McK. 106.]
Colla. T.p.+[3]+i–C.lxxxix.
Colo. ❧ Imprynted/at London in Fletestrete/at the signe of the George/Nexte to saynte Dunstones/Churche byWyllyam/ Powell./

T 341. The new boke/of Iustices of peace/made by Anthonie/Fitz Herbard iudge/lately translated out/of Frēch into Eng-/lishe, . . . /1554./

Colla. T.p.+2–173+[3].

Colo. Imprinted at Lon-/don in Fletestrete with-/in temple barre, at the signe of/the hande and starre, by/Richarde Tottle, the/xvii. day of Octo-/ber the yeare of/our lord./1554./

T 342. The/Newe Boke/of iustices of/peace made by Anthonie Fitz/herbard iudge, lately transla-/ted out of Frēch into Eng-/lishe and newlye cor-/rected. The yere/of our Lorde./1554./ ¶ Cum priuilegio ad impri-/mendum solum./

Colla. T.p.+2–173+[4].

Colo. Imprinted at Lon-/don in Fletestrete with-/in temple barre, at the signe of/the hande and starre, by/Richarde Tot-tyll, the/Vii. day of Februa-/ry the yeare of/our Lorde./1560./

T 343. The/Newe Boke/of Iustices of/peace made by Anthonie Fitz/Herbert iudge, lately transla-/ted out of Frēch into Eng-/lishe/ and newlye cor-/rected. The yere/of our Lorde./1554./ ¶ Cum priuilegio ad im-/primendum solum./

Colla. T.p.+2–173+[3].

Colo. Imprinted at London/in Fletestrete within Temple/ barre, at the signe of the/hand and starre, by/Richard Tottill,/ the/xiii day/of Iuly, the/yeare of/our/Lord./1566./

T 344. La nouvelle/Natura brevium/du Iudge tresreverend Monsieur An-/thoine Fitzherbert, . . . /Londini in aedibus Ri-/chardi Tottelli/Anno. 1553./ ¶ Cum Priuilegio ad imprimen-/dum solum./ [In McK. 108.]

Colla. T.p.+[32]+1–271+[1].

Colo. ☞ Imprinted/at London by Richarde Tottyl/dwellyng in Fletestreate at the signe/of the hand and starre wythin/ Temple Barre/.1553./ ¶ Cum Priuilegio ad imprimen-/dum solum.

T 345. La Nouvelle/Natura breviū du Iudge/tresreuerende Monsieur Anthonie/Fitzherbert, dernierement renu/ . . . / ¶ Londini in aedibus Ri-/chardi Tottelli./Anno. Do. 1553./ ¶ Cum priui-legio./ [In border 48.]

Colla. A–D 8's+1–271+[1].

Colo. ¶ Imprinted at London/by Richarde Tottyl dwellyng/ in Fletestreate at the signe of/the Hand and Starre/wythin Temple/Barre./1560./Cum Priuilegio./

T 346. La Nouuelle/Natura breuiū du iudge/tresreuerende Monsieur Anthonie/Fitzherbert, . . . / ¶ Londini in aedibus Ri-/chardi Tottelli./Anno Do. 1553./ ¶ Cum priuilegio./ [In border 48.]

Colla. A–D 8's+1–271+[1].

Colo. Imprinted at London by/Rycharde Tottell, dwelling in/ Fleetstreat at the signe of the/hand and starre within/Temple barre./1567./Cum priuilegio./

T 347. La Nouuelle/Natura breviũ du Iudge/tresreuerende Monsieur Anthonie/Fitzherbert, . . . / ¶ Londini in aedibus Ri-/chardi Tottelli./Añ Do. 1567./Cum priuilegio./ [In border 48.]
Colla. A–D 8's, +1–271+[1].
Colo. Imprinted at London by/Rycharde Tottill, dwelling in/ Fleetestreate, at the signe/of the Hand & Starre within/Temple Barre./1567./Cum priuilegio./

T 348. La Nouuelle/Natura breviũ du Iudge/tresreuerende Monsieur Anthonie/Fitzherbert, denierement renu &/corrige per lacteur, . . . / ¶ Londini in aedibus Ri-/chardi Tottelli./Añ Do. 1567./Cum priuilegio./ [In border 48.]
Colla. A–D 8's+1–271+[1].
Colo. Imprinted at London by/Rycharde Tottill, dwelling in/ Fleetestreate, at the signe/of the Hand & Starre within/Temple Barre./1576./Cum priuilegio./

T 349. La Nouuelle/Natura brevium du Iudge/tresreuerende Monsieur Anthonie/Fitzherbert, denierement renue &/corrige per laucteur, auecques/ . . . / ¶ Londini in aedibus Ri-/chardi Tottelli./Añ Do. 1581./Cum priuilegio./ [In border 48.]
Colla. A–D 8's+1–271+[1].
Colo. ¶ Imprinted at London by/Richarde Tottell, dwelling in/Fleetestreate, at the Signe of the/Hande and Starre within/ Temple Barre./1581./Cum Priuilegio ad impri-/mendum solum./

T 350. Le nouel Natura/Brevium du Iudge tresre-/uerende Monsieur An-/thony Fitzherbert, . . . /Londini;/In Aedibus Richardi Tottelli/Anno Domini/1588./Cum gratia & Priuilegio Regiae/ Maiestatis./
Colla. A–D 8's+1–271+[1].
Colo. ☙ Imprinted at London by/Rychard Tottell, dwelling in Fleete-/streate, at the Signe of the Hande/and Starre within Temple Barre./1588./Cum Priuilegio ad impri-/mendum solum./

T 351. La novel/Natura Brevium du Iudge/tresreuerend Monsieur An-/thony Fitzherbert/ . . . /Londini,/In Edibus Thomae Wight, &/Bonhami Norton./Anno Domini/1598./Cum gratia & Preuilegio Regiae/Maiestatis./
Colla. A–D 8's+1–271+1 bl.
Colo. None.

T 352. Sur/vey-/inge./❦/An. M.D.XXXIX./ [In border 28.]
Colla. A 4+1–60.
Colo. ☙ Londini in aedibus Thome Bertheleti/typis impress. Cum priuilegio/ad imprimendum solum./Anno. M.D.XXXIX./

T 352a. Surueyinge./❦/
Colla. [4] + 1–59.
Colo. I☙ Lindini in edibus Thome Ber-/theleti, prope aquagium sitis Sub intersigno Lucre-/cie Romane/excus./Cum Priuilegio.

T 353. Sur-/vey-/inge/❦/An. M.D.XLVI./ [In border 28.]
Colla. [4]+1–60.

Colo. ☙ Londini in aedibus Thome Bertheleti/typis impress. Cum priuilegio/ad imprimendum solum./Anno. M.D.XLVI./

T 353a. Here be/gynneth a ryght frutefull/matter: and hath to name/ the boke of Surueyinge &/improuemen-/tes./☞ ☜/ [In top and sill piece of No. 29, with made-up sides. The title is preceded by half of the common shell ornament.]

Colla. T.p.+[3]+1–52.

Colo. Imprinted at/London in Fletestrete at the/sygne of the Rose Gar-/lande by Wyllyam Copland./for Rychard Kele./

T 353b. ☙ The Boke of/Surueying, and Improue-/mentes . . . /¶ Im-prynted at London/in Fletestrete nere to s./Dunstanes Church/ by Thomas/Marshe./

Colla. [4]+1-54.

Colo. Imprynted at/London in Fletestrete nere to s. Dun-stanes/Churche by Tho-/mas Marshe./

T 353c. Sur/vey-/inge./❦/Anno Domini,/1567./

Colla. 1–67+[4].

Colo. None.

T 354. Annalium/tam Regum Ed-/wardi quinti, Ri/chardi tertii, & Hen-/rici septimi, quam Hen-/rici ocatui/ . . . / ¶ Studio & Labore Guilhelmi/Fletewoodi Recordatoris/Londinensis./ In aedibus Richardi Tottelli./1579./Cum priuilegio./

Colla. T.p.+[3]+A–Aa 8's, Bb 4.

Colo. ¶ Imprinted at London/in Fletestrete within/Temple Barre, at the signe/of the hande and Starre, by/Richard Tottle, the x./day of September./1579./ ¶ Cum Priuilegio./

T 355. Annalium/tam regum/Edwardi quinti . . . /Studio & Labori Guilhelmi/Fleetewoodi quondam Recor-/datoris Londimensis./ In Aedibus Ianae Yetsweirt./1597./

Colla. A–R 8's.

Colo. None.

T 356. Prenobolis/militis, cognomento Fo-/rescu, qui temporibus Henrici/sexti, floruit, de politica ad/ministratione, . . . / ¶ Excusum Londini tipis Edwardi/Whitechurche, et veneunt in/edibus Henrici Smyth/Bibliopole./Cum priuilegio ad im-/ primendum Solum.

Colla. T.p.+2–71+[3].

Colo. None.

T 357. ¶ A learned/commendation of the politique/lawes of Englande: wherein by moste/pitthy reasons & evident demonstrations they are/plainelye, . . .

Colla. T.p.+[2]+3–132+[3]

Colo. Imprinted at London/in Fletestrete within Temple/ Barre, at the signe of the/hand and starre, by/Rychard Tot-till,/1567./

T 358. ☙ A learned/commendation of the politique/lawes of England: wherein by most/pitthy reasons and evident demonstrations they are/plainelye, . . .

Colla. T.p.+[2]+3–132+[3].
Colo. Imprinted at Lond-/dō in Fletestrete, within Tem-/ple barre, at the signe of the Hande/and Starre, by Richarde/ Tottell. 1573./

T 359. A/learned/Commendation of the po-/litique Lawes of England: wherein,/by most pithie reasons and evident demon-/strations, . . . /London,/Printed by Thomas Wight, and Bonham/ Norton. 1599./Cum Priuilegio./
Colla. T.p.+[2]+3–132+[3].
Colo. None.

T 360. The/lawiers lo-/gike . . . /by/Abraham Fraunce./At London,/ Imprinted by William/How, for Thomas Gub-/bin, and T. Newman./1588./
Colla. T.p.+[8]+1–151.
Colo. None.

T 361. A/direction/or/Preparative to the study/of the Lawe:/ . . . / At London/Printed by Thomas Wight./Anno Domini. 1600./
Colla. T.p.+[3]+1–95.
Colo. None.

T 362. ¶ A treatise cō-/cernygne diuers/of the constitucy/ons prouynciall/and legantines./Printed at London by Tho-/mas Godfray. Cum pri-/uilegio regali./
Colla. A–F 8's, G 6.
Colo. None.

T 363. A treatyse/concernīge/the power/of the clergye, and/the lawes of the/Realme./*/Cū priuilegio regali./
Colla. A–H 8's, I 4.
Colo. Printed at Lōdon by Tho/mas Godfray. Cum pri-/ uilegio Regali./

T 364. De Legibus/Angliae municipalibus Li-/ber, . . . ¶ Laborem queras, vt laborem vites./
Colla. T.p.+[3]+1–371.
Colo. Imprinted at London with-/in Temple Barre, at the signe of the/Hande and Starre, by Richarde/Tottil, the ix. day of October,/Anno. 1583./ ¶ Cum priuilegio ad impri-/mendum solum./

T 365. Tractatus/de legibus et consuetidini-/bus regni Anglie, . . .
Colla. T.p.+[2]+1–113+1 bl.+Q–R 8's.
Colo. Londini in aedi-/bus Richardi/Totteli./Cum priuilegio ad impri-/mendum solum./

T 366. ¶ The auc-/thoritie of al Iustices/of peace . . . /Anno Domini/ 1580./
Colla. T.p.+2–249+[6].
Colo. ¶ Imprinted at London in/Fleetestrete within Temple barre/at ye signe of the Hande & Starre,/by Richard Tottell, the 16. day of Februarie./1579./

T 367. ¶ The Auc-/thoritie of al Iustices/of peace, with diuers/warrants . . . newly set foorth/by Iohn Kitchin of Graies Inne . . . /Anno Domini/1589./
Colla. T.p.+2–250+[6].
Colo. ¶ Imprinted at London in/Fleetestrete, within Temple barre,/at ye signe of the Hand & Starre,/by Richard Tottell, the/16. day of Februarie./1579./Cum priuilegio ad impri-/mendum solum./

T 368. Le court/Leete, et Court Ba-/ron, collect per Iohn/Kytchin, . . .
Colla. T.p.+[7]+1–250+[6].
Colo. Imprinted at London in/Fleetestrete, within Temple barre,/at ye signe of the Hand & Starre,/by Richard Tottell, the/16. day of Februarie/1579./Cum priuilegio.

T 369. ❧ Le court/Leete, et Court Baron,/collect per Iohn Kytchin . . . / ¶ In aedibus Richardi/Tottelli. Octobris quarto./Anno Dñi. 1580./Cum priuilegio ad imprimen-/dum solum./
Colla. T.p.+[5]+1–250+[6].
Colo. ¶ Imprinted at London in/Fleetestrete, within Temple barre,/at ye signe of the Hand & Starre,/by Richard Tottell, the/10. day of April./1580./Cum priuilegio ad impri-/mendum solum./

T 370. ❧ Le court/Leete, et Court Baron,/collect per Iohn Kytchin de/ . . . / ¶ In aedibus Richardi/Tottelli. Octobris quarto./Anno Dñi. 1581./Cum priuilegio ad imprimen-/dum solum.
Colla. T.p.+[5]+1–216.
Colo. None.

T 371. ¶ Le Court leete, et court/Baron, collect per Iohn Kit-/chyn, . . . / ¶ In aedibus Richardi Tottelli, Maij/sexto, Anno Do. 1585./ ¶ Cum priuilegio ad imprimendum solum./
Colla. T.p.+[11]+1–364.
Colo. None.

T 372. Le Court leete & Court/Baron collect per Iohn Kit-/chin, . . . /In aedibus Richardi Totelli,/Anno a virgineo partu,/ 1587./Primo Martij./Cum priuilegio ad/imprimendum solum./
Colla. T.p.+[11]+1–254.
Colo. None.

T 373. Le Court leete & Court/Baron collect per Iohn Kit-/chin, . . . /In aedibus Richardi Totelli,/Anno a virgineo partu,/ 1592./Primo Iulij./Cum priuilegio ad/imprimendum solum./
Colla. T.p.+[11]+1–254.
Colo. None.

T 374. ❧ Le court/leete et court/Baron collect per Iohn Kitchin/ . . . /In aedibus Thomae Wight, &/Bonhami Norton./1598./ Cum Priuilegio.
Colla. T.p.+[11]+1–289+3.
Colo. None.

T 375. ¶ Retourna/Brevium./Nouelment corrigee,/ . . . ¶ In aedibus Richardi Tottelli./1581./ ¶ Cum priuilegio./

Colla. T.p.+1–58+[2].
Colo. None.

T 376. Retourna/Brevium/Nouelment corrigee,/ . . . Collectes/per Iohannum Kitchin . . . / ¶ In aedibus Richardi Tottelli./ 1585./Cum priuilegio./
Colla. T.p.+2–58+[2].
Colo. None.

T 377. Retorna Bre-/uium nouelment/corrigee,/ . . . ¶ Collectes per Iohannem Kitchin/ . . . / ¶ In aedibus Richardi Tottelli./ 1587./Cum priuilegio.
Colla. T.p.+[1]+257–289+[3].
Colo. None.

T 378. Retorna/Breuium nouelment/corrigee,/. . . Collectes per Iohannem Kitchin/. . . /In Aedibus Richardi Tottelli./1592./Cum Priuilegio.
Colla. T.p.+256–289+[3].
Colo. None.

T 379. APXAIONOMIA,/sive/depriscis anglo-/rum legibus libri, . . . / Londini,/ex officina Joannis Daij./An. 1568./ ¶ Cum gratia et priuilegio/Regiae Maiestatis per Decennium./

Colla. A–D 4's, E 3+1–140+Qq II–IIII.
Colo. None.

T 380. The/Duties of Consta-/bles Borsholders, Tything-/men, and such other lowe Mi-/nisters of the Peace./. . . /Collected and penned by William Lambard/of Lincolnes Inne Gent. 1582./ [McK. 238.] ¶ Printed at London, by Roger Warde./
Colla. T.p.+2–83.
Colo. None.

T 381. The/Duties of Consta-/bles, Borsholders, Tithing-/men, and such other lowe/Ministers of the Peace./ . . . /Collected and penned by William Lambarde of/Lincolnes Inne Gent. 1582/ [McK. 202 b.] /Imprinted at London by Rafe Newberie/and Henrie Midleton. 1583./ [McK. 215.]
Colla. Paged, 1–78.
Colo. None.

T 382. The/Duties of Consta-/bles, Borsholders, Tithing-/men, and such other lowe/Ministers of the Peace./ . . . by William Lambarde . . . / [McK. 202 b.] Imprinted at London by Rafe Newberie/and Henrie Midleton, 1584./ [McK. 215.]
Colla. T.p.+[1]+4–78 (paged).
Colo. None.

T 383. The/Duties of Constables,/Borseholders, Tythingmen, and/ such other lowe Ministers/of the Peace./ . . . by William Lambard . . . /[McK. 202 b.]/Imprinted at London by Rafe Newberie/and Henrie Midleton, 1587./

Colla. T.p.+[1]+3–80 (paged).
Colo. None.

T 384. The/Duties of Constables, Borseholders . . . Imprinted at London by Rafe Newberie/and Henrie Midleton, 1591./
Colla. T.p.+[1]–80.
Colo. None.

T 384a. The/Duties of Constables, Bor-/sholders. . . . / ¶ Imprinted at London bẏ/Ralph Newberie. 1591.
Colla. T.p.+3–80.
Colo. None.

T 385. The/Dueties of Constables, Borshol-/ders, Tythingmen, and such/other lowe Ministers/of the Peace./ . . . /First collected and penned by William/Lamberd of Lincolnes Inne Gent. 1582./and now enlarged by the same Authour./Imprinted at London by/Charles Yetsweirt Esq./1594./Cum priuilegio Regiae/ Maiestatis./
Colla. Paged 1–80.
Colo. None.

T 386. The Dueties/of/Constables, Borsholders,/Tythingmen,/ . . . / London/Printed by Thomas Wight, and/Bonham Norton, 1599./
Colla. T.p. 2–52.
Colo. None.

T 387. Eirenarcha:/or of/The Office of the/Iustices of Peace, in/two Bookes:/ . . . /By William Lambard/ . . . /At London:/ Imprinted by Ra: Newbery and/H. Bynneman, by the ass. of/ R. Tot./& Chr. Bar./Anno. Dom. 1581./ [In border, McK. 185.]
Colla. T.p.+Aii–iiii+1–511+L18.
Colo. None. [No. 35 on last leaf.]

T 388. Eirenarcha:/or of/The office of the/Justices of Peace, in/two Bookes:/Gathered 1579. and now/reuised, and first published, in the/24. yeere of the peaceable/reigne . . . /By William Lambard . . . /At London:/Imprinted by Ra. Newberry, and/H. Bynneman, by the ass. of/R. Tot. and Chr. Bar./ Anno Dom./1582./ [In McK. 185.]
Colla. T.p.+[3]+1–511+L18's.
Colo. None. [No. 35 on reverse of last leaf.]

T 389. Eirenarcha:/or of/The office of the Iusti-/ces of Peace, in two/ Bookes:/ . . . /By William Lambard, . . . /At London:/ Imprinted by Ralf. Newbery,/and H. Binneman, by the assig./of Richard Tottell, and/Chr. Barker./1582./
Colla. T.p.+[3]+1–511+[7].
Colo. None. [No. 35 on reverse of last leaf.]

T 390. Title page lacking.
Colla. T.p.+[3]+1–511+[8].
Colo. Imprinted at London for/Rafe Newberie./1583./

T 391. Eirenarcha:/or of/The office of the Iustices/of Peace, . . . / By William Lambard,/ . . . /At London,/Printed by Ralph Newbery./Cum priuilegio./Anno Domini,/1588./ [In McK. 185.]
Colla. T.p.+2+1–627+Ss III–VIII, Tt–Yy 8's, Zz 6's.
Colo. Imprinted at London/by Ralph Newbery./1588./ [McK. 248.]

T 392. Eirenarcha:/or of/The office of the Iustices/of Peace, in foure/ Bookes:/ . . . /At London,/Printed by Ralph Newbery,/ Cum priuilegio./Anno Domini,/1591/ [In McK. 185.]
Colla. T.p.+[3]+1–627+Ss iii-VIII, Tt–ZZ 8's Last leaf blank.
Colo. Imprinted at London/by Ralph Newbery./1588./ [McK. 248.]

T 393. Eirenarcha:/or of/The office of the Iustices/of Peace in foure/Bookes./ . . . /By William Lam-/bard . . . /At London,/Printed by Ralph Newbery./Cum priuilegio./Anno Domini, 1592./ [In McK. 185.]
Colla. T.p.+1–600+Pp V–VIII, Qq–Vv 8's.
Colo. None.

T 394. Eirenarcha:/Or of/The office of the Iustices/of Peace in foure/ Bookes./Gathered 1579. first pub-/lished 1581: . . . / ¶ By William Lambard/ . . . /At London/Printed by Ralph Newbery./ ¶ Cum Priuilegio./Anno Domini,/1594./ [In McK. 185.]
Colla. T.p.+1–606+Qq–Vv 8's, Xx 4's.
Colo. None.

T 395. Eirenarcha:/Or of/The Office of the Iustices/of Peace, in foure/Bookes./First gathered 1579. pub-/lished 1581. and now fourthly/revised, corrected, . . . /By William Lam-/bard . . . /At London,/Printed by Thomas Wight, and/Bonham Norton, 1599./ ¶ Cum priuilegio./
Colla. T.p.+1–606+Rr–Xx 8's, Yy 3.
Colo. None.

T 396. A perambulation/of Kent:/ . . . by William Lambard, . . . / ¶ Imprinted at Lon-/don for Ralphe Newberie,/dwelling in Fleetestreete a/litle above the/Conduit./Anno. 1576./
Colla. T.p.+[8]+1–435.
Colo. Imprinted at London by Henrie/Middleton, for Rafe New-/bery dwelling in Fleetestreate, a litle/above the Con-duite./Anno Domini. 1576./

T 397. A Perambulation/of Kent:/ . . . by/William Lambarde . . . / . . . /Imprinted at London,/by Edm. Bollifant./1596./
Colla. T.p.+[4]+1–588+[3].
Colo. None.

T 398. a i blank; on reverse cut 1.
Colla. a^8, b^8, c^8, d^6, e^8, f^8, g^8, h^8, i^8, k^6, l^8, m^8, n^8, o^8, p^8, q^8, v^8, s^8, v^8, x^8, y^8, A^8, B^8, C^8, D^8, F^8, G^8, H^8, I^8, K^8, L^8, M^8, N^8, P^8, Q^8, R^8, S^{10}, aa^8, bb^8, cc^8, in 8's: d, k, p, t^6, z^6, E^6, O^6, dd^{10}.
Colo. None.

T 399. Constitutiones priuin/ciales ecclesie anglicāe./per. d Wilhelmū Lyndewode/utrinsqz iuris doctorē edite./Incipiunt feliciter./ [Over cut of bishop.]
Colla. A–X 8's.
Colo. Opus Preseus Fabricatum/est. Et diligenter correctum/ Per Wynandum de worde./Apud Westmonasteriū. In do/mo caxston./Anno Incarna/cionis Millesimo quadringē/tesimo nonagesimo sexto./Ultima die May acabatūqz./Gloria deo./ [McK. 2 on reverse.]

T 400. No title page. De sūma trinitate & fide catholica./
Colla. A–R 8's.
Colo. Impressum per Richardū Pynson./ [McK. 3.]

T 401. No title page.
Colla. a–v 8's, A 8, B 4.
Colo. Emprinted by Richard Pynson./ [McK. 3.]

T 402. Constitutiones prouincia-/les ecclesie anglicae. per d. Wil-/ helmum Lyndewode utriusqz/iuris doctorem edite. Iucipiunt/ feliciter.
Colla. A–S 8's.
Colo. Istud opus presens fabricatum est./Diligenter correctum. Impressum ꝑ/Wynandum de worde apud westmo-/ nasterium. Anno millesimo quadrin-/gentisimo nonagesimo nono die deci-/ma quinta Aprilis. [McK. 46 b.]

T 403. Prouinciale seu: Constitu/tiones Anglie . . . &c.
Colla. T.p.+ii–Cxcii,+ Table, a 6, b 6, c 8.
Colo. ¶ Explicitū est opus magistri wilhelmi lynde-/wode super cōstitutiones prouinciales Anglie summa diligen/tia & accurationi magr̄i Andree Bocard cū annotationibus et/castigationibus debitis, cūqz summariis suis locis ꝓpositis In/inclyta parisiana academia. Anno salutis nostre Millesimo/quingentesimoprimo. Maij vero die. xxviij./

T 404. Constitutiones legitime seu legatine regionis anglicani. [Cut of St. George.]
Colla. T.p.+Aii[viii]+B 8+ii–clv.
Colo. . . . Coimpressa/sunt solertissima accuratione atqz arte Magistri/wulfgangi hopilii: impēsis eiusdem: et ꝓbissimi/ bibliopole Ioānis cōfluetini: in inclyta Parrhi-/siorum academia. Ad laudem et gloriam . . . An-/no domini Millesimo quingentesimo quarto: ad/idus Semptembris./

T 405. Prouinciale, seu Cōstitutiones An-/glie: . . . ¶ Venales habentur Londoñ. apud bibliopolas/In Cimiterio sancti Pauli: in signo sanctissime/Trinitatis et sancte Anne matris marie. [In made up border containing McK. 16 & 17.]
Colla. T.p.+ii–Clxxxix.+Table,+[12] 6's.
Colo. ¶ Explicit preclarum opus wilhelmi Lyn/dewode eruditissimi viri, super constitutiones prouinciales Anglie:/ summa cura atqz diligentia wolffgangi Hopylii reuisum, emēdatū,/atqz In inclita Parisiorū Academia. Impressum: una cum annota/tionibus debitis: cūqz summariis suis locis prepositis.

Impēsis vero/et sumptibus honesti mercatoris Londoñ. wilhelmi Brettoñ. Anno/salutis nostre Millesimo quingētesimo quinto. xxiij. Martii./

T 406a. De summa trinitate z fide catholica./
No t.p.
Colla. A–E 8, F 10, last p. bl.
Colo. None.

T 406b. ℭ Hic incipiunt constitutiones dñi Othonis./
Colla. A–D 8, E 4.
Colo. ℭ Expliciunt constitutiones Legatum/cum Iohanne Othone. Impressum/per me Richardum Pynson./ [McK. 9 b.]

T 407. ℭ Incipiunt opera super cōstitu-/tiones prouinciales & Othonis./
Colla. A–M 8's.
Colo. Expliciūt constitutiones Legatum cum Iohan/ne O-thone. Impresse Londoñ. per me wynandum/de worde, in the fletestrete. in signo solis commorā/tem. Anno dñi M. CCCCC. xvii./ [McK. 25.]

T 408a. Legatine seu Constitutiones legitime/ . . . / ℭ Venales habentur Londoñ apud bibliopolas/In Cimiterio sancti Pauli. In signo sanctissime/Trinitatis, et sancte Anne matris marie./
Colla. T.p.+ii–lxxvi.
Colo. None.

T 408b. Prouinciale seu Cōsti-/tutiones Anglie . . . /Venales habētur Londoñ. in cimiterio san/cti Pauli: apud Franciscum bryckman./

Colla. T.p.+ii–cclv.+Table, A–C 8's, D 4.
Colo. ℭ Explicit preclarū opus Wilhelmi Lin-/dewode eruditissimi viri super constitutiones pro-/uinciales Anglie: summa cura atqz diligentia Chri/stophori Endouieñ. Antwerpie impressum. una cū/annotationibus debitis. cunqz summariis suis lo-/cis prepositis. Impensis vero Francisci Brickman/honesti mercatoris Anno salutis nostre Millesimo/quingentesimo vicesimo quinto. xx. die Decembris./

T 409. ℭ Incipiunt opera sup constitu-/tiones prouinciales et Othonis/
Colla. A–M 8's.
Colo. ℭ Habes candide lector has Legati constitutiones/cum Ioanne Othone nuper impressas/atqz cura/vigilantissima recognitas Londini apud huma-/nissimum virum winandum de worde. In vico fle-/testrete sub signo solari. Anno ab incarnatione xpi/M.D.xxix. vigesimo octauo die mensis Nouēbris./ [McK. 46 b.]

T 410. Constitu-/tions puincialles,/and of Otho, and/Octhobone,/ Translated in to/Englyshe./Cum priuilegio./ [In border, McK. 81.]
Colla. T.p.+[11]+woodcut+1–184.
Colo. ℭ Imprynted at London in Fle/testrete by me Robert Redman,/Anno. M.D. xxxiiii./Cum priuilegio./

T 411. Constitu/tiones Angliae pro-/uinciales ex diversis cantuariensium Archie-/piscoporum Synodalibus decretis, per Guili-/elmum Lyndewode, . . . Londini/Excudebat Thomas Marshe./2557.
Colla. T.p.+[19]+1–282+[1]–76+[3].
Colo. None.

T 412. A/Brefe Collection/of the Lawes of the Forest:/ . . . By Iohn Manwood,/ . . .
Colla. T.p.+[3]+1–372.
Colo. None. No name, no date. Probably privately printed.

T 413. A treatise/and discourse of/the Lawes of the Forrest: . . . / . . . By Iohn Manwood./At London/Printed by Thomas Wight and/Bonham Norton. 1598./Cum priuilegio./
Colla. T.p.+[7]+1–167+[7].
Colo. None.

T 414. A traictise/declaryng and plain-/ly prouyng, that the preten-/ded marriage of Priestes, and pro-/fessed persones, is no marriage . . . /By Thomas Martin, Doctour/of the Ciuile Lawes./¶ Excusum Londini in/aedibus Roberti Caly, Typographi./Mense Maii Anno. 1554./Cū priuilegio./ [In border 42.]
Colla. T.p.+[3]+A–Mm 4's.
Colo. None.

T 415. ¶ Incipit perutilis/tractat' magistri Iohīs Parkins/ . . . in edibus Roberti/Redman Anno salut' nr̄e/1528 die vero. 24. Octobris./ ¶ Cum gratia & pri-/uilegio a Rege/indulto./ [in made-up border].

Colla. T.p.+3+B–Y 8's [last two leaves blank.]
Colo. . . . in edi-/bus Roberti Redman/Anno salut' nostre 1528/die vero. 24. Octobris./ [No. 23 on reverse.]

T 416. ¶ Incipit perutilis tracta-/tus magistri Io. Parkins, &c. . . . / in edi-/bus Roberti Redm̄/An. dn̄i. 1532./mēse Octo/bris./ Cum privilegio./ [In made-up border. No. 34 on reverse.]
Colla. T.p.+[3]+1–188.
Colo. ¶ Impressus Londini in edibus/Roberti Redman. anno/dn̄i. 1532. mense/Octobr̄./

T 417. ¶ Incipit perutilis/tractatus magistri Ioh./Parkins interioris Tem-/pli socii sine explanatio/quorundam capitulorum/in tabula huius libelli co/tento grandi cum dilige-/tia et studio ad immenum/in formacionem valde ne-/cessaria nouiter edita/ magna diligentia/reuisa ac castigata/in edibus Wil-/helmi Myd-/dylton/Anno dn̄i. 1541./Cum priuilegio.
Colla. A 4, 1–188.
Colo. ¶ Impressus Londini in edibus/Wilhelmi Myddylton An./dn̄i. 1541. mense/Augusti./

T 418. ❧ Incipit per/utilis tractatus/magistri Iohannis Parkins, . . . in/edibus Henrici/Smyth./An. M.D.XLV./

Colla. T.p.+[3]+1–163.
Colo. ¶ Imprintyd at London by me Hen-/ry Smyth, dwellyng wyth/out Temple barre in saint/Clementes paryshe./

T 419. ¶ Here beginneth/a verie Profitable booke of/Master Iohn Perkins/ . . . /Londini in Aedibus Ricar-/di Totteli./1555./ Cum priuilegio ad im-/primendum solum./
Colla. T.p. 4+[19]+1–168.
Colo. Imprinted at Lon-/don in Fletestrete with-/in temple barre, at the signe of/the hande and starre, by/Richarde Tottle./

T 420. ¶ A profitable/booke of Maister Iohn/Perkins felow of the/ inner Temple,/ . . . /Apud Richardum/Tottell./Cum priuilegio./
Colla. T.p.+[19]+1–168.
Colo. Imprinted at London/in Fletestrete within Tem-/ple barre at the signe of the/hand & starre, by Ri-/chard Tottil./ 1567/

T 421. A profitable/Booke of Master John/Perkins felow of the Inner/ Temple treating of/the lawes of/England./Apud Richardum/ Tottell./Cum priuilegio./
Colla. A–B 8's, C 4, 1–168.
Colo. ¶ Imprinted at London in/Fletestrete within Temple Barre,/at the signe of the hande/and starre, by Ry-/charde Tottil./1567./

T 422. A profitable/Booke of Master/Iohn Perkins,/ . . . / ¶ Apud Richardum/Tottell./ ¶ Cum priuilegio./
Colla. T.p.+[19]+1–168.
Colo. ¶ Imprinted at London in/Fleetestrete, within Temple barre/at the signe of the hande and/Starre, by Richarde Tottel./ the 14. daye of/December./1576./

T 423. A profitable/Booke of Master/Iohn Perkins, . . . / ¶ Apud Richardum/Tottell./ ¶ Cum priuilegio./
Colla. T.p.+[19]+1–168.
Colo. ¶ Imprinted at London in/Fletestreete within Temple barre/at the signe of the Hand & Starre,/by Richarde Tottel, the/last day of August./1581./

T 424. A profitable/Booke of Master Iohn/Perkins, . . . ¶ Apud Richardum/Tottell./Cum priuilegio./
Colla. T.p.+[19]+1–168.
Colo. ¶ Imprinted at London in/Fletestreete within Temple barre/at the signe of the Hand & Starre/by Richarde Tottell./ 1586./

T 425. A profitable/Booke of Master Iohn Perkins, . . . /London./ ¶ Apud Richardum Tottell./Cum priuilegio./
Colla. A–B 8's+C 4+1–168.
Colo. ¶ Imprinted at London in/Fleetestreat within Temple barre,/at the signe of the Hand and/Starre by Richard/Tottel. 1593./

T 426. ¶ A profitable/booke of Maister Iohn/Perkins felowe of the/ inner Temple trea-/ting of the law-/es of Eng-/lande./Apud Richardum/Totell./ ¶ Cum priuilegio ad impri/mendum solum/

Colla. A–B 8's+C 4+1–165+[2].

Colo. ℭ Imprinted/at London in Fletestrete/within Temple barre, at the/signe of the hand & starre,/by Richard Tottel./

T 427. ¶ A profitable/booke of Maister Iohn/Perkins felowe of the/ inner Temple trea-/ting of the law-/es of Eng-/lande./Apud Richardum/Totell./ ¶ Cum priuilegio./

Colla. T.p.[19]+1–168.

Colo. Imprinted at Lon-/don in fletestrete with-/in temple barre, at the signe of/the hande and starre by/Richarde Tottle.

T 428. A profi-/table booke/of Master Iohn Per-/kins, Fellow of the/ Inner Temple./Treating of the Lawes of/England./Londini,/In aedibus Ianae Yetsweirt./Cum priuilegio./1597./

Colla. A–B 12's (table)+1–168.

Colo. None.

T 429. ℭ A newe/boke of Presidentes in/maner of a Register . . ./ 1543./

Colla. T.p.+aii–iv+[i]–cxviii.

Colo. Impressum Lōdini in edib' Edwardi/Whytchurche. Cum priuilegio ad/imprimendum solum: per/septennium./ ℭ These bookes be to sell at the west dore/of Paules, by Wyll-yam Tylotson./

T 429a. ℭ A new/boke of Presiden/tes, in maner of a Re-/gister . . ./

Colla. [8]+[i]–cliii.

Colo. ℭ Imprinted at London by/Edwarde Whitchurche./ Cum priuilegio ad impri-/mendum solum./Per Septenniū.

T 430. ℭ A booke of/Presidētes, . . ./Officina Richardi Graftoni./

Colla. T.p.+[19]+i–cc.lxxxviii.

Colo. Londini/Ex officina Richardi Graftoni/clarissimo principi Edouardo/a Typographia/Cum priuilegio ad impri-/mendum solum./

T 431. ☙ A Boke/of presidentes/ . . . /

Colla. A–B 8's+[1]-

Colo. ☙ Imprinted at/London in Fletestrete at the signe/ of the George next to Saynte/Dunstons churche by Wyl-/lyam Powell./

T 432. ℭ A boke of/Presidentes, . . . /❦/Anno Domini. 1550./

Colla. T.p.+[11]+A–V 8's, X 4's.

Colo. Londini/Ex officina Richardi Graftoni/clarissimo principi Eduar-/do a Typographia./Cum priuilegio ad impri-/mendum solum./

T 433. ❧ A boke/of presydentes/ . . .

Colla. T.p.+[15]+[i]–cc.xvi.

Colo. ℭ Imprinted at London in Elete/strete at the sygne of the George nexte to saint/Dunstons churche by Wyl/lyam Powell./ ℭ Cum priuilegio ad imprimendum solum./

T 434. ☙ A boke/of presydentes,/ . . . /
Colla. A–B 8's+[i]–clix.
Colo. ℭ Imprinted at London in Flete/strete at the sygne of the Prin-/ces armes by Thomas/Marshe./Anno. M.D.L.V./

T 435. ☙ A boke/of Presidentes/ . . . /
Colla. A–B 8's+[i]–Clix.
Colo. ℭ Imprinted at London in Flete/strete at the sygne of the Prin-/ces armes by Thomas/Marshe./Anno. M.D.L.V./

T 436. ¶ A Boke of presi-/dentes,/ . . . /
Colla. A–B 8's+[i]–clix.
Colo. ℭ Imprinted at London/in Fletestrete within Temple/barre, at the signe of the hande/and starre, by Richard/Tottyll./Anno. 1559./

T 437. T.p. lacking.
Colla. A 8, B 8, i–clix.
Colo. ℭ Imprinted at London/in Fletestrete within Temple/barre, at the signe of the hande/and starre, by Richard/Tottyll./Anno. 1561./

T 438. ☙ A Boke/of Presidentes exactelye written/in manner of a register newly/Imprinted augmen-/ted and corrected/ . . .
Colla. T.p.+[15]+i–clix.
Colo. ℭ Imprinted at London/in Fletestrete within Temple/barre, at the signe of the hande/and starre, by Richard/Tottyll./Anno. 1562./

T 439. ¶ A booke of/presidents,/ . . . /Anno do. 1569./Cum priuilegio./
Colla. A–B 8's+1–159.
Colo. ¶ Imprinted at London/in Fletestrete within Temple/Barre at the signe of the hand/and Starre by Ry-/charde Tottyl./1569./

T 440. ¶ A Booke of/Presidents/ . . . . /¶ Anno Domini/1572./In aedibus Richardi/Tottelli./¶ Cum Priuilegio./
Colla. [16]+1–159/.
Colo. ¶ Imprinted at London in/Fletestrete within Temple Barre,/at the signe of the hande/and starre by Ry-/chard Tottil./1572.

T 441. ¶ A Booke of/Presidens exactly wrytten/in maner of a Register . . . / ¶ Anno Domini./1575./ ¶ In aedibus Richardi/Tottelli./ ¶ Cum priuilegio/
Colla. T.p.+[15]+1–159.
Colo. ¶ Imprinted at London in/Fletestrete within Temple barre,/at the signe of the hande/and starre, by Ry-/chard Tottil./1575./

T 442. ¶ A booke of/Presidens,/ . . . / ¶ Anno Domini./1576./ ¶ In aedibus Richardi/Tottelli./ ¶ Cum priuilegio./
Colla. A–B 8's+1–159.
Colo. ¶ Imprinted at London in/Fleetestrete, within Temple barre,/at the signe of the Hand/and Starre, by Ri-/chard Tottell./1576./

T 443. ¶ A Booke of/Presidents, . . . / ¶ Anno Domini./1578./ ¶ In aedibus Richardi/Tottelli./ ¶ Cum priuilegio./
Colla. A–B 8's+1–159.
Colo. ¶ Imprinted at London in/Fleetestrete, within Temple Barre,/at ẏͤ signe of the Hand & Starre,/by Rychard Tottell, the/7. day of December./1581./

T 444. ☞ A Booke of/Presidents, . . . /Anno Domini./1583./ ¶ Imprinted at London, by/Iohn Charlewood, the assigne of/Richard Tottle/
Colla. T.p.+[15]+[i]–clix.
Colo. None.

T 445. ¶ A booke of Pre-/sidents, . . . / ¶ Anno Domini./1584./ ¶ In aedibus Richardi/Tottelli./ ¶ Cum priuilegio ad impri-/mendum solum./
Colla. T.p.+[11]+1–184, 4 bl.
Colo. Imprinted at London in Fleete-/strete within Temple Barre, at the signe/of the Hand and Starre, by Rychard/Tottel. An. 1584./ ¶ Cum priuilegio ad imprimendum solum./

T 446. A Booke of Pre-/sidents, . . . /Anno Domini./1586./ ¶ In aedibus Richardi/Tottelli./ ¶ Cum priuilegio ad imprimen-/dum solum./
Colla. T.p.+[11]+1–184.
Colo. ¶ Imprinted at London in Fleete-/strete within Temple Barre, at the signe/of the Hand and Starre, by Rychard/Tottel. An. 1584./Cum priuilegio ad imprimendum solum./

T 447. A/Booke of/Presidents/ . . . /Imprinted at London by/Thomas Wight. 1600./Cum Priuilegio./
Colla. T.p.+[7]+1–123.
Colo. None.

T 448. A colleccion/of entrees,/ . . . In aedibus Richar-/di Tottell./ Cum priuilegio./Anno salutis M.D.LXVI./decimo quarto die Maij./ [In border, McK. 196.]

Colla. T.p.+[4]+1–627.
Colo. In aedibus Richardi Tottell./Cum priuilegio./Anno salutis. 1566. decimoquarto Maij./

T 449. A collection/of entrees./ . . . / ¶ In aedibus Richardi/Tottel./ Cum priuilegio./ ¶ Anno. 1574. vicesimo se-/cundo Ianuarij./ [In border, McK. 196.]
Colla. T.p.+[3]+1–627.

Colo. In aedibus Richardi Tottell./Cum priuilegio./Anno dñi. 1574./

T 450. 1596./❧ A collection/of Entrees,/etc. . . . / ❡ In aedibus Iane Yetsweirt relictae Caroli/Yetsweirt Ar. nuper defuncti./Cum priuilegio Regiae/Maiestatis./ [In border, McK. 168, omitting mermaid.]
Colla. T.p.+[i]+1–704.
Colo. None.

T 451. Exposiciones tminoꝝ legū angloꝝ. et/natura breuium cū diuersis casibus re/gulis & fundamentis legum. . . .
Colla. A 8, B–F 6's, G 4, Folio.
Colo. /[McK. 37]./❡ Impryntyd at Lōdō ī chepe/syde at powlys gate . ˙ . ˙ . /Cum priuilegio regali . ˙ . / [McK. 37 on reverse.]

T 452. Exposiciones t̄minoꝝ legū angloꝝ. Et/natura breuiū cū diuersis casibus re-/gulis & fundamentis legum . . .
Colla. A 8, B–F 6's, G 4. Folio.
Colo. /[McK. 37.]/ ❡ Imprynted at Lōdō ī chepe/syde at powlys gate./Cum priuilegio regali . ˙ ./ [McK. 37 on reverse.]

T 453. Expositiones terminorū le-/gum anglorū. . . .
Colla. T.p.+[7]+i–ciii+[1].
Colo. Impressum. xv. die Iulii. anno dñi/M.V.C.xxvii./Cum priuilegio regali./ [Nos. 20 & 21 on last leaf.]

T 454. The exposicions/of the termes of the lawes of Eng-/land, . . . / 1563/ ¶ In aedibus Richar-/di Tottell./Cum priuilegio./
Colla. T.p.+[2]+1–140+[3].
Colo. Imprinted at London/in Fletestreete, within/Temple barre, at the/signe of the hand/& starre, by Ry-/chard Tottell./ the. xxix. day of Aprill./1563./Cum priuilegio./

T 455. The exposicions/of the termes of the lawes of Eng-/land, . . . / 1567/ ¶ In aedibus Richar-/di Tottell./Cum priuilegio./
Colla. T.p.+[2]+1–140+[3].
Colo. Imprinted at London/in Fletestrete within Teple/barre at the signe of the hand &/starre, by Richarde/Tottil, the 17. of/February./1567./Cum priuilegio./

T 456. The expositions of the Termes/of the Lawes of Englande, . . . /1572./ ¶ In aedibus Richar-/di Tottel./Cum priuilegio./
Colla. T.p.+[2]+1–138+[2].
Colo. Imprinted at London/in Fletestrete within Temple/ Barre at the signe of the hand/and Starre by Ry-/charde Tottyl./1572./

T 456a. ❡ The expositions of the termes/of the lawes of Englande. . . ./ 1575./ ❡ In aedibus Richar-/di Tottel./ ❡ Cum priuilegio./
Colla. T.p.+[2]+1–138+[2].
Colo. ❡ Imprinted at London/in Fletestrete within Temple/ Barre at the signe of the Hand/and Starre by Ry-/chard Tottyll./1575./

T 457. ¶ An exposi-/tion of certaine difficult/and obscure wordes, and termes of/the lawes of this Realme, . . . / ¶ In aedibus Richar-/di Tottelli./ ¶ Cum priuilegio./

Colla. T.p.+[3]+1–211.

Colo. ¶ Imprinted at Lon-/don, in Fleetestrete within/Temple Barre, at the Signe of/the Hand and Starre/by Richarde/Tottell./1579./

T 458. An/exposition of certaine diffi-/cult and obscure words and termes/of the Lawes of this Realme, . . . /In aedibus Richardi/Tottelli./Cum priuilegio./1592./

Colla. T.p.+[3]+1–196.

Colo. None.

T 459. An/exposition of cer-/taine difficult and obscure words,/and termes of the Lawes of this Realme, . . . /At London/Printed by th' Assignee of Charles/Yetsweirt Esq. deceased./Cum priu-ilegio Regiae/Maiestatis./1595./

Colla. T.p.+[3]+1–192.

Colo. None.

T 460. An/Exposition/of certaine diffi-/cult and obscure wordes, and/Termes of the Lawes of this Realme . . . /At London/Printed by Thomas Wight,/and Bonham Norton./1598./Cum priuilegio Regiae/Maiestatis./

Colla. T.p.+[4]+1–198.

Colo. None.

T 461. ¶ Dialogus de/fundamentis./legum An-/glie et de/conscientia./

Colla. T.p. ii–xci+[1]. No foliation on title page.

Colo. ¶ Explicit dialogus de fun-/damentis legum anglie & de consci/entia. Impressum Londini p/Iohannem Rastell. An/no Dñi. M.v.C./xxviii./ ¶ Cum priuilegio Regali./ [McK. 37 on reverse.]

T 462. Folio primo/ ¶ Dialogus de/fundamentis/legum An-/glie et de/conscientia./

Colla. T.p.+ii–xci+[1]+two leaves of errata.

Colo. (On reverse of first of unnumbered pages.) ¶ Explicit dialogus de fun-/damentis legum anglie & de consci/entia. Impressum Londini p/Iohannem Rastell. An/no Dñi. M.v.L./xxviii. /¶ Cum priuilegio Regali./ [McK. 37 on reverse.]

T 463. ¶ Hereafter fo-/loweth a Dyaloge in Englysshe,/bytwyxt a Doctoure of Dyvynyte,/and a Student in the Lawes of/Englande: . . . / [Over McK. 57.]

Colla. T.p.+2–50+[24].

Colo. ¶ Imprynted/by me Robert wyer, dwellynge/in seynt Martyns parysshe/in the felde, besyde Cha-/ryngcrosse, in the Bys/shop of Norwyche/Rentes./ [On reverse of S 5; then on S 6, McK. 57, and on reverse the following.] ¶ And these bokes be for to sell at/the sygne of seynt Johñ Euange/lyste in seynt Martyns parys-/she besyde Charyngcrosse./ [McK. 67 a.]

T 464. The fyrste dya-/loge in Englys/she, with newe addycons./ [Over McK. 57.]
Colla. T.p.+ii–lxxviii+[2].
Colo. ¶ Imprynted by me Robert wyer/dwellynge at the sygne of saynt/Johñ Evangelyste, in saynt/Martyns parysshe, besyde/Charyngcrosse, in the Bys/shop of norwych rentes./ [Over McK. 68, 69.]

T 465. ¶ Here after fo-/loweth a Dialoge in Englisshe/betwyxte a Doctour of Dyuynyte and a/student in the Lawes of Englãde:/ of the groũdes of the sayd lawes/and of Conseyence./ [No. 12.]
Colla. T.p.+[1]+iii–xxxix+[18].
Colo. ¶ Imprintyd by/me Robert Redman, dwellyng in/ Fletestrete in saynt Dunstones/parysshe nexte to the churche/ at yͤ sygne of the George./ [McK. 3.]

T 466. ¶ The fyrst dia/logue in Englisshe, with/newe additions./ [Over No. 11; No. 12 on reverse.]
Colla. T.p.+2–77+3.
Colo. ¶ Imprynted,/at Londõ in the Fletestrete, by me/ Robert Redman dwellynge in saint/Dunstones parysshe, nexte the/churche. In the yere of our/lorde god. M.CCCCC./XXXii. the fyrst day/of the moneth of/Iuly./ [McK. 41 on reverse.]

T 467. The secũde/dyaloge in Englysshe bytwene/a doctour of dyvynytye and/a student in the lawes of/Englande./ [In border 26.]
Colla. T.p.+2–147+[5].
Colo. ¶ Impryntyd at London in Southwarke by/Peter Treuerys In the yere of our lorde god/M.v.C.xxx. the. xxiiii day of Nouembre./

T 468. Here af-/ter foloweth a lytell/treatise called the/newe addi-/ cions./❦/ [In border 27.]
Colla. T.p.+2–30+[2].
Colo. Thomas Bertheletus regius impressor/excudebat, Anno domini. M./D.XXXi. Cum priuilegio/a rege indulto./

T 469. The secunde dya-/logue ĩ Englysshe/wyth new addy-/cyons, . . . /
Colla. T.p.+ii–clxvi+[6].
Colo. ¶ Impryntyd at London in Southwarke by/Peter Treveris/1531./

T 470. ¶ The se-/conde dyaloge in En-/glysshe bytwene a doc-/tor of dyuynyte and/a student in the lawes/of Englande./
Colla. T.p.+ii–cxv+[5].
Colo. ¶ Imprynted at London in Fletestrete, by me/Robert Redman, dwellynge in saint Dunstones paryssh, next the chur-/ che. In the yere of our lorde god/a tousande five hondred/and. xxxi. The. first day/of the moneth of/Iune. [McK. 3 on reverse.]

T 471. ¶ The seconde/dyalogue in Englysshe, bytwene/a doctour of divynyte and/a student in the lawes/of Englande, newly corrected and/imprinted/with/newe addy-/cions./ [Over No. 22.]
Colla. T.p.+2–156+[6].

Colo. ℭ Imprynted,/at Loddō in the Fletestrete, by me/ Robert Redman dwellynge in saint/Dunstones parysshe, nexte the/churche. In the yere of our/lorde god. M.CCCCC./XXXii. The fyrst day/of the moneth of/Iuly./ [McK. 3 on reverse.]

T 472. ❧ The dialo/gues in Englysshe, bytwene a/Doctour of dyvynyte & a Studēt in/the lawes of Englāde, . . . / [Over No. 25.]
Colla. T.p.+2–189+[6].
Colo. ℭ Imprynted/at London in Fletestrete at the/sygne of the George nexte to/saynt Dunstones church by/Wyllyam Myddyl-/ton, in the yere of/our Lorde a M./CCCCC./xliii./ ℭ Cum priuilegio/ad imprimen-/dum solum./ [McK. 93 on reverse.]

T 473. ℭ The dyaloges/in Englishe, betwene/a Doctour of divi-/nitie, and a Stu-/dent/in |the lawes of Englande,/ . . . / ¶ Cum priuilegio ad im/primendum solum./ [In border 48.]
Colla. T.p.+2–177+[4].
Colo. ¶ Londini in aedibus Richardi/Totteli. An. 1554./

T 474. The dya-/loges in En-/glishe, betwene a/Doctour of divi-/nitie and a studēt/in the lawes of/Englād, . . . [In McK. 105.]
Colla. T.p.+2–182+[4].
Colo. Londini in aedibus Ri-/chardi Toteli./An. 1554./Cum priuilegio ad impri-/mendum solum.

T 475. ¶ The dialoges/in English, betwene/a Doctour of divini-/tye, and a Stu-/dent/in the lawes of England,/ . . . / [In border 48.]
Colla. T.p.+2–177+[4].
Colo. ¶ Londini in aedibus Richardi/Tottelli. An. 1569./

T 476. ¶ The dialoges/in Englishe, betweene a/Doctor of Divinitie, and a/Student/in the lawes of Englande, . . . / [In border 46.]
Colla. T.p.+2–177+[4].
Colo. ¶ Londini in aedibus Richardi/Tottelli. Anno. 1575./

T 477. ¶ The Dialoges/in Englishe, betwene a/Docter of Divinitie, and a/Student/in the lawes of Englande./ . . . / [In border 46.]
Colla. T.p.+2–177+[4].
Colo. ¶ Londini in Aedibus Richardi/Tottelli Anno 1580./

T 478. ¶ The Dialoges/in English, betwene a/Docter of Diuinity, and/ a Student/in the lawes of England./Newly corrected and/imprinted, with/new additi-/ons./ ¶ Cum priuilegio.
Colla. T.p.+2–176+[4].
Colo. ¶ Londini in Aedibus Richardi/Tottelli. Anno 1580./

T 479. The/Dialogue in English, be-/tweene a Doctor of Divinitie,/ and a Student in the Lawes of/England, . . . / ¶ Imprinted at London in/Fleetestreete, within Temple Barre/at the signe of the Hand and Starre by/Richard Tottill./1593./
Colla. T.p.+2–176+[4].
Colo. None.

T 480. The/dialogue in En-/glish, betweene a Doctor of/Divinitie, and a student in the/Lawes of England:/ . . . /At London,/ Printed by Thomas Wight,/and Bonham Norton./1598./Cum priuilegio Regiae/Maiestatis./
Colla. T.p.+2–176+[4].
Colo. None.

T 481. De/Republica/Anglorum./The maner of gouernement or/ policie of the Realme of Eng-/land, compiled by the Honora-/ble man Thomas Smyth . . . /At London,/Printed by Henrie Midleton/for Gregorie Seton./Anno Domini/1583./
Colla. T.p.+[1]+1–119. Thomas Smyth at end.
Colo. None.

T 482. De/Republica/Anglorum./The maner of Gouernement or/ policie of the Realme of Eng-/land, . . . /At London,/Printed by Henrie Midleton/for Gregorie Seton/Anno Domini/1584./
Colla. T.p.+[3]+1–119.
Colo. None.

T 483. The/Common-welth/of England, and/maner of government/ thereof./Compiled by the honorable Sir Thomas Smith, Knight,/ . . . / . . . [McK. 261.]/At London/Inprinted by Iohn Windet for Gregorie Seton, and/are to be solde at his shoppe under/ Aldersgate. 1589./
Colla. T.p.+[1]+1–148.
Colo. None.

T 484. The/Common-wealth/of England and/maner of government/ thereof./Compiled by the honorable Sir Thomas Smith, Knight/ . . . /[McK. 261.]/At London,/Printed by Valentine Simmes, for Gregorie Seton,/and are to be solde at his shoppe under/ Aldersgate. 1594./
Colla. T.p.+[1]+7–148.
Colo. None.

T 485. Les plees del coron/ . . . /1557/in aedibus Richardi/ Tottelli./ Cum priuilegio ad impri-/mendum solum./ [In border 49.]
Colla. T.p.+[3]+1–198.
Colo. Imprinted at London in fletestrete/within Temple barre at the signe of the hand/and starre by Rychard Tottyll./ An. do. 1557./Cum priuilegio ad imprimendum solum./

T 486. Les plees del coron:/ . . . /1557/In aedibus Richardi/Tottelli./ Cum priuilegio ad impri-/mendum solum./ [In border 49.]
Colla. T.p.+[13]+1–193.
Colo. ☛ Imprinted at London in Flete-/strete within temple Barre at the signe of/the hand and starre, By Richard/Tottel. An. 1574./Cum priuilegio./

T 487. ¶ Les Plees Del Coron:/ . . . /Anno domini 1560./In aedibus Richardi/Tottelli./ ¶ Cum priuilegio./ [In border 49.]
Colla. T.p.+[13]+1–198.
Colo. Imprinted at London in Fletestrete/within Temple

barre at the signe of/the hande and starre/by Richard Tottyll./ An. do. 1560./Cum priuilegio./

T 488. ¶ Les plees del coron:/ . . . /Anno domini 1567./In aedibus Richardi/Tottelli./Cum priuilegio./ [In border 49.]
Colla. T.p.+[13]+1–198.
Colo. ❧ Imprinted at Lon/don in fletestrete within temple/ Barre at the signe of the hand & starre./by Rychard Tottel, An./1567./Cum priuilegio./

T 489. Les Plees del Coron,/ . . . par le tres reverend Iudge Monsieur/Guilliaulme Staundforde . . . /Anno Domini 1574./ In aedibus Richardi/Tottelli./ ¶ Cum priuilegio./ [In border 47.]
Colla. T.p.+[13]+1–198.
Colo. ❧ Imprinted at London in Flete-/strete within temple Barre at the signe of/the hand and starre, by Richard/Tottel, An. 1574./Cum priuilegio./

T 490. Les Plees del Coron,/ . . . per le tres reverend Iudge Monsieur/ Guilliaulme Staundforde, . . . /Anno Domini 1583./In Aedibus Richardi/Tottelli./ ¶ Cum priuilegio./ [In border 47.]
Colla. T.p.+[11]+1–196.
Colo. ❧ Imprinted at London in Fleete-/strete within Temple Barre, at the signe of/the Hand and Starre, by Rychard/ Tottel. An. 1583./ ¶ Cum priuilegio ad imprimendum solum./

T 491. ¶ An exposicion of/the kinges prerogative, . . . /1567./
Colla. T.p.+[4]+5–85.
Colo. Imprynted at Lon-/don in flete strete within temple/ Barre at the signe of the hand & starre./by Rychard Tottel, An./ 1567./Cum priuilegio./

T 492. An exposicion of/the kinges prerogative, . . . /1568./
Colla. T.p.+[5]+6–85.
Colo. Imprynted at Lon-/don in flete strete within temple/ Barre at the signe of the hand & starre./by Rychard Tottel, An./1568./Cum priuilegio./

T 493. ❧ An exposition of/the Kinges Prerogative, . . . By William Staunforde, . . . /1573./Imprinted at London in Fleete-/streate within Temple barre at/the signe of the Hande and/ Starre, by Richarde/Tottle./Cum priuilegio ad impri-/mendum solum./
Colla. T.p.+[5]+6–83+[2].
Colo. ¶ Imprinted at London in Fleetestreate/within Temple barre at the signe of the Hand/and Starre by Richard Totttle./ Anno Dom 1573./Cum priuilegio ad impri-/mendum solum.

T 494. ¶ An exposicion of/the kinges prerogative . . . /1568./
Colla. T.p.+[5]+6–85.
Colo. ¶ Imprinted at London in Fleetestreate/within Temple barre at the signe of the Hand/and Starre by Richarde Tottle./ Anno Dñi 1577./Cum priuilegio ad imprimen-/dum solum./

T 495. ❧ An exposition of/the Kinges Prerogative, . . . by Sir William Staunford, . . . /1577./ ¶ Imprinted at London in Fleete-/

streate within Temple barre/at the signe of the Hand and Starre, by Ri-/chard Tottel./ ¶ Cum priuilegio ad impri-/mendum solum./
Colla. T.p.+[4]+5–85.
Colo. ¶ Imprinted at London in Fleetestreate/within Temple barre at the signe of the Hand/and Starre by Richarde Tottle./ Anno Dñi 1577./Cum priuilegio ad imprimen-/dum solum./

T 496. An/exposition of the kinges/praerogative, . . . by Sir William Staunford, . . . /☞ Imprinted at London in Fleet-/streat within Temple Barre at the/Signe of the hand & Starre/by Richard Totthil./1590./
Colla. T.p.+[1]+6–84.
Colo. None.

T 497. The/Practice, Pro-/ceedings, and/Lawes of armes, . . . / Imprinted at Lon-/don by the Deputies of Christopher/Barker Printer to the Queenes most ex-/cellent Maiestie./1593/
Colla. T.p.+[11]+1–342.
Colo. None.

T 498. A briefe treatise/of testaments and/last willes,/ . . . /London/ Printed by Iohn Windet. 1590./
Colla. T.p.+[11]+[1]–293+[13].
Colo. Printed at London by I. Windet, 1591./

T 499. Le digest des/Briefes originals, et des/chose concernants eux/ compose per Simon/Theloall./Londini./In Aedibus Richardi Tottelli./Octobris decimo quarto./1579./Cum priuilegioad impri-/mendum solum./
Colla. T.p.+[7]+1–424.
Colo. ¶ Imprinted at London within/Temple barre at the Signe of the Hand/and Starre by Richard Tottell./the 14. day of October./1579./

T 500. (Symbolaeography, or Law Formes by William West.)
Title-page lacking.
Colla. T.p.+[3]+A–Y 8's, Aa–Qq 8's, Rr 6's.
Colo. None.

T 501. A Discourse/uppon usurye, by waye of/Dialogue and orations . . . /By Thomas Wilson . . . /1572./
Colla. T.p.+[17]+[1]–201+[3].
Colo. ¶ Londini in aedibus Ry-/chardi Tottelli./1572./

CHAPTER IV

Printers and Their Law Books

No effort at original investigation into the lives of the English printers has been made. The descriptions in this chapter are abridged from Duff's "Century of the English Book Trade" (1905), and McKerrow's "Dictionary of Printers and Booksellers" (1910).

In attempting to fix a date for the books printed, use has been made of various peculiarities of the printers. The style of type, the style of the initial letters, the amount of wear shown by type or by woodcuts, the use of devices, have all been studied, and in the case of printers who printed many law books the result may be stated with considerable confidence. In the case of printers who printed only a few books, the date, unless it appears in title-page or colophon, is only conjectural. Great help has been derived in dating Pynson's books from McKerrow's "Printers' and Publishers' Devices" (London, 1913). In dating Berthelet's Statutes, Proctor's essay, in the "Transactions of the Bibliographical Society," v, 255, has been the basis of the arrangement.

John Allde

An apprentice to Richard Kele; printed from 1560 to 1582. His only known law book (printed for John Waley) is

1573.	T 304, 305.	The Office of Sheriffs.

Anonymous Printers

[1550].	T 319.	The order for Swannes.
1556.	T 48.	Littleton's Tenures in English (probably Marsh).
1574.	T 280.	Institutions or principal grounds. [Rycharde Bankes.] (Cannot be Bankes; this is copied from an earlier edition.)
n. d.	T 412.	Manwood's Forest Laws.
1591.	T 34.	Littleton's Tenures.
n. d.	T 261.	Brief treatise of oaths.

Richard Bankes

Printed irregularly from 1523 at various places in London; from 1539 to 1542 he was printing for Taverner. He had some connection with Grafton.

His principal law books were the first two editions of "Institutions or Principal Grounds of the Law." The first of these is apparently in de Worde's type. The second was printed in a smaller type with Grafton's compartment, McK. 91.

1530.	T 252.	Assize of Bread.
1540.	T 269.	Institutions or Principal Grounds.
1542.	T 270.	Institutions or Principal Grounds.
[154-].	T 307.	Ordinal or Statute concerning artificers.

Christopher Barker

Printed in London from about 1576 to 1599; during the last years printing usually by deputy. In 1577 he became Queen's Printer in succession to Jugge. His law books were:

1578. S 294. Statutes 13 Eliz.
1579. S 66. Rastell's Statutes.
S 74. Pulton's Statutes.
1581. S 299. Statutes 23 Eliz.
S 75. Pulton's Statutes.
1583. T 325, 326. Cecil's Justice in England (two editions).
S 67. Rastell's Statutes.
[1583]. S 68. Rastell's Statutes.
1585. S 300. Statutes 27 Eliz.
1586. S 76. Pulton's Statutes.
1587. S 301. Statutes 29 Eliz.
S 31. Statutes at Large.
1588. S 69. Rastell's Statutes (by deputies).
1589. S 302. Statutes 31 Eliz. (by deputies).
[158–]. S 77. Pulton's Statutes.
1591. S 69a. Rastell's Statutes.
1592. S 77a. Pulton's Statutes.
1593. T 497. Sutcliffe's Laws of Arms.
S 305. Statutes 35 Eliz. (by deputies).
T 249. Apology for Sundry Proceedings.
1594. S 70. Rastell's Statutes (by deputies).
1595. T 250e. Articles to be enquired of (by deputies).
1597. T 248. Court of Requests (by deputies).
T 262. Capitula sive Constitutions.
S 307. Statutes 39 Eliz. (by deputies).
1599. T 267. Injunctions.

Robert Barker

Succeeded his father Christopher on the latter's death in 1599. In 1600 he printed his only law book within the period.

1600. T 251. Articles to be enquired of in the visitation.

Thomas Berthelet

Began to print on his own account about 1527, in Fleet Street, "nere to ye cundite at ye signe of Lucrece." He was appointed King's Printer, in succession to Pynson, in 1530, and acted as such until the end of the reign of Henry the Eighth. He died in 1555. His nephew Thomas Powell and his apprentice Henry Wykes apparently succeeded to his right to print the statutes of Henry the Eighth.

As a printer he was neat and tasteful. His types were apparently new. He used few woodcuts. His device of the Lucrece (McK. 80) was used in a few statutes; otherwise he printed without device. He used in the statutes also a cut of the King's Arms (17) and a black block (18). He used several borders. His law books were:

1527. R 11. Year Book 21 Ed. 3.
1528. R 95. Year Book 7 H. 6.
R 97. Year Book 8 H. 6.

1529. R 404. Year Book 14 H. 7.
[1529]. R 405. Year Book 15 H. 7.
1530. T 75. Old Tenures.
T 14. Littleton.
T 114. Articuli ad Narr. Novas.
T 124. Diversity of Courts.
T 141. Book for a Justice.
T 167a. Carta Feodi.
[1530]. S 134. Statutes 22 H. 8.
1531. T 88. Natura Brevium.
T 468. Doctor and Student (two editions).
S 59. Magna Carta.
[1531]. S 141. Statutes 23 H. 8.
1532. R 14. Year Book 22–28 Ed. 3.
S 21. Secunda pars.
T 115. Articuli ad Narr. Novas.
[1532]. S 149. Statutes 24 H. 8.
[1533]. S 155. Statutes 25 H. 8.
1534. T 89. Natura Brevium.
[1534]. T 253. Assize of Bread.
S 161. Statutes 26 H. 8.
[1534–7]. S 135. Statutes 22 H. 8.
S 142–144. Statutes 23 H. 8 (three issues).
S 156. Statutes 25 H. 8.
S 162, 163. Statutes 26 H. 8 (two issues).
S 175. Statutes 28 H. 8.
T 190a. Court Baron.
T 253a. Assize of Bread.
1535. T 126. Diversity of Courts.
T 236a. Ordinance of Exchequer.
[1535]. S 168. Statutes 27 H. 8.
[1536]. S 174. Statutes 28 H. 8.
T 142. Justice of the Peace.
T 170a. Carta Feodi.
1537. T 237. Ordinance of the Exchequer.
1538. T 76. Old Tenures.
T 41. Littleton in English.
T 116. Articuli ad Narr. Novas.
T 226, 227. Returna Brevium.
T 314. Statutes for a Justice of the Peace.
S 150. Statutes 24 H. 8.
1539. T 144. Justice of the Peace.
T 171. Carta Feodi.
T 352. Fitzherbert. Surveying.
S 180, 181. Statutes 31 H. 8 (two issues).
1540. S 187. Statutes 32 H. 8.
T 193. Court Baron.
T 238. Ordinance of the Exchequer.
T 315. Statutes for a Justice of the Peace.
S 22. Secunda pars.
1541. T 16. Littleton's Tenures.
S 12. Magna Carta.
1542. S 193–195. Statutes 33 H. 8 (three issues).
1543. T 173. Carta Feodi.
S 32, 33. Statutes of Henry 8 (Title page and table: two issues).
S 27. Statutes to Henry 8.
T 316. Statutes for a Justice of Peace.

	T 312.	Grants and Ordinances for Romney Marsh.
[1543].	S 112.	Statutes 1 H. 8.
	S 118.	Statutes 3–7 H. 8.
	S 123.	Statutes 14–15 H. 8.
	S 130.	Statutes 21 H. 8.
	S 136, 137.	Statutes 22 H. 8 (two issues).
	S 145.	Statutes 23 H. 8.
	S 157.	Statutes 25 H. 8.
	S 164.	Statutes 26 H. 8.
	S 169.	Statutes 27 H. 8.
	S 177.	Statutes 28 H. 8.
	S 188.	Statutes 32 H. 8.
1543.	S 199.	Statutes 34–35 H. 8.
1544.	S 205.	Statutes 35, H. 8.
	T 145.	Book for a Justice.
	T 194.	Court Baron.
	T 239.	Ordinance of the Exchequer.
	T 318.	Statutes for War.
[1544].	T 228.	Returna Brevium.
	S 189.	Statutes 32 H. 8.
	S 200.	Statutes 34–35 H. 8.
1546.	S 151.	Statutes 24 H. 8.
	S 170.	Statutes 27 H. 8.
	S 182.	Statutes 31 H. 8.
	S 211.	Statutes 37 H. 8.
	T 353.	Fitzherbert. Surveying.
1547.	S 201.	Statutes 34–35 H. 8.
1551.	S 34.	Statutes of Henry 8 (Title page and table).
[1552].	S 113.	Statutes 1 H. 8.
	S 119.	Statutes 3–7 H. 8.
	S 124.	Statutes 14–15 H. 8.
	S 131.	Statutes 21 H. 8.
	S 138.	Statutes 22 H. 8.
	S 146.	Statutes 23 H. 8.
	S 158.	Statutes 25 H. 8.
	S 165.	Statutes 26 H. 8.
	S 176.	Statutes 28 H. 8.
	S 183.	Statutes 31 H. 8.
	S 190.	Statutes 32 H. 8.
	S 196.	Statutes 33 H. 8.
1552.	S 207.	Statutes 35 H. 8.
1553.	S 37.	Statutes of Edward 6. (Title page and table).

Bollifant

1596.	T 397.	Lambarde, Perambulation of Kent.

Bocard

1504.	T 403.	Lyndwode.

Bretton

1505.	T 405.	Lyndewde.

Brickman

1525.	T 408.	Lyndewde.

John Butler

A journeyman of de Worde, who is reported to have printed one law book, the "Expositions" of 1527. This was printed without signature to the "Prologus" of John Rastell. Duff ("Westminster and London Printers," p. 152), says that this work is "clearly the work of [John] Rastell." This does not seem at all clear to me. To be sure, most of the lower case letters are identical with those used by Rastell in Fitzherbert's "Abridgement" and in his bilingual "Expositiones." On the other hand, the capitals are quite distinct, the format is different, smaller than Rastell ever used, and the omission of ascription of the Prologue to Rastell is almost conclusive. I have noticed no other font of type with capitals like those used in this book, the "A," "E," and "M" being quite distinctive.

On the other hand, the type is very similar to Wyer's (e. g. in the "Doctor and Student"); but with slight differences.

The woodcuts used, the Job and the St. John Evangelist (39 & 40) are also distinctive. Butler printed at the sign of St. John the Evangelist. It is to be said, however, that he used a different cut of St. John (McK. 72). His one law book:

1527. T 453. Terms of the law.

John Byddell

An apprentice of de Worde, who printed from 1535 to 1544, at de Worde's old house, at the sign of the Sun. So far as is known he printed only one law book, in de Worde's type 1.

[1538]. T 268. Institutions in the laws of England.

Henry Bynneman

Printed in London from 1566 to 1583. For Ralph Newbery, their names being given as joint printers, he printed the following law books:

1581. T 387. Lambard's Eirenarcha.
1582. T 388. Lambard's Eirenarcha.
T 389. Lambard's Eirenarcha.

Caley

1554. T 414. Martin, Marriage of Priests.

John Cawood

Printed from 1546; in 1553 was appointed royal printer by Queen Mary; continued under Elizabeth, jointly with Richard Jugge. He died in 1572.

1554–59. S 240–247, S 251–254, S 257–259, S 262–265. All the statutes of Mary and of Philip and Mary.
1560–72. Statutes of Elizabeth (see Jugge).

William Caxton

Caxton, the first English printer, who printed from 1477 till his death in 1491, appears to have printed only one law book, in his type numbered "6" in Duff's "Early Printed Books."

[1490]. S 97. Statutes 1–4 Henry 7.

John Charlewood

Printed from about 1556 to 1593. So far as is known he printed two law books, both for other publishers.

1583. T 444. Phaer, Book of Precedents (for Tottell).
1587. T 333. Crompton. Short declaration (for Gubbin and Newman).

Robert Copeland

An assistant of de Worde, who printed many books for him from 1514 to 1535. He died in 1547-48. At de Worde's office, the sign of the Sun, he issued the "Court Baron"; and the "Justice of the Peace" at his own shop, at the sign of the Rose Garland. In his law books he used de Worde's woodcuts, the King and Judges and the royal arms but on the reverse of the last leaf his own device (McK. 36). His law books are:

[1515]. T 182. Court Baron.
1515. T 134. Justice of the Peace.

In them he used the type used by de Worde for printing his quarto tracts.

John Day

Printed in London from 1546 to 1580. He printed three law books:

1568. T 379. Lambard's Archaionomia.
1571. T 308. Reformation of the Ecclesiastical Law.
T 259. Book of Canons.

William Faques

The works of this printer were few but beautiful. In 1504 he was King's Printer, the first to hold that office; and as such he printed his only legal work.

[1506]. S 106. Statutes 19 Henry 7.

This is printed in three styles of beautiful clear-cut type, the text of each page being surrounded by a neat border in the shape of a chain. At the end is his device [McK. 14, 15]. He died as early as 1508, when Pynson succeeded him.

Richard Faques

This printer succeeded William Faques, but printed at the sign of the Maiden's Head, near St. Paul's, where later several printers were located. His only known legal work is a fragment of a statute.

[1510]. S 111. Statutes 1 Henry 8.

Thomas Gaultier

Printed for booksellers from 1550 to 1553. In that time he printed a copy of the "Great Abridgement," to be sold respectively (with the names inserted in the Colophon) by Powell, Kele and Seres. He used Whitechurch's border.

1551. S 53, 54, 55. Great Abridgement.

Thomas Godfray

Printed in London from 1535 for several years; his books are undated. His only law books are:

[1536]. T 362. Constitutions provincial and legantine.
T 363. The power of the clergy.

Richard Grafton

Began printing about 1535. He was made King's Printer in 1547, but removed from office on the accession of Mary, and printed little if anything afterwards until his death in 1573. His son-in-law, Richard Tottel, succeeded to his types and woodcuts. He printed the following law books:

[1547].	T 266.	Injunctions given by Edward 6.
	T	Articles to be enquired.
	T 430.	Phaer's Book of Presidents.
1548.	T	Articles to be enquired of.
[1548].	T 264.	Exhortation to the Justices of Peace.
	T 247.	An admonition or warning.
1550.	T 432.	Phaer's Book of Presidents.
[1548–53].	S 215–218a, S 221–224, S 226–228, S 230–238.	Statutes all the years of Edward 6.

Nicholas Hyll

A native of the Netherlands, who printed from about 1546; he died in 1553. His printing was principally for others, and he may have been the printer of the following series, which (unchanged except for the names) bore the names of Hyll, Kele, Smyth, Toye, and Walye.

1546.	T 147.	Justice of the peace.
	T 176.	Carta feodi.
	T 196.	Court baron.
	T 212.	Hundred court.
	T 241.	Ordinance of the Exchequer.
	T 274.	Office of Sheriffs.
[1546].	T 307.	Ordinal for Artificers.

William How

Printed in Fleet Street from 1565 to 1590. His only law book (in some copies said to have been printed for Gubbin and Newman) was:

1588. T 360. Fraunce's The lawiers logike.

Adam Islip

Printed in London from 1591 to 1640. He was an apprentice to Hugh Jackson. He printed

1594. T 327. Clarke's Trial of Bastardy.

Hugh Jackson

An apprentice to William Powell, who printed from 1576 to 1616, at St. John the Evangelist in Fleet Street near the Conduit. He printed

[1587]. T 257. Assize of Bread.

Richard Jugge

Printed from 1547. He became royal printer, jointly with John Cawood, on the accession of Queen Elizabeth. He died in 1577.

He printed the following books jointly with Cawood, and after Cawood's death, alone:

1559. T 250. Articles to be enquired.
[1565]. T 263. Defence of priest's marriages.
[1572–75]. S 271. Statutes 1 Elizabeth.
S 273, 274. Statutes 1 Elizabeth.
S 282–284. Statutes 5 Elizabeth.
S 286–288. Statutes 8 Elizabeth.
S 292, 293. Statutes 13 Elizabeth.
1572. S 295, 296. Statutes 14 Elizabeth.
1575. S 297, 298. Statutes 18 Elizabeth.

[With John Cawood]

1559. S 267–270. Statutes 1 Elizabeth.
1563. S 275–280. Statutes 5 Elizabeth.
[1565]. S 272. Statutes 1 Elizabeth.
S 281. Statutes 5 Elizabeth.
1566. S 285. Statutes 8 Elizabeth.
1571. S 289–291. Statutes 13 Elizabeth.

Richard Kele

Printed from 1542 until his death in 1552. His law books are:

1546. T 215. Hundred Court.
T 295. Ordinance of the exchequer.

(These six tracts were printed, probably by Hyll, for Kele, Smyth, Toye, and Waley, and were identical except for the names.)

1551. S 53. Great Abridgement. [See Gaultier.]
1552. T 293. Office of Sheriffs.

King

[1555]. T 299. Office of sheriffs.

John Lettou and William de Machlinia

These printers were established together in London about 1481, and printed at Flete-bridge, near the church of All Saints. Lettou and Machlinia together printed, all in Duff's types "1" and "2":

[1481]. T 3. Littleton, Tenores novelli.
[1482]. S 39. Abbreviamentum statutorum.
T 182, 195, 202. Year Books 33, 35, and 36 Henry 6.

Lettou ceased to print law books before 1485; from that time Machlinia printed alone until the end of 1486, when he apparently ceased to print. Machlinia alone printed, in Duff's types "1" and "2":

[1485]. T 4. Littleton. Tenores novelli.
S 1. Nova statuta.

He then moved to Holborn and printed in Duff's types "4" and "5":

[1486]. S 96. Statutes 1 Richard 3.
T 189, 208. Year Books 34 and 37 Henry 6.

THOMAS MARSHE

Began printing in Fleet Street about 1554, and printed until 1587. He used no woodcuts or devices in his law books, but used a border which had been used by Petyt and afterwards by Seres; if indeed the printing was not done by them jointly. He also used a rough border of his own, and for his statutes a plain border of straight lines. His law books were:

1555. T 434, 435. Phaer's Book of Presidents (two issues). Institutions or principal grounds.
[1555]. T 294, 295, 296. Office of Sheriffs (three issues).
1556. T 47, 48. Littleton. Tenures, in English (two issues).
S 14, 23. Magna Carta and Secunda Pars.
T 277a. Institutions or principal grounds.
1557. T 411. Lyndewode.
T 353b. Surveying.
1562. T 301. Office of Sheriffs.
1573. S 36. Statutes of Henry 8, Title and Table.
1577. S 30. Statutes to Henry 8.
[1577]. S 115. Statutes 1 Henry 8.
S 121. Statutes 3–7 Henry 8.
S 126. Statutes 14–15 Henry 8.
S 133. Statutes 21 Henry 8.
S 140. Statutes 22 Henry 8.
S 148. Statutes 23 Henry 8.
S 154. Statutes 24 Henry 8.
S 160. Statutes 25 Henry 8.
S 167. Statutes 26 Henry 8.
S 173. Statutes 27 Henry 8.
S 179. Statutes 28 Henry 8.
S 186. Statutes 31 Henry 8.
S 192. Statutes 32 Henry 8.
S 198. Statutes 33 Henry 8.
S 204. Statutes 34–35 Henry 8.
S 210. Statutes 35 Henry 8.
S 214. Statutes 37 Henry 8.

HENRY MIDDLETON

Printer in London, 1567 to 1587. He was son of William Middleton. He printed law books for booksellers:

1. For Gregory Seton:

1583. T 481. Smith's De Republica Anglorum.
1584. T 482. Smith's De Republica Anglorum.

2. For Ralph Newberry:

1576. T 396. Lambard's Perambulations of Kent.
1584. T 260. The Customs of London.

3. By Ralph Newbery and Henry Middleton:

1583. T 381. Lambard's Duties of Constables.
1584. T 382. Lambard's Duties of Constables.
1587. T 383. Lambard's Duties of Constables.
1591. T 384. Lambard's Duties of Constables.

William Middleton

Successor of Robert Redman at the sign of the George on Fleet Street, used his type and cuts, though with his own devices. Most of his legal treatises are dated, but all his Year Books are without date, and with no indication in which part of his short career they belong. He printed from 1541 to 1547; and was succeeded by his wife's immediate new husband, William Powell. His legal works were:

1541.	T 417.	Perkin's profitable book.
1542.	S 51.	Great Abridgement of the Statutes.
	S 85, 94.	Abridgement, 24–25, 33 Hen. 8.
1543.	T 338.	Fitzherbert's New Justice.
	T 472.	Doctor and Student.
	T 127.	Diversity of Courts.
	T 229.	Returna brevium.
	T 271.	Institutions or principal grounds.
1544.	T 103.	Natura Brevium, in English.
	T 42.	Littleton in English.
	T 174.	Carta feodi.
	T 195.	Court baron.
	T 211.	Hundred court.
[1544].	T 91.	Natura Brevium.
	T 240.	Ordinance of the exchequer.
	T 146.	Justice of the peace.
	T 128.	Diversity of Courts.
1544.	T 272.	Institutions or Principal grounds.
1545.	T 18.	Littleton.
[1545].	T 77.	Old tenures.
1545.	T 175.	Carta feodi.
	T 291.	Office of Sheriffs.
	T 273.	Institutions or principal grounds.
1547.	T 275.	Institutions or principal grounds.
	T 200.	Court Baron.
	T 216.	Hundred Court.
[1541–47].	R 77.	Year Books. 2 Hen. 6.
	R 99.	7 & 8 Hen.
	R 112.	10 Hen. 6.
	R 123.	12 Hen. 6.
	R 128.	14 Hen. 6.
	R 139.	19 Hen. 6.
	R 173.	30–31 Hen. 6.
	R 178.	32 Hen. 6.
	R 204.	36 Hen. 6.
	R 210.	37 Hen. 6.

R 219. 39 Hen. 6.
R 227. 1 Ed. 4.
R 243. 3 Ed. 4.
R 251. 4 Ed. 4.
R 282. 8 Ed. 4.
R 365. 22 Ed. 4.
R 427. 18 & 19 Hen. 8.
R 436. 26 Hen. 8.
R 445. 27 Hen. 8.
S 26. Great Books of the Statutes.

Ralph Newbery

A bookseller in London, 1560 to 1607. He probably never printed, though his name occurs alone as printer of several books, but usually with that of Henry Middleton or Henry Bynneman, which see. The law books in which his name alone occurs are:

1. Printed by Ralph Newbery:

1588. T 391. Lambard's Eirenarcha.
1591. T 392. Lambard's Eirenarcha.
1592. T 393. Lambard's Eirenarcha.
1594. T 394. Lambard's Eirenarcha.
T 384a. Lambard's Constables.

2. Printed for Ralph Newbery:

1583. T 390. Lambard's Eirenarcha.

Bonham Norton

Printed in London from 1594 to 1635. All his law books to 1600 were printed in partnership with Thomas Wight, q.v.

Julian Notary

A printer at Westminster from 1496 to 1500, when he moved to the Strand outside Temple Bar. He appears to have printed for de Worde. It is probable that his only law books were:

1507. S 99. Statutes 1–4 Henry 7.
S 101. Statutes 7 Henry 7.
S 104. Statutes 11 Henry 7.
S 107. Statutes 19 Henry 7.

Thomas Orwin

Printed in London, 1587 to 1593. He was in constant trouble with the law, and his press was seized in 1592; but the next year, in partnership with the bookseller William Kirckham, he printed his one law book:

1593. T 322. Adames' Court Leet.

John Oswen

Printed first at Ipswich in 1548, then moved to Worcester, where he printed until 1553. His only law book is:

1553. S 239. Statutes 7 Ed. 6.

Henry Pepwell

This printer's shop was at the sign of the Trinity, in St. Paul's churchyard. He began to print in 1518, and died in 1539; his only known law book, existing only as a fragment, is

[1521]. T 184. Court Baron.

Thomas Petyt

Printed from 1536 to 1554. His law books are:

1541.	T 337.	Fitzherbert's New Book of Justices.
1542.	S 52.	Great Abridgement.
1543.	T 290.	Office of Sheriffs.
	S 95.	Abridgement 33 H. 8.
1544.	T 101.	Natura Brevium in English.
[1545–51].	T 46.	Littleton in English.
	T 102.	Natura Brevium in English.
1552.	S 13.	Magna Carta.
	S 56.	Great Abridgement.
	T 95.	Abridgement 33 H. 8.

Thomas Powell

Nephew of Thomas Berthelet, who succeeded him in business, printing from 1556 to 1563. His only law books are issues of the Statutes of Henry 8, which he printed with the type and borders of Berthelet.

[1556].	S 152.	Statutes 24 Henry 8.
	S 202.	Statutes 34–35 Henry 8.
1557.	S 171.	Statutes 27 Henry 8.
	S 212.	Statutes 37 Henry 8.
[1562–63].	S 114.	Statutes 1 Henry 8.
	S 120.	Statutes 3–7 Henry 8.
	S 125.	Statutes 14, 15 Henry 8.
	S 132.	Statutes 21 Henry 8.
	S 139.	Statutes 22 Henry 8.
	S 147.	Statutes 23 Henry 8.
	S 153.	Statutes 24 Henry 8.
	S 159.	Statutes 25 Henry 8.
	S 166.	Statutes 26 Henry 8.
	S 172.	Statutes 27 Henry 8.
	S 178.	Statutes 28 Henry 8.
	S 185.	Statutes 31 Henry 8.
	S 191.	Statutes 32 Henry 8.
	S 197.	Statutes 33 Henry 8.
	S 203.	Statutes 34–35 Henry 9.
	S 209.	Statutes 35 Henry 8.
	S 213.	Statutes 37 Henry 8.
1563.	S 35.	Table to Statutes of Henry 8.

William Powell

Succeeded Middleton on his marriage with Middleton's widow, two months after Middleton's death. He printed from 1547 to 1567, using Middleton's type, woodcuts and devices. His law books are:

1547.	T 339.	Fitzherbert's New Book of Justices.
	T 119.	Articuli ad Narr. Novas.
1548.	T 44.	Littleton in English.
[1548].	T 431.	Phaer's Book of Presidents.
1549.	T 292.	Office of Sheriffs.
1550.	T 151.	Justice of the Peace.
1551.	T 151a.	Justice of the Peace.
	T 45.	Littleton in English.
	T 276.	Institutions or principal grounds.
	T 340.	Fitzherbert's New Book of Justices.
	S 55.	Great Abridgement. [Gaultier's name printed out of title.]
1552.	T 201.	Court Baron.
	T 246.	Ordinance of the Exchequer.
	T 298.	Office of Sheriffs.
[1552].	T 231.	Returna Brevium.
1553.	T 19.	Littleton.
	T 104.	Natura Brevium.
[1553].	T 433.	Phaer, Book of Presidents.
[1547–53].	R 64.	Year Book 9 Hen. 5.
	R 107.	Year Book 9 H. 6.
	R 299.	Year Book 11 Ed. 4.
	R 302.	Year Book 12 Ed. 4.
	R 309.	Year Book 13 Ed. 4.
	R 333.	Year Book 17 Ed. 4.
	R 370.	Year Book Long quinto.
	R 416.	Year Book 12 & 13, Hen. 8.

Richard Pynson

Pynson began to print about 1490, when his shop was in St. Clement's parish, outside Temple Bar. In 1500 he moved to Fleet Street, within Temple Bar, in St. Dunstone's parish, where he continued to print until his death, 1529–30. He became King's Printer in 1508.

Pynson was the first printer to print law books in considerable numbers; the early books being folios, and (from 1499) smaller books also. The text of all his law books printed by him in the fifteenth century was in type "2" of Duff's reproductions.

Fifteenth-Century English Books

The headlines, etc., were successively in types "1" (to 1492), "5" (1496), and "7" (1500). Before Pynson printed law books himself he secured two at least to be printed in Rouen by Tailleur; these were printed in the Tailleur type reproduced by Duff.

Pynson paid great attention to ornamental two- and three- line capitals, which he used to mark the successive topics of his text.

In the first decade of the century he was using (1) large, plain, square initials in white on black; and (2) a set of plain heavy-faced initials. This was succeeded, about 1510, by (3) a set of square initials, black on white, most of them either with a grotesque face, or with a flower; the earlier initials being still used, but with the block badly worn or wormed. About 1518 he began the use of a set (4) of larger square initials, 7-line, white on black ground. List of books from Pynson's press:

[1490].	R 455.	Statham's Abridgement (Tailleur) fo.
	T 5.	Littleton. (Tailleur) fo.
[1492].	R 223.	Year Book 1 Ed. 4, fo. [Types 1 & 2.]
	R 287.	Year Book 9 Ed. 4, fo. [Types 1 & 2.]
[1493].	T 317.	Statutes of War. 4°. [Type 4.]
[1495].	R 240.	Year Book 3 Ed. 4, fo. [Types 2 & 5.]
	R 248.	Year Book 4 Ed. 4, fo. [Types 2 & 5.]
	R 256.	Year Book 5 Ed. 4, fo. [Types 2 & 5.]
	R 263.	Year Book 6 Fd. 4, fo. [Types 2 & 5.]
	R 271.	Year Book 7 Ed. 4, fo. [Types 2 & 5.]
	R 279.	Year Book 8 Ed. 4, fo. [Types 2 & 5.]
[1496].	T 6.	Littleton, fo. [Cut 10. Type 2.]
	T 108.	Nove Narrationes, fo. [Type 2.]
	T 79.	Natura Brevium, fo. [Types 2 & 5.]
	T 68.	Old Tenures, fo. [Type 2.]
	S 105.	Statutes 11 Hen. 7, fo. [Type 6, 7.]
	R 224.	Year Book 1 Edw. 4.
[1499].	T 80.	Natura Brevium, fo. [Type 2.]
1499.	T 400, 401.	Lyndewode (2 issues), 8°. [Types 2, 3, 6, 7.]
	S 40, 41.	Abbreviatio Statutorum (two issues), 8°. [Types 2, 5.]
[1499].	R 47.	Liber Assissarum. 8°. [Types 3, 7.]
[1500].	R 103.	Year Book 9 Hen. 6, fo. [Types 2, 7.]
	R 143.	Year Book 20 Hen. 6, fo. [Type 2.]
	R 297.	Year Book 11 Ed. 4, fo. [Type 2.]
[1502].	R 400.	Year Book 1–8 H. 7, fo. [Type 11.]
	S 109.	Statutes 1–19 H. 7, fo. [Type 11.]
	R 241.	Year Book 3 Ed. 4, fo.
	R 249.	Year Book 4 Ed. 4, fo.
	R 257.	Year Book 5 Ed. 4, fo.
	R 264.	Year Book 6 Ed. 4, fo.
	R 272.	Year Book 7 Ed. 4, fo.
	R 280.	Year Book 8 Ed. 4, fo.
[1503].	R 144.	Year Book 20 H. 6, fo.
[1504].	S 2.	Nova Statuta.
	T 7.	Littleton, fo.
	T 81.	Natura Brevium, fo.
	T 69.	Old Tenures, fo.
[1506].	T 130.	Justice of Peace. 4°.
	T 158.	Carta Feodi. 4°.
	T 180.	Court Baron. 4°.
1508.	S 3.	Magna Carta.
[1508].	R 54.	Year Book 7 H. 4, fo.
	R 55.	Year Book 8 H. 4, fo.
	R 57.	Year Book 11 H. 4, fo.
	R 58.	Year Book 12 H. 4, fo.
	R 59.	Year Book 14 H. 4, fo.
	R 63.	Year Book 9 H. 5, fo.
	R 183.	Year Book 33 H. 6, fo.
	R 196.	Year Book 35 H. 6, fo.
	R 225.	Year Book 1 Ed. 4, fo.
	R 233.	Year Book 2 Ed. 4, fo.
	R 258.	Year Book 5 Ed. 4, fo.
	R 265.	Year Book 6 Ed. 4, fo.
	R 294.	Year Book 10 Ed. 4.
	R 300.	Year Book 12 Ed. 4.

	R 307.	Year Book 13 Ed. 4.
	R 363.	Year Book 22 Ed. 4.
	R 374.	Year Book 1 Ed. 5.
	R 391.	Year Book 2 Rich. 3.
	R 402.	Year Book 9 H. 7.
	R 403.	Year Book 12 H. 7.
	R 418.	Year Book 14 H. 8.
[1509].	R 161.	Year Book 27 H. 6.
[1510].	S 110.	Statutes 1 Hen. 8.
1510.	T 283.	Intrationum liber, fo.
	T 406.	Lyndewode 8°.
1510.	R 82.	Year Book 3 H. 6.
	R 89.	Year Book 4 H. 6.
[1512].	T 226.	Year Book 1 Ed. 4.
1514.	S 4.	Magna Carta.
[1516].	S 116, 117.	Statutes 1–7 H. 8.
1516.	T 8.	Littleton, fo.
	T 70.	Old Tenures, fo.
	T 183.	Court Baron. 4°.
	T 217.	Returna Brevium. 4°.
[1516–18].	R 30.	Year Book 40 Ed. 3.
	R 32.	Year Book 41 Ed. 3.
	R 34.	Year Book 42 Ed. 3.
	R 35.	Year Book 43 Ed. 3.
	R 36.	Year Book 44 Ed. 3.
	R 37.	Year Book 45 Ed. 3.
	S 117a.	Statutes 6 H. 8.
1517.	R 38.	Year Book 46 Ed. 3.
[1517].	R 47.	Year Book Lib. Ass.
1518.	R 40.	Year Book 48 Ed. 3.
[1518].	R 41.	Year Book 49 Ed. 3.
	R 42.	Year Book 50 Ed. 3.
	R 1.	Year Book 7 Ed. 3.
[1518–19].	R 75.	Year Book 2 H. 6.
	R 145.	Year Book 20 H. 6.
	R 234.	Year Book 2 Ed. 4.
	R 242.	Year Book 3 Ed. 4.
	R 273.	Year Book 7 Ed. 4.
	R 281.	Year Book 8 Ed. 4.
	R 296.	Year Book 10 Ed. 4.
	R 392.	Year Book 2 Ri. 3.
1519.	S 5.	Magna Carta. 12°.
[1519].	T 82.	Natura Brevium, fo.
1520.	R 24.	Year Book 38 Ed. 3.
[1520].	R 10.	Year Book 21 Ed. 3.
	R 39.	Year Book 47 Ed. 3.
	R 68.	Year Book 1 H. 6.
	R 83.	Year Book 3 H. 6.
	R 104.	Year Book 9 H. 6.
	R 111.	Year Book 10 H. 6.
	R 122.	Year Book 12 H. 6.
	R 133.	Year Book 18 H. 6.
	R 150.	Year Book 21 H. 6.
	R 155.	Year Book 22 H. 6.
	R 167.	Year Book 28 H. 6.
	R 190.	Year Book 34 H. 6.
	R 203.	Year Book 36 H. 6.

	R 209.	Year Book 37 H. 6.
	R 218.	Year Book 39 H. 6.
	R 250.	Year Book 4 Ed. 4.
	R 288.	Year Book 9 Ed. 4.
	R 314.	Year Book 14 Ed. 4.
	R 320.	Year Book 15 Ed. 4.
	R 326.	Year Book 16 Ed. 4.
	R 339.	Year Book 18 Ed. 4.
	R 345.	Year Book 19 Ed. 4.
	R 351.	Year Book 20 Ed. 4.
	R 357.	Year Book 21 Ed. 4.
	R 364.	Year Book 22 Ed. 4.
1521.	S 42.	Great Abridgement. 8°.
	T 135.	Justice of Peace. 4°.
[1521].	T 203.	Hundred Court. 4°.
	T 219.	Returna Brevium. 4°.
	T 164.	Carta Feodi.
1525.	T 9.	Littleton. 8°.
	T 72.	Old Tenures. 8°.
	T 83.	Natura Brevium. 8°.
[1525].	T 111.	Articuli Nov. Narr. 8°.
1526.	T 122.	Diversity of Courts. 8°.
1527.	S 7.	Magna Carta.
1528.	T 10.	Littleton. 8°.
	T 84.	Natura Brevium. 8°.
	S 43.	Great Abridgement.
[1529].	S 127.	Statutes 21 H. 8. fo.

John Rastell

Rastell began to print about 1514. About 1520 he moved to an establishment at the sign of the Mermaid, next to St. Paul's gate. He seems not to have printed — law books at least — after 1529. His son began printing in 1530.

He seems to have used four types in his law books:

1. The type of the text of Fitzherbert's Abridgement.
2. The type of the table (in Vol. 1) and the headings of the same work.
3. A small square black-letter, with gothic features, used in his editions of the Great Abridgement.
4. A larger type, in black-letter, used on several title-pages.

He used two devices: (1) a large one [McK.37], which was recut about 1527, being a trifle wider and one eighth of an inch higher; and (2) a smaller one, J. R. and the motto Justicia Regat, in a ribbon on black ground. [McK.40.]

A controversy of long standing about the printer of Fitzherbert's Abridgement may here be noticed. In many authorities it is stated that Pynson printed the first edition in 1514, and that the 1516 edition of Rastell was a separate work. No Pynson edition, and no edition dated 1514, can be found in either of the libraries alleged to contain it. It is significant, however, that the woodcuts which form the frontispieces of the first and third volumes are identical with the cuts often used by Pynson — are in fact printed from the same block, as is shown by the breaks in the cut being the same. In the third volume there are two issues of the title-page; one is printed from Pynson's block, the other is recut, and this recut block is also used in the second volume.

It may be conjectured therefore that Pynson had some connection with the printing of this work.

John Rastell's works were:

[1514].	R 48, 49.	Liber Assissarum (two impressions).
[1514–16].	R 456, 461.	Fitznerbert's Abridgement.
[1515].	R 4, 7.	Year Books 17 & 18 Ed. 3.
	R 295.	Year Book 10 Ed. 4.
	R 373.	Year Book 1 Ed. 5 & 1 R. 3.
[1518].	R 462.	Table to Fitz. Abr.
[1520].	T 71.	Old Tenures.
	T 451, 452.	Terms of the Law (two issues).
[1527].	T 137.	Book of the Justyce of Peas.
	T 165.	Carta Feodi.
	T 186.	Court Baron.
	T 205.	Hundred Court.
	T 220.	Returna Brevium.
	T 232.	Ordinance of the Exchequer.
1527.	S 44.	Great Abridgement of the Statutes.
1528.	T 461, 462.	Doctor & Student (two issues).
	T 13.	Littleton's Tenures (fragment).
	S 45.	Great Abridgement of the Statutes.
1529.	S 129.	Statutes 21 Hen. 8.

William Rastell

Printed between 1530 and 1534, when he gave up the art to enter the bar. He printed few law books. He used one compartment. He had three types: (1) an elegant italic with a light face; (2) a slightly heavier elegant black-letter; (3) a small neat black-letter. In addition to these, he used for titles and headings some of the heading-types of his father, John Rastell. He had no device.

A peculiarity in one of his works requires consideration. The original of his Register of Writs was, according to the colophon, to be sold at his house or at Redman's. The same edition was reissued by Tottel without the first colophon, but with a colophon by Tottel on a separate leaf. In a copy of this in the Harvard Law Library an uninked impression of Rastell's colophon may be plainly seen in the place it occupies in the original issue. His books were:

1531.	T 309.	Register of all writs.
[1533].	S 47.	Abridgement of the Statutes.
[1534].	S 82, 84.	Abridgement of Statutes 22–24 Hen. 8.
	T 1, 2.	Twelve tracts (two issues, in single and double columns. Type not reset).

Robert Redman

This printer began to print in St. Clement's parish, outside Temple Bar, about 1525. He assumed Pynson's sign (the George) and printed the law books which Pynson was accustomed to print, and as a result a bitter controversy sprang up, which continued active on Pynson's side until his death in 1530. Redman at once bought out his business, and used his type and devices; apparently also Redman assumed to be his successor as King's Printer, though he was soon prevented from so acting. He died in 1540. The business continued to be carried on by his wife, Elizabeth (sometimes using her maiden name, Elizabeth Pickering), for about a year, when the office passed to William Middleton.

His first set of type was perhaps bought, as one of his earliest borders certainly was, from Julian Notary, whose office he may have taken in the early twenties. In 1530 he succeeded to Pynson's cuts and type.

Redman used several woodcuts and devices besides those he bought from Pynson's Estate. Those found in his law books are:

1. A device of the Trinity.
2. A device of the Christ-child.
3. A crowned Tudor rose.

His law books were:

1525.	S 6.	Magna Carta.
[1525].	T 11.	Littleton.
1527.	T 206.	Hundred Court.
	R 84.	Year Book 3 Hen. 6.
	T 166.	Carta Feodi.
	T 187.	Court Baron.
	T 138.	Book for a Justice of Peace.
	T 221.	Returna Brevium.
[1527].	S 46.	Great Abridgement in French.
1528.	T 415.	Perkins' Profitable Book.
	T 73.	Old Tenures.
	T 12.	Littleton.
	S 47.	Great Abridgement in English.
[1528].	T 113.	Articuli ad narr. novas.
	T 123.	Diversity of Courts.
1529.	T 187.	Natura Brevium.
[1529].	S 128.	Statute 21 H. 8.
[1525–28].	R 17.	Year Book 24 Ed. 3.
	R 69.	Year Book 1 H. 6.
	R 76.	Year Book 2 H. 6.
	R 90.	Year Book 4 H. 6.
	R 127.	Year Book 14 H. 6.
	R 134.	Year Book 18 H. 6.
	R 138.	Year Book 19 H. 6.
	R 151.	Year Book 21 H. 6.
	R 156.	Year Book 22 H. 6.
	R 289.	Year Book 9 Ed. 4.
	R 301.	Year Book 12 Ed. 4.
	R 308.	Year Book 13 Ed. 4.
	R 321.	Year Book 15 Ed. 4.
	R 327.	Year Book 16 Ed. 4.
	R 340.	Year Book 18 Ed. 4.
	R 352.	Year Book 20 Ed. 4.
	R 358.	Year Book 21 Ed. 4.
[1530].	S 80, 81.	Abridgement Statutes 21, 22 H. 8.
1530.	T 167.	Carta Feodi.
[1530].	S 48.	Great Abridgement.
	S 25.	Great Book of Statutes.
	T 139.	Boke for a Justice of Peace.

	T 188.	Court Baron.
	T 207.	Hundred Court.
	T 222.	Returna Brevium.
	T 233.	Ordinance of the Exchequer.
[1530–38].	R 18.	Year Book 29 Ed. 3.
	R 21.	Year Book 30 Ed. 3.
	R 27.	Year Book 39 Ed. 3.
	R 33.	Year Book 41 Ed. 3.
	R 117.	Year Book 11 H. 6.
	R 162.	Year Book 27 H. 6.
	R 168.	Year Book 28 H. 6.
	R 172.	Year Book 30–31 H. 6.
	R 177.	Year Book 32 H. 6.
	R 184.	Year Book 33 H. 6.
	R 197.	Year Book 35 H. 6.
	R 214.	Year Book 38 H. 6.
	R 235.	Year Book 2 Ed. 4.
	R 266.	Year Book 6 Ed. 4.
	R 274.	Year Book 7 Ed. 4.
	R 298.	Year Book 11 Ed. 4.
	R 315.	Year Book 14 Ed. 4.
	R 332.	Year Book 17 Ed. 4.
	R 346.	Year Book 19 Ed. 4.
	R 406.	Year Book 21 H. 7.
	T 140a.	Book for a Justice.
[1531].	T 465.	Doctor & Student. First dialogue.
1531.	T 470.	Doctor & Student. Second dialogue.
1532.	T 466.	Doctor & Student. First dialogue.
	T 471.	Doctor & Student. Second dialogue.
1532.	T 74.	Old Tenures.
	T 98.	Natura Brevium.
	T 120.	Diversity of Courts.
	T 39.	Littleton in English.
	T 223.	Returna Brevium.
	T 416.	Perkins' Profitable Book.
1533.	T 168.	Carta Feodi.
	T 140.	Boke of Justices of Peace.
	T 189.	Court Baron.
	T 234.	Ordinance of Exchequer.
	T 125.	Diversity of Courts.
1534.	T 410.	Lyndewode.
	R 31.	Year Book 40 Ed. 3.
	S 10.	Magna Carta.
	S 86.	Abridgment Stat. 24–25 H. 8.
	T 324.	Britton.
	T 90.	Natura Brevium. fo.
1535.	T 99.	Natura Brevium.
1537.	T 224.	Returna Brevium.
[1538].	T 143.	Boke for a Justice of Peace.
	T 288.	Office of Sheriffs.
1538.	T 169.	Carta Feodi.
	T 170.	Carta Feodi.
	T 190.	Court Baron.
	T 208.	Hundred Court.
	T 209.	Hundred Court.
	T 235.	Ordinance of the Exchequer.
	T 236.	Ordinance of the Exchequer.

T 334. L'office et auctoryte des J. P.
T 335. Fitzherbert's Justice of Peace.
S 49. Great Abridgement.
1539. T 15. Littleton.
T 117. Articuli ad Narr. Novas.
S 8. Magna Carta.
S 87, 88, 89, 90. Abridgement. 26 (2 copies) and 27–28 (2 copies) H. 8.
1540. T 100. Natura Brevium.
[1540]. R 383. Year Book 1 R. 3.
R 401. Year Book 1–8 H. 7.
R 406. Year Book 21 H. 7.
R 415. Year Book 12–13 H. 8.
R 419. Year Book 14 H. 8.
S 50. Great Abridgement.
S 91, 92. Abridgement 31 H. 8 (2 copies).
1541. T 172. Carta Feodi.
T 225. Returna Brevium.

ELIZABETH (PICKERING) REDMAN

1540. T 336. Fitzherbert, Justice.
[1541]. S 11. Magna Carta.
T 289. Office of Sheriffs.
S 83, 93. Abridgement Statutes 23, 32 H. 8.

ROBERT ROBINSON

Began to print in Fetter Lane about 1580, and printed until about 1597. His only law book is:

1585. R 478. Bellewe's Reports.

THEODORIC ROOD

Printed at Oxford from 1478 to 1486, and in that time issued one law book in types "2," "3," "4," and "5."

[1481]. T 398. Lyndewode, W. Constitutiones provinciales.

WILLIAM SERES

Printed from 1546 to 1577. His only law book was a copy of the Great Abridgement printed for him by Gaultier, whose mane is on the title-page.

1551. S 54. Great Abridgement.

VALENTINE SIMMES

A printer in London from 1585 to 1622. He printed:

1594. T 484. West's Symboleography.
1600. T 287. The Laws of the Stannary of Devon.

JOHN SKOT

Began to print in St. Sepulchre's parish in 1521, and he was in St. Paul's Churchyard in 1528–9. He assisted Wynkyn de Worde. He printed the

"Justice of Peace" series in the style of de Worde, with the title in a ribbon, using the cut of the King's arms but not that of the King and Justices. On the reverse of the last leaf he used his device (McK.59). In his Carta Feodi he uses the crowned rose (46).

1521.	T 136.	Justice of the Peace.
	T 185.	Court Baron.
[1521].	T 163.	Carta Feodi.
[1522–9].	T 185a.	Court Baron.
	T 204.	Hundred Court.

He uses the same type de Worde used for the tracts.

Henry Smyth

Was a son-in-law of Redman, who printed outside Temple Bar in 1545 and 1546. He used some of the material of William Rastell. His law books were:

[1545].	T 78.	Old Tenures.
	T 17.	Littleton.
	T 92.	Natura Brevium.
	T 118.	Articuli ad Narr. Novas.
	T 129.	Diversity of Courts.
1545.	T 418.	Perkins' Profitable Book.
	T 356.	Fortescue, de politica.
	T 284.	Intrationum Liber.
[1545–46].	R 70.	Year Book 1 H. 6.
	R 78.	Year Book 2 H. 6.
	R 85.	Year Book 3 H. 6.
	R 91.	Year Book 4 H. 6.
	R 96.	Year Book 7 H. 6.
	R 98.	Year Book 8 H. 6.
	R 105, 106.	Year Book 9 H. 6 (two issues).
	R 113.	Year Book 10 H. 6.
	R 118.	Year Book 11 H. 6.
1546.	T 178.	Carta Feodi.
	T 198.	Court Baron.
	T 230 a.	Returna Brevium.
	T 293.	Ord. of Exchequer.
	T 148.	Book for a Justice of Peace.

Richard Tottell

Printed in London from 1552 to 1593. At the beginning of his career he received a patent to print law books, and most of the law books printed in England for forty years were from his press. The patent did not include Statutes which were printed by the King's Printer; but about 1577, after the death of Jugge, he is said to have claimed the right to print them also, and to have printed several of them, until Barker received the appointment of Printer to the Queen in the same year.

Tottell was son-in-law of Richard Grafton; and when Grafton was removed from office as King's Printer and imprisoned, on the accession of Queen Mary, Tottell took over his type and wood cuts. The type which Grafton used for his statutes, and Tottell for his Year-Books, has two very distinctive capital letters, the D and T, by condition of which an approximate date of the Year-Books can be traced. The T had originally a long member on the left reaching down to the line; this was soon worn off. Tottell got a new supply of this letter early in his printing, but by 1570 it was all worn, and from that time all the capital T's were without the prolongation on the left line. The capital D had a perpendicular hair-line next the left-hand down-stroke of the D which lasted throughout Grafton's time and until about 1570; by that time it was worn away in all cases.

Tottell's name was spelled in at least eleven different ways (not counting a misprint, Totttle): Tathill, Tothill, Tottel, Tottil, Tottyl, Tottell, Tottill, Tottyll, Tottle, Totel, and Totell. The spelling commonly used on his title-pages is Tottell, and this has been here adopted. There have been many conjectures as to the reasons for these misspellings, but no sound explanation exists. No uniform method is found even in a single edition of the Year-Books; but in most cases where several years were printed together one spelling prevailed (not without exceptions), and this fact has proved a help in fixing the date of certain years.

Most of the Year-Books are dated; but dates of earlier years cannot be trusted. If a year was printed before 1560, or even 1570, a later reprint of the year was likely to copy the date of the earlier issue. It is therefore necessary, in one of the ways suggested, or by considering the way in which years were bound together in volumes, to fix a conjectural date. All these methods have been employed in the conjectural dates suggested below.

Another help in determining the true date of his Year-Books is the form of his colophons. These fall into four general classes:

I. Colophons having a long first line: "Imprinted at London in fletestrete within," or perhaps with the last word divided. This is the form adopted in all the "hand and star" books, and in several others dated 1558–60; and in two later ones, 22 Ed. 4 of 1572 and 12–14 H. 8, 1567. These must be accounted for as hasty copies of old forms.

II. Colophons in bold type, in a stereotyped form, of which the first line is: "Imprinted at London." This was first used in several editions between 1555 and 1561, with two examples dated 1562, and one dated 1566; next in an edition of the years of Edward 4 dated 1572; and then in a number of editions from 1574 to 1585.

III. Colophons in still bolder type, the first line being "Imprinted (Imprynted) at Lon-". This appears in several books dated 1562, and in books which must be placed between that date and 1570.

Two books dated and indubitably ascribed to 1556 (26 & 27 Hen. 8) are in this form, and must be regarded as an accidental variant from type II.

IV. A somewhat smaller colophon, of which the first line reads "Imprinted at London in". This form is used somewhat irregularly: a few times in 1566–68; several times in irregularly-dated books ascribed to 1572, and forming, with similar books in form II, a complete set of the books of Edward 4; and in a few books dated from 1580 to 1585. From the fact that these books all appear to form part of a series of which the other colophons are in form II, it would seem that this form is a typographical variant of form II.

As a result of these various tests, the colophon test having been applied after the others had been used to fix a tentative relation between the books and approximate dates, the following schedule of dates may be put forward as probably substantially correct:

Part II. 1–10 Ed. 3.

The only edition of this part by Tottell is dated 1562, and has colophon in form II. This is the earliest edition known of all the years (except year 7) of this part, and was therefore probably printed directly from the manuscripts, except for year 7, which had been printed by Pynson in 1518.

Part III. 17–39 Ed. 3.

There appear to have been two editions of this part, one printed in 1561. Years 17 and 18 have no date or colophon. 21 is dated 1561, and has colophon in form II, and 29, 30, 38 and 39 are of the same date and form. The book 22–28 seems not to have been printed at this time, but was printed later, dated 1567, with colophon III.

A second Tottell edition of this part was printed about 1585. Years 17 and 18 were again printed without date or colophon; 21 was dated 1584, with colophon IV; 22–28, 29, 30, 38 and 39 were dated 1585, with the same form of colophon.

Part IV. 40–50 Edward 3.

Tottell published three editions of this part, all of which had previously been printed by Pynson, and the first two years by Redman. Tottell printed no separate years.

The first edition is dated 1555, and has colophon II. The second is dated 1565, and has colophon III. The third, dated 1576, has colophon II.

Part V. Liber Assissarum.

This part, which was first printed by Rastell, was twice reprinted in full by Tottell. The first edition was dated 1561, and the second 1580; both have colophon II.

Part VI. This part was printed by Tottell in two portions.

Henry IV. The years of this reign were printed together by Tottell three times, apparently from manuscript, as only scattered years had been printed by Pynson and Wyre. Tottell printed the years first in 1553, with colophon II; again in 1562–63, with colophon III; and in 1575, with colophon II.

The years of Henry V (of which year 9 only had previously been printed, by Pynson and by Powell) were printed three times: in 1563, with colophon III; in 1570 (with a title-page newly set, but dated 1563), with colophon III; and again in 1587, with colophon II.

Part VII. The first part of Henry VI (1–20) was printed by Tottell in three editions.

The first, between 1556 and 1562, with colophon II, except as follows: colophon I, — 3, 11, 19; colophon III, — 9, 12, 14 (1562); 18, with an early short form of colophon, not elsewhere found, about 1559. Year 20 was printed twice: in 1553 and 1559.

The second edition was printed between 1567 and 1570, with colophon III. Years 12 and 14 of this edition have colophon II, and 18 has a colophon in the same form as the first edition.

The third edition was printed between 1582 and 1587, with colophon II except years 9, 14 and 20 (without colophon). Year 19 is dated 1567, but was independently ascribed to 1585. Year 18 has a colophon as in the other editions.

Part VIII. The second part of Henry VI (21–39) is also in three editions.

The first, dated 1556–57, is as follows: years 21, 22, 27, 28 with colophon I, undated hand & star editions ascribed to 1556; 30, 32, 33, 34, 35, 38, dated 1556, and 36, 39, dated 1557, colophon II; 37, undated, colophon I.

The second edition, in 1566 or 1567, with colophon III. Three of the years (33, 34, 35) were wrongly dated 1556, but ascribed to 1566. A second issue of year 27 is found, dated 1562.

The third edition, dated 1575 to 1578, has colophon II. A second issue of year 22 is found, dated 1578.

This was printed in four editions.

First, 1556 to 1559; all with colophon II except years 2, 3, 4, 10–12, 13, 21 which have colophon I. A second issue of year 6 was printed, the two being dated 1556 and 1557.

Second, 1565 to 1567, with colophon III. Many of these years were dated earlier, but all have been independently ascribed to one of the dates named. Year 15 has colophon II. Two copies of year 1 of this edition have been found, dated 1556 (1565) and 1565.

Third, in 1572 (some of the years variously dated, but all ascribed to this year). Of this edition years 1, 3, 4, 5, 7, 8, 10–12, 16, 19, 20, 21 have colophon IV; years 2, 6, 9, 13, 14, 15, 17, 18 have colophon II; year 22 has colophon I.

Fourth, 82–84, with colophon II; except year 1 (colophon IV). Year 22 is dated 1578.

Part X. Long Quint.

Tottell printed only one edition of the Long Quint, dated 1587, with colophon II.

Part XI. The reigns which together make up part XI of the later printers were differently and irregularly printed by Tottell, and offer most of the difficulties which arise in dating the books of this printer. As these were the most recent reigns, and therefore contained the books most in demand, frequent issues of the books of these reigns were called for, and they cannot be grouped in larger units than those of each reign.

Edward V.

Seven editions may be distinguished.
1555; colophon II.
1559; colophon II.
1564 (dated 1559); colophon III.
1568; colophon III.
1572 (dated 1558); colophon IV.
1579 and another dated 1558; colophon IV.
1585; colophon IV.

Richard III. Seven editions.

1558–59 (two issues, without date); colophon II.

1561 (without date), and 1568; colophon III.
1574, 1581 and 1587; colophon II.

Henry VII. Eight editions.
1–3, 1555 (three editions); colophon II.
4–5, 1560 (dated 1555) and 1567, colophon III.
6–8, 1567, 1580, 1585/3; colophon IV.

Henry VIII. At least eight editions.
1556; colophon II.
1559–60; there have been found 12–14, 1560, and 18–19, hand and star, with colophon I. Year 26, with colophon II, perhaps belongs to this edition; no correspondent year 27 has been found. Two other issues of year 18–19, without date, with colophon I, exist.
1566; 12–14 with colophon II, and the remaining years with colophon III. Another issue of 26 and 27, misdated 1556, with colophon III, is also found.
1567; 12–14 with colophon I, the remaining years with colophon IV.
1569; with colophon III.
1579; with colophon II.
1583; with colophon II. Only year 27 of this edition has been found.
1591; with colophon II.

The General Table of Tottell's Books is as follows:

1553. T 310. Registrum omnium brevium.
T 344. Fitzherbert's new natura brevium.
R 60. Year Book 1–14 H. 4.
R 146. Year Book 20 H. 6.
1554. T 20. Littleton's Tenures.
T 473. Doctor and Student.
T 474. Doctor and Student.
T 341. Fitzherbert's Justice of Peace.
T 365. Glanville.
1555. T 419. Perkins' Profitable Book.
R 52. Year Book Liber Assissarum abridged.
R 53. Year Book Liber Assissarum abridged.
R 43. Year Book 40–50 Ed. 3.
R 375. Year Book 1 Ed. 5.
R 407, 408, 409. Year Book 1–21 H. 7.
1556. T 152. Book for a Justice of Peace.
T 49. Littleton in English.
S 16, 17, 24. Magna Carta (two issues), and Secunda Pars.
R 72. Year Book 1 H. 6.
R 79. Year Book 2 H. 6.
R 86. Year Book 3 H. 6.
R 92. Year Book 4 H. 6.
R 124. Year Book 12 H. 6.
R 147. Year Book 20 H. 6.
R 169. Year Book 28 H. 6.
R 174. Year Book 30–31 H. 6.
R 179. Year Book 32 H. 6.
R 185. Year Book 33 H. 6.
R 191. Year Book 34 H. 6.
R 198. Year Book 35 H. 6.
R 215. Year Book 38 H. 6.
R 228. Year Book 1 Ed. 4.

R 275. Year Book 7 Ed. 4.
R 283. Year Book 8 Ed. 4.
R 290. Year Book 9 Ed. 4.
R 316. Year Book 14 Ed. 4.
R 322. Year Book 15 Ed. 4.
R 341. Year Book. 18 Ed. 4.
R 347. Year Book 19 Ed. 4.
R 353. Year Book 20 Ed. 4.
R 366. Year Book 22 Ed. 4.
R 420. Year Book 12–14 H. 8.
R 428. Year Book 18–19 H. 8.
R 437–9. Year Book 26 H. 8.
R 446–8. Year Book 27 H. 8.
[1556]. R 119. Year Book 11 H. 6.
R 129. Year Book 14 H. 6.
R 152. Year Book 21 H. 6.
R 157. Year Book 22 H. 6.
R 163. Year Book 27 H. 6.
R 211. Year Book 37 H. 6.
R 303. Year Book 10–12 Ed. 4.
R 359. Year Book 21 Ed. 4.
1557. T 21, 22, 23. Littleton's Tenures (3 issues).
T 125. Natura Brevium in English.
T 93. Natura Brevium.
T 485, 486. Staunford Pleas of the Crown.
S 557. Rastell's Statutes.
R 205. Year Book 36 H. 6.
R 220. Year Book 39 H. 6.
R 259. Year Book 5 Ed. 4.
R 267. Year Book 6 Ed. 4.
R 328. Year Book 16 Ed. 4.
R 334, 335. Year Book 17 Ed. 4.
1558. R 236. Year Book 2 Ed. 4.
R 244. Year Book 3 Ed. 4.
R 252. Year Book 4 Ed. 4.
R 376. Year Book 1 Ed. 5.
[1558]. R 384, 393. Year Book 1, 2 R. 3.
1559. T 153, 154. Book for a Justice of Peace.
T 436. Book of Presidents.
S 58, 59. Rastell's Statutes (two copies).
R 100. Year Book 7–8 H. 6.
R 310. Year Book 13 Ed. 4.
R 377. Year Book 1 Ed. 5.
R 440. Year Book 26 H. 8.
[1559]. R 135. Year Book 18 H. 6.
R 140. Year Book 19 H. 6.
R 385. Year Book 1 R. 3.
R 394. Year Book 2 R. 3.
1560. T 342. Fitzherbert's Justice of Peace.
T 345. Fitzherbert's natura Brevium.
S 72. Pulton's Statutes.
T 487. Staunford's Pleas of the Crown.
R 421, 422. Year Book 12–14 H. 8 (two issues).
[1560]. T 426. Perkins' Profitable Book.
R 410. Year Book 1–21 H. 7.
R 429, 430, 431. Year Book 18–19 H. 8 (three issues).
T 110. Novae narrationes.

T 437. Book of presidents.
R 12, 19, 22, 25, 28. Year Books 21, 29, 30, 38, 39 Ed. 3.
R 50. Year Book Liber Assisarum.
R 114. Year Book 10 H. 6.
[1561]. R 5, 8. Year Books 17, 18 Ed. 3.
R 386, 395. Year Books 1, 2 R. 3.
1562. T 438. Book of presidents.
T 300. Office of Sheriffs.
R 2. Year Book 1–10 Ed. 3.
R 61. Year Book 1–14 H. 4.
R 108. Year Book 9 H. 6.
R 125. Year Book 12 H. 6.
R 130. Year Book 14 H. 6.
R 164. Year Book 27 H. 6.
1563. T 454. Terms of the Law.
R 65. Year Book 1–9 H. 5.
[1564]. R 378. Year Book 1 Ed. 5.
1565. R 463, 464, 465. Fitzherbert's Abridgement and Table.
S 60. Rastell's Statutes.
R 44. Year Book 40–50 E. 3.
R 229. Year Book 1 Ed. 4.
[1565]. S 219. Statutes 1 Ed. 6.
S 225. Statutes 2–3 Ed. 6.
S 229. Statutes 3–4 Ed. 6.
S 249. Statutes 1 Mary 2d Par.
S 255. Statutes 1–2 P. & M.
1566. T 448. Rastell's Entries.
T 343. Fitzherbert's Justice of Peace.
S 61. Rastell's Statutes.
R 180. Year Book 32 H. 6.
R 216. Year Book 38 H. 6.
R 237. Year Book 2 Ed. 4.
R 245. Year Book 3 Ed. 4.
R 260. Year Book 5 Ed. 4.
R 304. Year Book 10–12 Ed. 4.
R 311. Year Book 13 Ed. 4.
R 360. Year Book 21 Ed. 4.
R 423. Year Book 12–14 H. 8.
R 432. Year Book 18–19 H. 8.
R 441. Year Book 26 H. 8.
R 449. Year Book 27 H. 8.
[1566]. R 186. Year Book 33 H. 6.
R 192. Year Book 34 H. 6.
R 199. Year Book 35 H. 6.
R 230. Year Book 1 Ed. 4.
R 253. Year Book 4 Ed. 4.
R 268. Year Book 6 Ed. 4.
R 317. Year Book 14 Ed. 4.
R 323. Year Book 15 Ed. 4.
R 329. Year Book 16 Ed. 4.
R 354. Year Book 20 Ed. 4.
R 367. Year Book 22 Ed. 4.
1567. T 346, 347. Fitzherbert's Natura Brevium (two issues).
T 353C. Fitzherbert's Surveying.
T 278. Institutions or principal grounds.
T 357. Fortescue.
T 420, 421. Perkins' Profitable Book.

	T 24.	Littleton's Tenures.
	T 94.	Natura Brevium.
	T 455.	Terms of the Law.
	T 488.	Staunford's Pleas of the Crown.
	T 491.	Staunford's Prerogative.
	R 15.	Year Book 22–28 Ed. 3.
	R 120.	Year Book 11 H. 6.
	R 141.	Year Book 19 H. 6.
	R 153.	Year Book 21 H. 6.
	R 158.	Year Book 22 H. 6.
	R 165.	Year Book 27 H. 6.
	R 170.	Year Book 28 H. 6.
	R 175.	Year Book 30–31 H. 6.
	R 206.	Year Book 36 H. 6.
	R 212.	Year Book 37 H. 6.
	R 221.	Year Book 39 H. 6.
	R 276.	Year Book 7 Ed. 4.
	R 411, 412.	Year Book 1–21 H. 7.
	R 424.	Year Book 12–14 H. 8.
	R 433.	Year Book 18–19 H. 8.
	R 442.	Year Book 26 H. 8.
[1567].	R 284.	Year Book 8 Ed. 4.
	R 291.	Year Book 9 Ed. 4.
	R 336.	Year Book 17 Ed. 4.
	R 342.	Year Book 18 Ed. 4.
	R 348.	Year Book 19 Ed. 4.
1568.	T 51, 52.	Littleton in English.
	T 492.	Staunford's Prerogative.
	S 62.	Rastell's Statutes.
	R 87.	Year Book 3 H. 6.
	R 93.	Year Book 4 H. 6.
	R 136.	Year Book 18 H. 6.
	R 379.	Year Book 1 Ed. 5.
	R 387, 396.	Year Books 1, 2 R. 3.
1569.	T 155, 156.	Book for a Justice of Peace.
	T 25.	Littleton's Tenures.
	T 439.	Book of Presidents.
	T 475.	Doctor and Student.
	T 323.	Bracton.
	R 425.	Year Book 12–14 H. 8.
	R 434.	Year Book 18–19 H. 8.
	R 443.	Year Book 26 H. 8.
	R 451.	Year Book 27 H. 8.
1570.	T 279.	Institutions or principal grounds.
	T 301, 302, 303.	Office of sheriffs.
	R 66.	Year Book 1–9 H. 5.
	R 73.	Year Book 1 H. 6.
	R 80.	Year Book 2 H. 6.
	R 101.	Year Book 7–8 H. 6.
	R 109.	Year Book 9 H. 6.
	R 115.	Year Book 10 H. 6.
	R 148.	Year Book 20 H. 6.
1571.	R 484.	Plowden's Reports.
	T 286.	Laws concerning Liveries.
[1571].	S 220.	Statutes 1 Ed. 6.
	S 250.	Statutes 1 Mary (2d Par).
	S 256.	Statutes 1–2 P. & M.

	S 260.	Statutes 2, 3 P. & M.
	S 266.	Statutes 4, 5 P. & M.
	S 38.	Statutes Ed. 6 — Eliz. (t.p. and table).
1572.	T 26.	Littleton's Tenures.
	T 95.	Natura Brevium.
	T 440.	Book of Presidents.
	T 456.	Terms of the Law.
	T 501.	Wilson on Usury.
	S 63.	Rastell's Statutes.
	R 238.	Year Book 2 Ed. 4.
	R 269.	Year Book 6 Ed. 4.
	R 292.	Year Book 9 Ed. 4.
	R 312.	Year Book 13 Ed. 4.
	R 318.	Year Book 14 Ed. 4.
	R 324.	Year Book 15 Ed. 4.
	R 337.	Year Book 17 Ed. 4.
	R 343.	Year Book 18 Ed. 4.
	R 368.	Year Book 22 Ed. 4.
[1572].	R 231.	Year Book 1 Ed. 4.
	R 246.	Year Book 3 Ed. 4.
	R 254.	Year Book 4 Ed. 4.
	R 261.	Year Book 5 Ed. 4.
	R 277.	Year Book 7 Ed. 4.
	R 285.	Year Book 8 Ed. 4.
	R 305.	Year Book 10–12 Ed. 4.
	R 330.	Year Book 16 Ed. 4.
	R 349.	Year Book 19 Ed. 4.
	R 355.	Year Book 20 Ed. 4.
	R 361.	Year Book 21 Ed. 4.
	R 380.	Year Book 1 Ed. 5.
1573.	T 358.	Fortescue.
	T 493.	Staunford's Prerogative.
	R 469, 470.	Brooke's Abridgement.
1574.	T 157.	Book for a Justice of Peace.
	T 27.	Littleton's Tenures (two issues).
	T 53.	Littleton in English.
	T 489.	Staunford's Pleas of the Crown.
	T 449.	Rastell's Entries.
	S 64.	Rastell's Statutes.
	R 126.	Year Book 12 H. 6.
	R 131.	Year Book 14 H. 6.
	R 388, 397.	Year Books 1, 2 R. 3.
1575.	T 441.	Book of presidents.
	T 476.	Doctor and Student.
	R 62.	Year Book 1–14 H. 4.
	R 154.	Year Book 21 H. 6.
	R 159.	Year Book 22 H. 6.
	R 166.	Year Book 27 H. 6.
	R 171.	Year Book 28 H. 6.
	R 176.	Year Book 30–31 H. 6.
	R 187.	Year Book 33 H. 6.
	Y 193.	Year Book 34 H. 6.
	R 200.	Year Book 35 H. 6.
	R 207.	Year Book 36 H. 6.
	R 213.	Year Book 37 H. 6.
	R 217.	Year Book 38 H. 6.
	R 222.	Year Book 39 H. 6.

1576. T 348. Fitzherbert's Natura Brevium.
T 54. Littleton in English.
T 106. Natura Brevium in English.
T 422. Perkins' Profitable Book.
T 442. Book of Precedents.
R 471, 472. Brooke's Abridgement.
S 18, 19. Magna Carta (two copies).
R 45. Year Book 40–50 Ed. 3.
R 181. Year Book 32 H. 6.
1577. T 28. Littleton's Tenures.
T 494, 495. Staunford's Prerogative.
T 281. Institutions or Principal Grounds.
S 73. Pulton's Statutes.
S 65. Rastell's Statutes.
R 466, 467, 468. Fitzherbert's Abridgement and Table.
1578. R 485. Plowden's Commentaries.
R 479. Brooke's New Cases.
R 160. Year Book 22 H. 6.
R 369. Year Book 22 Ed. 4.
1579. T 354. Fleetwood's Annals.
T 368. Kitchin's Court Leet.
T 29. Littleton's Tenures.
T 457. Terms of the Law.
T 499. Theloall, Writs.
R 486. Plowden's Reports.
S 74. Pulton's Statutes.
[1579]. S 74a. Pulton's Statutes.
R 381. Year Book 1 Ed. 5.
R 426. Year Book 12–14 H. 8.
R 435. Year Book 18–19 H. 8.
R 444. Year Book 26 H. 8.
R 452. Year Book 27 H. 8.
1580. T 282. Institutions or principal grounds.
T 369. Kitchin's Court Leet.
T 366, 367. Kitchin's Justice of Peace.
T 96. Natura Brevium.
T 477, 478. Doctor and Student.
R 51. Year Book Liber Assissarum.
R 413. Year Book 1–21 H. 7.
[1580]. T 107. Natura Brevium in English.
1581. T 349. Fitzherbert's Natura Brevium.
T 370. Kitchin's Court Leet.
T 375. Kitchin's Returna Brevium.
T 30. Littleton's Tenures.
T 55. Littleton in English.
T 423. Perkins' Profitable Book.
T 72, 73, 76, 77. Index of Littleton.
T 443. Book of Precedents.
S 75. Pulton's Statutes.
R 389, 398. Year Books 1, 2 R. 3.
R 88. Year Book 3 H. 6.
R 94. Year Book 4 H. 6.
R 110. Year Book 9 H. 6.
R 121. Year Book 11 H. 6.
R 232. Year Book 1 Ed. 4.
R 286. Year Book 8 Ed. 4.
R 293. Year Book 9 Ed. 4.

R 313. Year Book 13 Ed. 4.
R 319. Year Book 14 Ed. 4.
R 325. Year Book 15 Ed. 4.
R 344. Year Book 18 Ed. 4.
R 356. Year Book 20 Ed. 4.
[1582]. R 132. Year Book 14 H. 6.
R 350. Year Book 19 Ed. 4.
1583. T 364. Gregory de Legibus.
T 329. Crompton's Justice of Peace.
T 31. Littleton's Tenures.
T 56. Littleton in English.
T 490. Staunford's Pleas of the Crown.
R 247. Year Book 3 Ed. 4.
R 255. Year Book 4 Ed. 4.
R 331. Year Book 16 Ed. 4.
R 338. Year Book 17 Ed. 4.
R 414. Year Book 1–21 H. 7.
R 417, 419a. Year Book 12–14 H. 8.
R 453. Year Book 27 H. 8.
1584. T 330. Crompton's Justice of Peace.
T 97. Natura Brevium.
T 445, 446. Book of Precedents.
R 487. Plowden's Reports.
R 13. Year Book 21 Ed. 3.
R 74. Year Book 1 H. 6.
R 81. Year Book 2 H. 6.
R 102. Year Book 7–8 H. 6.
R 239. Year Book 2 Ed. 4.
R 262. Year Book 5 Ed. 4.
R 278. Year Book 7 Ed. 4.
R 306. Year Book 10–12 Ed. 4.
R 362. Year Book. 21 Ed. 4.
[1584]. R 488. Table to Plowden's Reports.
R 149. Year Book 20 H. 6.
R 270. Year Book 6 Ed. 4.
1585. T 371. Kitchin's Court Leet.
T 376. Kitchin's Returna Brevium.
T 32. Littleton's Tenures.
T 64, 65. Index to Littleton.
R 481. Dyer's Reports.
R 16. Year Book 22–28 Ed. 3.
R 20. Year Book 29 Ed. 3.
R 23. Year Book 30 Ed. 3.
R 26. Year Book 38 Ed. 3.
R 29. Year Book 39 Ed. 3.
R 382. Year Book 1 Ed. 5.
[1585]. R 6, 9. Year Books 17, 18 Ed. 3.
R 37. Year Book 18 H. 6.
R 142. Year Book 19 H. 6.
R 188. Year Book 33 H. 6.
R 194. Year Book 34 H. 6.
R 201. Year Book 35 H. 6.
1586. T 57. Littleton in English.
T 424. Perkins' Profitable Book.
R 473, 474, 475, 476. Brooke's Abridgement (two issues).
1587. T 331. Crompton's Justice of Peace.
T 372. Kitchin's Court Leet.

	T 377.	Kitchin's Returna Brevium.
	S 20.	Magna Carta.
	R 67.	Year Book 1-9 H. 5.
	R 116.	Year Book 10 H. 6.
	R 371.	Year Book Long Quint.
	R 399.	Year Book 2 R. 3.
	R 480.	Plowden's Reports.
[1587].	R 390.	Year Book 1 R. 3.
1588.	T 350.	Fitzherbert's Natura Brevium.
	T 33.	Littleton's Tenures.
	R 489.	Plowden's Reports.
	R 483a.	Dyer's Reports.
1589.	T 367.	Kitchin's Justice of Peace.
1590.	T 496.	Staunford's Prerogative.
1591.	T 35.	Littleton's Tenures.
	R 482.	Dyer's Reports.
	R 454.	Year Books, 12-27 H. 8.
1592.	T 373.	Kitchin's Court Leet.
	T 378.	Kitchin's Returna Brevium.
	T 458.	Terms of the Law.
1593.	T 58.	Littleton in English.
	T 332.	Crompton's Justice of Peace.
	T 425.	Perkins' Profitable Book.
	T 479.	Doctor and Student.
n.d.	T 427.	Perkins' Profitable Book.

Robert Toye

Issued books from 1542 to 1555, most of them printed by others. His only law books consisted of the series printed probably by Nicholas Hyll, for several printers.

1546.	T 150.	Justice of the Peace.
	T 199.	Court baron.
	T 214.	Hundred Court.
	T 230b.	Returna brevium.
	T 244.	Ordinance of the Exchequer.
	T 274.	Office of sheriffs.

Peter Treveris

Was an obscure printer in Southwark, about 1530, who seems to have had some connection with Wyer. While the latter printed "Doctor and Student," "First Dialogue," "Treveris" in the same years and apparently with the same type printed the second dialogue.

In these books, the only law books he printed, Treveris used no device; in the first edition he used Compartment 51. His law books are:

1530.	T 467.	Doctor & Student, Second Dialogue.
1531.	T 469.	Doctor & Student, Second Dialogue.

Tysdale

[1562].	T 265.	Form of Indentures.
1562.	T 308.	Ordinal for Artificers.

John Waley or Walley

Printed from 1546 to 1585. The only law book he printed himself is:

[1560]. T 285. The Form of Making Indentures.

He was one of the printers for whom were printed (probably by Hyll) the following series:

1546. T 149. Justice of the Peace.
T 177. Carta feodi.
T 197. Court baron.
T 213. Hundred Court.
T 230c. Returna brevium.
T 242. Ordinance of the Exchequer.

Roger Warde

An apprentice to Thomas Marsh, who printed in various places in London from 1577 to 1598. In 1582, at the Talbot, by Holborn Conduit, he printed his only known law book:

1582. T 380. Lambard's Duties of Constables.

Edward Whitechurch

Printed in London from 1541 to 1553. He printed, so far as is known, only two law books, both to be sold by others.

1543. T 429. Phaer's Book of Presidents. To be sold by Tylotson.
[1545]. T 356. Fortescue. To be sold by Smyth.

J. Wight

1556. T 297. Office of Sheriffs.

Thomas Wight

Bookseller and printer in London from 1580 to 1608. In 1599 he and Bonham Norton succeeded Yetsweirt in the patent for printing law books. He printed alone the following:

1600. T 61. Littleton's Tenures in English.
T 447. Book of Presidents.
T 361. Fulbeck's Preparative.
S 79. Pulton's Statutes.
R 46. Year Book 40–50 Ed. 3.
R 483. Table to Plowden's Reports.

In partnership with Norton:

1598. T 351. Fitzherbert's Natura Brevium.
T 413. Manwood's Forest Law.
T 460. Terms of the Law.
T 480. Doctor and Student.
T 374. Kitchin's Court Leet.
S 71. Rastell's Statutes.

1599. T 38. Littleton's Tenures.
T 359. Fortescue's Laws of England.
T 386. Lambard's Duties of Constables.
T 395. Lambard's Eirenarcha.
R 372. Year Book 1–22 Ed. 4.
R 477. Gregory's Abridgement.
R 490. Plowden's Reports.

JOHN WINDET

Printed in London from 1584 to 1611. His law books are:

1589. T 483. Smyth's Commonwealth of England. [For Gregory Seton.)
1590–1. T 498. Swinburn on Wills.
1600. T 258. Assize of Bread.
[1567]. T . Reginald Wolfe. Advertisements partly for due order.

REGINALD WOLFE

[1567]. T . Advertisements partly for due orders.

JOAN WOLFE

1579. T 313. Statutes &c for Romney Marsh.

WYNKYN DE WORDE

An assistant of Caxton, who at the latter's death in 1491 took over his office in Westminster; he stayed here until 1500, when he moved to Fleet Street, and printed there at the sign of the Sun. He died in 1535.

He used numerous devices, being modifications of Caxton's. His woodcuts in law books were three separate cuts of a bishop, two at least of the king's arms, and a cut of a king and judges which he seems to have acquired from Notary, (or perhaps he lent it to Notary).

His types before 1500 will be found in Duff. In his law books from that time to 1520 he used (1) a conventional legal black-letter, with rather distinctive capitals. In some of his later law books he employed (2) a fine black-letter. His known legal works were:

[1492–96]. S 98. Statutes 1–4 H. 7. [1493.] Type 4.
S 100. Statutes 7 H. 7. [1495.] Types 4 & 6.
S 102, 103. Statutes 11 H. 7. [1496.] Types 4 & 6.
1496. T 399. Lyndewode, Provinciale. Types, Duff 2 & 4.
1499. T 402. Lyndewode, Provinciale. Types, Duff 2 & 4.
1508. S 108. Statutes 1–19 Henry 7. 1508. Tract type 1.
1510. T 131, 132. Justice of Peace (2 issues). Tract type 1.
[1510]. T 159, 160, 161, 162. Carta Feodi (4 issues). Tract type 1.
T 181. Court Baron. Tract type 1.
1515. T 133. Book for a Justice.
1517. T 407. Lyndewode, Provinciale. Type 2.
1519. T 215. Returna Brevium. Type 1.
1529. T 409. Lyndewode Provinciale. Type 2.

ROBERT WYER

This printer took the sign of St. John Evangelist, in the "Bishop of Norwich's Rents" (after 1536 the Duke of Suffolk's), in St. Martin's parish. He printed several law books, using his devices in McKerrow (67–70), and also a cut of the royal arms (McK. 57) ascribed by McKerrow to Siberch, the Cambridge printer, in 1521, and used a few years later by Antwerp printers. It passed to Wyer before 1530. I cannot see the slightest variation between Wyer's block and that of Siberch (in Duff's "Provincial Printers" p. 82) even in the smallest lines (unless possibly a flower? over the portcullis in the right side near the bottom, which I do not find in his facsimile). If Wyer's block was recut, it was cleverly done.

Wyer used several styles of type.

1. In his "Doctor and Student" and other earlier books, a fine black-letter not unlike J. Rastell's or Butler's, but with capitals very like those used by de Worde. The large title type seems to be that of J. Rastell in his "Great Abridgment." Treveris used the same in his "Second Dialogue." These two rather obscure printers may have bought the type from de Worde and Rastell.

2. The type of his Assize of Bread appears to be the black-letter type of de Worde's tracts, afterwards used by Copland and Pepwell. Wyer's legal works were:

[152–].	R 56.	Year Book 9 H. 4.
1530.	T 463.	Doctor and Student. First Dialogue.
[1532].	T 464.	Doctor and Student. First Dialogue.
[1535].	T 40.	Littleton.
[1540].	T 254.	Assise of Bread.
[1545].	T 306.	Ordinal or Statutes concerning Artificers.
[1550].	T 255.	Assize of Bread.
[1553].	T 256.	Assize of Bread.

Henry Wykes

An apprentice of Berthelet, who put his name on one book of statutes (printed with Berthelet's type and woodcut) during the latter's lifetime, and another after his successor, Thomas Powell, had ceased to print.

1551.	S 28.	Statutes to 1 H. 8.
1564.	S 29.	Statutes to 1 H. 8.

Charles Yetsweirt

Succeeded Tottell as patentee for law books in 1594; he died in 1595, and his widow, Jane, continued to print under the patent until 1597. His law books were:

1594.	T 328.	Crompton's Jurisdiction of Courts.
	T 385.	Lambard's Duties of Constables.
	T 36.	Littleton's Tenures.
	T 59.	Littleton's Tenures in English.
	R 489a, b, c	Plowden.
1595.	T 459.	Terms of the law.
	S 70a.	Rastell's Statutes.

Jane Yetsweirt

1595.	T 311.	Registrum omnium brevium.
1596.	T 450.	Rastell's Entries.

	S 78.	Pulton's Statutes.
	R 3.	Year Book 1–10 Ed. 3.
1597.	T 355.	Fleetwood's Annals.
	T 60.	Littleton's Tenures in English.
	T 428.	Perkins' Profitable Book.
	R 454.	Year Book Ed. 5 to H. 8.
[1597].	T 37.	Littleton's Tenures.
	R 491.	Plowden's Reports, Abridgement.
	R 480.	Brooke's New Cases.

APPENDIX I

WOODCUTS REFERRED TO IN THE DESCRIPTIONS

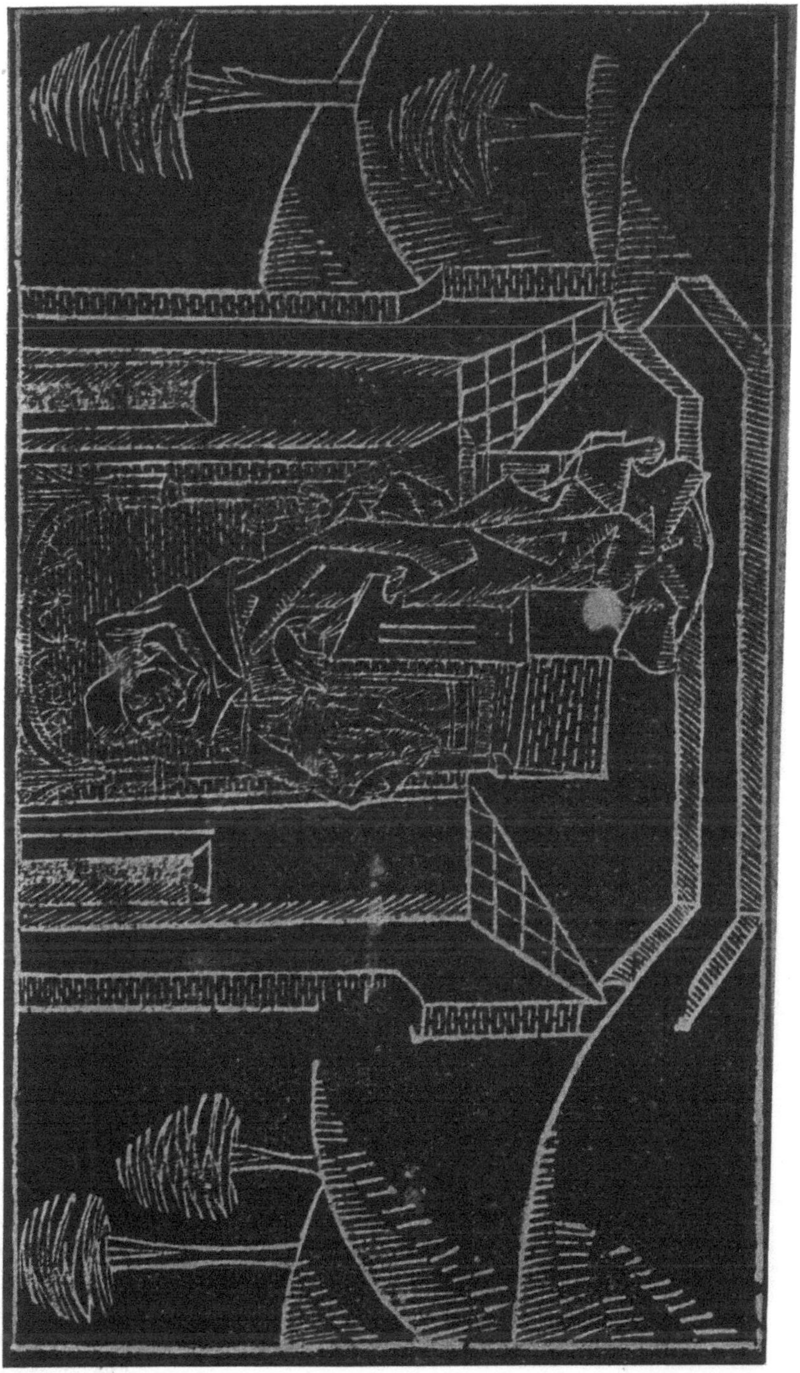

No. 1. Rood's Lyndewood, T 398.

No. 2. Tailleur's Mark, on books printed by him for Pynson: Statham's Abridgement, R 455. Littleton, T 5.

No. 3. de Worde's Lyndwode, T 399.

No. 4 (reduced). Pynson's Old Tenures, 1496, T 68.

No. 5. Notary's Statutes of Henry 7: S 99, 101, 104, 107. Redrawn in de Worde's Statutes of Henry 7, S 102, 108/, and in Pynson's and de Worde's Justice of Peace, T 130, 131.

No. 6. Same as **5**.

No. 7 (reduced). First used by Pynson in his folio editions of Littleton and the Natura Brevium, 1496–1508: T 6, 7, 8, 82; in his early Statute, 19 Hen. 7, S 109; and in his Year-Book, 2 R 3, R 391. He then apparently lent it to J. Rastell for Fitzherbert's Abridgement, Vol. 1, R 456.

On Pynson's death it passed to Redman, who used it in his Year-Books of 40 Ed. 3, R 31, and 1 R 3, R 383, and in his Great Book of Statutes, S 25.

On Redman's death it passed to his successor, W. Middleton, who used it in his Great Book of Statutes, S 26.

No. 8 (reduced). First used by Pynson in his Statutes, 3, 6 Henry 8, S 116, 117a; then in his Littleton, 1516, T 8, his Natura Brevium, 1519, T 82, and his Year-Book of 7 Ed. 3, R 1. It was also used by Rastell. in his edition of Fitzherbert's Abridgement, in one impression of Vol. II, R 457, and in two impressions of Vol. III, R 459, 461. In a new draft, with the rose filled in and with minor differences, Rastell used it in one impression of Vols. II and III of Fitzherbert's Abridgement, R 458, 460.

It eventually passed from Pynson to Redman, who used it in his Great Book of Statutes, S 25.

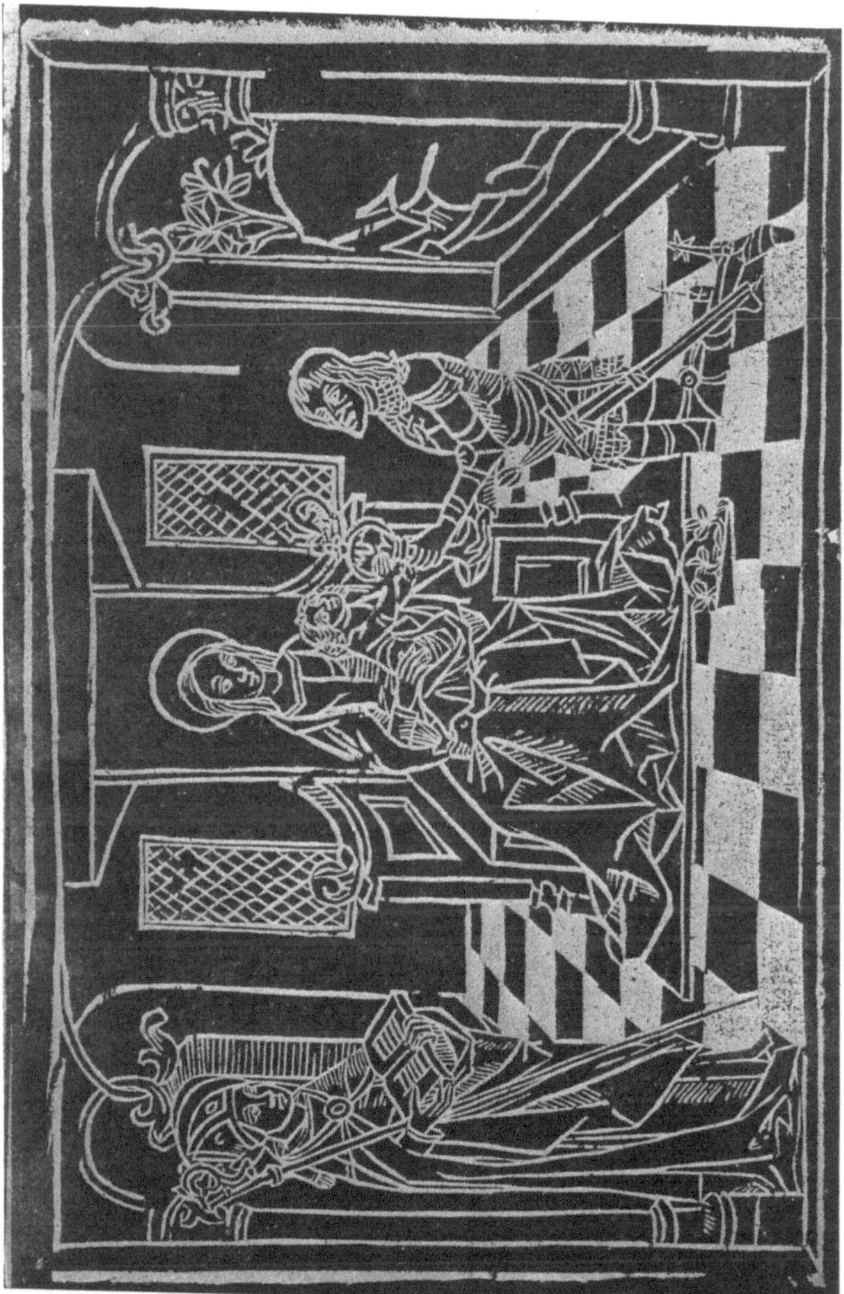

Nos. 9 and **10** were used by Berthelet in his Year-Book, 1 Ed. 5 and 1 R 3, R 373.

No. 10 Same as **9**.

No. 11. First used by Pynson in his tracts, 1521–1528: T 9, 10, 72, 83, 84, 122, 135, 203. They then passed to Redman, who used them in editions of the tracts, 1530–1541: T 39, 98, 99, 120, 125, 167, 169, 172, 188, 189, 207, 208, 222, 223, 224, 233, 235, 236. He also used it in his Doctor and Student, 1532, T 466, and in his Britton, T 324.

Redman's successor, Middleton, used it in tracts, T 229, 240; and his successor, Petit, used it in two editions of the Natura Brevium, T 101, 102.

No. 12. First used by Pynson, T 111. Then used by Redman in editions of the tracts, 1528–1535: T 12, 73, 74, 87, 98, 99, 113, 123, 168. He also used it in editions of Doctor and Student: T 465, 466.

No. 13. Rastell's Table to Fitzherbert's Abridgement, R 462.

No. 14. In Wyer's editions of the Assize of Bread: T 254, 255, 256.

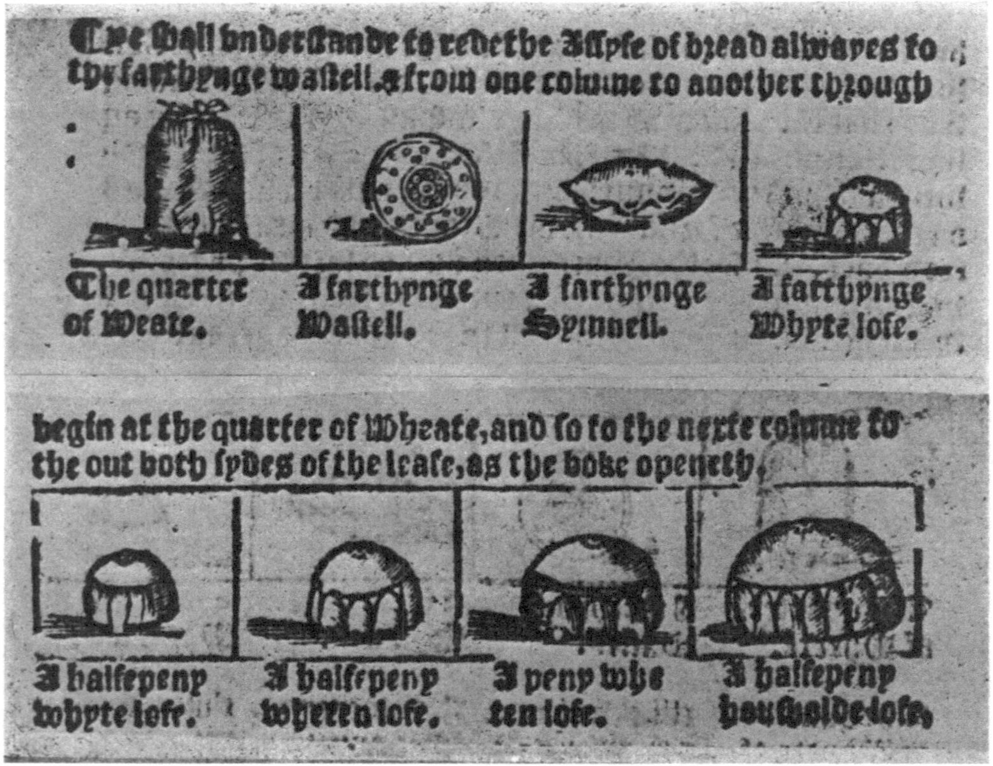

No. 14a. In Wyer's editions of the Assize of Bread: T 254, 255, 256.

No. 15. In an edition of Carta Feodi, probably by Pynson, T 164.

No. 16. Used by Berthelet in Statutes of Henry 8: S 112, 118, 123, 142.

No. 17. Used by Berthelet in the Statutes of Henry 8. State 1, perfect: 23, 24, and 25 H. 8, S 141, 149, 155, 156.

State 2, top line damaged: 24, 26, 27, and 28 H. 8, S 150, 161, 162, 168, 176.

State 3, two small gaps in left side border-line, and one on right: 3–7, 27, 31 H. 8, S 118, 169, 170, 180, 181.

State 4, top line mended, but large break on left side, and both top corners injured: 24, 25, 28, 32 and 33 H. 8, S 151, 157, 177, 189, 193, 194, 195.

No. 17a. State 5, outer line all cut away, but fleur-de-lis whole: 3–7, 23, 31, and 37 H. 8, s 119, 144, 182, 211.

State 6, fleur-de-lis broken at the top. By Berthelet, 25, 31, 33, and 34–35 H. 8, s 158, 183, 196, 201. By his successor, H. Powell, 23, 24, 27, 28, 31, 33, 37 H. 8, s 147, 153, 171, 172, 178, 185, 197, 201, 212, 213. And by Marsh, 28 H. 8, s 179. [See Proctor in 5 Transactions Bibliographical Society, 255; see also 35 Harvard Law Review 519.]

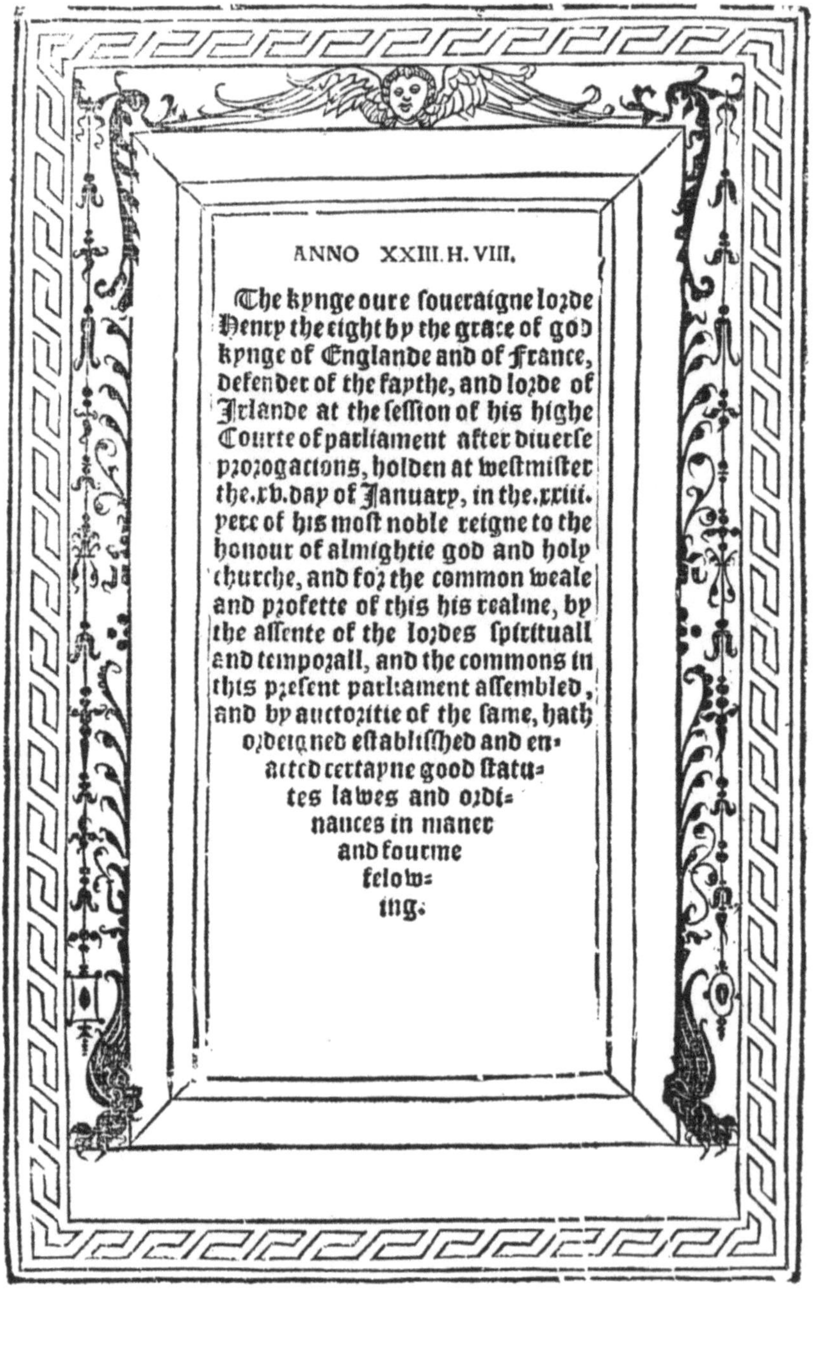

ANNO XXIII. H. VIII.

The kynge oure ſoueraigne loꝛde
Henry the eight by the grace of god
kynge of Englande and of France,
defender of the faythe, and loꝛde of
Irlande at the ſeſſion of his highe
Courte of parliament after diuerſe
pꝛoꝛogacions, holden at weſtmiſter
the .xv. day of January, in the .xxiii.
yere of his moſt noble reigne to the
honour of almightie god and holy
churche, and foꝛ the common weale
and pꝛofette of this his realme, by
the aſſente of the loꝛdes ſpirituall
and tempoꝛall, and the commons in
this pꝛeſent parliament aſſembled,
and by auctoꝛitie of the ſame, hath
oꝛdeigned eſtabliſſhed and en-
acted certayne good ſtatu-
tes lawes and oꝛdi-
nauces in maner
and fourme
felow-
ing.

No. 18. Used first by Berthelet in his Statutes of Henry 8.

State 1, perfect: 23 H. 8, S 141.

State 2, inside line at base broken: 1, 23, 26, 27, 28 H. 8, S 142, 143, 161, 162, 168, 174, 175, 176.

State 3, inside line at base gone, slight breaks in outside border: 21, 26, 27, 33 H. 8, S 130, 163, 169, 193, 194.

State 4, larger breaks in outside border: 21, 23, 26, 27, 28, 33 H. 8, S 131, 144, 165, 170, 177, 196. It was lent in this state to Berthelet's apprentice, Wykes, to use in an edition of the Statutes to Henry 8, S 28; and to Cawood to print the earliest impressions of the first two Parliaments of Mary, S 240, 241, 247.

State 5, still larger breaks, border warped: used by Berthelet's successor, H. Powell, in an edition of the Statutes of Henry 8: 1, 3–7, 14–15, 21, 23, 24, 25, 26, 27, 28, 31, 33, 34–35, and 37 H. 8, S 120, 126, 132, 147, 153, 159, 166, 171, 172, 178, 185, 197, 203, 213.

It was finally used by Tottell in a Table to the Statutes Ed. 6 to Eliz., S 38. [See 5 Trans. Bibl. Soc. 255; 35 Harv. L. Rev. 519.]

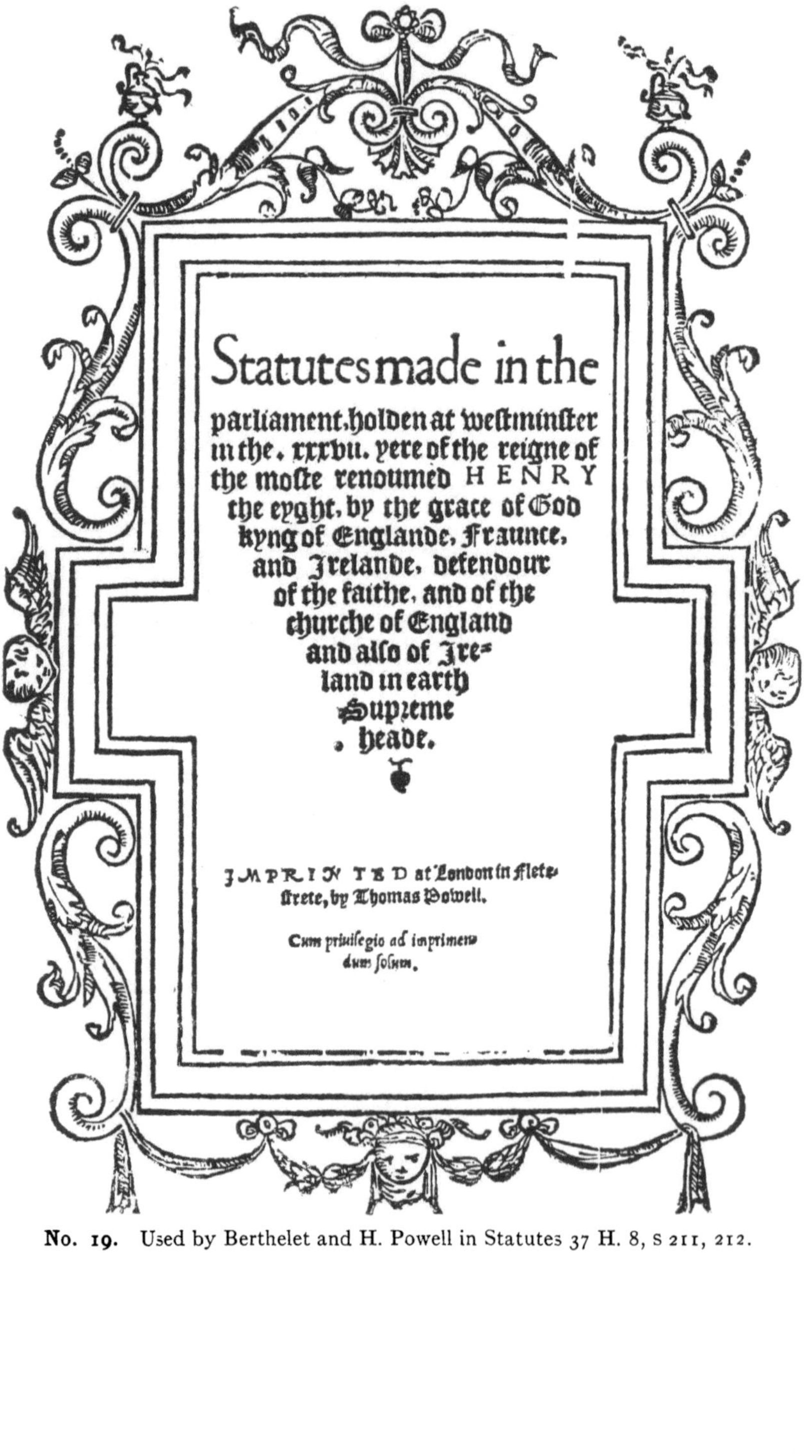

Statutes made in the parliament, holden at westminster in the. xxxvii. yere of the reigne of the moste renoumed HENRY the eyght, by the grace of God kyng of Englande, Fraunce, and Irelande, defendour of the faithe, and of the churche of England and also of Ireland in earth Supreme heade.

IMPRINTED at London in Fletestrete, by Thomas Powell.

Cum priuilegio ad imprimendum solum.

No. 19. Used by Berthelet and H. Powell in Statutes 37 H. 8, S 211, 212.

Nos. 20, 21. Used by Butler (?) in his edition of Rastell's Terms of the Law, T 453.

No. 22. Used by Redman in abridgements of the Statutes: S 50, 86, 87; and in Doctor and Student, T 471. Then by his successor, W. Middleton, in tracts, T 175, 338; then by W. Powell, in small treatises and tracts: T 44, 45, 201, 292, 339.

No. 23. Used by Redman before 1530: Year Book 4 H. 6, R 90; Perkins' Profitable Book, T 415; Natura Brevium, T 87.

No. 24. Used by Middleton as an ornament, T 338.

No. 25. Used by Redman in tracts: T 100, 190, 225, 288; by his widow in Magna Carta, S 11; by W. Middleton, in small treatises and tracts: T 77, 91, 103, 127, 200, 216, 472; then by W. Powell, T 292.

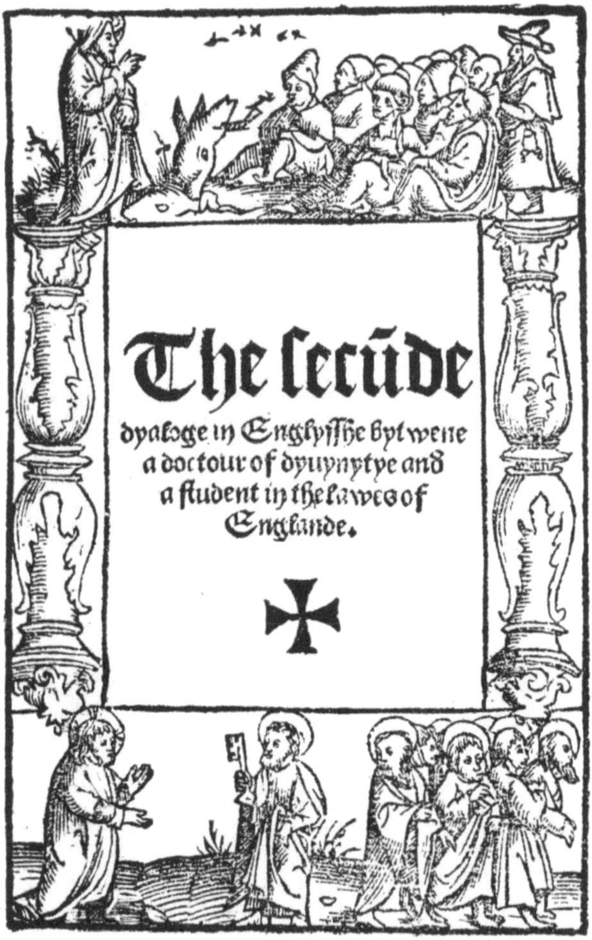

No. 26. Used by Treveris in the Second Dialogue of Doctor and Student (1530), T 467.

No. 27. Used by Berthelet in tracts, T 141, 468, and in Statutes, S 9, 20

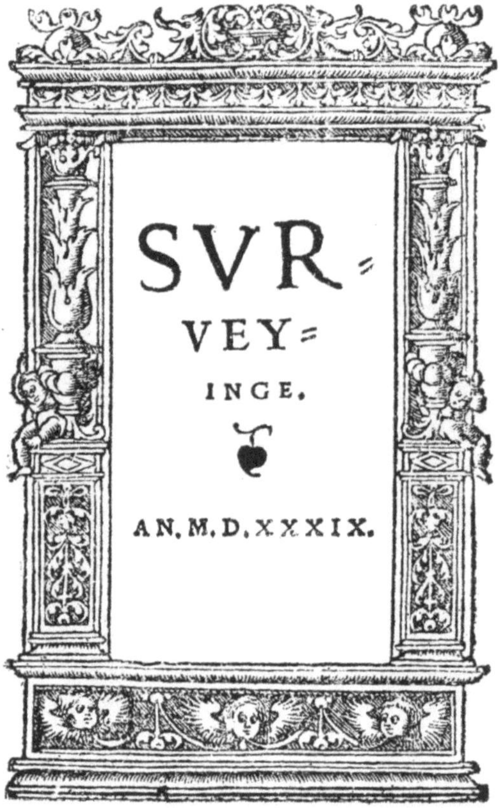

No. 28. Used by Berthelet in tracts and small treatises: T 171, 174, 193, 194, 226, 227, 239, 352, 353.

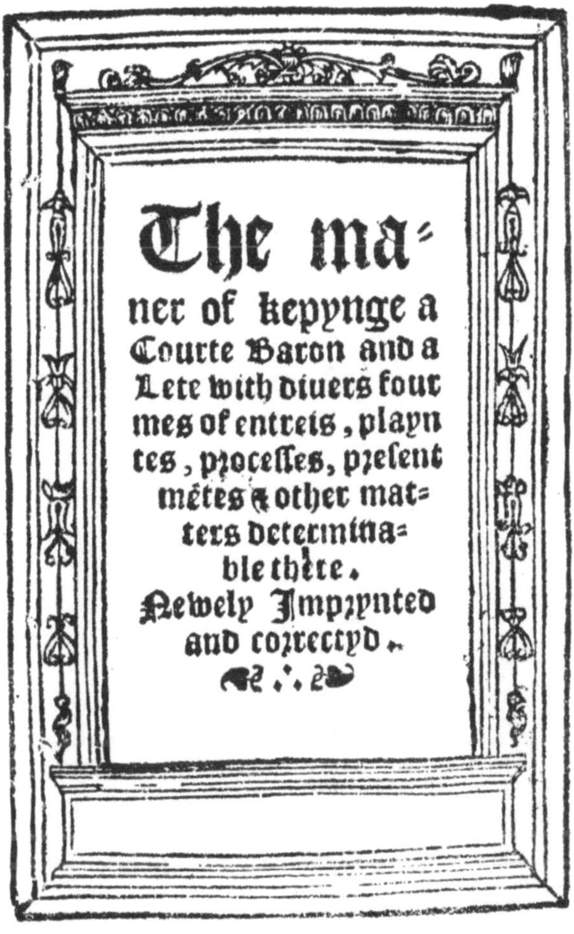

No. 29. Used by Redman in tracts and small treatises, and collected statutes: T 143, 172, 190, 288, 334, S 10, 11, 49. Then used by W. Middleton in tracts and small treatises: T 146.

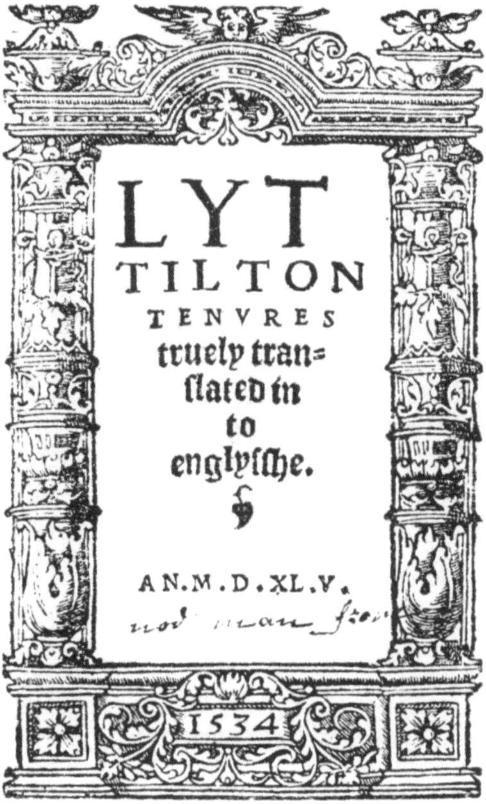

No. 30. Used by Berthelet in editions of Littleton and tracts: T 43, 76, 116, 126, 141, 228, 237, 238, 314.

It was then used by Hyll (with the date in the bottom panel erased) in printing an edition of the tracts for Smith, Waley, Toye and Kele: T 147, 176, 196, 230.

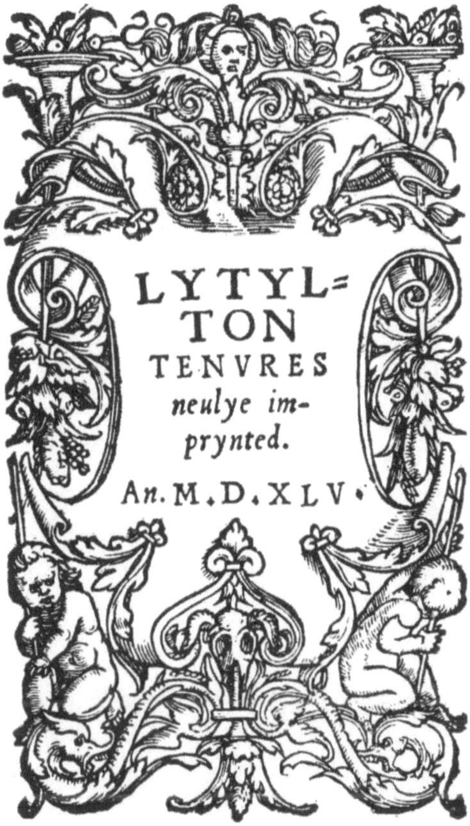

No. 31. Used by Smyth in a Littleton, T 17, and a Diversity of Courts, T 129.

No. 32. Used by Petit in small treatises, T 46, 337.

No. 33. Used by Hyll (printing also for Smyth, Waley, Toye, and Kele) in his Book for a Justice, T 147.

No. 34. Used by Redman in Perkins' Profitable Book, T 416.

No. 35. Used by Hyll, Ordinance for Exchequer, T 241.

ANNO PRIMO REGI-
NAE ELIZABETHE.

AT THE
parliament be-
gonne at Westmynster, the
xxiii. of January in the fyrste
yeare of the reigne of oure So-
ueraigne Ladye, Elizabeth by the
grace of God, of England, Fraunce
and Ireland, Quene, defen-
doure of the Faithe, &c.
And there proroged tyll the xxv. of the
same moneth, and then and there holden,
kept, and continued untill the dissolution
of the same, beyng the eyght day of May,
then nexte ensuynge, were enac-
ted as foloweth.

Anno. 1.5.5.9.

No. 36. Used by Grafton in the earliest editions of the Statutes 1 Ed. 6, s 215, 216; then by Jugge and Cawood in the first editions of the Statutes 1 Elizabeth: s 267, 268, 269, 270.

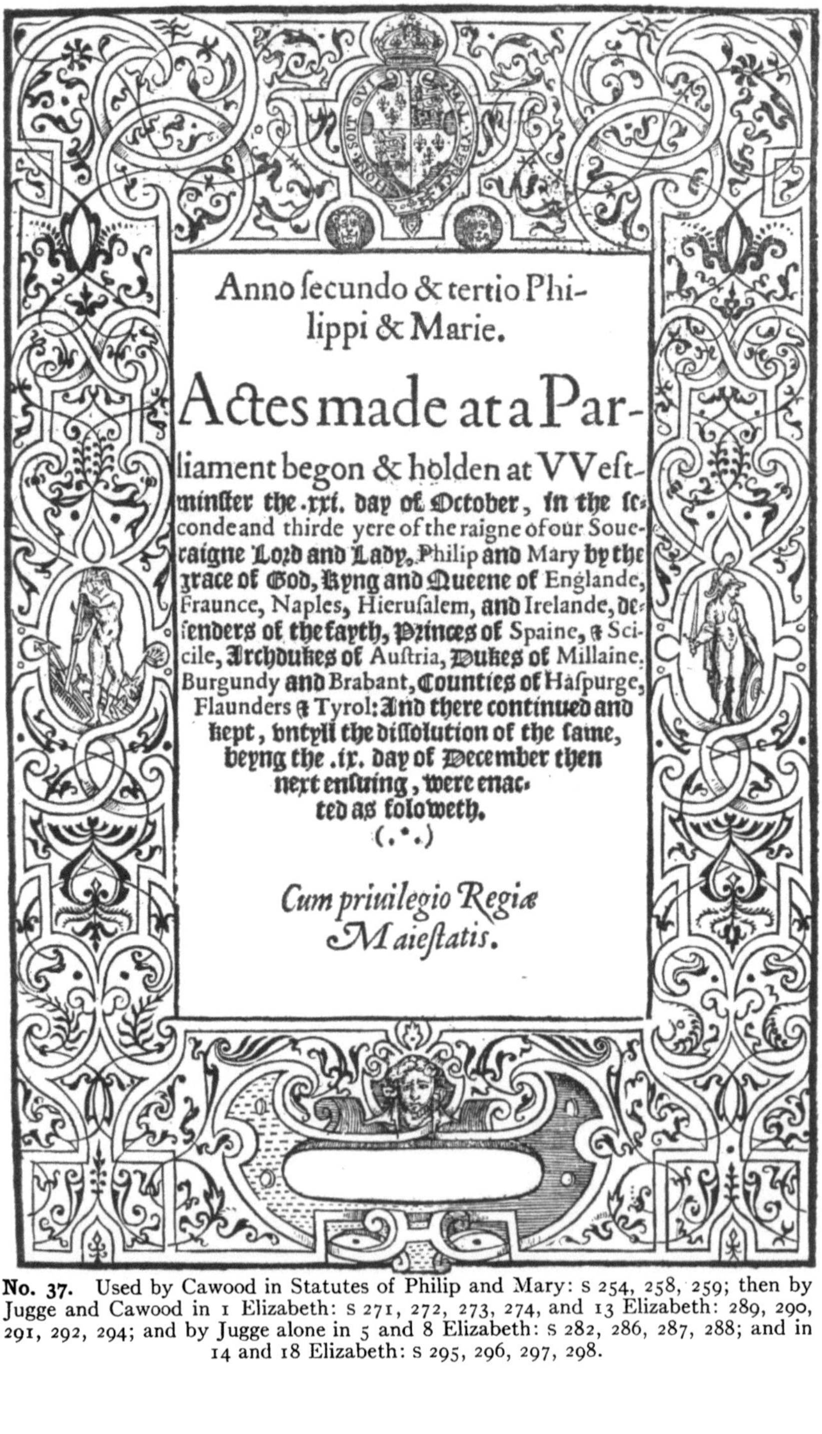
Anno ſecundo & tertio Phi-
lippi & Marie.

Actes made at a Par-
liament begon & holden at VVeſt-
minſter the .xxi. day of October, in the se-
conde and thirde yere of the raigne of our Soue-
raigne Lord and Lady, Philip and Mary by the
grace of God, Kyng and Queene of Englande,
Fraunce, Naples, Hieruſalem, and Irelande, de-
fenders of the fayth, Princes of Spaine, & Sci-
cile, Archdukes of Auſtria, Dukes of Millaine,
Burgundy and Brabant, Counties of Haſpurge,
Flaunders & Tyrol: And there continued and
kept, untyll the diſſolution of the ſame,
beyng the .ix. day of December then
next enſuing, were enac-
ted as foloweth.
(.*.)

Cum priuilegio Regiæ Maieſtatis.

No. 37. Used by Cawood in Statutes of Philip and Mary: S 254, 258, 259; then by Jugge and Cawood in 1 Elizabeth: S 271, 272, 273, 274, and 13 Elizabeth: 289, 290, 291, 292, 294; and by Jugge alone in 5 and 8 Elizabeth: S 282, 286, 287, 288; and in 14 and 18 Elizabeth: S 295, 296, 297, 298.

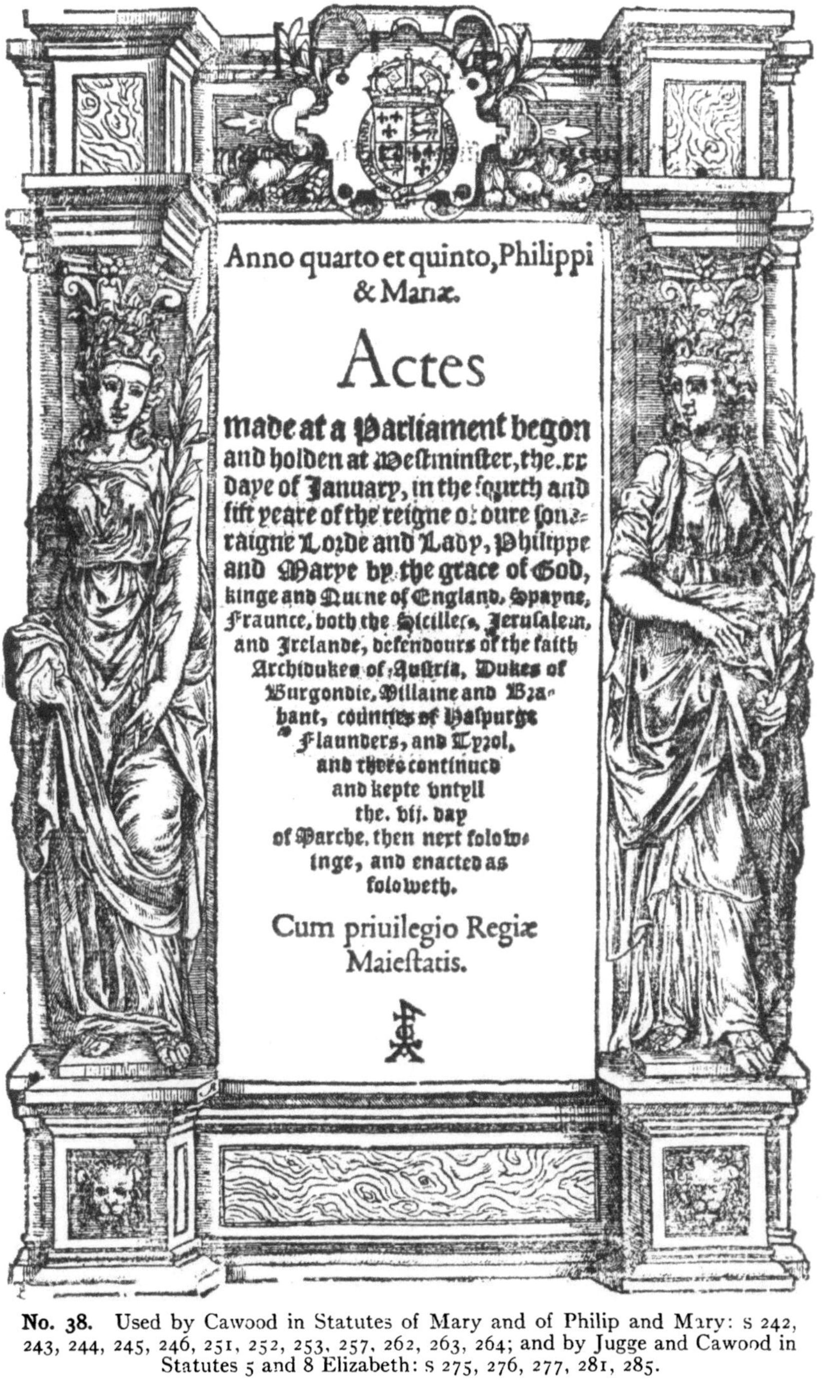

No. 38. Used by Cawood in Statutes of Mary and of Philip and Mary: S 242, 243, 244, 245, 246, 251, 252, 253, 257, 262, 263, 264; and by Jugge and Cawood in Statutes 5 and 8 Elizabeth: S 275, 276, 277, 281, 285.

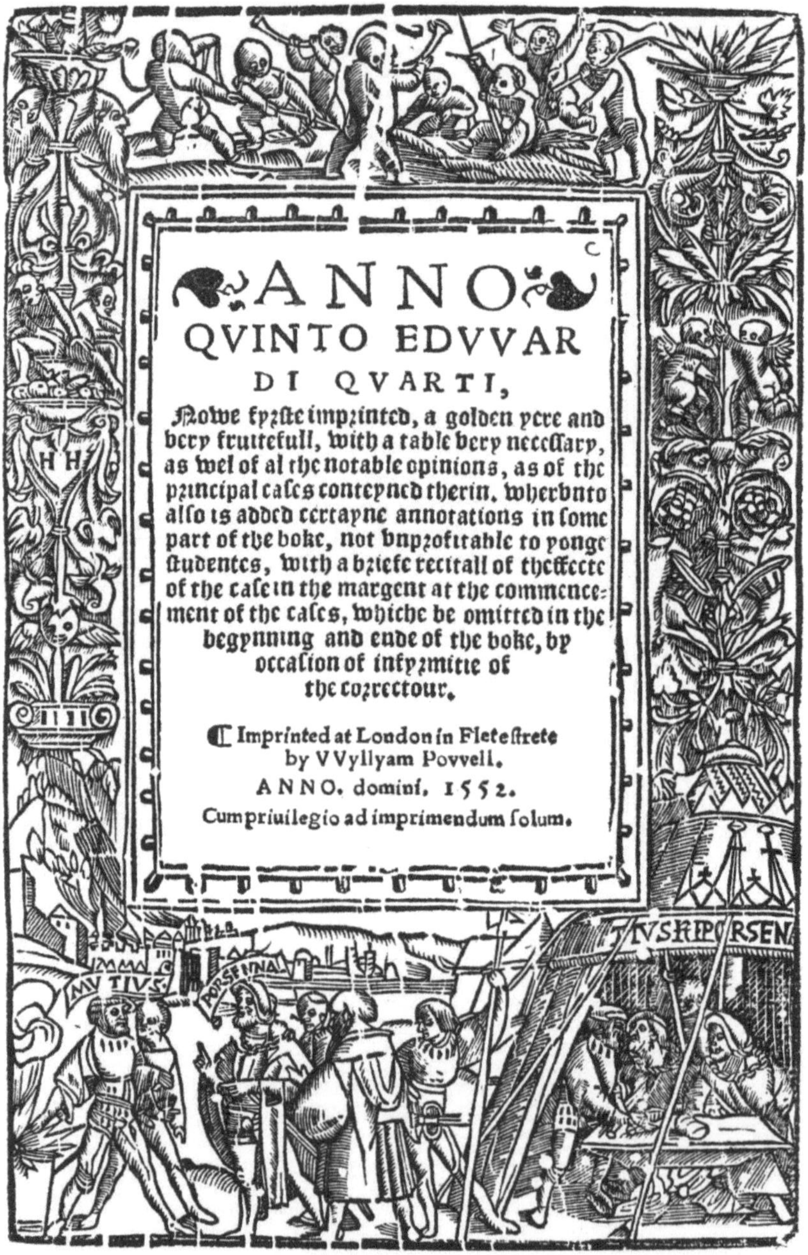

ANNO
QVINTO EDVVAR
DI QVARTI,
Nowe fyrſte imprinted, a golden yere and very fruitefull, with a table very neceſſary, as wel of al the notable opinions, as of the principal caſes conteyned therin. wherunto alſo is added certayne annotations in ſome part of the boke, not unprofitable to yonge ſtudentes, with a briefe recitall of theffecte of the caſe in the margent at the commencement of the caſes, whiche be omitted in the begynning and ende of the boke, by occaſion of infyrmitie of the correctour.

¶ Imprinted at London in Fleteſtrete by VVyllyam Povvell.
ANNO. domini. 1552.
Cum priuilegio ad imprimendum ſolum.

No. 39. Used by Pynson, Year Book 1 Ed. 5, R 374; and by W. Powell, Long Quint, T 370.

No. 40. Used in Tottell's edition of the Registrum, T 310.

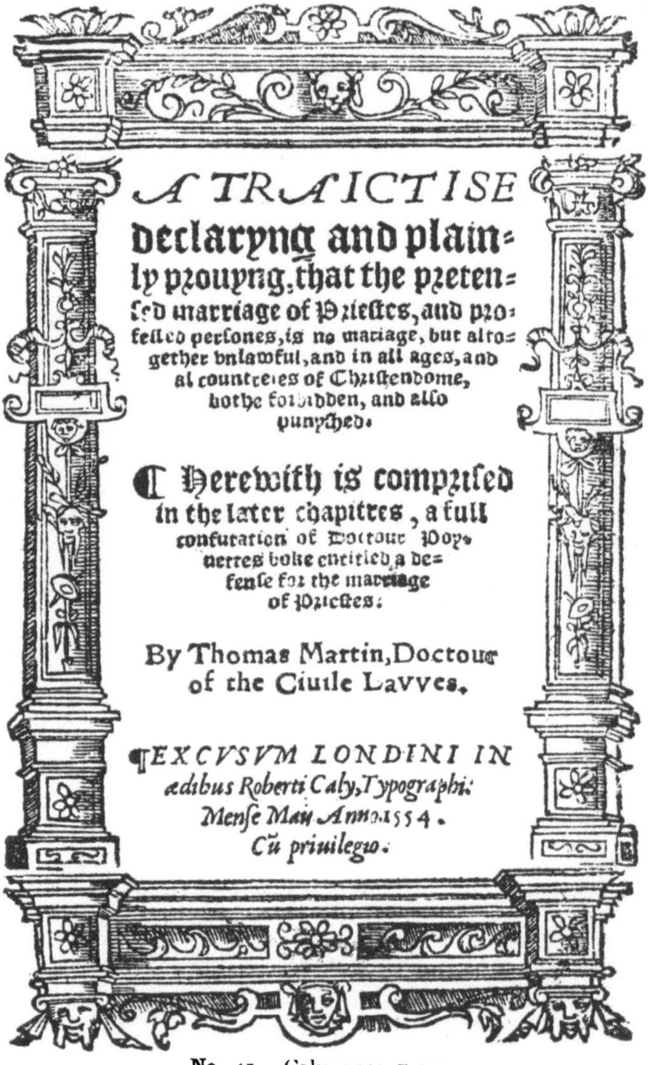

A TRAICTISE declaryng and plainly prouyng, that the pretensed marriage of Priestes, and professed persones, is no mariage, but altogether vnlawful, and in all ages, and al countreies of Christendome, bothe forbidden, and also punyshed.

¶ Herewith is comprised in the later chapitres, a full confutation of Doctour Poynettes boke entitled, a defense for the marriage of Priestes.

By Thomas Martin, Doctour of the Ciuile Lavves.

¶EXCVSVM LONDINI IN ædibus Roberti Caly, Typographi: Mense Maii Anno 1554.
Cũ priuilegio.

No. 41. Caly. 1554. T 414.

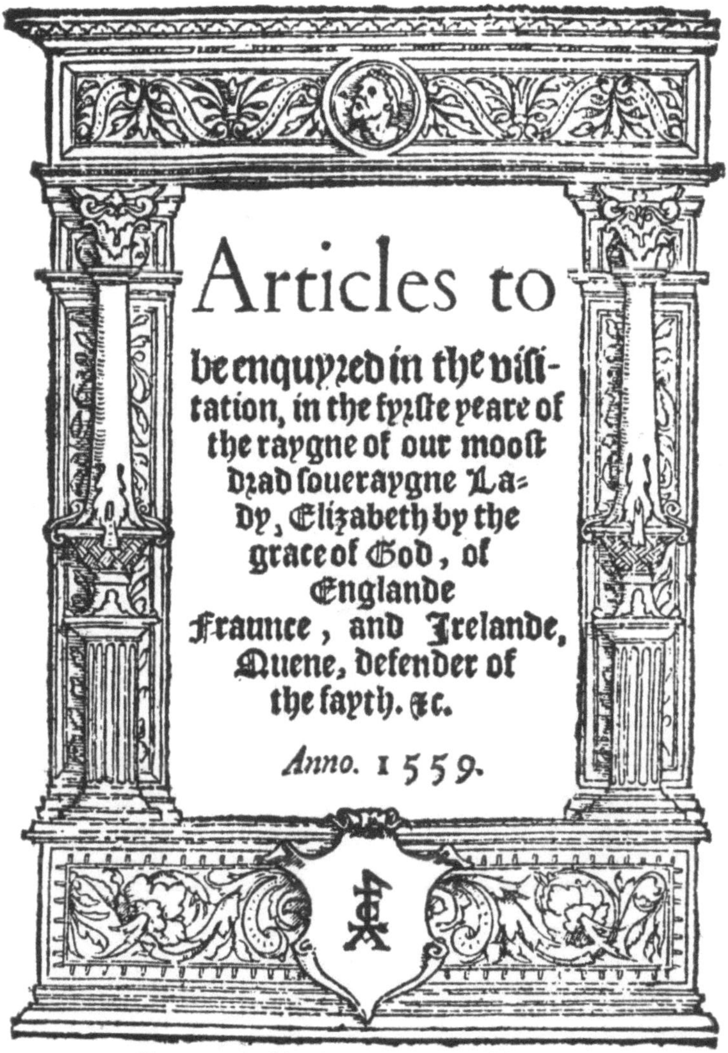

Articles to
be enquyred in the visi-
tation, in the fyrste yeare of
the raygne of our moost
drad souerayne La-
dy, Elizabeth by the
grace of God, of
Englande
Fraunce, and Irelande,
Quene, defender of
the fayth. &c.

Anno. 1559.

No. 42. Used by Cawood in the Articles, T 250.

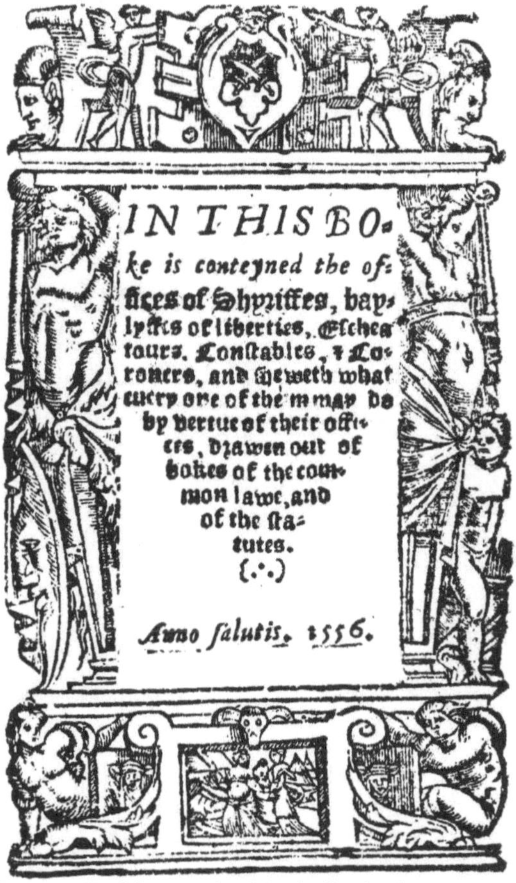
IN THIS BO-
ke is conteyned the of-
fices of Shyriffes, bay-
lyffs of liberties, Eschea-
tours, Constables, & Co-
roners, and sheweth what
every one of them may do
by vertue of their offi-
ces, drawen out of
bokes of the com-
mon lawe, and
of the sta-
tutes.
(.·.)

Anno salutis. 1556.

No. 43. Used in 1555 by Marsh, Institutions, T 277; and in 1556 by J. Wight, Office of Sheriffs, T 297.

No. 44. Used by Redman in his folio edition of Littleton, T 11.

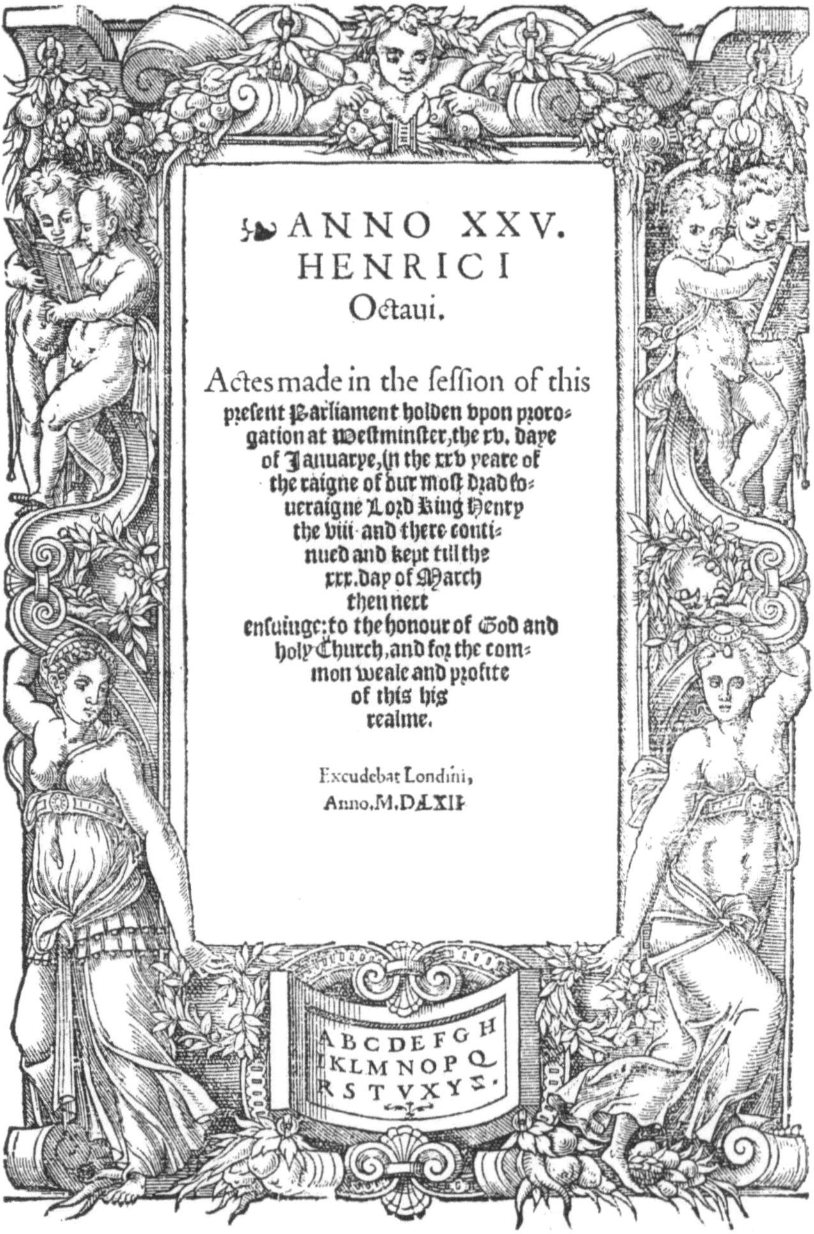

ANNO XXV.
HENRICI
Octaui.

Actes made in the session of this present Parliament holden vpon prorogation at Westminster, the xv. daye of Januarye, in the xxv yeare of the raigne of our most drad souerai̇gne Lord King Henry the viii. and there continued and kept till the xxx. day of March then next ensuinge: to the honour of God and holy Church, and for the common weale and profite of this his realme.

Excudebat Londini,
Anno. M.D.LXII.

No. 45. Used by Marsh in 1577 in an edition of the Statutes to Henry 8, s 30; of the Statutes 25 H. 8, s 160; and in an edition of the Statutes of Mary and of Philip and Mary: s 249, 250, 255, 256, 260, 266.

No. 46. Used by Tottell, 1575–1580, in editions of Doctor and Student, T 476, 477, and in Brooke's New Cases, R 479.

Les Plees del Coron, diuisees in plusors titles & common lieux. Per queux home plus redement & plenairement trouera quelque chose qu'il quira, touchaunt les dits Plees, composees par le tresreuerend Iudge Monsieur Guilliaulme Staundforde Chiualer, dernierment corrigee auecques vn table parfaicte des choses notables contenues en ycelle, nouuelment reueu et corrigee.

Anno Domini 1574.

In ædibus Richardi Tottelli.

¶ Cum priuilegio.

R.T.

No. 47. Used by Tottell in the later editions of Staunford's Pleas of the Crown, T 489, 490.

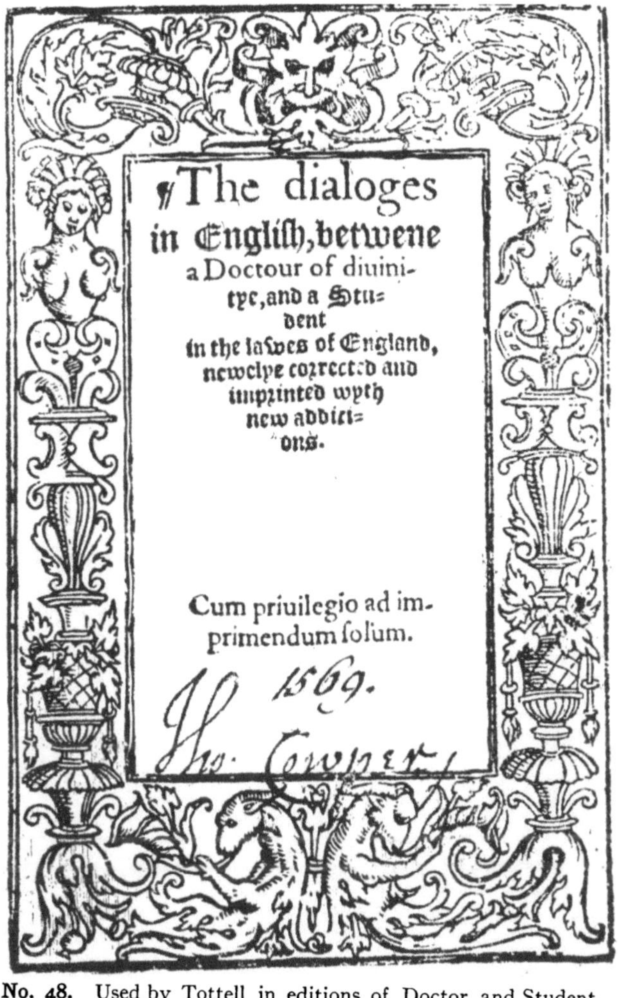

No. 48. Used by Tottell in editions of Doctor and Student, T 473, 475, and of Fitzherbert's Natura Brevium: T 345, 346, 347, 348, 349.

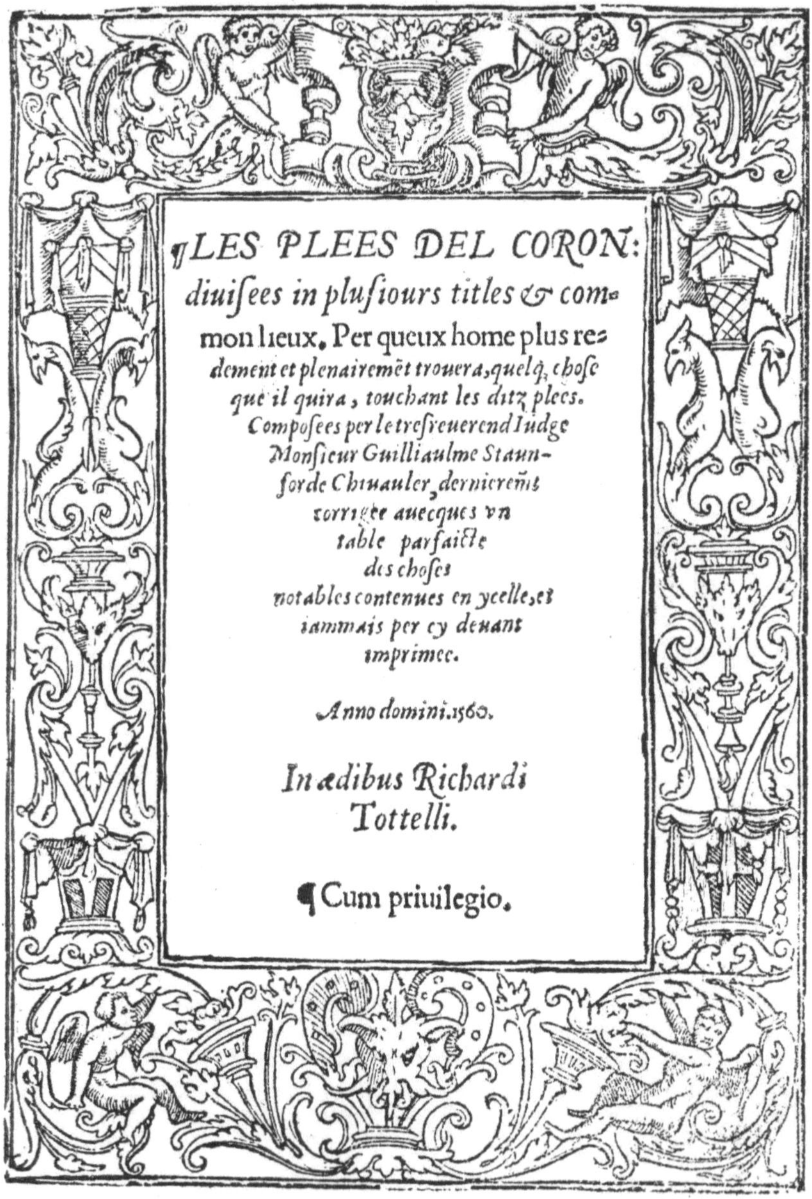
¶LES PLEES DEL CORON:
diuisees in plusiours titles & common lieux. Per queux home plus redement et plenairemēt trouera, quelq; chose que il quira, touchant les ditz plees. Composees per le tresreuerend Iudge Monsieur Guilliaulme Staunforde Chiualer, dernieremēt corrigee auecques vn table parfaicte des choses notables contenues en ycelle, et iammais per cy deuant imprimee.

Anno domini.1560.

In ædibus Richardi Tottelli.

¶Cum priuilegio.

No. 49. Used by Tottell in the earlier editions of Staunford's Pleas of the Crown: T 485, 486, 487, 488.

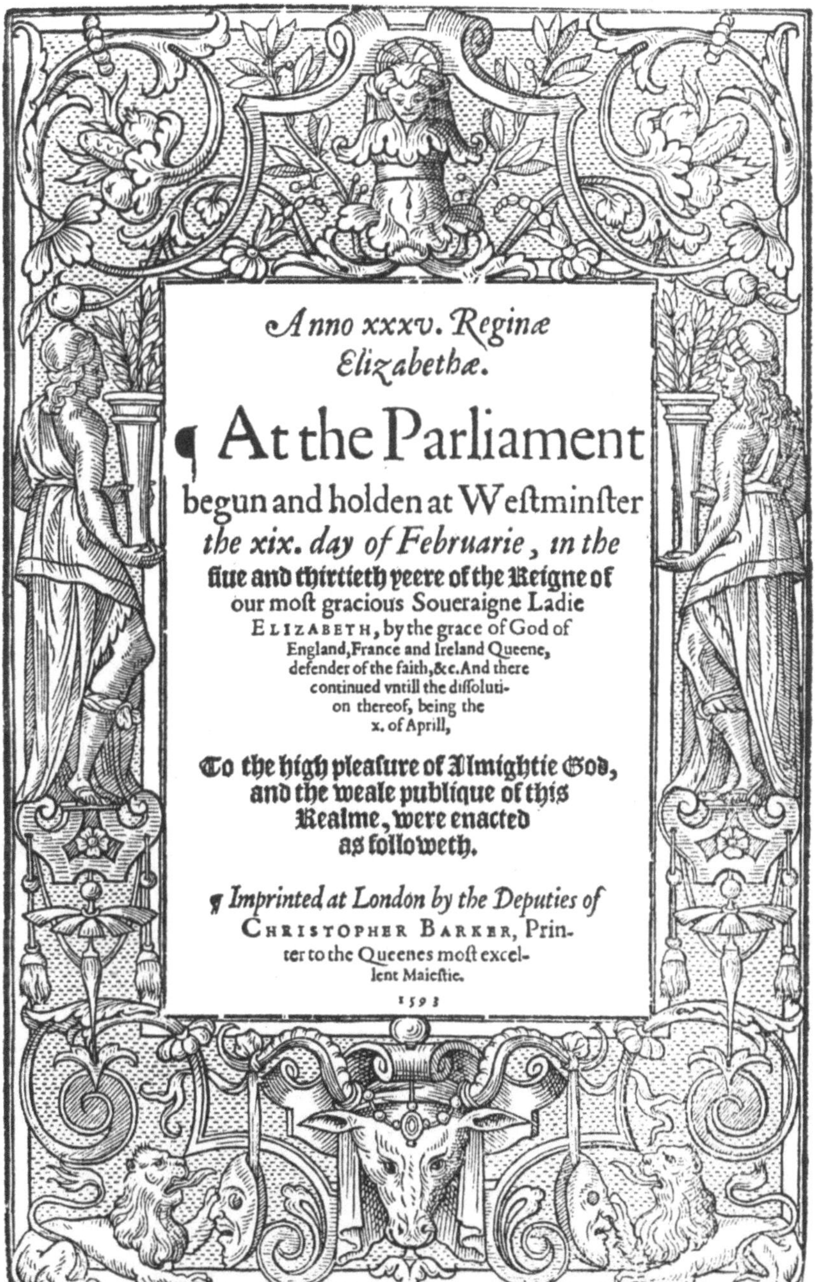

Anno xxxv. Reginæ Elizabethæ.

¶ At the Parliament begun and holden at Westminster the xix. day of Februarie, in the fiue and thirtieth yeere of the Reigne of our most gracious Soueraigne Ladie ELIZABETH, by the grace of God of England, France and Ireland Queene, defender of the faith, &c. And there continued vntill the dissolution thereof, being the x. of Aprill,

To the high pleasure of Almightie God, and the weale publique of this Realme, were enacted as followeth.

¶ Imprinted at London by the Deputies of CHRISTOPHER BARKER, Printer to the Queenes most excellent Maiestie.

1593

No. 50. Used by Christopher Barker and his deputies in printing the Statutes: 23, 27, 29, 31, 35 and 39 Elizabeth: S 299, 300, 301, 302, 303, 304, 305, 306, 307.

APPENDIX II

TABLES

These Tables include in condensed form most of the information about books described in the preceding chapters; and they also indicate where the books may be found in libraries in England and America accessible to the public.

In the first column is a brief title of the book; in the second, its number in this bibliography; in the third, the name of the printer; in the fourth, the date of publication, a conjectural date being placed in brackets; in the fifth, the libraries in which it has been found; and in the sixth such information as is necessary to distinguish between editions of the same date, or otherwise so similar as to lead to confusion.

The list of libraries searched, with their abbreviations, is as follows:

B: British Museum, London.
C: The University Library, Cambridge, England.
CH: The Library of Trinity Hall, Cambridge.
CJ: The Library of St. John's College, Cambridge.
CK: The Library of King's College, Cambridge.
CM: The Pepysian Library, Magdalen College, Cambridge.
CP: The Library of Pembroke College, Cambridge.
CT: The Library of Trinity College, Cambridge.
F: The San Francisco County Law Library.
G: The Huntington Library, San Gabriel, Cal.
H: The Library of the Harvard Law School.
I: The Library of the Inner Temple, London.
J: The J. P. Morgan Library, New York, N. Y.
L: The Library of Lincoln's Inn, London.
N: The State Library of New York, Albany, N.Y.
O: The Bodleian Library, Oxford University, England.
OA: The Library of All Souls College, Oxford.
OB: The Library of Brasenose College, Oxford.
OE: The Library of Exeter College, Oxford.
OQ: The Library of Queen's College, Oxford.
P: The Library of Lambeth Palace, London.
R: The Rylands Library, Manchester, England.
S: Sandhurst College Library.
U: The Law Library of Columbia University, New York.
W: The Congressional Library, Washington, D. C.

PART I. TABLE OF THE STATUTES

I. COLLECTIONS

Name	Number	Printer	Date	Libraries	Distinguishing Marks
NOVA STATUTA	S 1	Machlinia	[1485]	B: C: G: H: I: J: O: OA: OB: OC: R	
	S 2	Pynson	[1500]	C: G: H: N: O	
MAGNA CARTA	S 3	Pynson	1508	B: G: O	
	S 4	Pynson	1514	B: H	
	S 5	Pynson	1519	B: C: H: R	
	S 6	Redman	1525	H: O	
	S 7	Pynson	1527	H	
	S 8	Berthelet	1531	B: G: H: N: O: W	
	S 9	Redman	1534	N: G: H	
	S 10	Redman	1539	B: G: H: N: W	
	S 11	E. Redman	[1540]	B: C: G: H: O	
	S 12	Berthelet	1541	G: H: O: U	
	S 13	Petit	1542	B: CJ: CP: G: H: N: O: U: W	
	S 14	Petit	1552		
	S 15	Marsh	1556	B: CP: G: H: N: OQ: U	
	S 16	Tottell	1556^1	B: G: H: N: U: W	12 Iun. 1556
	S 17	Tottell	1556^2	B: CT: G: U: W	12 Inn. 1556
	S 18	Tottell	1576^1	B: C: G: H: U: W	¶ Magna Carta
	S 19	Tottell	1576^2	H	❧ Magna Carta
	S 20	Tottell	1587	G: H: N: O: U: W	❧ Secunda pars
SECUNDA PARS	S 21	Berthelet	1532	B: H: N: O: W	
	S 22	Berthelet	1540	G: H: U	
	S 23	Marsh	1556	CP: G: H: U	
	S 24	Tottell	1556^1	B: CT: G: H: U: W	
	S 24a	Tottell	1556^2	G	❧ Secunda pars
GREAT BOOK	S 25	Redman	[153–]	H	
	S 26	Middleton	[154–]	B: H: CM	

TABLE OF THE STATUTES—*Continued*

Name	Number	Printer	Date	Libraries	Distinguishing Marks
Statutes to Henry VIII	s 27	Berthelet	1543	B: CJ: G: H: O: U: W	in officina Thomae Berthe-
	s 28	Wykes	1551	H	
	s 29	Wykes	1564	CJ: G: H: W	
	s 30	Marsh	1577	B: G: H	
	s 31	Barker	1587	B: CJ: CP: F: G: H: W	
Statutes at Large Collected Statutes Henry VIII	s 32	Berthelet	1543 [1]	B: C: CJ: H: W	conteyninge
	s 33	Berthelet	1543 [2]	CJ: H	conteyning
	s 34	Berthelet	1551	B: G: H	
	s 35	Powell	1563	C: H	
	s 36	Marsh	1575	B: G	
Edward VI	s 37	Berthelet	1553	B: C: H	
	s 38	Tottel	[1571]	B: C: CH: G: H: W	

II. Abridgments

Name	Number	Printer	Date	Libraries	Distinguishing Marks
The Great Abridgment	s 39	[Lettou & Machl.]	[1485]	B: CJ: O: OA: R	
	s 40	Pynson	1499 [1]	B: H: J	(Colo.) Explicit abbreviamentum
	s 41	Pynson	1499 [2]	C: G: H: R: W	(Colo.) Explicit abbreviamentū
	s 42	Pynson	1521	B: C: H	
	s 43	Pynson	1528	B: C: H: R: W	
	s 44	J. Rastell	1527	B: H: O: R	
	s 45	J. Rastell	1528	C: H: P: W	
	s 46	Redman	[1527]	C: H	Le bregemēt
	s 47	Redman	1528	B:	
	s 48	W. Rastell	1533	B: H	
	s 49	Redman	[1538]	B: CJ: H	¶ : The greate abbrydgement
	s 50	Redman	n.d.[3]	H: U	*Colo.* ¶ Imprynted by R. R.
	s 51	Middleton	1542	B: C: H: O	
	s 52	Petit	1542	B: C: H: O: W	
	s 53	Gaultier-Kele	1551	H	
	s 54	Gaultier-Seres	1551	C	
	s 55	[Gaultier] Powell	1551	H: N: W	
	s 56	Petit	1552		

TABLE OF THE STATUTES—*Continued*

Name	Number	Printer	Date	Libraries	Distinguishing Marks
RASTELL'S STATUTES	s 57	Tottel	1557	B	
	s 58	Tottel	1557/9[1]	H: W	1557.)...... ¶ In aedibus R. T.
	s 59	Tottel	1557/9[2]	B: CJ: CP: H	1557)......In aedibus R. T.
	s 60	Tottel	1565	B: G: H	
	s 61	Tottel	1566	H	
	s 62	Tottel	1568	B: U	
	s 63	Tottel	1572	G: H	
	s 64	Tottel	1574	B: G: H: W	
	s 66	Barker	1579	B: G	
	s 67	Barker	1583	B: G: H: U	
	s 68	Barker	n. d. [1583]	H: W	
	s 69	Barker (dep.)	1588	B: H	
	s 69a	Barker (dep.)	1591	H	
	s 70	Barker (dep.)	1594	B: CP: H	
	s 71	Yetsweirt	1595	G: H	
	s 71a	Wight & Norton	1598	B: G: H	
PULTON'S PENAL STATUTES	s 72	Tottel	1560		
	s 73	Tottel	1577[1]	CJ: H	Nov. 1, 1777
	s 73a	Tottel	1577[2]	G	Jan. 27, 1777
	s 74	Barker	1579	B: H	
	s 75	Barker	1581	B: G: H: W	
	s 76	Barker	1586	B: H: U	
	s 77	Barker	n. d.	H: W	
	s 77a	Barker (dep.)	1592	G: U	
	s 78	Yetsweirt	1596	H	
	s 79	Wright	1600	H: W	

TABLE OF THE STATUTES—*Continued*

Name	Number	Printer	Date	Libraries	Distinguishing Marks
SESSION-LAWS					
21 HENRY VIII	s 80	[Redman]	n. d.	C: W	
22	s 81	Redman	n. d.	C: W	
22	s 82	[W. Rastell]	n. d.	B: H	
23	s 83	E. Redman	n. d.	C: P	
23–24	s 84	W. Rastell	1534	H	
24–25	s 85	Middleton	n. d.	C	
24–25	s 86	Redman	n. d.	H: W	
26	s 87	Redman	n. d.[1]	C	¶ Imprynted at London in Fletestrete
26	s 88	Redman	n. d.[2]	H: W	¶ Imprynted by me
27–28	s 89	Redman	n. d.[1]	C	Imprynted at London in Fletestrete
27–28	s 90	Redman	n. d.[2]	H: W	¶ Imprinted by me
31	s 91	Redman	n. d.[1]	B	❧ The Abregement
31	s 92	[Redman]	n. d.[2]	C	¶ The abregement
32	s 93	E. Redman	n. d.	B: C	
33	s 94	Middleton	n. d.	B: H	
33	s 95	Petit	1542	B: H: W	

III.—SESSION-LAWS

Regnal Year	Number	Printer	Date	Libraries	Distinguishing Marks
Rich. III					
1	S 96	[Machlinia]	[1486]	B: G: R	
Henry VII					
1–4	S 97	[Caxton]	[1490]	B: I: R	
	S 98	de Worde	[1492]	CK	
	S 99	Notary	1507	H	
7	S 100	de Worde	[1492]	CK	
	S 101	Notary	1507	B: H	
11	S 102	de Worde	[150–]	B: H: R	
	S 103	de Worde	[150–]	CK	
	S 103	Notary	1507	B: H	
19	S 104	de Worde	[1492]	H	
	S 105	Pynson	[150–]	O	
	S 106	Faques	[150–]	B	
	S 107	Notary	1507	H	
1–19	S 108	de Worde	1508	B: H	
	S 109	Pynson	[150–]	B: H: CM	
Henry VIII					
1	S 110	Pynson	[1510]	B: H	
	S 111	R. Faques	[1510]	H	
	S 112	Berthelet	[1543]	B: C: CJ: CM: H: W	Title in 18 lines: Colo. T. B. r. i. excud.
	S 113	Berthelet	[1552]	B: H: O: U	Title in 16 lines: Colo. T. B. excud.
	S 114	Powell	[1562]	H: W	
	S 115	[Marsh]	[1573]	B: H: U	
3–4	S 116	Pynson	[1513]	B: H: N: O	
6	S 117	Pynson	[1515]	C: H	
7	S 117a	Pynson	[1516]	H	
3–7	S 118	Berthelet	[1543]	B: C: CJ: G: H: W	Soverayn: Colo: T. B. r. i. excud.
	S 119	Berthelet	1552	B: H: U	Soverayne: Colo. T. B.
	S 120	Powell	[1562]	CH: H: W	
7	S 121	[Marsh]	[1573]	B: H: U	

SESSION-LAWS —*Continued*

Regnal Year	Number	Printer	Date	Libraries	Distinguishing Marks
14–15	S 122	Pynson	[1524]		
	S 123	Berthelet	[1543]	B: C: CJ: CM: H: W	Soverayne: Colo. T. B. r. i. excud.
	S 124	Berthelet	[1552]	B: H: U	Soveraine: Colo. T. B. excud.
	S 125	[Powell]	[1562]	CH: H: W	
	S 126	[Marsh]	[1573]	B: H: U	
21	S 127	Pynson	[1529]	B: H	Device at end.
	S 128	[Redman]	[1529]	B	No device at end.
	S 129	Rastell	[1529]	B	
	S 130	Berthelet	[1543]	B: C: CJ: CM: G: H: W	Colo. Bertheleti
	S 131	Berthelet	[1552]	B: H: U: W:	Colo. Bertholeti
	S 132	[Powell]	1562	B: H: W	
	S 133	[Marsh]	1573	B: H: U	
22	S 134	Berthelet	[1530]	B	Anno XXII. Colo. T. B.
	S 135	Berthelet	[153–]	B: H	Anno XXII. Colo. ¶ T. B.
	S 136	Berthelet	[1543]	B: C: CJ: CM: G: H: W	Anno vicesimo secundo. Title l. 20, primū
	S 137	Berthelet	[1543]	H: W	Fourth line of title, Statuta bonum
	S 138	Berthelet	[1552]	B: H: U: W	Anno vicesimo secundo. Title l. 20, primum
	S 139	Powell	[1562]	B: C: H	
	S 140	[Marsh]	[1573]	B: H: U	
23	S 141	Berthelet	[1531]	B: H	Colo. ¶Imprinted. Signatures A-D
	S 142	Berthelet	[1531]	H	Colo. ¶Imprinted. Signatures A-E
	S 143	Berthelet	[153–]	B: CJ: W	Colo. ¶Imprynted
	S 144	Berthelet	[153–]	B	God saue the kynge.
	S 145	Berthelet	[1543]	B: C: CJ: CM: H: W	
	S 146	Berthelet	[1552]	B: H: U	❧ God save the Kynge.
	S 147	[Powell]	[1562]	B: C: H: W	
	S 148	[Marsh]	[1573]	B: H: U	❧ God save the Kynge. ❧
24	S 149	Berthelet	[1532]	B	Parlyamente. ❧ Londini.
	S 150	Berthelet	1538	B: CJ: H: W	Parlyamente. ❧ Londini.
	S 151	Berthelet	1546	B: C: CJ: CM: H: W	Parliament
	S 152	Powell	[1562]	H	Line 16 of title, Londini in aedibus Thomae
	S 153	[Powell]	[1562]	B: C: H: U: W	
	S 154	[Marsh]	[1573]	B: H: U	

SESSION-LAWS —*Continued*

Regnal Year	Number	Printer	Date	Libraries	Distinguishing Marks
25	s 155	Berthelet	[1533]	B: H	☙ Londini
	s 156	Berthelet	[153–]	B: H	Londini
	s 157	Berthelet	[1543]	B: C: CJ: CM: H: W	❧ Londini. Typis
	s 158	Berthelet	[1552]	B: H: O: W	❧ Londini. Tipis
	s 159	[Powell]	1562	B: CH: H: W	
	s 160	[Marsh]	[1573]	B: H: U	
26	s 161	Berthelet	[1534]	B	Parlyament. Device of Lucrece
	s 162	Berthelet	[153–]	B: C	Parlyament. Table (reverse of title) ends Finis tabulæ)
	s 163	Berthelet	[153–]	B: H: W	Parlyament. Table ends Finis Tabule
	s 164	Berthelet	[1543]	B: C: CJ: CM: G: H: W	
	s 165	Berthelet	[1552]	B: H: U	Parliament
	s 166	Powell	[1562]	B: H: W	
	s 167	[Marsh]	[1573]	B: H: U	
27	s 168	Berthelet	[1535]	B: H	a ii, first line, Gloucester
	s 169	Berthelet	[1543]	B: CJ: H: W	a ii, first line, Glocester
	s 170	Berthelet	1546	B: C: CJ: CM: H: W	
	s 171	Powell	1557	H: U	
	s 172	Powell	1562	B: H: W	
	s 173	[Marsh]	[1573]	B: H: U	
28	s 174	Berthelet	[1536]	B: H: O	No "Arma Regis" cut
	s 175	Berthelet	[153–]	C: G	
	s 176	Berthelet	[1543]	B: H: W	daye: T. B. excud.
	s 177	Berthelet	[1552]	B: C: CJ: CM: H: W	Leaves not numbered
	s 178	[Powell]	[1562]	B: H: U: W	day
	s 179	[Marsh]	[1573]	B: H: U	
31	s 180	Berthelet	1539	B: CJ: W	❧ Anno: Kynge ∴ ∴
	s 181	Berthelet	1539	C: CM	❧ Anno.: Kynge ❧ ☙ ❦
	s 182	Berthelet	1546	B: C: H: W	❧ Anno: Kyng
	s 183	Berthelet	[1552]	H	☙ Anno.
	s 184	Berthelet	[1552]	B: H: U	☙ Anno. Londidi in imprint
	s 185	[Powell]	[1562]	B: H: W	
	s 186	[Marsh]	[1573]	B: H: U	
32	s 187	Berthelet	1540	B: CM: W	XXVIII of Apryl, the xxxi yere: No leaf.

SESSION-LAWS —*Continued*

Regnal Year	Number	Printer	Date	Libraries	Distinguishing Marks
	S 188	Berthelet	[154-]	B: CJ: H: U: W	XXVIII of Apryll, the xxxi yere:
	S 189	Berthelet	[1543]	B: H	the xxxii yere. Colo. God save the Kinge.
	S 190	Berthelet	[1552]	B: H	the xxxii yere. Colo. God save the Kynge.
	S 191	[Powell]	[1562]	B: C: H: W	the xxxii yeare.
	S 192	[Marsh]	[1573]	B: H: U	Anno XXXII.
33	S 193	Berthelet	1542	B: CM	Victoryouse . . . folowynge
	S 194	Berthelet	1542	C: H: O: U: W	Vyctoryouse . . . folowinge
	S 195	Berthelet	1542	B: CJ: H: W	Vyctoryouse . . . folowynge
	S 196	Berthelet	[1552]	B: H	Victoriouse . . . folowyng
	S 197	[Powell]	[1562]	B: H: W	Anno XXXIII.
	S 198	[Marsh]	[1573]	B: H: U	
34-35	S 199	Berthelet	1543	B: CM	Colo. Imprinted
	S 200	Berthelet	[154-]	B: CJ: H: W	Colo. T. B. r. i. excud.
	S 201	Berthelet	1547	B: C: F: H: L: W	Colo. Imprinted
	S 202	[Powell]	[1556]	H: U	No colo
	S 203	[Powell]	[1562]	B: H: W	
	S 204	[Marsh]	[1573]	B: H: U	
35	S 205	Berthelet	1544	B: C: CJ: CM: G: H: W	Kyng
	S 206	Berthelet	1547	H: W	Kynge: Colo. Thomas
	S 207	Berthelet	[1552]	B: H: U: W	Kynge: Colo. Imprinted: rpynter
	S 208	Berthelet	[1552]	H	Colo. prynter
	S 209	[Powell]	[1562]	F: H	Kynge: Colo. ❡Imprinted
	S 210	[Marsh]	[1573]	B: U	Colo. Yeare
37	S 211	Berthelet	1546	B: C: CJ: CM: F: H: U: W	
	S 212	Powell	1557	H: U	
	S 213	Powell	[1562]	B: H	
	S 214	[Marsh]	[1573]	B: H: U	
Edward VI					
1	S 215	Grafton	1548	B: C: CM	Parliamēt
	S 216	Grafton	1548	B	Parliamente
	S 217	Grafton	[155-]	B: O	¶Anno primo: Colo. Excusum

SESSION-LAWS —*Continued*

Regnal Year	Number	Printer	Date	Libraries	Distinguishing Marks
	S 218	Grafton	[155–]	B: G: H: W	Anno primo: Westminstre
	S 218a	Grafton	[155–]	F: G	¶ Statutes: Parliament
	S 219	[Tottel]	[156–]	B: C: CJ: CH: H	Anno primo: Westminster
2–3	S 220	[Tottel]	[157–]	B: CJ: W	¶Anno primo: Colo. ¶ Excusum
	S 221	Grafton	1549	C: H	Parliament: Colo. Mense Aprilis
	S 222	Grafton	1549	B: C: G	Parliament: Colo. Mense Iunii
	S 223	Grafton	1552	B: F: H	Parlament: Colo. R. G.
	S 224	Grafton	1552	B: CJ: CM: G: O: W	¶Actes: parliament
	S 225	[Tottel]	[156–]	B: CJ: CH: H: W	Parlament: Colo. ¶ R. G.
3–4	S 226	Grafton	1550	B: C: F: H	Anno tertio
	S 227	Grafton	1553	B: H	Anno III
	S 228	Grafton	1553	B: CJ: CM: F: G: H: OW	¶Anno III: Edwardi sexti
	S 229	[Tottel]	[156–]	B: CH: CJ: H: W	¶Anno III: Edwardi sfxti
5–6	S 230	Grafton	1552	C: H	Colo. Mense Aprili MDLII
	S 231	Grafton	1552	C: CM	Colo Mense Aprili 1552
	S 232	Grafton	1552	B	Anno quinto. Colo Mense Iunii MDLII
	S 233	Grafton	1552	B: H	Present parlamente Colo. Mense Iunii MDLII
	S 234	Grafton	[155–]	B: CH: CJ: G: H: O: W	Presét parlamente Colo. Mense Iunii 1552
	S 235	Grafton	[155–]	B: CJ: H	Presét parlamente Colo. Mense Iunii MDLII
7	S 236	Grafton	1553	B: CJ: CM: G: H	Parlament
	S 237	Grafton	1553	B: C: CJ: F: H	Parlamente
	S 238	Grafton	1553	B: CH: H: O: W	Parliament
	S 239	Oswen	1553	C	
Mary					
1, 1st	S 240	Cawood	1554	B: C: CM: F: G: H	Actes: begonne: catchword a ii, or
	S 241	Cawood	1554	B: G: H	Actes: begonne: catchword a ii, by
	S 242	Cawood	[155–]	CH: H	Actes: begon
	S 243	Cawood	[155–]	B: CJ: G: W	Actes: begun
	S 244	Cawood	[155–]	G: O	¶Actes: begun
1, 2d	S 245	Cawood	1554	B: CM: G: H	Parliament
	S 246	Cawood	1554	B: C: CH: H: L	Parlyamente
	S 247	Cawood	1554	F: G: H	Colo. Excusum

SESSION-LAWS —*Continued*

Regnal Year	Number	Printer	Date	Libraries	Distinguishing Marks
	S 248	Cawood	1554	CJ	Colo. ☞Excusum
	S 249	[Tottel]	[156-]	B	Colo. ¶Excusum
	S 250	[Tottel]	[157-]	B: CJ: O: W	Colo. Excusum
Philip & Mary 1, 2	S 251	Cawood	1555	B: H	Table (reverse of title): An Act touchyng
	S 252	Cawood	1555	C: G: H	Table: An Acte touchinge
	S 253	Cawood	[155-]	H	Anno primo et secūdo
	S 254	Cawood	[155-]	H	
	S 255	[Tottel]	[157-]	B: CH: CJ	Colo. Excusum
	S 256	[Tottel]	[157-]	B: CJ: O: W	Colo. ¶Excusum
2, 3	S 257	Cawood	1555	B: CH: CJ: CM	
	S 258	Cawood	1555	G: H	Begon
	S 259	Cawood	1555	B: CJ: G: O: W	Begunne
	S 260	[Tottel]	[157-]	B: C: H	
4, 5	S 261	Cawood	1558	CM: H	☞ Actes
	S 261a	Cawood	1558	H	Parlyamente
	S 262	Cawood	1558	B: C: CH: CJ	Actes: Colo. ¶Excusum
	S 263	Cawood	[156-]	B: G: H	Actes: Colo. ☞ Excusum
	S 264	Cawood	[156-]	H	
	S 265	[Tottel]	[157-]	B: CJ: G: O	
Elizabeth 1	S 267	Jugge & Cawood	1559	H	Colo. Imprynted
	S 268	Jugge & Cawood	1559	H	Colo. ¶Imprinted
	S 269	Jugge & Cawood	1559	B: H: W	Colo. ☞ Imprinted
	S 270	Jugge & Cawood	1559	B: CH: CJ: CM: H	Colo. ¶Imprinted
	S 271	Jugge & Cawood	[156-]	B: G: H: O	Colo. ☞ Imprinted
	S 272	Jugge & Cawood	[156-]	C	Colo. ¶Imprinted
	S 273	Jugge	[1572-5]	B: CJ: W	Yeere
	S 274	Jugge	[1572-5]	B: H: U	Yere
5	S 275	Jugge & Cawood	1563	B: CM: W	Colo. ☞ Imprinted
	S 276	Jugge & Cawood	1563	B	Colo. ¶Imprynted
	S 277	Jugge & Cawood	1563	CJ: G	Colo. ¶Imprinted: Jhon Cawood

SESSION–LAWS—*Continued*

Regnal Year	Number	Printer	Date	Libraries	Distinguishing Marks
	s 278	Jugge & Cawood	1563	H	Colo. Powles
	s 279	Jugge & Cawood	1563	H	Colo. Ihon Cawood
	s 280	Jugge & Cawood	1563	C: CH: U	Colo. Poules
	s 281	Jugge & Cawood	[156–]	B	Colo. ¶ Imprinted: John Cawood
	s 282	Jugge	[1572–5]	H	
	s 283	Jugge	[1572–5]	B: H: O	Fyfth yeere
	s 284	Jugge	[1572–5]	B: CJ: G	Fifth yeere
8	s 285	Cawood & Jugge	1566	CH: CM: H	
	s 286	Jugge	[1572–5]	B: C: CJ: G: H	Anno: Colo. Rycharde Iugge
	s 287	Jugge	[1572–5]	B: CJ: G: O	¶ Anno.
	s 288	Jugge	[1572–5]	B	Anno: Colo. Richard Iugge
13	s 289	Jugge & Cawood	1571	B	The seconde of April
	s 290	Jugge & Cawood	1571	CJ: CM: H	The second of Apryll: Colo. Powles
	s 291	Jugge & Cawood	1571	B: CH: H: U	The second of Apryll: Colo. Poules
	s 292	Jugge	[1572–5]	B: G: W	
	s 293	Jugge	[1572–5]	B	
	s 294	Barker	1578	CJ: G	
14	s 295	Jugge	1572	B: CJ: G	The eight of May
	s 296	Jugge	1572	B: CJ: CM: G: H: O: U: W	The eyght of May
18	s 297	Jugge	1575	CJ: CM	
	s 298	Jugge	1575	B: CJ: CM: G: H: O: U: W	
23	s 299	Barker	1581	B: CJ: CM: G: H: O: U	
27	s 300	Barker	1585	B:CJ:CM:CP:G:H:O:U:W	
29	s 301	Barker	1587	B: CJ: CM: CP: G: H: O: W	
31	s 302	Barker (dep.)	1589	B: CJ: G: O: W	Ladie: Colo. 3d line italic.
	s 303	Barker (dep.)	1589	CP: G	Ladie: Colo. 2d line italic.
	s 304	Barker (dep.)	1589	G: H	Lady
35	s 305	Barker (dep.)	1593	B: CJ: CM: G: L: O	Colo. Imprinted
	s 306	Barker (dep.)	1593	G: H: W	Colo. ❧ Imprinted
39	s 307	Barker (dep.)	1597	B: CP: CM: G: H: O: W	

PART II.—DECISIONS

Section 1.—Year Books

Regnal Year	Number	Date	Printer	Libraries	Distinguishing Marks
Edward III					
7	R 1	1518	Pynson	B: G: H: L: CT: W	
7–10	R 2	1562	Tottyll	B: C: G: H: U: W	
	R 3	1596	Yetsweirt	F: G: H: U: W	
17	R 4	[1515]	J. Rastell	B: JH: L: CT: W	
	R 5	[1561]	[Tottell]	B: G: H: U: W	Capitals in early form : Anno xvii.
	R 6	[1585]	[Tottell]	B: F: H: O: U: W	Capitals in late form : Anno xvij.
18	R 7	[1515]	J. Rastell	B: CT: H: L: W	
	R 8	[1561]	[Tottell]	B: F: G: H: U: W	¶De termino
	R 9	[1585]	[Tottell]	B: G: H: O: U: W	¶De termino
21	R 10	[1520]	Pynson	B: CT: G: H: L: U: W	
	R 11	1527	Berthelet	B: CT: W	
	R 12	1561	Tottyll	B: F: G: H:O: W	
	R 13	1584	Tottyll	B: G: H: O: U: W	
22–28	R 14	1532	Berthelet	B: CT: G: H: L: O: U: W	
	R 15	1567	Tottel	F: G: H: W	
	R 16	1585	Tottyl	B: H: O: U: W	
24	R 17	[1525–8]	Redman	B: CT: G: H: L: U: W	
29	R 18	[1527]	Redman	B: CT: G: H: L: U: W	
	R 19	1561	Tottyll	B: F: G: H: O: W	
	R 20	1585	Tottyl	B: G: H: O: U: W	
30	R 21	[153–]	Redman	B: CT: H: L: W	
	R 22	1561	Tottyll	B: F: G: H: O: U: W	
	R 23	1585	Tottell	B: G: H: O: U: W	
38	R 24	1520	Pynson	B: CT: G: H: L: W	
	R 25	1561	Tottyll	B: F: G: H: O: U: W	
	R 26	1585	Tottel	B: H: O: U: W	
39	R 27	[153–]	Redman	B: CT: H: W	
	R 28	1561	Tottyll	B: F: G: H: O: U: W	
	R 29	1585	Tottill	B: H: O: U: W	

PART II.—SECTION I —*Continued*

Regnal Year	Number	Date	Printer	Libraries	Distinguishing Marks
Edward III					
40–50	R 43	1555	Tottel	CT: F: G: H: W	
	R 44	1565	Tottel	B: H: L: U: W	
	R 45	1576	Tottel	B: C: CT: G: H: U: W	With Table
	R 46	1600	Wight	F: H: U: W	
40	R 30	[1516–18]	Pynson	B: L	
	R 31	1534	Redman	G: L	
41	R 32	[1516–18]	Pynson	B: L	
	R 33	[153–]	Redman	G: L	
42	R 34	[1516–18]	Pynson	B: G: H: L	
43	R 35	[1516–18]	Pynson	B: G: L	
44	R 36	[1516–18]	Pynson	B: G: H: L	
45	R 37	[1516–18]	Pynson	B: G: L: W	
46	R 38	1517	Pynson	B: G: L	
47	R 39	1520	Pynson	B: G: L: W	
48	R 40	1518	Pynson	B: G: H: L	
49	R 41	[1518]	Pynson	B: G: L	
50	R 42	[1518]	Pynson	B: G: L: W	
Lib. Ass.	R 47	[1500]	Pynson	B: H: R: L	
	R 48	[1514][1]	J. Rastell	B: C: H: W	With Colophon
	R 49	[1514][2]	J. Rastell	H	Without Colophon
	R 50	1561	Tottyll	B: CP: F: G: H: U: W	
	R 51	1580	Tottel	F: G: H: U: W	
Abridg.	R 52	1555	Tottell	F: H: W	
	R 53	1555	Tottel	G: H: N: U: W	
Henry IV					
1–14	R 60	1553	Tathyll	B: CT: L: U: W	
	R 61	1562–3	Tottell	B: G: H: L: W	
	R 61a	1562	Tottell	H	Same with uninked colo.
	R 62	1575–6	Tottell	B: CP: CT: F: H: U: W	
7	R 54	[1508]	Pynson	L	
8	R 55	[1508]	Pynson	L	

PART II.— SECTION 1 —*Continued*

Regnal Year	Number	Date	Printer	Libraries	Distinguishing Marks
Henry IV					
9	R 56	[152–]	Wyre	L	
11	R 57	[1508]	[Pynson]	L	
12	R 58	[1508]	[Pynson]	L	
14	R 59	[1508]	[Pynson]	L	
Henry V					
1–9	R 65	1563	Tottell	B: G: H: W	
	R 66	1563–70	Tottyl	B: CP: CT: F: H: L: U: W	
	R 67	1587	Tottyll	H	
9	R 63	[1508]	[Pynson]	L	
	R 64	[154–]	Powell	G: W	
Henry VI					
1	R 68	[1520]	Pynson	G: H: L: W	
	R 69	[1525]	Redman	B: CP: H	
	R 70	[154–]	Smyth	C: H	
	R 71	[154–]	Myddylton	G: W	
	R 72	1556	Tottyll	B: F: H: U: W	
	R 73	1570	Tottyl	CT: H: OA: U	
	R 74	1584	Tottyl	B: H: L: W	
2	R 75	[1518]	Pynson	B: C: CP: H: L	
	R 76	[1528]	Redman	B: G: W	
	R 77	1547	Myddilton	G: H	
	R 78	[154–]	Smyth	C: H: W	
	R 79	1556	Tottyll	B: F: H: U: W	
	R 80	1570	Tottyl	CT: H: OA: U: W	
	R 81	1584	Tottyl	B: H: L: W	
3	R 82	1510	Pynson	C: H: W	
	R 83	[1520]	Pynson	CP: G: H: W	
	R 84	1527	Redman	B: G: L	
	R 85	[154–]	Smyth	C: H: W	
	R 86	[1556]	Tottill	B: F: H: U: W	
	R 87	1568	Tottel	H: OA: U	

PART II.—Section 1—*Continued*

Regnal Year	Number	Date	Printer	Libraries	Distinguishing Marks
Henry VI					
	R 88	1582	Tottell	B: H: L: W	
4	R 89	[1510]	Pynson	G: H	
	R 90	1528	Redman	B: CP: G: H: L: W	
	R 91	[154-]	Smyth	C: H: W	
	R 92	1556	Tottel	B: F: H: U: W	
	R 93	1568	Tottel	H: OA: U	
	R 94	1582	Tottell	B: H: L: W	
7	R 95	1528	Berthelet	G: L: W	
	R 96	[154-]	Smyth	H	
8	R 97	1528	Berthelet	G: L: W	
	R 98	[154-]	Smyth	H	
7 & 8	R 99	[154-]	Myddylton	B: C: G: H: W	
	R 100	1559	Tottyll	B: F: G: H: U: W	
	R 101	1570	Tottyl	H: L: OA: U	
	R 102	1584	Tottyl	B: H: W	
9	R 103	[1500]	Pynson	H: OE	
	R 104	[1520]	Pynson	C: G: H: L: W	
	R 105	[154-]	Smyth	B: C: H: W	Anno regni Regis
	R 106	[154-]	Smyth	H	Anno nono
	R 107	[154-]	Powell	CP: F: G	
	R 108	1562	Tottell	H: U: W	
	R 109	1570	Tottyl	H: OA: U: W	
	R 110	[1582]	[Tottell]	B: L: O: W	
10	R 111	[1520]	Pynson	G: H: L: W	
	R 112	[154-]	Myddylton	G: H	
	R 113	[154-]	Smyth	B: C: H: W	
	R 114	1561	Tottyll	B: F: G: H: U: W	
	R 115	1570	Tottyl	H: OA: U	
	R 116	1587	Tottyll	B: H: L: W	
11	R 117	[153-]	Redman	B: CP: G: H: L: W	
	R 118	[1541]	Smyth	C: H: W	

PART II.—SECTION 1—*Continued*

Regnal Year	Number	Date	Printer	Libraries	Distinguishing Marks
Henry VI					
	R 119	[1556]	Tottill	B: F: G: H: U: W	
	R 120	1567	Tottill	H: L: OA: U: W	
	R 121	1582	Tottel	B: H: W	
12	R 122	[1520]	Pynson	B: G: H: L: W	
	R 123	[154–]	Myddylton	B: C: G: H: W	
	R 124	[1556]	Tottle	F: G: H	
	R 125	1562	Tottell	B: CP: H: U: W	
	R 126	1574	Tottel	H: OA: U: W	
14	R 127	[1528]	Redman	B: G: L: W	
	R 128	[154–]	Meddelton	B: C: G:H	
	R 129	[1556]	Tottel	F: H: W	
	R 130	1562	Tottell	B: H: U: W	
	R 131	1574	Tottel	H: OA: U: W	
	R 132	[1582]	[Tottell]	B: G: H: L: W	
18	R 133	[1520]	Pynson	B: G: H	
	R 134	[1528]	Redman	C: CP: G: H: L: W	
	R 135	[1559]	Tottel	B: F: G:H:L:O: OA: U: W	De termino pasche
	R 136	[1568]	Tottel	CT: H: U	¶De termino pasche
	R 137	[1585]	Tottel	H: W	¶ De termino pasche
19	R 138	[1528]	Redman	G: H: L: W	
	R 139	[154–]	Myddylton	C: G: H: N	
	R 140	[1559]	Tottel	B: CP: F: G: H: O: U: W	
	R 141	1567	Tottill	B: CJ: H: U	¶De termino Michælis
	R 142	[1585]	Tottel	CT: L: O: OA: U: W	¶ De termino Michælis
20	R 143	[1500]	[Pynson]	OE	Anno xx°
	R 144	[1503]	[Pynson]	C: H: L: W	
	R 145	[1518]	Pynson	G: H	
	R 146	1553	Tottyll	B: H: W	
	R 147	1556	Tottyll	B: CP: F: G: H: O: U: W	
	R 148	1570	Tottyl	H: OA: U: W	
	R 149	[1584]	[Tottell]	C: H: L: O: W	

PART II.—SECTION I—*Continued*

Regnal Year	Number	Date	Printer	Libraries	Distinguishing Marks
Henry VI					
21	R 150	[1520]	Pynson	G: H: L: W	
	R 151	[1528]	Redman	B: H	
	R 152	[1556]	Tottill	B: H: U: W	
	R 153	1567	Tottill	B: G: H: U: W	
	R 154	1575	Tottel	CT: G: H: L :O: U: W	
22	R 155	[1520]	Pynson	G: H: W	
	R 156	[1528]	Redman	B: H: L	
	R 157	[1556]	Tottill	H: U: W	
	R 158	1567	Tottill	B: CJ: G: H: U: W	
	R 159	1575	Tottel	G: H: L: U: W	
	R 160	1578	Tottel	CT: O: W	
27	R 161	[1509]	Pynson	C: CP: H: L	
	R 162	[153-]	Redman	B: G: H: W	
	R 163	[1556]	Tottel	H: W	
	R 164	1562	Tottell	G: H: U: W	
	R 165	1567	Tottill	B: H: O: W	
	R 166	1575	Tottel	G: H: L: U: W	
28	R 167	[1520]	Pynson	C: CP: H: L	
	R 168	[153-]	Redman	B: G: H: W	
	R 169	1556	Tottle	G: H: U: W	
	R 170	1567	Tottel	B: H: O: U: W	
	R 171	1575	Tottel	G: H: L: U: W	
30–31	R 172	[153-]	Redman	B: G: H: L	
	R 173	[154-]	Myddylton	B: H	
	R 174	1556	Tottel	CP: G: H: U: W	
	R 175	1567	Tottel	B: H: U: W	
	R 176	1575	Tottel	G: H: L: O: U: W	
32	R 177	[153-]	Redman	B: G: H: L	
	R 178	[154-]	Myddylton	H	
	R 179	1556	Tottel	CP: G: H: U W	
	R 180	1566	Tottel	B: H: U: W	

PART II.—SECTION 1—*Continued*

Regnal Year	Number	Date	Printer	Libraries	Distinguishing Marks
Henry VI					
	R 181	1576	Tottel	G: H: L: O: U: W	
33	R 182	[148–]	Lettou & Mach.	B: C	
	R 183	[1508]	Pynson	C: CP	
	R 184	[153–]	Redman	B: G: H: L: W	
	R 185	1556	Tottel	CP: G: H: U: W	❧De termino
	R 186	[1566]	Tottell	B: H: U: W	¶De termino
	R 187	1575	Tottel	G: H: L: O: U: W	
	R 188	[1585]	[Tottell]	CT	
34	R 189	[148–]	Maclyn	B: C: OE	
	R 190	[1520]	Pynson	B: G: H: L: W	
	R 191	1556	Tottel	CP: G: H: U: W	❧De termino
	R 192	[1566]	Tottel	B: H: U: W	¶De termino
	R 193	1575	Tottel	G: H: L: O: U: W	
	R 194	[1585]	[Tottell]	CT	
35	R 195	[148–]	[Lettou & Mach.]	B: C	
	R 196	[1508]	[Pynson]	C: L	
	R 197	[153–]	Redman	B: G: H: L: W	
	R 198	1556	Tottel	CP: G: H: U: W	¶ De termino
	R 199	[1566]	Tottell	B: H: U: W	¶De termino
	R 200	1575	Tottel	G: H: L: O: U: W	
	R 201	[1585]	[Tottell]	CT	
36	R 202	[148–]	[Lettou & Mach.]	B: C	
	R 203	[1520]	Pynson	B: G: H: L	
	R 204	[154–]	Myddylton	H	
	R 205	1557	Tottle	CP: G: H: U: W	
	R 206	1567	Tottel	B: CT: H: U: W	
	R 207	1575	Tottel	G: H: L: O: U: W	
37	R 208	[148–]	[Machlinia]	C: OE	
	R 209	[1520]	Pynson	B: G: H: L: W	
	R 210	[154–]	Myddylton	CP: H	
	R 211	[1556]	Tottill	G: H: U: W	

PART II.—SECTION 1—*Continued*

Regnal Year	Number	Date	Printer	Libraries	Distinguishing Marks
Henry VI					
	R 212	1567	Tottill	B: H: U: W	
	R 213	1575	Tottel	G: H: L: O: U: W	
38	R 214	[153–]	Redman	B: G: H: L: W	
	R 215	1556	Tottel	CP: G: H: U: W	
	R 216	1566	Tottel	B: H: O: U: W	
	R 217	1575	Tottel	G: H: L: U: W	
39	R 218	1520	Pynson	B: G: H: L	
	R 219	154–	Myddylton	H	
	R 220	1557	Tottle	CP: G: H: U: W	
	R 221	1567	Tottill	B: H: O: U: W	
	R 222	1575	Tottel	CT: G: H: L: U: W	
Edward IV					
1–22	R 372	1599	Wight & Norton	B: F: G: H: OA: U: W	
1	R 223	1492	Pynson	B	De tmino Michis
	R 224	1496	Pynson	B: R	Edwardi iiii
	R 225	1508	[Pynson]	H: W	De termino scti Mich.
	R 226	1514	Pynson	L	¶De termino Michaelis
	R 227	154–	Myddylton	B: H	
	R 228	1556	Tottill	B: G: H: U: W	De termino
	R 229	1565	Tottel	O: W	
	R 230	[1566]	Tottel	B: CP: F: H: U: W	☙ De termino
	R 231	[1572]	Tottel	B: H: W	¶De termino
	R 232	1582	Tottel	H: W	
2	R 233	1508	Pynson	B: C: H: W	De termio pasche
	R 234	1520	[Pynson]	C: H: L	Colo. secundus
	R 235	153–	[Redman]	H: L	
	R 236	1558	Tottyll	F: G: H: L: O: U: W	
	R 237	1566	Tottell	H: O: U: W	
	R 238	1572	Tottel	H: U: W	
	R 239	1584	Tottel	H: W	
3	R 240	1496	[Pynson]	B: R	De termino sce Trin

PART II.—SECTION I—*Continued*

Regnal Year	Number	Date	Printer	Libraries	Distinguishing Marks
Edward IV					
	R 241	1502	[Pynson]	H: L: W	¶De termino sce Trinitatis
	R 242	1518	Pynson	H: W	De termino Trinitatis
	R 243	[154–]	Myddylton	B	
	R 244	1558	Tottell	B: CP: F: G: H: U: W	
	R 245	1566	Tottell	B: H: U: W	
	R 246	[1572]	Tottill	B: H: U: W	
	R 247	1583	Tottel	B: H: W	
4	R 248	[1496]	[Pynson]	B: R	De termino pasch
	R 249	[1502]	[Pynson]	H: L: W	¶De termino Pasche
	R 250	[1520]	Pynson	C: H: L: W	
	R 251	[154–]	Myddylton	B	
	R 252	1558	Tottyll	B: CP: F: G: H: O: U: W	
	R 253	[1566]	Tottell	B: H: U: W	
	R 254	[1572]	Tottill	B: H: O: U: W	
	R 255	1583	Tottel	B: H: W	
5	R 256	[1496]	[Pynson]	B: R	De termino pasche A° v.
	R 257	[1502]	[Pynson]	C: H: L: W	¶De termino Pasche. anno v.
	R 258	[1508]	[Pynson]	B: H: L: W	De termino Pasche. Anno v.
	R 259	1557	Tottle	B: CP: F: G: H: O: U: W	
	R 260	1566	Tottell	B: H: U: W	
	R 261	[1572]	Tottill	B: H: U: W	
	R 262	1584	Tottel	B: H: W	
6	R 263	[1496]	[Pynson]	B: R	A° vi.
	R 264	[1502]	[Pynson]	H: L	Anno vi°
	R 265	[1508]	[Pynson]	B: H: L: W	Anno vi.
	R 266	[153–]	[Redman]	B	
	R 267	1557	Tottle	B: F: G: H: U: W	
	R 268	[1566]	Tottell	H: O: U: W	
	R 269	1572	Tottel	B: H: U: W	
	R 270	[1584]	Tottell	B: H: W	
7	R 271	[1496]	[Pynson]	B: R	De termino pasche

PART II.—SECTION 1—*Continued*

Regnal Year	Number	Date	Printer	Libraries	Distinguishing Marks
Edward IV					
	R 272	[1502]	[Pynson]	H: L: W	¶De termino Pasche
	R 273	[1518]	Pynson	B: H: W	
	R 274	[153-]	Redman	B: F: L: H: O: W	
	R 275	1556	Tottyll	B: CP: G: H: U: W	
	R 276	1567	Tottill	H: U: W	¶De termino Pasche
	R 277	[1572]	Tottill	B: H: U: W	¶ De termino Pasche
	R 278	1584	Tottel	B: H: W	
8	R 279	[1496]	[Pynson]	B: R	De termio pasche
	R 280	[1502]	[Pynson]	H: W	Edwardi. iiii.
	R 281	[1518]	[Pynson]	B: H: L: W	
	R 282	[154-]	Myddylton	B	
	R 283	1556	Tottel	B: CP: G: H: U: W	¶De termino
	R 284	[1567]	Tottel	B: H: O: W	¶De termino
	R 285	[1572]	Tottill	B: F: H: O: U: W	De termino
	R 286	1582	Tottell	H: W	¶De termino Paschae
9	R 287	[1492]	Pynson	B: H: R	Colo. Explicit annnus
	R 288	[1520]	Pynson	B: H: W	Colo. Explicit Annus
	R 289	[1528]	Redman	B: H: L	
	R 290	1556	Tottel	CP: F: G: H: O: U: W	
	R 291	[1567]	Tottell	H: O: W	
	R 292	1572	Tottel	B: U: W	
	R 293	1582	Tottel	B: H: W	
10–12	R 303	[1556]	Tottill	G: H: U: W	
	R 304	1566	Tottell	H: O: U: W	
	R 305	[1572]	Tottill	B: H: U: W	
	R 306	1584	Tottyl	H: U: W	
10	R 294	[1508]	Pynson	B: F: W	¶De termino Pache
	R 295	[1515]	[Rastell]	B: H: L: W	De termino Pach.
	R 296	[1518]	[Pynson]	H: L: W	De termino Pasche
11	R 297	[1500]	[Pynson]	R	De termino sancte Trinitatis
	R 298	[153-]	Redman	B: H: L: W	

PART II.—Section 1—*Continued*

Regnal Year	Number	Date	Printer	Libraries	Distinguishing Marks
Edward IV					
	R 299	[154–]	[Powell]	F: H: W	
12	R 300	[1508]	Pynson	B: H: L: W	
	R 301	[1528]	Redman	H	
	R 302	[154–]	[Powell]	F: H: W	
13	R 307	[1508]	Pynson	F: H: W	
	R 308	[1528]	Redman	B: H: L	
	R 309	[154–]	Powell	H: W	
	R 310	1559	Tottill	CP: G: H: U: W	
	R 311	1566	Tottill	H: O: U: W	
	R 312	1572	Tottel	B: C: U: W	
	R 313	1582	Tottel	H: W	
14	R 314	[1520]	Pynson	B: H: L: W	
	R 315	[153–]	Redman	B: H: L	
	R 316	1556	Tottel	B: CP: F: G: H: U: W	
	R 317	[1566]	Tottell	B: H: O: W	
	R 318	1572	Tottel	B: U: W	
	R 319	1582	Tottel	B: H: W	
15	R 320	[1520]	Pynson	H: L: W	
	R 321	[1528]	Redman	B	
	R 322	1556	Tottel	CP: F: G: H: O: U: W	¶ De termino
	R 323	1566	Tottel	B: H: W	¶De termino
	R 324	1572	Tottel	B: U: W	
	R 325	1582	Tottel	H: W	
16	R 326	[1520]	Pynson	B: H: L	
	R 327	[1528]	Redman	H: W	
	R 328	1557	Tottle	CP: F: G: H: O: U: W	
	R 329	[1566]	Tottell	H: O: U: W	
	R 330	[1572]	Tottill	H: U: W	
	R 331	1583	Tottel	B: H: W	
17	R 332	[153–]	Redman	B: H: L: W	
	R 333	[154–]	Powel	H: L	
	R 334	1557	Tottel	B: CP: F: G: H: U	¶ De termino

PART II.—SECTION 1—*Continued*

Regnal Year	Number	Date	Printer	Libraries	Distinguishing Marks
Edward IV					
	R 335	1557	Tottel	H: W	De termino
	R 336	[1567]	Tottel	B: H: O: U: W	¶De termino
	R 337	1572	Tottel	H: U: W	
	R 338	1583	Tottel	H: W	
18	R 339	[1520]	Pynson	B: H: L	
	R 340	[1529]	Redman	B: H: W	
	R 341	1556	Tottel	B: CP: F: G: H: O: U: W	
	R 342	[1567]	Tottell	H: O: W	
	R 343	1572	Tottel	H: U: W	
	R 344	1582	Tottell	H: W	
19	R 345	[1520]	Pynson	B: H: L: W	
	R 346	[153–]	Redman	B: W	
	R 347	1556	Tottle	B: CP: F: G: H: O: U: W	
	R 348	[1567]	Tottel	H: O: U: W	
	R 349	[1572]	Tottill	H: U: W	
	R 350	[1582]	Tottell	H: W	
20	R 351	[1520]	Pynson	B: H: L: W	
	R 352	[1528]	Redman	H: L	
	R 353	1556	Tottel	B: CP: F: G: H: O: U: W	
	R 354	[1566]	Tottell	B: H: O: W	
	R 355	[1572]	Tottill	B: U: W	
	R 356	1582	Tottyll	B: H: W	
21	R 357	[1520]	Pynson	B: H: L: W	
	R 358	[1528]	Redman	B: F: G: H: L	
	R 359	[1556]	Tottyll	B: G: H: U: W	
	R 360	1566	Tottell	H: O: U: W	
	R 361	[1572]	Tottill	H: U: W	
	R 362	1584	Tottel	H: W	
22	R 363	[1508]	Pynson	B: H: L: W	¶De termino
	R 364	[1520]	Pynson	B: L	De termino
	R 365	[154–]	Myddylton	B	
	R 366	1556	Tottel	B: CP: F: G: H: O: W	❧De termino

PART II.—SECTION I—*Continued*

Regnal Year	Number	Date	Printer	Libraries	Distinguishing Marks
Edward IV					
	R 367	[1566]	Tottel	B: H: O: U: W	¶De termino
	R 368	1572	Tottle	B: H: U: W	
	R 369	1578	Tottel	H: U: W	
Long Quint.	R 370	1552	Powell	F: H: W	
	R 371	1587	Tottyll	B: H: OA: U: W	
1 Edw. V & 1 Rich. III	R 373	[1517]	J. Rastell	B: L	
Edward V					
1	R 374	[1508]	Pynson	L	
	R 375	1555	Tottel	G: H	
	R 376	1558	Tottyll	B: H	Colo.
	R 377	1559	Tottyll	B: CP: H: U: W	
	R 378	[1564]	Tottell	B: H: U: W	
	R 379	1568	Tottill	B: G: H: O: U: W	
	R 380	[1568]	Tottill	H: W	
	R 381	1579	Tottyll	B: H: U	
	R 382	1585	Tottyl	B: F: H: W	
Edward V, Richard III, Henry VII, Henry VIII	R 454	1597	Yetsweirt	B: F: H: L: U	
Richard III	R 373	[1517]	J. Rastell	B: L	
1	R 383	[153–]	Redman	H: L	
	R 384	[1558]	Tottyll	H: U: W	
	R 385	[1559]	Tottel	CP: G: H	
	R 386	[1561]	Tottell	H: O: U: W	
	R 387	1568	Tottel	B: G: H: U	
	R 388	1574	Tottel	B: H: W	
	R 389	1581	Tottel	B: G: H: O: U	
	R 390	[1587]	[Tottell]	B: F: H: W	
2	R 391	[1508]	[Pynson]	B: H	
	R 392	[1514]	Pynson	H: L	
	R 393	[1558]	Tottyll	H: U: W	
	R 394	[1559]	Tottel	CP: G: H	
	R 395	[1561]	Tottell	H: O: U: W	

PART II.—SECTION I—*Continued*

Regnal Year	Number	Date	Printer	Libraries	Distinguishing Marks
Richard III					
	R 396	1568	Tottel	G: H: U: W	
	R 397	1574	Tottel	B: H: W	
	R 398	1581	Tottel	B: G: H: O: U	
	R 399	1587	Tottyll	B: F: H: W	
Henry VII					
1–8	R 400	[1502]	[Pynson]	H	
	R 401	[153–]	Redman	L	
9	R 402	[1508]	Pynson	L	
12	R 403	[1508]	Pynson	L	
14	R 404	1529	Berthelet	L	
15	R 405	[1529]	Berthelet	L	
21	R 406	[153–]	Redman	L	
1–21	R 407	1555	Tottyl	B: CP: H: L	¶ Londini in aedibus
	R 408	1555	Tottyl	H: W	Londini in aedibus
	R 409	1555	Tottel	G: H: W	
	R 410	[1560]	Tottell	B: U: W	Colo. ¶ Imprinted
	R 411	1567	Tottill	H	Colo. ❧ Imprinted
	R 412	1567	Tottill	B: H: O: U: W	
	R 413	1580	Tottle	B: H: U: W	
	R 414	1583	Tottel	B: F: H: O: W	
Henry VIII					
12–13	R 415	[1540]	Redman	L	
	R 416	1548	Powell	B: H	
	R 417	[1583]	Tottel	G: H	
14	R 418	[1508]	Pynson	L	
	R 419	1540	Redman	B: H	
	R 419a	[1583]	Tottel	G: H	
12–14	R 420	1556	Tottel	B: F: H: O: U: W	
	R 421	1560	Tottyll	B: H: U: W	Colo. ¶ Imprinted
	R 422	1560	Tottyll	CP: H: W	Colo. ¶Imprinted
	R 423	1566	Tottell	B: H: W	
	R 424	1567	Tottill	H: U: W	

PART II.—SECTION 1—*Continued*

Regnal Year	Number	Date	Printer	Libraries	Distinguishing Marks
Henry VIII					
	R425	1569	Tottel	B: G: H	
	R426	1579	Tottel	B: H: W	
12–27	R454	1591	Tottell	H: W	
18–19	R427	154–	Myddylton	B	
	R428	1556	Tottel	B: F: G: H: O: U: W	
	R429	1560	Tottill	B: H: W	
	R430	1560	Tottel	CP: H	
	R431	1560	Tottil	H: U: W	
	R432	1566	Tottell	B: H: W	
	R433	1567	Tottel	H: U: W	
	R434	1569	Tottel	B: G: H	
	R435	1579	Tottel	B: H	
26	R436	154–	Myddylton	B	
	R437	1556	Tottell	H: U: W	¶De termino Pasche
	R438	1556	Tottel	B: H: O: U	¶ De termino Paschae
	R439	1556	Tottel	CP: G: H	De termino pasche
	R440	1559	Tottyll	H: U: W	
	R441	1566	Tottell	H: O: W	
	R442	1567	Tottel	H: U: W	
	R443	1569	Tottel	B: G: H	
	R444	1579	Tottel	B: H	
27	R445	154–	Myddylton	B	
	R449	1566	Tottell	H: W	¶De termino
	R446	1556	Tottell	H: U: W	☙De termino
	R447	1556	Tottel	CP: G: H	De termino
	R448	1566	Tottill	B: O: W	
	R450	[1583]	Tottel	H: W	
	R451	1569	Tottel	B: G: H: U: W	Colo. Imprynted
	R452	1579	Tottel	H	
	R453	1583	Tottel	B: H: O: U: W	

Section 2.—Abridgments

Author	Number	Date	Printer	Libraries	Distinguishing Marks
Statham	R 455	[1490]	Pynson-Tailleur	B: G: H: L: N: U: W	
Fitzherbert	R 456–461	1516	J. Rastell	B: G: H: N: O: W	
	R 463, 464	1565	Tottell	G: H: U: W	
	R 466, 467	1577	Tottell	G: H: U: W	
Table to F.	R 462	1518	[J. Rastell]	H	
	R 465	1565	Tottell	G: H: U: W	
	R 468	1577	Tottel	H: U: W	
Brooke	R 469, 470	1573	Tottell	G: H: U: W	
	R 471, 472	1576	Tottell	G: H: U: W	
	R 473, 474	1586 [1]	Tottell	H: U	vicesimo nono die Septembris
	R 475, 476	1586 [2]	Tottell	G: H: W	vicesimo nono die Septemb.
Gregory	R 477	1599	Wight & Norton	H: N: U: W	

Section 3.—Reports

Author	Number	Date	Printer	Libraries	Distinguishing Marks
Plowden	R 484	1571	Tottyl	G: U	
	R 485	1578	Tottell	G: H: U: W	
	R 486	1579	Tottell	G: H: W	Appendix
	R 486a	1584	Tottell	G: U	Appendix
	R 487	1584	Tottell	G: H: U: W	Part II
	R 488	[1584]	[Tottell]	H: U: W	Table
	R 489	1588	Tottyll	G: H: U	
	R 489a	1594	Yetsweirt	H: U	
	R 489b	1594	Yestweirt	H	Appendix
	R 489c	[1594]	Yestweirt	H	Table to Part II
	R 490	1599	Wight & Norton	CT: G: H	
	R 491	[1596]	J. Yetsweirt	H:	Abridgment
Dyer	R 481	1585	Tottell	G: H: W	
	R 482	1591	Tottyll	H	
	R 483a	1588	Tottell	U	
	R 483	1600	Wight	G: H	Table
Bellewe	R 478	1585	Robinson	G: H: U: W	
Brook's New Cases	R 479	1578	Tottel	CT: G: H: U: W	
	R 480	1587	Tottel	H: U: W	
	R 480a	1597	Yetsweirt	CT: G: H: W	

PART III.—TREATISES

Section 1.—Rastell's Anonymous Tracts

Name	Number	Printer	Date	Libraries	Distinguishing Marks
Rastell's Tracts	T 1	W. Rastell	1534	B: G: H: N: O: U: W	Double column
	T 2	W. Rastell	1534	H	Single column
Articuli at Narr. Nov.	T 111	Pynson	1525	B: H: W	
	T 112	Redman	1525		
	T 113	Redman	1528	B	
	T 114	Berthelet	1530	B: C: H	
	T 115	Berthelet	1532	H	
	T 116	Berthelet	1538	B	
	T 117	Redman	1539	B: H	
	T 118	Smyth	[1545]	B: H	
	T 119	Powell	1547	B	
Book for a Justice	T 130	Pynson	[1506]	H: S	
	T 131	de Worde	1506	G	
	T 132	de Worde	1510	B: G: O	
	T 133	de Worde	1515	G	
	T 134	Copland	1515	C: O	
	T 135	Pynson	1521	C	
	T 136	Skot	1521	R	
	T 137	J. Rastell	[1527]	B: O	
	T 138	Redman	1527	O	
	T 139	Redman	[1530]	C: H	
	T 140	Redman	[1533]	H: O: W	
	T 140a	Redman	[153–]	H	
	T 141	Berthelet	[1530]	C: H	
	T 142	Berthelet	[1536]	H	
	T 143	Redman	[1538]	H	
	T 144	Berthelet	1539	B: H	
	T 145	Berthelet	1544	B: C: G: H: O	
	T 146	Middleton	[1544]	B: H	
	T 147	Hyll	1546	H	
	T 148	Smyth	1546		

PART III.—SECTION I—*Continued*

Name	Number	Printer	Date	Libraries	Distinguishing Marks
	T 149	Waley	1546	B	
	T 150	Toye	1546	B	
	T 151	Powell	1550	H	
	T 151a	Powell	1551	C	
	T 152	Tottle	1556	B: H	
	T 153	Tottil	1559[2]	B: H: U	this boke. Fyrst
	T 154	Tottil	1559[1]	G: H: O	this booke. Fyrste
	T 155	Tottel	1569[1]	B	
	T 156	Tottyl	1569[2]	I	
	T 157	Tottyl	1574	B: H: N: W	
Carta Feodi	T 158	Pynson	[1506]	H: S	
	T 159	de Worde	[1510][1]	B: G: H: O	¶Carta feodi simplicis cum Colo. ¶Impressa London per W. de W. in
	T 160	de Worde	[1510][2]	B: C: L: R	¶Carta feodi simplicis Colo. ¶Impressa London per W. de W. in
	T 161	de Worde	[1510][3]	C: G	¶Carta feodi simplicis cum Colo. ¶Impresa London per W. de W. in vico
	T 162	de Worde	[1510][4]	O	¶Carta feodi simplicis cum Colo. ¶Impressa London per W. de W.
	T 163	Skot	[1521]	R	
	T 164	Pynson	[1516]	B: H	
	T 165	J. Rastell	[1527]	O	
	T 166	Redman	1527	O	
	T 167	Redman	1530	B: C: H	
	T 167a	Berthelet	[1530]	H	
	T 168	Redman	1533	G: H: O: W	
	T 169	Redman	1538[1]	B: H	¶Paruus libellus
	T 170	Redman	1538[2]	H: O	❧Paruus libellus
	T 170a	Berthelet	[1536]	H	
	T 171	Berthelet	1539	B: H	
	T 172	Redman	1541	H: L	

PART III.—SECTION 1—*Continued*

Name	Number	Printer	Date	Libraries	Distinguishing Marks
	T 173	Berthelet	1543	B: H	
	T 174	Myddylton	1544	B	
	T 175	Myddylton	1545	H	
	T 176	Hyll	1546	H	
	T 177	Waley	1546	B	
	T 178	Smyth	1546	H	
Court Baron	T 180	Pynson	[1506]	B: H	
	T 181	de Worde	[1510]	B: O	
	T 182	Copeland	[1515]	C: G	
	T 183	Pepwell	[1521]	C: R	
	T 184	Pynson	[1516]	B: O	
	T 185	Skot	[1521]	C: G	
	T 186	J. Rastell	[1527]	O	
	T 187	Redman	1527	O	
	T 188	Redman	1530	C: H	
	T 189	Redman	1533	G: H: O: R: W	
	T 190	Redman	[1538]	B: G: H: W	
	T 190a	Berthelet	153–	H	
	T 193	Berthelet	1540	B: H	
	T 194	Berthelet	1544	B: H: O	
	T 195	Myddylton	1544	B: H	
	T 196	Hyll	1546	H	
	T 197	Waley	1546	B	
	T 198	Smyth	1546	H	
	T 199	Toye	1546	B	
	T 200	Middilton	1547	H	
	T 200a	W. Powell	1552	H	
Diversity of Courts	T 122	Pynson	1526	H	
	T 123	Redman	1528	H	
	T 124	Berthelet	1530	C: G: H	
	T 120	Redman	[1532]	H: W	
	T 125	Redman	1533	G: H: O: W	
	T 126	Berthelet	1535	H	

PART III.—SECTION I—*Continued*

Name	Number	Printer	Date	Libraries	Distinguishing Marks
	T 127	Myddylton	1543	H: W	
	T 128	Middleton	[1544]	B	
	T 129	[Smyth]	[1545]	H	
Hundred Court	T 203	Pynson	[1521]	C: O	
	T 204	Skot	152–	G	
	T 205	J. Rastell	[1527]	B: O: W	
	T 206	Redman	1527	O	
	T 207	Redman	[1530]	C: H: O	
	T 208	Redman	1538 [1]	B: G: H	¶Modus tenēdi
	T 209	Redman	1538 [2]	H: O	¶Modus tenendi
	T 211	Myddylton	1544	B: H	
	T 212	Hyll	1546	H	
	T 213	Waley	1546	B	
	T 214	Toye	1546	B	
	T 215	Kele	1546	O	
	T 216	Myddylton	1547	H: W	
Natura Brevium	T 79	Pynson	1496	CK: G	
	T 80	Pynson	1499	C	
	T 81	Pynson	1504	G: H: L	
	T 82	Pynson	1519	B: C: H	
	T 83	Pynson	1525	B: H	
	T 84	Pynson	1528	B: G: H	
	T 87	Redman	1529	H: W	
	T 88	Berthelet	1531	B	
	T 89	Berthelet	1534	R	
	T 90	Redman	[1534]	B: H	folio
	T 91	Myddylton	[1544]	B: H	
	T 92	Smyth	1545	B: H	
	T 93	Tottill	1557	B: H: N: W	
	T 94	Tottell	1567	B: G: H: N: W	
	T 95	Tottle	1572	B: H: W	
	T 96	Tottle	1580	H: N: W	
	T 97	Tottle	1584	B: C: G: H: U: W	

PART III.—SECTION 1—*Continued*

Name	Number	Printer	Date	Libraries	Distinguishing Marks
N. B. in English	T 98	Redman	1532	H	
	T 99	Redman	1535	B: H	
	T 100	Redman	1540	B: CJ: G: H	
	T 101	Petit	1544	B: CP	
	T 102	Petit	[1544]	B: C: H	
	T 103	Myddylton	1544	B: H: W	
	T 104	W. Powell	1553	H	
	T 105	Tottell	1557	B: H	
	T 105a	Tottil	1557	H	
	T 106	Tottill	1576	H: U	
	T 107	Tottill	[1580]	G: H: U: W	
Novae Narrationes	T 108	Pynson	[1496]	B: C: G	
	T 110	Tottil	1561	B: G: H: N: U: W	
Old Tenures	T 68	Pynson	[1496]	B: H	Has colo.
	T 69	Pynson	[1504]	G	No colo. 7-line initial.
	T 70	Pynson	[1516]	B: H: L	No colo. Heavy plain initial
	T 71	J. Rastell	[1520]	H	
	T 72	Pynson	1525	B: H: W	
	T 73	Redman	1528	H	
	T 74	Redman	1532	B: H: W	
	T 75	Berthelet	[1530]	C: H	
	T 76	Berthelet	1538	B: W	
	T 77	Myddylton	[1545]	H	
	T 78	Smyth	[1545]	H	
Ordinance of Exchequer	T 232	J. Rastell	[1527]	O	
	T 233	Redman	[1530][1]	C: H	¶This is a true copy of the or-
	T 234	Redman	[1533][2]	B: H: W	¶This is a......ordynaunce
	T 235	Redman	[1538][3]	G: O	☙This is a......ordynaunce
	T 236	Redman	[1538][4]	B: H	¶This is a......ordinaunce
	T 236a	Berthelet	1535	H	
	T 237	Berthelet	1537	B: H	
	T 238	Berthelet	1540	H	
	T 239	Berthelet	1544	B: H	

PART III.—Section 1—*Continued*

Name	Number	Printer	Date	Libraries	Distinguishing Marks
Returna Brevium	T 240	Myddylton	[1544]	B	
	T 241	Hyll	[1546]	H: O	
	T 242	Waley	[1546]	B	
	T 243	Smyth	[1546]	B	
	T 244	Toye	[1546]	H	
	T 245	Kele	[1546]	B	
	T 246	W. Powell	1552	B: H	
	T 217	Pynson	1516	O	
	T 218	de Worde	1519	G: R	
	T 219	Pynson	1521	C	
	T 220	J. Rastell	[1527]	B: O	
	T 221	Redman	1527		
	T 222	Redman	[1530]	CT: G: W	
	T 223	Redman	1532	C: H	
	T 229	Myddylton	1543	B	
	T 226	Berthelet	[1538][1]	H	❦Leaves not numbered
	T 227	Berthelet	[1538][2]	H	❦
	T 228	Berthelet	[1544][3]	B: H	❦Leaves numbered
	T 224	Redman	1537	B: H	
	T 225	Redman	1541	H	
	T 230a	[Waley]	1546	B: G	
	T 230b	[Smyth]	1546	H	
	T 230c	[Toye]	1546	H	
	T 230d	W. Powell	[1552]	H	

Section 2.—Other Anonymous Treatises

Admonition or warning	T 247	Grafton	[1548]	H	
Ancient State	T 248	[Barker]	1597	B: G: H	
Apology for Proceedings	T 249	Barker	1593	G: H: U: W	
Articles of Visitation	T 249a	Grafton	1547	B: H	
	T 250	Jugge & Cawood	1559	B: H	

PART III.—SECTION 2—*Continued*

Name	Number	Printer	Date	Libraries	Distinguishing Marks
	T 250a	Jugge	[158–]	B: H	
	T 250b	C. Barker	[158–]	B: G	
	T 250c	C. Barker	1583	B: H	
	T 250d	C. Barker	1591	B: H	
	T 250e	C. Barker	1595	B: G	
	T 251	R. Barker	1600	B: G: H	
Articuli de quibus	T 251a	[Day]	1575	H	
Assize of Bread	T 252	Bankes	[1530]	CM	
	T 253	Berthelet	[1534]	C	The Assyse
	T 253a	Berthelet	n. d.	G	¶ The Assise
	T 254	Wyer	[1540]	B: W	
	T 255	Wyer	[1550]	B	
	T 256	Wyer	[1553]	C: H	
	T 256a	Colwell		G	
	T 257	Jackson	[1587]	B	
	T 258	Windet	1600	H	
Book of Canons	T 259	Day	1571	B: G	
Breefe Discourse	T 260	Midleton	1584	G: H	
Brief Treatise of Oathes	T 261	n. n.	n. d.	H	
Capitula sine Constitutiones	T 262	Barker	1597	B: H	
	T 262a	Barker	1599	B: G: H	
Defence of Priest's Marriages	T 263	Jugge	[1565]	H	
	T 262b	Kingston	156–	G	
Division between Spirituality and Temporality	T 263a	Berthelet	[1530]	G: H	
Exhortation to J. P.	T 264	Grafton	1548		
Indentures	T 265	Tysdale	n. d.		
Injunctions by E. 6	T 266	Grafton	1547	B: G: H	
Injunctions by the Queen	T 267	Jugge & Cawood	1559	B	
	T 267a	Jugge	[157–]	B	
	T 267b	Kyngston	[158–]	B: H	
	T 267c	C. Barker	[1591]	B: H	
	T 267d	C. Barker	[1595]	B: H	

PART III.—SECTION 2 — *Continued*

Name	Number	Printer	Date	Libraries	Distinguishing Marks
	T 267e	[Barker]	[1599]	B: G: H: W	
	T 267f	[Barker]	158–	G	
Institutions &c.	T 268	Byddell	[1538]	C	
	T 269	Banks	1540	H	
	T 270	Banks	1542	H	
	T 271	Myddylton	1543	C: G: H	
	T 272	Myddylton	1544	B	
	T 273	Myddylton	1545	H	
	T 274	Hyll	1546		
	T 275	Myddylton	1547	H: W	
	T 276	W. Powell	1551	H	
	T 277	Marshe	1555	H: W	
	T277a	Marshe	1556	.H	
	T 278	Tottel	1567	H: U	
	T 279	Tottyl	1570	B: H	
	T 280	Banks	1574	C	
	T 281	Tottell	[1577]	W	
	T 282	Tottell	1580	H	
Intrationum Liber	T 283	Pynson	1510	G: H: N: W	
	T 284	Smyth	1545	H: N: U: W	
Form of Indentures	T 285	Waylye	[1560]	C	
Laws Concerning Liveries	T 286	Totell	1571	G	
Office of Sheriffs	T 288	Redman	1538	H	
	T 289	Pickering	[1540]	B	
	T 290	Petyt	1543	O	
	T 291	Myddylton	1545	B: H	
	T 292	W. Powell	1549	H: R	
	T 293	Kele	1552	C	
	T 294	Marche	[1555][1]	C: H	❧In this
	T 295	Marshe	[1555][2]	H	In this booke. *Colo.* Dunstanes
	T 296	Marshe	[1555][3]	H	In this booke. Colo. Dunstons
	T 297	J. Wright	1556	G: H	

PART III.—*Section 3*—*Other Treatises*

Name	Number	Printer	Date	Libraries	Distinguishing Marks
	T 298	W. Powell	1552		
	T 299	King	1555	H: W	
	T 300	Tottell	1562		
	T 301	Marche	1562	H	
	T 302	Tottyl	1570 [1]	H	*Colo.* Rychard Tottyl
	T 303	Tottyl	1570 [2]	H	*Colo.* Rycharde Tottyl
	T 304	Alde	1573	B	
Orders devised	T 304a	Barker	1586	B: G: H	
	T 304b	C. Barker	1594	B	
Ordinal	T 305	Bankes	[154–]	B	
	T 306	Wyer	[1545]	B: C	
	T 307	Hyll	n. d.		
	T 307a	Tysdale	1562		
Reformatio	T 308	Day	1571	B: H: W	
Registrum	T 309	W. Rastell	1531	C: CJ: G: H: N: U: W	
	T 310	Tottel	1553	B: G: H: N: U: W	
	T 311	J. Yetsweirt	1595	B: C: G: H: U: W	
Stannaries of Devon	T 287	Simmes	1600	H: W	
Romney Marsh Ordinances	T 312	Berthelet	1543		
	T 313	J. Wolfe	1579	G	
Statutes for a Justice	T 314	Berthelet	1538	B: H	
	T 315	Berthelet	1540	H	
	T 316	Berthelet	1543	B	
Statutes for war	T 317	Pynson		B: G	
	T 318	Berthelet	1544	B	
Swans, order for	T 319	[Woodcoke]	[1585]	B: G	
ADAMS, Court Leet	T 322	Orwin-Kirckham	1593	B: C: H	
BRACTON, de Legibus	T 323	Tottell	1569	B: G: H: N: U: W	
BRITTON	T 324	Redman	[1534]	B: G: H: N: U: W	
CECIL, Justice	T 325	Barker	1583 [1]	B: CT: G	
	T 326	Barker	1583 [2]	B: CT: G: H: W	"Secondly"
CLARKE, Bastardy	T 327	Islip	1594	B: G: H	
COUSINS, Apology	T 249	Barker	1593	W	See *Apology*

PART III.—Section 3—*Continued*

Name	Number	Printer	Date	Libraries	Distinguishing Marks
Crompton, Jurisdiction	T 328	C. Yetsweirt	1594	B: G: H: N: U: W	
Crompton, Justices	T 329	Tottill	1583	CP: G: H: U: W	
	T 330	Tottel	1584	CJ: G: H: W	
	T 331	Tottell	1587	G: H: W	
	T 332	Tottell	[1593]	B: CJ: H: U	
Crompton, Short Declaration	T 333	Charlewood	1587	B: G	
Fitzherbert, L' office	T 334	Redman	1538	B: G: H: O: U	
Fitzherbert, Justice	T 335	Redman	1538	B: C: H: O	
	T 336	E. Redman	1540	B	
	T 337	Petyt	1541	H	
	T 338	Myddylton	1543	H	
	T 339	W. Powell	1547	H	
	T 340	W. Powell	1551	H: W	
	T 341	Tottle	1554	G: H	
	T 342	Tottyll	1560	H	
	T 343	Tottill	1566	B: G: H: W	
Fitzherbert, Natura Brevium	T 344	Tottyl	1553	B: G: H: W	
	T 345	Tottyl	1560	B: G: H: U	
	T 346	Tottell	1567 [1]	CP: H: W	T. p. Anno Do. 1553
	T 347	Tottill	1567 [2]	B: CJ: G: H: U: W	T. p. Añ. Do. 1567
	T 348	Tottill	1576	H	
	T 349	Tottell	1581	G: H: W	
	T 350	Tottell	1588	G: H: W	
	T 351	Wight & Norton	1598	G: H	
Fitzherbert, Surveying	T 352	Berthelet	1539	B: G: H	
	T 352a	W. Copland	154–	G: H	
	T 353	Berthelet	1546	B: G	
	T 353a	Berthelet	n.d.	G	
	T 353b	Marsh	[1557]	G	
	T 353c	[Tottel]	1567	G	
Fleetwood, Annals	T 354	Tottle	1579	B: H: N: U: W	
	T 355	J. Yetsweirt	1597	B: G: W	

PART III.—SECTION 3—*Continued*

Name	Number	Printer	Date	Libraries	Distinguishing Marks
FORTESCUE, de Politica	T 356	Smyth	[1545]	B: H: U: W	
FORTESCUE, Laws of England	T 357	Tottill	1567	B: G: H: W	
	T 358	Tottell	1573	B: CP: G: H: W	
	T 359	Wight & Norton	1599	B: G: H: N: U: W	
FRAUNCE, Lawyers' Logic	T 360	How	1588	B: CT: G: H: U	
FULBECK, Preparative	T 361	Wight	1600	B: CJ: G: H: W	
GODFRAY, Constitutions	T 362	Godfray	[1536]	CT: G: H	
GODFRAY, Power of Clergy	T 363	Godfray	[1536]	H: U	
GREGORY, de Legibus	T 364	Tottil	1583	H	
GLANVILLE, Tractatus	T 365	Tottel	[1554]	B: CT: G: H: U: W	
KITCHIN, Justices	T 366	[Tottel]	1580/79	B: CJ: W	
			1580/80	CJ: U	
	T 367	[Tottell]	1580	H	
KITCHIN, Court Leet	T 368	Tottell	1579	H	
	T 369	Tottell	1580	CJ: G: H: W	
	T 370	Tottell	1581	H: N: W	
	T 371	Tottell	1585	C: CP: G: H: U	
	T 372	Totell	1587	G: H: U	
	T 373	Totell	1592	B: H	
	T 374	Wight & Norton	1598	H: N: W	
KITCHIN, Returna Brevium	T 375	Tottell	1581	B: H	
	T 376	Tottell	1585	C: G: H: U	
	T 377	Tottell	1587	G: H: U	
	T 378	Tottell	1592	H	
LAMBARD, Archaionomia	T 379	Day	1568	G: H: U: W	
Constables	T 380	Warde	1582	CT	
	T 381	Newberie & Middleton	1583	B: H	
	T 382	Newberie & Middleton	1584	B: G: H	
	T 383	Newberie & Middleton	1587	B: CT: H	

PART III.—Section 3—*Continued*

Name	Number	Printer	Date	Libraries	Distinguishing Marks
Lambard, Eirenarcha	T 384	Newberie & Middleton	1591	G	
	T 384a	Newberie	1591	G: U	
	T 385	C. Yetsweirt	1594	B: H	
	T 386	Wight & Norton	1599	B: H: U: W	
	T 387	Newbery & Bynneman	1581	B: G: H: U	
	T 388	Newbery & Bynneman	1582[1]	B: H: N: U	Ra Newbery, and H. Bynneman
	T 389	Newbery & Bynneman	1582[2]	B: G: H	Ralf. Newbery, and H. Binneman
	T 390	Newberie	1583	H	
	T 391	Newbery	1588[1]	B: CJ: CT: G: H: N	T. p. 1588
	T 392	Newbery	1588[2]	CP: H	T. p. 1591
	T 393	Newbery	1592	G: H: U: W	
	T 394	Newbery	1594	B: G: H: U	
	T 395	Wight & Norton	1599	B: H: U: W	
Lambard, Perambulation	T 396	Middleton-Neuberie	1576	G: H: W	
	T 397	Bollifaut	1596	G: H	
Littleton, Tenures	T 3	Lettou & Machlinia	[1480]	B: C: W	
	T 4	Machlinia	[1485]	B: W	
	T 5	Tailleur-Pynson	[1490]	B: C	
	T 6	Pynson	[1496]	G: H	¶Expliciunt Tenores Lytylton
	T 7	Pynson	[1504]	B: C: G: H	¶Tenorum Lytylton Lector iam cernito Finem
	T 8	Pynson	1516	B: C: H: R: W	
	T 9	Pynson	1525	H	
	T 10	Pynson	1528	H	
	T 12	Redman	1528	B: H	
	T 13	[J. Rastell]	[1528]	B: C	
	T 14	Berthelet	1530	C: H: W	
	T 15	Redman	1539	H	
	T 11	Redman	[1540]	B: H: N	folio

PART III.—SECTION 3—*Continued*

Name	Number	Printer	Date	Libraries	Distinguishing Marks
	T 16	Berthelet	1541	W	
	T 17	Smyth	1545	H	
	T 18	Myddylton	1545	B: H	
	T 19	W. Powel	1553	H	
	T 20	Tottel	1554	B	
	T 21	Tottil	1557[1]	H: U: W	T. p. Tottele *Colo.* ¶Imprinted
	T 22	Tottil	1557[2]	G: H	T. p. Tottel *Colo.* ¶Imprinted
	T 23	Tottill	1557[3]	B: H	*Colo.* ¶Imprinted
	T 24	Tottil	1567	B	
	T 25	Tottill	1569	G: H	
	T 26	Tottill	1572	CT: H	
	T 27	Tottyl	1574	G: H: U: W	
	T 28	Tottyl	1577	H	
	T 29	Tottyl	1579	H: W	
	T 30	Tottel	1581	G: H: U	
	T 31	Tottill	1583	B: G: H	
	T 32	Tottill	1585	G: H: U: W	
	T 33	Tottell	1588	G: H: W	
	T 34	n. p.	1591	C: G: H: W	
	T 35	Tottell	1591	H: U: W	
	T 36	C. Yetsweirt	1594	H	
	T 37	J. Yetsweirt	[1597]	G: H	
	T 38	Wight & Norton	1599	H: N	
LITTLETON, Tenures in English	T 39	Redman	[1532]	B: CJ	
	T 40	Wyer	[1535]		
	T 41	[Berthelet	1538	B]	
	T 42	Middleton	1544	H: O	
	T 43	[Berthelet]	1545	CJ: H	
	T 44	W. Powell	1548	B: C: H	
	T 45	W. Powell	1551	H	
	T 46	Petyt	[1551]	CT: H: N: U: W	
	T 47	Marshe	1556	B: H: N	Colophon
	T 48	[Marshe]	1556	C: H: N: W	No colophon

PART III.—SECTION 3—*Continued*

Name	Number	Printer	Date	Libraries	Distinguishing Marks
	T 49	Tottle	1556[1]	B: H	T. p. ❧ Littleton
	T 50	Tottell	1556[2]	G: H	T. p. Littleton
	T 51	Tottill	1568[1]	H	¶ Cum privilegio
	T 52	[Tottell]	[1568][2]	B	¶ Cum privilegio
	T 53	Tottyl	1574	C: G: H: W	
	T 54	Tottyl	1576	H: W	
	T 55	Tottel	1581	H: U	
	T 56	Tottill	1583	H: U: W	
	T 57	Tottill	1586	B: G: H: W	
	T 58	Tottill	1593	H: W	
	T 59	C. Yetsweirt	1594	H: N: W	
	T 60	J. Yetsweirt	1597	H	
	T 61	Wight	1600	B: H: W	
Index	T 62	[Tottel]	1581[1]	G: H	¶ Index Littleton
	T 63	[Tottill]	1581[2]	H	Littleton
	T 64	[Tottill]	1585[1]	G: H: W	Index Littleton
	T 65	[Tottell]	1585[2]	H: W	Index [line
	T 66	[Tottell]	1581[3]	H: W	Index Littleton. At end 1581 on separate
	T 67	[n. p.]	1581[4]	H: W	Index Littleton. 1581 not on separate line
LYNDEWODE, Provincial	T 398	[Rood]	[1481]	B: C: CJ: CK: H: O: OU: R	
	T 399	de Worde	1496	B: C: H: M: O: OC: OJ: P: R	
	T 400	Pynson	[1496]	B: R: W	Impressum per R. P.
	T 401	Pynson	[1499]	B: H: M: O: R	Emprinted by R. P.
	T 402	de Worde	1499	O: OC: P: R	
	T 403	Bocard	1501	B: G: H: W	
	T 404	Hopyl-Confluens	1504	H	
	T 405	Hopyl-Breton	1505	B: G: H: W	
	T 406	Pynson	[1510]	B	
	T 407	de Worde	1517	C: G	
	T 408	Endovien-Brickman	1525	B: G: H: W	
	T 409	de Worde	1529	H	

PART III.—SECTION 3—*Continued*

Name	Number	Printer	Date	Libraries	Distinguishing Marks
	T410	Redman	1534	H	
	T411	Marshe	1557	CJ: G: H: W	
MANWOOD, Forest Laws	T412	n. p.	[159–]	B: H	
	T413	Wight & Norton	1598	B: G: H: N: U: W	
MARTIN, Marriage	T414	Caly	1554	B: G: H: W	
PERKINS, Profitable Book	T415	Redman	1528	B: C: H	
	T416	Redman	1532	G: H	
	T417	Myddylton	1541	C: G	
	T418	Smyth	1545	G: H: U	
	T419	Tottle	1555	H	
	T420	Tottel	1567 [1]	H: W	¶ A profitable
	T421	Tottil	1567 [2]	CT: H: W	A profitable
	T422	Tottel	1576	CP: H: W	
	T423	Tottel	1581	G: H: W	
	T424	Tottell	1586	C: G: H: W	
	T425	Tottel	1593	G: H: U: W	
	T426	Tottel	n. d.	H	*Colo.* ¶ Imprinted
	T427	Tottle	n,d.	H: O: U: W	*Colo.* Imprinted
	T428	J. Yetsweirt	1597	G: H: U: W	
PHAER, Book of Precedents	T429	Whytchurche	1543	B: C: W	
	T429a	Whytchurche	n. d.	G	
	T430	Grafton	[1547]	H	
	T431	W. Powell	[1548]	H	
	T432	Grafton	1550	G: H: W	
	T433	W. Powell	1553	H	
	T434	Marshe	1555 [1]	H: W	presydentes
	T435	Marshe	1555 [2]	H: W	presidentes
	T436	Tottyll	1559	H: U: W	
	T437	Tottyll	1561	L	
	T438	Tottyll	1562	H	
	T439	Tottyl	1569	H	
	T440	Tottel	1572	H	
	T441	Tottil	1575	CJ: G	

PART III.—SECTION 3—*Continued*

Name	Number	Printer	Date	Libraries	Distinguishing Marks
	T442	Tottell	1576	H	
	T443	Tottell	1581	H	
	T444	Charlewood	1583	G: H: U	
	T445	Tottel	1584[1]	G: H: U	¶ A booke
	T446	Tottel	1584[2]	C: CP: H	A booke
	T447	Wight	1600	H	
RASTELL, Entries	T448	Tottell	1566	B: G: H: U: W	
	T449	Tottell	1574	B: H: U: W	
	T450	C. Yetsweirt	1596	B: G: H: U	
RASTELL, Terms of the Law	T451	J. Rastell	[1520][1]	B: H	T. p. second line breuium
	T452	J. Rastell	[1520][2]	H	T. p. second line breuiū
	T453	[Butler]	1527	C: G: H: O: W	
	T454	Tottell	1563	H	
	T455	Tottil	1567	H	
	T456	Tottyl	1572	CT: G: H: W	
	T456a	Tottel	1575	G: H	
	T457	Tottell	1579	C: CJ: G: H	
	T458	Tottell	1592	CJ: G: H: W	
	T459	C. Yetsweirt	1595	H: U: W	
	T460	Wight & Norton	1598	O: H	
ST. GERMAN, Doctor & Student	T461	J. Rastell	1528[1]	H	No foliation on t. p.
	T462	J. Rastell	1528[2]	B: C: H	"Folio primo" on t. p.
	T463	Wyer	[1530]	B: C: H	¶Hereafter foloweth
	T464	Wyer	[1531]	B: C: H	The fyrste dyaloge
	T465	Redman	[1531]	O	¶Hereafter foloweth
	T466	Redman	1532	B: G: N: H	The fyrst dialogue
	T467	Treverys	1530	C: G: H	The secūde dyaloge
	T468	Berthelet	1531	C: H	New additions
	T469	Treveris	1531	C: H	The secunde dyalogue
	T470	Redman	1531	O	¶The seconde dyaloge
	T471	Redman	1532	G: H	¶The seconde dyalogue
	T472	Myddylton	1543	B: G: H	

PART III.—SECTION 3—*Continued*

Name	Number	Printer	Date	Libraries	Distinguishing Marks
	T473	Tottel	1554[1]	B: G: H: W	¶The dyaloges
	T474	Totel	1554[2]	H	The dyaloges
	T475	Tottell	1569	B: G: H: U: W	
	T476	Tottell	1575	G: H: U: W	
	T477	Tottell	1580[1]	B: H: N	¶ The dialoges in Englishe
	T478	Tottell	1580[2]	G: R: W	¶ The dialoges in English
	T479	Tottill	1593	G: H: N: U	
	T480	Wight & Norton	1598	B: G: H: N: U: W	
SMYTH, De Republica	T481	Midleton	1583	B: CP: CT: G: H: W	
	T482	Midleton	1584	B: CJ: H: W	
	T483	Windet	1589	B: CJ: G: H	
	T484	Simmes	1594	B: G: H: W	
STAUNFORD, Pleas of the Crown	T485	Tottyll	1557[1]	H: W	*Colo.* Imprinted
	T486	Tottel	1557[2]	H	*Colo.* Imprinted
	T487	Tottyll	1560	B: G: H: W	
	T488	Tottel	1567	B: G: H: U: W	
	T489	Tottel	1574	B: CP: G: H: U: W	
	T490	Tottel	1583	B: G: H: N: U: W	
Prerogative	T491	Tottel	1567	B: G: H: W	
	T492	Tottel	1568	B: G: H: W	
	T493	Totttle	1573	B: G: H: U: W	
	T494	Tottle	1577[1]	B: H: W	T. p. 1568
	T495	Tottle	1577[2]	G: H: N: W	T. p. 1577
	T496	Totthil	1590	B: H: W	
SUTCLIFFE, Laws of Arms	T497	Barker	1593	B: G: H	
SWINBURN, Wills	T498	Windet	1590	B: CJ: G: H: U	
THELOALL, Writs	T499	Tottell	1579	C: CP: G: H: N: U: W	
WEST, Symboleography	T500	?	?	B: G: H	
WILSON, Usury	T501	Tottell	1594	B: H	

Bei Fragen zur Produktsicherheit wenden Sie sich bitte an:
If you have any questions regarding product safety,
please contact:

Walter de Gruyter GmbH
Genthiner Straße 13
10785 Berlin
productsafety@degruyterbrill.com